Contested Constitutionalism

Law and Society Series
W. Wesley Pue, General Editor

The Law and Society Series explores law as a socially embedded phenomenon. It is premised on the understanding that the conventional division of law from society creates false dichotomies in thinking, scholarship, educational practice, and social life. Books in the series treat law and society as mutually constitutive and seek to bridge scholarship emerging from interdisciplinary engagement of law with disciplines such as politics, social theory, history, political economy, and gender studies.

A list of the titles in this series appears at the end of this book.

Edited by James B. Kelly and
Christopher P. Manfredi

Contested Constitutionalism
Reflections on the *Canadian Charter of Rights and Freedoms*

UBCPress · Vancouver · Toronto

20 19 18 17 16 15 14 13 12 11 10 09   5 4 3 2 1

Printed in Canada with vegetable-based inks on FSC-certified ancient-forest-free paper (100 percent post-consumer recycled) that is processed chlorine- and acid-free.

Printed in Canada on acid-free paper

Library and Archives Canada Cataloguing in Publication

Contested constitutionalism : reflections on the Canadian Charter of Rights and Freedoms / edited by James B. Kelly and Christopher P. Manfredi.

(Law and society series, 1496-4953)
Includes bibliographical references and index.
ISBN 978-0-7748-1674-8

1. Canada. Canadian Charter of Rights and Freedoms. 2. Civil rights – Canada. 3. Canada – Politics and government – 1984-1993. 4. Canada – Politics and government – 1993-2006. I. Kelly, James B. (James Bernard), 1968- II. Manfredi, Christopher P. (Christopher Philip), 1959- III. Series: Law and society series (Vancouver, B.C.)

KE4381.5.C65 2009   342.7108′5   C2008-907949-3
KF4483.C519C65 2009

Canadä

UBC Press gratefully acknowledges the financial support for our publishing program of the Government of Canada through the Book Publishing Industry Development Program (BPIDP), and of the Canada Council for the Arts, and the British Columbia Arts Council.

This book has been published with the help of a grant from the Canadian Federation for the Humanities and Social Sciences, through the Aid to Scholarly Publications Programme, using funds provided by the Social Sciences and Humanities Research Council of Canada.

UBC Press
The University of British Columbia
2029 West Mall
Vancouver, BC V6T 1Z2
604-822-5959 / Fax: 604-822-6083
www.ubcpress.ca

To Michèle and Fiona
To Paula and Sophie

Contents

Acknowledgments

Many of the chapters in this volume originated from a conference, *The Charter @ 25/La Charter @ 25*, hosted by the McGill Institute for the Study of Canada in February 2007 in Montréal. The Advisory Committee of the conference deserves special thanks for their dedication and hard work: Denise Chong, Pearl Eliadis, James Kelly, L. Ian MacDonald, Roderick Macdonald, Antonia Maioni, Christopher Manfredi, Doug Mitchell, Simon Potter, Kent Roach, Colleen Sheppard, and Roger Tassé. The committee was fortunate to have the support and commitment of the staff at the McGill Institute for the Study of Canada, particularly Johanne Bilodeau, Adriana Goreta, Linda Huddy, and Luke Moreau. James Kelly and Christopher Manfredi would like to thank Randy Schmidt at UBC Press for once again serving as their editor and Megan Brand for serving as production editor. Finally, they would like to thank Stacy Belden for her work copy editing this volume.

Introduction

1

Should We Cheer? Contested Constitutionalism and the *Canadian Charter of Rights and Freedoms*

James B. Kelly and Christopher P. Manfredi

More than twenty-five years after its controversial entrenchment as part of the Trudeau government's "people's package," the critical debate surrounding the *Canadian Charter of Rights and Freedoms* continues.[1] What began as a concern that the *Charter* would lead to the "Americanization" of Canada through an empowerment of the Supreme Court of Canada and the formalization of constitutional supremacy[2] has now become a consideration of the implications of *Charter* dialogue between the Supreme Court of Canada, Parliament, and the provincial legislatures.[3] The initial attempt to strengthen Canadian unity through a national statement on rights and freedoms[4] has now become a consideration of the appropriateness of the Court in divisive policy debates such as same-sex marriage, the constitutionality of public health care, the accommodation of religious freedom in public education, and the co-existence of the *Charter of the French Language* and the Canadian *Charter*.[5] Finally, what began as a concern that the *Charter* would centralize the federation[6] has now become a demonstration of a concern that the asymmetrical application of the *Charter* comes at the expense of equal public services among the provinces and notions of equal citizenship.[7] Instead of transcending the institutions of the federation and unifying Canadians, the *Charter* has become embedded in its institutions and the fundamental political and constitutional debates of the Canadian state. Controversy continues – but for reasons very different from those surrounding the *Charter's* entrenchment in 1982.

Shortly after the patriation of the *Constitution Act* in 1982, an edited volume – *And No One Cheered* – captured academic views on the agreement entrenched without the consent of the Quebec National Assembly.[8] In many ways, the contributors to *Contested Constitutionalism: Reflections on the Canadian Charter of Rights and Freedoms* all ask whether the *Charter* should be cheered as a positive addition to the constitutional system. It is not surprising that the answers to this simple question vary among the volume's contributors, who present a diversity of approaches to understanding the *Charter*.

This volume presents a critical reflection on the *Charter* after more than twenty-five years and focuses on three themes: governance and institutions; policy-making and the courts; and citizenship and identity. Peter Russell remarked that before its introduction in 1982, the *Charter* "represents a further flight from politics, a deepening disillusionment with the procedures of representative government and government by discussion as means of resolving fundamental questions of political justice."[9] The selected themes analyze the implications of this flight from parliamentary politics that now co-exists with judicial politics.[10] Perhaps more importantly, this volume refrains from being a celebration of the *Charter* and, instead, seeks to understand whether it is in fact the "dangerous deed" that Donald Smiley suggested the 1982 agreement represented for Canadian constitutionalism.[11]

Constitutionalism and the Supreme Court of Canada

The contributors to this volume, therefore, consider the implications of the judicialization of politics and whether the growth and influence of the Supreme Court of Canada has strengthened the institutions of Canadian democracy, increased the tenor of policy discourse, and strengthened notions of citizenship and identity. The judicialization of politics refers to the greater participation by the judiciary in fundamental policy debates that occur when courts determine the constitutionality of public policy by their consistency with rights and freedoms.[12] Further, this phenomenon occurs when decision-making processes incorporate judicial values and frame policy debates as involving competing rights discourses "so that debates as to the wisdom of legislation have been replaced by debates about constitutional compliance."[13]

Evidence of the judicialization of politics is found in the former Chrétien government's defence of the *Anti-Terrorism Act* introduced in 2001.[14] Then minister of justice Anne McLellan defended the proposed *Anti-Terrorism Act* before a parliamentary committee as a measured approach that balanced security with freedom in a manner consistent with the *Charter*: "I wish to assure this Committee that this bill has been subject to a very thorough review on *Charter* grounds and that its measures have been designed so that they will respect the values embodied in the *Charter*, and, we expect, survive legal challenges."[15] The Chrétien government's defence of the *Anti-Terrorism Act* supports Alec Stone Sweet's conclusion that "governing with judges also means governing like judges"[16] because it was premised on its compliance with legal values and the *Charter*. While this phenomenon is suggested to transfer decision making authority from the parliamentary to the judicial arena, Russell cautions that the effects should not be overstated: "The main impact of a constitutional bill of rights on the political system, if Canada's experience is a guide, may be less of a transfer of power to the judiciary than a general transfer of the nature of political life."[17] Indeed, the *Charter* has produced two approaches to governing with rights: parliamentarians who govern like judges when they design legislation that is constitutionally compliant and members of the judiciary who govern like parliamentarians when they base constitutionality on the reasonable limits clause of the *Charter*, since this act requires the judiciary to establish the characteristics of a free and democratic society as the justification for limiting a right or freedom. Governing like parliamentarians occurs most explicitly, however, when the judiciary employ remedies that effectively amend statutes determined unconstitutional by the court in question.

While the introduction of the *Charter* is viewed as the emergence of the judicialization of politics, it has been a constant feature of Canadian federalism since the early days of Confederation. The decline of the Senate as an effective intra-state institution regulating disputes between the two orders of government and integrating provincial interests into federal institutions resulted in political actors using the courts to mediate inter-governmental conflict.[18] The judicialization of politics began with the rise of the provincial rights movement under the leadership of Ontario premier Oliver Mowat in the 1870s, which challenged federal domination in provincial areas of jurisdiction as being inconsistent with the federal principle before the Judicial Committee of the Privy Council (JCPC), the imperial body that served as Canada's highest court until 1949.[19] This structure continued during the Great Depression when the JCPC ruled the *Employment and Social Insurance Act ultra vires* (beyond their power),[20] requiring the Parliament of Canada to seek a formal constitutional change to assume this responsibility from the provinces. Further, the federal government sought constitutional advice on whether it could abolish appeals to the JCPC and allow the Supreme Court of Canada to become the highest court of appeal in 1947.[21]

The judicialization of politics intensified, however, during the period of mega-constitutional politics in Canada, starting in the 1960s.[22] The Supreme Court of Canada was drawn into fundamental debates between the national and provincial governments through increasing use of the reference procedure, which allows either level of government to submit constitutional questions to their highest court for resolution. In this period, the Supreme Court of Canada decided whether the federal or provincial governments had ownership over offshore mineral resources,[23] determined the constitutionality of the *Anti-Inflation Act* introduced by the Parliament of Canada,[24] considered whether the federal government had the ability to alter the composition of the Senate,[25] whether Quebec possessed a historical veto over constitutional change,[26] and, finally, whether the federal government could unilaterally patriate the Constitution.[27] While contemporary critics of the judicialization of politics attribute its rise to the fact that the courts were acting as strategic political actors, Rainer Knopff, Dennis Baker, and Sylvia LeRoy argue in Chapter 4 that it should not be forgotten that the courts were first used by the governments of Canadian federalism to achieve strategic policy victories in periods of inter-governmental conflict.

Judicial Power and the *Charter*

Although the judicialization of politics has been present throughout Canadian constitutional politics, it has significantly changed since the *Charter*'s introduction. There are a number of factors that account for this transformation: constitutional provisions explicitly authorizing judicial participation in public policy; judicial approaches to governing with the *Charter*; changing approaches to governance by parliamentary actors; and, finally, greater recourse to the courts by citizens seeking policy changes denied by parliamentary politics.[28] Unlike the *Canadian Bill of Rights*, which is a statutory document applicable only to the federal government that did not authorize judicial review, a more robust judicial role is authorized by the *Constitution Act, 1982*, of which the *Charter* is a significant component. Section 52 of the *Constitution Act, 1982*, articulates the principle of constitutional supremacy by establishing that "[t]he Constitution of Canada is the supreme law of Canada" and, further, authorizes judicial invalidation of inconsistent laws as unconstitutional because "any law that is inconsistent with the provisions of the Constitution is, to the extent of that inconsistency, of no force or effect."[29]

The scope of judicial review, therefore, is significantly different from that which existed under the *British North America Act, 1867, (BNA Act)*, where judicial review was confined to the division of powers and the Supreme Court of Canada articulated its role as the umpire of federalism.[30] In this role, the Court evaluated government action for its consistency with the division of powers and whether the governments of Canadian federalism acted *intra vires* (within their power) or *ultra vires* (beyond their power). Today, the Supreme Court of Canada articulates its role as the "guardian of the Constitution," and the validity of government action is determined largely by its consistency with the *Charter*. Thus, the judicialization of politics is captured in how the Court has evolved as an institution and how it conceptualizes its role as constitutional guardian in relation to the *Charter* and not simply as the umpire of federalism.

While section 52 of the *Constitution Act, 1982*, does not explicitly authorize judicial determinations of constitutionality, section 24 of the *Charter* clearly establishes the judiciary as the institution to remedy laws determined "of no force or effect" under the *Constitution Act, 1982*. Section 24(1) provides that once a right or freedom guaranteed in the *Charter* has been infringed, an individual "may apply to a court of competent jurisdiction to obtain such remedy as the court considers appropriate and just in the circumstances."[31] Thus, there is tremendous discretion available to the judiciary in fashioning remedies that are *appropriate and just in the circumstances*, and this has been an important basis of judicial power since 1982. The range of remedies employed by the Supreme Court of Canada, however, demonstrates that the *Charter*'s introduction has not transferred sole decision-making authority from Parliament to the Court but has resulted in what Russell suggests would be a general transformation of political life. Three remedies have been employed by the Court when statutes have been found to violate the *Charter*: invalidation, suspended declarations of unconstitutionality, and, finally, judicial amendment of legislation through the reading-in/reading-down provision, or what Christopher Manfredi refers to as micro-constitutional amendment.[32]

The most common remedy employed by the Supreme Court of Canada remains the invalidation of legislation as being inconsistent with the *Charter*. This is arguably the least political remedy employed by the Court since it simply determines that an act is unconstitutional because it is a violation of the *Charter* and invalidates the act, rendering it immediately "of no force or effect." The remaining remedies are clearly political acts on the part of the Court, with suspended declarations representing an indirect political remedy and micro-constitutional amendments being a direct political remedy of an unconstitutional statute. The use of a suspended declaration of unconstitutionality is an indirect political remedy because the Court is conscious of the implications of invalidating a particular statute and factors the political context into its remedy. Instead of immediate invalidation, the Court determines that an act is unconstitutional but suspends its judgment for a period of time to allow the responsible legislative body an opportunity to draft amendments before the suspended decision expires.

This remedy was employed in *R. v. Swain,* when the Court invalidated section 542(2) of the *Criminal Code,* which provided for indefinite incarceration of individuals found not guilty by reason of insanity.[33] The Court determined that this provision violated the principles of fundamental justice protected under section 7 of the *Charter* since the designation not criminally responsible (NCR) due to mental capacity required periodic review to determine its continued applicability to an individual. Recognizing that the invalidation of this provision under section 24(1) would release individuals detained in psychiatric institutions into the general public, as their continued detainment would no longer be constitutional, the Court suspended its decision for six months. During this period, the *Criminal Code* was amended to provide for periodic review of individuals detained via section 542(2) to ensure its consistency with the principles of fundamental justice. Indeed, in a subsequent challenge to the amended section 542(2), the Court upheld its constitutionality, finding the provision "carefully crafted to protect the liberty of the NCR to the maximum extent compatible with the person's current situation and the need to protect public safety."[34]

The use of suspended declarations of unconstitutionality by the Supreme Court of Canada increased significantly during the second decade of *Charter* review and saw Kent Roach challenge the position that Canadian judges were engaged in American-style remedial activism as "the courts have often deferred to governments with gentle, patient, flexible remedies."[35] Indeed, the use of suspended declarations challenges the notion that the *Charter*'s introduction has transferred final decision-making authority to the Court. While suspended declarations do limit the force of judicial power, this remedy does, to a limited degree, result in the politicization of the judiciary since it requires a court to move beyond a consideration of the legal merit of an argument to the political merit of temporarily sustaining an unconstitutional policy to offset the potential implications to the public good that invalidation would produce, as the *Swain* decision demonstrates.

The third – and most controversial – remedy, a micro-constitutional amendment, sees the Supreme Court of Canada transition from a legal actor to a constitutional framer and a policy architect. The Court functions as a constitutional framer when it alters the text of the *Charter* either through sections of the document that authorize judicial amendment or through judicial review that changes the meaning of rights and freedoms. The Court functions as a policy actor when it amends legislation through the reading-in/reading-down remedy created by the courts through section 24(1) of the *Charter* because this remedy changes the architecture of public policy to ensure its constitutionality. Further, the ability under section 24(2) of the *Charter* to exclude in criminal proceedings evidence that "undermines the reputation of justice" is another dimension of the Court as a policy architect because the Court – and not Parliament – establishes the rules governing the constitutional gathering of evidence by the police.

The Supreme Court of Canada as constitutional framer is limited to section 15(1) since equality rights are enumerated (defined) *and* analogous (undefined). The placement of the phrase "in particular" before the enumerated grounds in section 15(1) was included to ensure that, as was not the case in previous drafts of the *Charter*, this protection was open-ended as the listed grounds were simply illustrations of the characteristics protected against discrimination.[36] Thus, equality rights provide for a micro-constitutional amendment because the provision was drafted to allow for new grounds to be added through judicial review if the courts determine that an emerging characteristic is analogous – or similar to – the existing enumerated categories.[37] This construction resulted in sexual orientation being added to section 15(1) in *Egan v. Canada* because the Court determined this characteristic to be analogous to the enumerated grounds for protection: "[I]t is a deeply personal characteristic that is either unchangeable or changeable only at unacceptable personal costs, and so falls within the ambit of s. 15 protection as being analogous to the enumerated grounds."[38] The Court has acted as a constitutional framer in three additional instances involving section 15(1): recognizing citizenship,[39] marital status,[40] and off-reserve band status as analogous grounds.[41] While the micro-constitutional amendment of equality rights clearly demonstrates the judicialization of politics in the post-*Charter* period, there is a strong textual basis to justify the Court acting as a constitutional framer with equality rights.

The controversy sounding the Supreme Court of Canada as a post-entrenchment framer of the *Charter* generally involves the alteration of rights or freedoms where they are not authorized by the text. The explicit rejection of the legislative intent of section 7, the principles of fundamental justice, represents the most telling example of micro-constitutional change by the Court in direct opposition to legislative intent. Unlike the *Canadian Bill of Rights*, which provides for the protection of legal rights in accordance with the due process of law, the *Charter* provides similar protection but in accordance with the principles of fundamental justice. The term "principles of fundamental justice" was used instead of "due process" to avoid a substantive interpretation of legal rights and to ensure a narrower, procedural approach.[42] This approach to section 7 was categorically rejected by the Court in *Reference re B.C. Motor Vehicle Act,* when it refused to be bound by the legislative intent of the principles of fundamental justice articulated before the Special Joint Committee on the Constitution of Canada by then justice minister Jean Chrétien and his officials.[43] According to Justice Antonio Lamer, "[i]f the newly planted 'living tree' which is the *Charter* is to have the possibility of growth and adjustment over time, care must be taken to ensure that historical materials, such as the Minutes of Proceedings and Evidence of the Special Joint Committee, do not stunt its growth."[44] While opinions are divided on a substantive approach to section 7, the debate on micro-constitutional amendments is generally more about policy *outcomes* and less about institutional *procedures*.

The issue of freedom of expression demonstrates the ability of the judiciary to change the meaning of entrenched rights simply through case law and highlights the controversy surrounding judicialized policy outcomes. Freedom of expression has been given the largest and most liberal interpretation by the Supreme Court of Canada, evolving from a right protecting expression that is considered to be essential to a democratic society to "all content of expression, irrespective of the meaning or message sought to be conveyed."[45] Indeed, the Court has extended section 2(b) to include hate literature,[46] solicitation for the purposes of prostitution,[47] and tobacco advertising[48] and has ruled that "[t]he possession of child pornography is a form of expression protected by s. 2(*b*) of the *Charter*."[49] While the Court ruled in *R. v. Sharpe* that child pornography had a much lower level of protection than political expression, the Court included the possession of child pornography within the ambit of section 2(b) and acted as a policy architect, reading down the *Criminal Code* to ensure its constitutionality with the right to possess child pornography.

These controversial social matters divide the Court just as they divide Canadian society, none more so than the *Tobacco Products Control Act* (*TPCA*), which was introduced by the Parliament of Canada to prohibit tobacco advertising as a means to protect the health of Canadians by discouraging new smokers.[50] As a result of the expansive approach to freedom of expression, the *TPCA* violated section 2(b), and the Court elevated the ability of multinational corporations to advertise cigarettes to the status of a fundamental freedom – a controversial decision given the peripheral connection between tobacco advertising and the expression necessary to facilitate a democratic society. While the Court was unanimous that the *TPCA* violated freedom of expression, a narrow majority (five to four) determined that the restriction did not constitute a reasonable limitation. The Court divided on the merits of the *TPCA* and the instruments chosen to advance the legislative intentions. The minority opinion accepted Parliament's policy justification that a total prohibition on tobacco advertising was necessary to achieve the objective of dissuading young smokers,[51] whereas the majority rejected that a total ban was necessary and disputed Parliament's assertion that a causal connection existed between tobacco advertising and consumption.[52] In particular, Justice Beverley McLachlin criticized the Crown for simply asserting the link between advertising and consumption and for failing to provide scientific evidence demonstrating causality.

If suspended decisions limit judicial power, then micro-constitutional amendments through the remedy of reading-in or reading-down provisions unquestionably politicize the judiciary. Similar to suspended declarations of unconstitutionality, the reading-in/reading-down remedy increased significantly during the second decade of *Charter* review by the Supreme Court of Canada and suggests, contrary to Roach's opinion, the emergence of American-style remedial activism, as it is not a gentle, patient, or flexible remedy.[53] This remedy sees the Court transition from being a *legal* actor concerned with questions of constitutionality to a *legislative* actor concerned with designing policy instruments that are constitutional – a subtle yet significant shift in the judicial function under the *Charter*.[54] Again, the issue of sexual orientation demonstrates the politicized nature of judicial review since the *Charter*'s introduction. The exclusion of sexual orientation as a protected ground against discrimination in Alberta's provincial human rights code was challenged as a violation of equality rights in *Vriend v. Alberta*.[55] At this time, several provincial human rights codes (Alberta, Newfoundland and Labrador, and Prince Edward Island) – which protect against discrimination in housing, employment, and education – did not recognize sexual orientation as a protected category. At issue in *Vriend*, therefore, was not government action resulting in discriminatory treatment but, rather, government inaction or legislative silence resulting in discrimination.

Finding that the under-inclusion of the *Individual's Rights Protection Act* (*IRPA*) violated section 15(1) of the *Charter*, the Supreme Court of Canada employed the most controversial remedy created under section 24(1), reading sexual orientation into Alberta's human rights code.[56] In justifying this remedy, which denied Alberta the opportunity to decide whether and how to amend the *IRPA*, Justice Frank Iacobucci invoked the dialogue metaphor, arguing that the final word still rested with the provincial legislature: "Moreover, the legislators can always turn to s. 33 of the *Charter*, the override provision, which in my view is the ultimate 'parliamentary safeguard.'"[57] The judicialization of politics, according to the Court, is simply incorrect because of the structure of the *Charter*. According to Roach, "[w]hen the Court has the last word, it is because the legislature and the people have let it have the last word."[58]

This defence of judicial activism as a dialogue between courts and legislatures is the contemporary debate regarding the *Charter*. Dialogue as advanced policy discourse is refuted by Grant Huscroft as underestimating the ability of the Supreme Court of Canada to have the final word through judicial decisions that determine the legislative response enacted by Parliament: "Not only can the Supreme Court of Canada strike down legislation, it has the power to make its decisions stick – to preclude any legislative response other than enactment of the Court's decision – if it chooses to do so."[59] Similar to an earlier debate that considered whether judicial review by the JCPC or the Supreme Court of Canada centralized or decentralized the federation, the *Charter* dialogue debate considers whether judicial review is democratically enhancing or debilitating for the federation.

The Parliamentary Response to the *Charter*

During his presentation before the Special Joint Committee on the Constitution of Canada, which reviewed the draft *Charter*, Peter Russell remarked: "I believe that a Charter only guarantees a change in the way in which certain decisions are made. It does not guarantee rights or freedoms, it guarantees a change in the way in which decisions are made about rights and freedoms."[60] The judicialization of politics has also resulted because of the decisions by parliamentary actors on how to govern with the *Charter*. This is evident in the transformation of parliamentary debates from policy discourses to rights discourses, where legislation is defended in the public interest only when it is determined to be *Charter* compliant. Former justice minister Irwin Cotler defended same-sex marriage as constitutionally required because the Court, in *Reference re Same-Sex Marriage*, determined that it was constitutional: "We had judgments of courts in eight jurisdictions that expressly held that the opposite-sex requirement for marriage was unconstitutional, a matter affirmed and referenced by the Supreme Court of Canada ... The court affirmed unanimously the constitutionality of that policy option of extending civil marriage to gays and lesbians as being not only consistent with the charter but indeed as flowing necessarily from it."[61] The judicialization of policy discourse by parliamentarians is further demonstrated by the government's reasoning about why civil unions would not be an acceptable policy alternative to same-sex marriage: "The courts have said that civil union is a lesser form of equality, and that individuals with access to civil unions but not civil marriages would be less respected under the law in terms of their values and their minority rights."[62]

By adopting the language of rights to justify policy in the public interest, parliamentarians govern like judges, and this further flight from politics is the result of elected officials "judicializing from within."[63] A review of parliamentary transcripts from the committee system reveals the presence of *Charter* dialogue between ministers and parliamentarians during the scrutiny of legislation and the legalization of policy debates. For instance, the parliamentary scrutiny of the *Anti-terrorism Bill* saw the minister of justice's certification that the bill was *Charter* compliant challenged by members of the committee and by witnesses called before the Justice and Human Rights Committee of the House of Commons. Discussions of the relationship between the *Charter* and the *Anti-terrorism Bill* dominated the proceedings of the parliamentary committee, and opposition to the bill was couched in the language of the *Charter*. Many provisions were argued to violate the *Charter* and to constitute an unreasonable limitation on section 7, the principles of fundamental justice.[64]

Judicialization from within is also evident inside the machinery of government and, according to James Kelly, from the emergence of the Department of Justice as a central agency that uses *Charter* compliance as a framework to evaluate whether policy is in the public interest.[65] For instance, the minister of justice is required to scrutinize all bills before they are introduced into the House of Commons and "report any such inconsistency to the House of Commons at the first convenient opportunity."[66] The Department of Justice is central to ensuring that legislation introduced into the House of Commons is, in the opinion of the minister of justice, *Charter* compliant, as the legislative initiatives of all government departments must be vetted by the Department of Justice for their *Charter* consistency before being sent to the Cabinet for discussion. The *Charter*, therefore, has had a transformative effect on the development of public policy, on the discourse surrounding public policy, and on the nature of parliamentary scrutiny. While former Chief Justice Brian Dickson argued that the *Charter* was not the dawn of a new era, the parliamentary response to the *Charter* suggests otherwise.[67]

Citizens and the *Charter*

Alan Cairns describes the *Charter* as the "citizens' constitution" and contrasts it with the "government's constitution" that existed before 1982. For Cairns, the *BNA Act* was a "government's constitution" because it simply distributed jurisdictional responsibilities between the governments of Canadian federalism and was largely silent about the rights of individuals.[68] Part of the popularity of the *Charter* is derived from the close personal attachment that many Canadians associate with this document. Indeed, the judicialization of politics is advanced by the status given to the *Charter* and the steps taken by citizens to defend their rights against government encroachment.

Charles Epp argues that the entrenchment of a bill of rights does not account for the judicialization of politics or the growing proportion of rights cases decided by supreme courts.[69] It is the use of litigation strategies by interest groups that, according to Epp, accounts for the increased involvement of the courts in policy debates. Epp refers to this process as the creation of a legal mobilization support structure that facilitates the transmission of societal demands to the courts for policy resolution. Indeed, the National Association for the Advancement of Coloured People is used to illustratrate that the judicialization of politics requires the presence of interest groups employing litigation in addition to lobbying strategies to achieve their policy goals.

The role of interests groups in advancing the judicialization of politics exists in Canada but in a somewhat different fashion than in the United States. The creation of the Court Challenges Program in 1977 by the Trudeau government facilitated the judicialization of politics since this program funded interest groups, such as Alliance Quebec, that challenged the language policies of the Parti Québécois government of Réne Lévesque. The parameters of the Court Challenges Program were broadened by the Mulroney government to include funding for equality rights-based litigation in the 1980s.[70] In Chapter 10, Troy Riddell analyzes the litigation strategies of minority language groups outside of Quebec. For instance, minority language education groups such as the Association canadienne-fraçaise de l'Alberta appeared as an intervenor in *Mahé v. Alberta,* a case involving the scope of section 23 of the *Charter* in regard to what level of services must be provided for French-language education in Edmonton.[71] In *Mahé,* the Supreme Court of Canada decided that a sliding scale approach must be adopted to determine what level of services are warranted by minority language communities – an approach that Christopher Manfredi contends makes "possible a significant degree of judicial management of education policy through remedial decrees."[72]

The interest group that has achieved significant policy victories through the courts is the Women's Legal Education and Action Fund (LEAF), a feminist interest group that appears as an intervenor in many cases involving section 15 of the *Charter*. Indeed, feminist legal mobilization demonstrates the dual strategies – lobbying and litigation – that are characteristics of the judicialization of politics associated with the introduction of the *Charter*. The Special Joint Committee on the Constitution of Canada was successfully used by feminist organizations such as the National Action Committee on the Status of Women to challenge the draft *Charter* and the inclusion of procedural equality. Feminist organizations opposed the entrenchment of procedural equality because of their dissatisfaction with *Bliss v. Canada (Attorney General)* and *Attorney-General of Canada v. Lavell* – two Supreme Court of Canada decisions that undermined, according to feminist organizations, the progressive potential of equality rights to address the unfair treatment of women.[73] As a result of important presentations before the Special Joint Committee on the Constitution of Canada, advocating substantive equality and the inclusion of analogous grounds in addition to enumerated grounds, feminist organizations transformed equality rights and are largely responsible for the final wording in section 15(1).[74] Once substantive equality was entrenched, LEAF emerged as an organization committed to defending its interpretation of the *Charter* beyond the confines of section 15(1). LEAF has been successful in advancing its position in the following areas: freedom of expression and the regulation of pornography, reproductive rights, and sexual orientation.[75]

The issue of sexual orientation and the litigation strategy of the federal government are analyzed by Matthew Hennigar in Chapter 11. The involvement of EGALE Canada – which stands for equality for gays and lesbians everywhere – further illustrates the importance of the Canadian version of the legal mobilization support structure and its contribution to the judicalization of politics. EGALE has appeared as an intervenor in every major case involving sexual orientation, such as the recognition of sexual orientation as being analogous to the enumerated grounds of section 15(1) in *Egan*, the reading-in of sexual orientation into Alberta's human rights code in *Vriend* and *Reference re Same-Sex Marriage*. In fact, Miriam Smith contends that gay and lesbian groups in Canada have been more successful than their counterparts in the United States in framing this issue within the emerging policy discourse on equality.[76]

In recent years, the judicialization of politics has involved the health care system, as Christopher Manfredi and Antonia Maioni discuss in Chapter 7. The issue of freedom of religion within the public education system was also addressed in *Multani v. Commission scolaire Marguerite-Bourgeoys*, a 2006 case involving whether the ban on the kirpan – a Sikh religious dagger – in the public school system was an unreasonable limitation on freedom of religion.[77] In *Multani*, the school board banned authentic kirpans because of safety concerns but allowed Gurbaj Singh to wear a plastic or wooden kirpan under his clothes. In its decision, the Supreme Court of Canada found the actions of the school board violated freedom of religion because the inability to wear an authentic kirpan required the appellant to choose between his religious beliefs and leaving the public school system: "Forced to choose between leaving his kirpan at home and leaving the public school system, Gurbaj Singh decided to follow his religious convictions and is now attending a private school. The prohibition against wearing his kirpan to school has therefore deprived him of his right to attend a public school."[78] Unable to find that this infringement constituted a reasonable limitation, the Supreme Court of Canada invalidated the decision of the school board.

The issue of reasonable accommodation of religious beliefs in public services is a contemporary debate, particularly in the province of Quebec with the launching of the Bouchard-Taylor Commission in 2007, which had a mandate to conduct public hearings and issue a report to Quebec's National Assembly. While the issue of reasonable accommodation has returned to the public domain, *Multani* was an important decision that raised this issue to the level of public consciousness. The ability to frame public discourse, therefore, is an important dimension of the judicialization of politics in Canada at the present time.

Organization of This Study

This study is organized into three sections: governance and institutions, policy making and the courts, and citizenship and identity. The selection of themes clearly demonstrates the importance of the Supreme Court of Canada after more than twenty-five years of *Charter* review. The initial analysis of the *Charter* at the period of entrenchment in 1982 generally involved whether the *Charter* would act as an instrument of national unity and, second, whether the *Charter* posed a challenge for provincial autonomy by centralizing the federation through rights-based review. The *Charter* debate now considers the complexity of the institutional response to the *Charter* by judicial, parliamentary, bureaucratic, and societal actors such as interest groups. Second, it considers the implications of the judicialization of politics for the policy process and the greater use of litigation by interest groups to achieve desired policy outcomes. Finally, the *Charter* and the *Constitution Act, 1982,* have altered conceptions of citizenship and identity by transforming individuals into rights bearers that can use the judicial arena to advance their conception of the community. The efforts by Aboriginals to have an inherent right to self-government recognized by the courts demonstrate the transformation of identity and citizenship since the entrenchment of the *Constitution Act, 1982.*

Governance and Institutions

The first part of this volume considers changing patterns of governance since the *Charter*'s introduction and the complex relationships created as a result of *Charter* dialogue between courts and legislatures. In Chapter 2, Andrew Petter opens the volume with a critical appraisal of the legalization of politics and its impact on governance. Of particular concern for Petter is the changing policy discourse within parliamentary institutions and the machinery of government, which has taken a strong legal quality. Petter contends that the most significant changes are the transformation of rights from a political to a legal nature, as well as the resolution of competing rights claims in the judicial arena instead of the parliamentary arena. Petter is generally concerned that the legalization of politics has serious consequences for the framing of public policy and the resolution of competing policy claims when they are expressed as rights discourses, which privileges those with a legal background. For Petter, this dialogue comes at the expense of democratic engagement because it has led to the legalization of the policy-making process and the growing importance of the Department of Justice and the attorney general, a concern that is shared by James Kelly in Chapter 5.

Petter points to three important implications of *Charter* dialogue as rights discourse: the legalization of government policy making; the growing importance of the attorney general's independence by reason of *Charter* litigation; and, finally, the legalization of political advocacy and discourse by interest groups. In his conclusion, Petter acknowledges that the legalization of politics was foreseen at the *Charter's* entrenchment but contends that now, after twenty-five years, it is well established. On the question of democratic dialogue, Petter ends with a caution for those who defend judicial review as an institutional dialogue between courts and legislatures: "It is, after all, not much of a dialogue, and hardly democratic, if the same legal norms and interpretations are driving decisions at both ends."[79]

In Chapter 3, Grant Huscroft presents a critique of the "mischief" of dialogue theory and argues that, in its present form, it cannot serve as a justification for judicial review under the *Charter*. At the heart of Huscroft's critique is a concern that dialogue theory obscures the dominance of the Supreme Court of Canada as a constitutional actor and downplays the structural influence of judicial decisions on legislative responses enacted by parliamentary bodies. Indeed, Huscroft contends that *Charter* dialogue cannot result in weak-form judicial review because it is premised on judicial supremacy and the dominant role of the Court in determining the meaning of constitutional guarantees. For Huscroft, the proponents of dialogue theory downplay the significance of judicial invalidation of legislation and how this drastically limits the policy responses available to Parliament or the provincial legislatures. To illustrate how judicial invalidation can frame a legislative response, Huscroft discusses the invalidation of tobacco advertising restrictions in *RJR-MacDonald Inc. v. Canada* and argues that the legislative response demonstrates the "mischief" of dialogue theory since Parliament simply followed the constitutional prescription offered by the Court in its majority decision to save the offending legislation. As a result of the reluctance of elected officials to use the notwithstanding clause, Huscroft argues that Canada has strong-form constitutionalism because judicial decisions generally represent the final word on the meaning of the *Charter*.

The Supreme Court of Canada as a strategic actor in constitutional politics is explored by Rainer Knopff, Dennis Baker, and Sylvia LeRoy in Chapter 4. Adopting Peter Russell's thesis of "bold statescraft, questionable jurisprudence," Knopff, Baker, and LeRoy argue that legal reasoning as political rhetoric is a strategy adopted by the Supreme Court of Canada to justify decisions with questionable legal merit.[80] The authors contend that legal reasoning fails to explain controversial decisions by the Supreme Court of Canada, such as the *Reference re a Resolution to Amend the Constitution (Patriation Reference)*, *Reference re Amendment to the Canadian Constitution,* or the *Reference re Secession of Quebec*.[81] Instead, Knopff, Baker, and LeRoy contend that the decisions must be understood as political calculations by judges to justify the outcomes for two audiences: the internal audience, such as the coalitions that the justices attempt to develop before a decision is rendered, and the external audience, such as the prime minister and premiers during the reference procedure or interest groups that participate as intervenors in *Charter* decisions.

For Knopff, Baker, and LeRoy, it is strategic calculation – and not legal merit – that explains judicial outcomes when judges court controversy: "Time and again, purely legal considerations fail to explain judgements. In fact, the legal surface is often perplexing in its own terms, and can be satisfactorily explained only in terms of unacknowledged political calculation with respect to external or internal audiences."[82] Viewing the Supreme Court of Canada as a strategic political actor has implications for *Charter* dialogue, as demonstrated by Knopff, Baker, and LeRoy in their analysis of prisoners' voting rights in *Sauvé v. Canada (Chief Electoral Officer)* and the legislative response that was revisited by the Supreme Court of Canada in the second *Sauvé* decision (known as *Sauvé I* and *Sauvé II*).[83] For Knopff, Baker, and LeRoy, strategic judicial decision making demonstrates the "mischief" of dialogue, as *Sauvé II* was less a dialogue between the Court and Parliament on whether any restrictions on prisoners' voting rights could be consistent with the *Charter* and more of an internal dialogue between the justices to preserve the Court's initial invalidation of the *Canada Elections Act* nine years earlier in *Sauvé I*.[84]

The last two chapters in the first part of this volume broaden the discussion of governance and institutions beyond the confines of the Supreme Court of Canada to consider the parliamentary response to the *Charter* (Chapter 5) and the unrealized potential of the notwithstanding clause for *Charter* dialogue and Canadian constitutionalism (Chapter 6). In Chapter 5, James Kelly argues that the characterization of dialogue between courts and legislatures misrepresents the complexity of dialogue within Parliament and its dominance by the Cabinet through the machinery of government. Though Kelly disputes that *Charter* dialogue has undermined democratic engagement through the legalization of politics, he concludes that the Cabinet's decision to govern with the *Charter* from the centre has led to a further marginalization of Parliament as an institution. Agreeing with Andrew Petter that democratic engagement has been undermined by the *Charter's* introduction, Kelly attributes this result to the political response to the *Charter* and not to the legalization of politics, as contended by Petter in Chapter 2.

The importance of *Charter* vetting by the Department of Justice on behalf of the Cabinet, and the lack of transparency in the *Charter* certification process by the minister of justice to Parliament, undermine the democratic engagement by parliamentarians outside the Cabinet – this is the basis of the democratic deficit as it relates to the *Charter* and not the Supreme Court of Canada's approach to *Charter* dialogue. Drawing upon the lessons of New Zealand and its parliamentary bill of rights, Kelly argues that the failure to link constitutional reform with parliamentary reform is the fundamental failure of the *Charter* project. Arguing that the next period of *Charter* analysis should be devoted to ensuring a transparent and parliamentary dialogue on the *Charter*, Kelly proposes three changes to the present cabinet-centred approach to the *Charter*: a reorganization of the Department of Justice to address its monopolization of *Charter* vetting within the machinery of government; the appointment of separate parliamentarians as attorney general and minister of justice within Cabinet; and, finally, the creation of a *Charter* scrutiny committee to allow parliamentarians to assess the internal Cabinet dialogue on the *Charter*. In this sense, Kelly challenges the reform agenda that has centred on the appointment of judges to the Supreme Court of Canada that is based on the experiences of the United States. Since the Canadian *Charter* operates within a parliamentary structure, more pertinent lessons can be drawn from the experiences of other Westminster democracies that have introduced bills of rights, such as New Zealand, the United Kingdom, and the Australian state of Victoria.

Part 1 concludes with Janet Hiebert's analysis of the notwithstanding clause and the competing narratives surrounding the inclusion of section 33 in the final version of the *Charter*, once the patriation issue returned to the institutions of executive federalism in November 1981. In Chapter 6, Hiebert argues that our understanding of the notwithstanding clause has been compromised by two dominant narratives as well as by our continued constitutional myopia that fails to recognize section 33 as part of a new constitutional understanding of bills of rights within the parliamentary tradition. For Hiebert, the legitimacy of the notwithstanding clause has been undermined by the narrative that views section 33 as a compromise of political necessity within executive federalism, which allowed the Trudeau government to achieve substantial provincial consent, as required by the *Patriation Reference*. This perception of the notwithstanding clause as a suspect constitutional instrument is also the result of its inconsistency with the dominant constitutional view of the time, what Hiebert refers to as a compromise of principles – the position that bills of rights are legal projects that require both judicial review and judicial finality to ensure a robust level of rights protection. Instead of recognizing the value of section 33 as being consistent with alternative constitutional principles, it has been rejected as being inconsistent with the dominant "strong-form" view of bills of rights that existed twenty-five years ago.

For Hiebert, the dominant narratives obscure the fact that, by including section 33 as part of the *Charter*, Canada was at the forefront of a new model of constitutionalism in 1982 – a model based neither on judicial supremacy nor parliamentary supremacy, but one that allowed judicial and political conceptions of rights to co-exist. The value of section 33 can only be rediscovered, therefore, by returning to the views of the premiers who articulated an alternative model in which political mechanisms co-exist with judicial review for the protection of rights. Relying on the political philosophy of former Saskatchewan premier Allan Blakeney, Hiebert develops an alternative understanding of section 33 and links it to the contemporary debate surrounding "parliamentary" bills of rights in Australia, New Zealand, and the United Kingdom.

Policy Making and the Courts

The second part of this volume considers the growing role of the Supreme Court of Canada as a policy actor in the Canadian federation and focuses on the following areas: health care policy (Chapter 7); national security and the *Charter* (Chapter 8); official languages policy (Chapter 9); minority language education policy (Chapter 10); and same-sex marriage (Chapter 11). In Chapter 7, Christopher Manfredi and Antonia Maioni argue unequivocally that the distinction between law and politics does not exist, stating that "[t]he Supreme Court of Canada is, and always has been, a policymaking institution. Moreover, it makes policy not as an accidental byproduct of adjudicating legal disputes, but by explicitly determining which legal rules will produce the most socially beneficial results."[85] For Manfredi and Maioni, as for Knopff, Baker, and LeRoy, the significant increase in the policy-making functions of the Supreme Court of Canada is largely the result of discretionary choices made by its justices, which has seen the Court emerge as a strategic policy actor in health care and social policy.

To demonstrate the Court as a strategic policy actor, Manfredi and Maioni present an analysis of *Chaoulli v. Québec*, a 2005 decision that invalidated the restrictions on private health insurance as a violation of the Quebec

Charter of Human Rights and Freedoms but upheld the restrictions as consistent with the Canadian *Charter*.[86] The majority decision by Justice Marie Deschamp is described as "an unexpected reversal" because, unlike the lower court decisions, which considered the issue only in relation to the Canadian *Charter*, the decision made by Justice Deschamp was based on the Quebec *Charter*. Manfredi and Maioni are particularly critical of the use of the Commission on the Future of Health Care in Canada (Romanow Commission) and the Senate Standing Committee on Social Affairs, Science and Technology (Kirby Committee) by the majority decision. Instead of reviewing the merits of the previous decisions, the majority decision reframed the constitutional questions considered in *Chaoulli* and based its decision on social science evidence that was not presented – or challenged – before the lower courts. They argue that the recent judicial foray into health care policy in *Chaoulli* "lays the foundation for an even more aggressive judicial role in policymaking, especially in the health care field, during the Charter's next quarter century."[87]

Indeed, Manfredi and Maioni are concerned that the Supreme Court of Canada lacks the institutional capacity to participate in substantive policy debates such as public health care and, further, that the use of litigation narrows the range of policy alternatives available to decision makers, thus resulting in policy with structural weaknesses. As does Huscroft, Manfredi and Maioni suggest that the legislative response to *Chaoulli* by the Charest government demonstrates the continued presence of strong-form judicial review in Canada, as the Court's decision significantly narrowed the policy manoeuvrability available to Quebec, thus widening the scope of public-private partnerships in the health care sector and challenging the public monopoly on this public service.

In Chapter 8, Kent Roach considers the evolution of national security policy in Canada after more than twenty-five years of *Charter* review by the Supreme Court of Canada. In many respects, Roach's chapter is a defence of the Supreme Court of Canada and judicial activism in the context of national security policy. Roach challenges the critical position presented by Huscroft and argues that *Charter* dialogue has created a more robust policy context since the *Charter* has required Parliament to confront rights issues that it might otherwise have ignored. Using the *Anti-Terrorism Act*, Roach contends that without the *Charter*, the act would have been less restrained in the powers provided to the police to fight domestic and international terrorism and would not have provided important procedural safeguards for those accused of terrorist activities.[88] Thus, the dialogue on national security policy has increased accountability and respect for the rights of unpopular individuals such as terrorism suspects.

While Roach does acknowledge the virtues of the *Charter* in structuring national security policy, there are limitations with the present approach to

Charter dialogue. For instance, Roach is critical of the growing use of immigration law as anti-terrorism law because it allows the Canadian government to interact with foreign governments that may not respect the rights of those accused of terrorism offences. Since the challenge of terrorism is global in nature and requires the Canadian government to coordinate with foreign governments to defend against it, the virtues of the *Charter* may be limited to the domestic realm, which may prove to be peripheral to the development of security policy within an international context. For Roach, this may come at the expense of the rule of law and the rights of the accused. Within the domestic realm, Roach is critical of the attempts to "*Charter* proof" legislation as this may simply result in Parliament meeting the minimum standards established by the *Charter* and may place less emphasis on the effectiveness or workability of national security policy. While Roach is supportive of the Supreme Court of Canada rejecting calls for deference in national security policy, he is concerned that the present judicial-centred approach to understanding this policy area obscures the need for a continuous review of the agents of law enforcement. Finally, Roach calls for the greater empowerment of independent review bodies to ensure that the *Charter* is applied to the state's secret security activities.

The chapters by Graham Fraser and Troy Riddell consider the issue of language rights, the policy-making role of the Supreme Court of Canada, and interest groups that pursue litigation strategies. In Chapter 9, Graham Fraser – the commissioner of official languages – presents the entrenchment of official languages as the latest chapter in a national conversation on language that began with the joining of Upper and Lower Canada in 1841 and was reflected in the *Consitution Act, 1982*, and the language guarantees in section 133. Arguing that language rights are equality rights in the Canadian context, Fraser recounts the efforts by the Pearson government in the 1960s to ensure that Parliament reflected the equality of English and French as languages. This effort was followed by the establishment of the Royal Commission on Bilingualism and Biculturalism in 1963, which resulted in the *Official Languages Act* of the Trudeau government in 1969.[89] The entrenchment of language rights in the *Charter*, therefore, is suggested by Fraser to be the latest manifestation of the national conversation on language as an equality right.

As a former journalist who covered the constitutional politics surrounding the patriation of the Constitution, Fraser was originally opposed to the final agreement because Quebec was not a signatory. Reflecting the dominant criticism of the entrenchment period, Fraser argued that the *Charter*, through the empowerment of the courts, would lead to the "Americanization" of Canadian political institutions as it posed a serious challenge to existing parliamentary practices. In his chapter, Canada's official languages commissioner argues that these fears were misguided because the development of language rights has been the result of a three-way dialogue between Parliament, the courts, and the provincial legislatures. While Quebec did not agree to constitutional changes in 1982, Fraser argues that section 23 (minority language education rights) is respectful of the ongoing language debate within Quebec, demonstrated by the recent decisions in *Solski (Tutor of) v. Quebec (Attorney General)* and *Gosselin (Tutor of) v. Quebec (Attorney General)*, which upheld the constitutionality of the *Charter of the French Language* or Bill 101. This dialogue on language rights is significant, as it resulted in the *Official Languages Act* being amended in 2005 to provide minority language communities with legal recourse to ensure that the federal government advances their interests. Thus, according to Graham Fraser, the national conversation on language has emerged as a dialogue of respect between Parliament, the Supreme Court of Canada, and the provincial governments.

In Chapter 10, Troy Riddell presents a critical appraisal of minority language education policy outside Quebec and the role of legal mobilization and judicial decisions in transforming section 23. While Riddell acknowledges that significant policy changes have occurred, he argues that this was not an inevitable development, as the framers of the *Charter* explicitly refused to grant "management and control" responsibilities to minority language education groups because of provincial opposition. Noting that great variation existed among provincial government over the provision of minority language education policy before the *Charter*, Riddell contends that the landmark decision *Mahé v. Alberta* in 1990 represents a turning point and the beginning of homogenous policy responses by the provinces.[90] In this decision, the Supreme Court of Canada revised section 23 to include "management and control" for official minority language groups, and this action has led to the development of very similar minority language education regimes at the provincial level. Riddell uses minority languge education policy as a case study to demonstrate the policy impact of legal mobilization and judicial decisions. In his chapter, he argues that minority language policy changes are the result not only of "top-down" structural factors such as the entrenchment of section 23, judicial victories, and federal government funding for minority language education groups but also "bottom-up" structural factors such as the activities of minority language education groups, policy and legal discourse, and contingent historical dynamics. Thus, Riddell argues that minority language education policy cannot be explained solely by judicial victories but also by the judicial-societal nexus that has resulted in a significant transformation – and homogenization – of minority language education policy in a federal state.

In Chapter 11, Matthew Hennigar considers one of the most significant constitutional events that has occurred since the entrenchment of the *Charter* – the recognition of sexual orientation as an equality right protection and the subsequent extension of same-sex marriage to gay and lesbian couples in 2003. Hennigar argues that it is unlikely that the framers of the *Charter* foresaw the development of equality rights in this direction. As minister of justice and the parliamentarian responsible for defending the draft *Charter*, Jean Chrétien resisted efforts to include sexual orientation as an equality right when the *Charter* was being drafted, although he did recognize this as a possibility through the analogous branch of section 15. Nearly twenty-five years later and following Chrétien's term as prime minister, Hennigar considers the Chrétien government's response to *Halpern v. Canada (Attorney General)* and *Barbeau/EGALE v. Canada (Attorney General)*, the reversal of its opposition to same-sex marriage and the decision to refer a draft bill to the Supreme Court of Canada.[91] Instead of viewing the Supreme Court of Canada as a strategic actor, Hennigar adopts George Tsebelis' "nested games" approach to illustrate the government's litigation strategy as the product of decision making within several overlapping contexts or games: partisan competition in Canadian politics; the Liberal leadership contest; and Cabinet's desire to retain decision-making authority on this issue. While Hennigar acknowledges the significant rights issues raised by same-sex marriage, he contends that the litigation strategy pursued by the federal government was the result of six nested games that structured the Chrétien government's response to *Halpern* and *Egale*, eventually resulting in the submission of a draft same-sex marriage bill to the Supreme Court of Canada before it had been reviewed by the House of Commons.

Citizenship and Identity

The third part of this volume considers the impact of the *Charter* on conceptions of citizenship, changing notions of constitutionalism and the emergence of identity politics among Aboriginal nations and multinational Canada. In Chapter 12, Sujit Choudhry presents a critical analysis of former Prime Minister Pierre Elliott Trudeau's original justification for introducing the *Charter* – as an instrument of national unity that provided Canadians with a common set of values to transcend provincial identities. Using the recent debate on whether to recognize Quebec as a nation, initiated by Michael Ignatieff during the 2006 Liberal leadership convention, Choudhry argues that the reaction to this proposal demonstrates the mixed legacy of the *Charter* as an instrument of national unity. It is argued that the *Charter* has emerged as an instrument of national unity outside Quebec but has failed to confront Quebec nationalism, as envisioned by Trudeau. According to Choudhry, "[h]ad the *Charter* been effective at combating Quebec nationalism and serving as the glue of a pan-Canadian national identity, the last twenty-five years of constitutional politics would not have happened."[92] Indeed, the failures of the Meech Lake Accord, and the Charlottetown Accord, and the strong reaction against the concept of Quebec as a nation within Canada are argued to be the result of the *Charter* and the competing patterns of national identity in Canada and Quebec that reinforce the centrifugal pressures of the federation. For Choudhry, Canada provides a cautionary tale for multinational states that envision a bill of rights as an instrument of national unity.

In Chapter 13, Guy Laforest argues that the Canada of the *Charter* has resulted in the internal exile of Quebecers within the federation. This internal exile occurs because the distinctive identity of Quebecers is not properly recognized in the *Constitution Act, 1982*. Perhaps more critically, Laforest contends that the *Charter* was intended to deny the specificity of Quebecers and represents a dangerous deed for the federal spirit and principle of Canada. For Laforest, this internal exile is especially troubling because it occurred at the hands of a Quebecer, Pierre Elliott Trudeau, after his emergence as a Canadian sovereigntist at the expense of his federalist credentials. To end the internal exile, Laforest argues that the *Charter* must be amended to recognize Quebec as a distinct society by altering section 1 to recognize Canada as a "free and democratic *federation*" rather than as a "free and democratic *society*." As well, Quebec should follow the example of other free and democratic federations, such as Spain and the Catalans, and adopt an internal constitution that recognizes its distinct status within the federation to end this internal exile.

In Chapter 14, Kiera Ladner and Michael McCrossan are critical of the road taken by the Supreme Court of Canada as it relates to Aboriginal rights. For Ladner and McCrossan, the judicialization of politics has not led to a re-imagining of the Canadian constitution to ensure its consistency with Aboriginal readings of the Canadian constitutional order. Instead, as argued in Chapter 14, although "the early literature signalled an acceptance of this reading and a commitment to decolonization, the courts have nevertheless abandoned the path set before them in favour of sustaining Canada's colonial legacy."[93] In a damning analysis of the impact of judicial review, Ladner and McCrossan conclude that there is nothing to cheer since the Court's interpretation of the *Constitution Act, 1982*, represents a dangerous deed because it is fundamentally inconsistent with Aboriginal understandings of the Canadian constitutional order. For Ladner and McCrossan, "[s]imply put, the Court has rendered obsolete everything Aboriginal people fought to achieve in the *Constitution Act, 1982*, and in subsequent constitutional negotiations."[94] Indeed, the authors contend that the Supreme Court of Canada has developed questionable Aboriginal rights jurisprudence that is bold statecraft because it is fundamentally at odds with indigenous constitutional visions.

Conclusion

It is only fitting that the concluding contribution to this volume is presented by Peter Russell in Chapter 15. Much of the scholarship in what is now called "law and politics" is derived from Russell's original research that considered the important role played by the Supreme Court of Canada in the evolution of Canadian constitutionalism. More than twenty-five years ago, Russell agreed with Donald Smiley that the *Charter*, as it related to Canadian democracy, was a dangerous deed. For Russell, questions of social and political justice would be transformed into technical legal issues resolved by those with a legal background. Further, the policy-making role of courts would weaken the "sinews of Canadian democracy" because Canadians would abdicate the resolution of policy conflicts to the courts. Russell concludes that the *Charter* has not been a dangerous deed.[95] At times, there have been bold statescraft and questionable jurisprudence by all actors that govern with the *Charter*: Parliament, the courts, and citizens. The dangerous deed is assuming that the *Charter* is solely responsible for the significant transformation of Canada's governing institutions, the public policy process, and conceptions of citizenship and identity.

In his chapter, Russell asks whether there are more serious threats to Canadian democracy than the judicialization of politics and whether the *Charter* has affected the quality of democracy in ways hoped for and those not anticipated at the time of entrenchment of the *Constitution Act, 1982*. He challenges that judicial decisions close off political debates, and he presents both a critique and defence of *Charter* dialogue. For Russell, judicial decisions have not only closed off debates between parliamentarians because of their reaction to the *Charter*, but they have also resulted in robust debates among Canadians on important social issues. Using same-sex marriage as an illustration of this dialogic dichotomy, Russell contends that political considerations on the part of both the Liberals and Conservatives have resulted in rather muted responses to the courts, and *Charter* dialogue has suffered because of the parliamentary response to same-sex marriage. While Russell acknowledges that "Charter patriotism" has resulted in a more rights-conscious and democratic constitutionalism, he argues that the *Charter* has not been the "quick fix" for national unity alluded to by Pierre Trudeau during the latter part of mega-constitutional politics.[96]

Finally, Russell identifies what he believes is the most pressing challenge to Canadian democracy since the *Charter*'s entrenchment – the growing centralization of power within the office of the prime minister and the central agencies that support this parliamentarian. Indeed, he admonishes the academic community for overlooking this development: "It is remarkable that the debate and discussion about the dangers to democracy posed by judicial activism showed so little awareness of centralization of power that was occurring in our parliamentary system."[97] In doing so, Russell suggests that the debate must come full circle – the flight from parliamentary politics that occurred during the first twenty-five years of the *Charter* must return to a consideration of parliamentary institutions as the cause of Canada's democratic deficit and not the judicialization of politics. Failure to do so, moreover, may represent the dangerous deed of the *Charter* for the next twenty-five years.

Notes

1 *Canadian Charter of Rights and Freedoms,* Part 1 of the *Constitution Act, 1982,* being Schedule B to the *Canada Act 1982* (U.K.), 1982, c. 11.
2 Michael Mandel, *The Charter of Rights and the Legalization of Politics in Canada* (Toronto: Thompson Educational Publishing, 1984), 5.
3 Peter W. Hogg and Allison A. Bushell, "The *Charter* Dialogue between Courts and Legislatures (Or Perhaps the Charter Isn't Such a Bad Thing after All)," *Osgoode Hall Law Journal* 35 (1997): 75-124.
4 Peter H. Russell, "The Political Purposes of the Canadian Charter of Rights and Freedoms," *Canadian Bar Review* 61 (1983): 31-43.
5 Allan Hutchinson, "Condition Critical: The Constitution and Health Care," in Colleen M. Flood, Kent Roach, and Lorne Sossin, eds., *Access to Care, Access to Justice: The Legal Debate over Private Health Insurance in Canada* (Toronto: University of Toronto Press, 2005), 101-15; F.L. Morton and Rainer Knopff, *The Charter Revolution and the Court Party* (Peterborough: Broadview Press, 2000), 33-58; and Guy Laforest, *Trudeau and the End of a Canadian Dream* (Montreal and Kingston: McGill-Queen's University Press, 1995), 125-49. *Charter of the French Language,* R.S.Q. c. C-11.
6 Donald Smiley, "A Dangerous Deed: The Constitution Act, 1982," in Keith Banting and Richard Simeon, eds., *And No One Cheered: Federalism, Democracy and the Constitution Act* (Toronto: Methuen, 1983), 78 and 90.
7 Lorne Sossin, "Towards a Two-Tier Constitution? The Poverty of Health Rights," in Flood, Roach, and Sossin, *supra* note 5, 161-83; and James B. Kelly, "The Courts, the Charter, and Federalism," in Herman Bakvis and Grace Skogstad, eds., *Canadian Federalism: Performance, Effectiveness and Legitimacy*, 2nd edition (Don Mills: Oxford University Press, 2008), 58-59.
8 Banting and Simeon, *supra* note 6. *Constitution Act, 1982* (U.K.), 1982, c. 11, s. 59.
9 Peter H. Russell, "The Effect of a Charter of Rights on the Policy-Making Role of Canadian Courts," *Canadian Public Administration* 25:1 (1982): 32.
10 Peter H. Russell, "Canadian Constraints on Judicalization from Without," *International Political Science Review* 15:2 (1994): 165.
11 Smiley, *supra* note 6, 74.
12 Torbjörn Vallinder, "The Judicialization of Politics – A World-Wide Phenomenon: Introduction," *International Political Science Review* 15:2 (1994): 91.
13 Danny Nicol, "The Human Rights Act and the Politicians," *Legal Studies* 24 (2004): 453.
14 *Anti-Terrorism Act,* S.C. 2001, c. 41.
15 The Honourable Anne McLellan, Minister of Justice and Attorney General of Canada, *Notes for the Minister of Justice's Appearance before the House of Commons Justice and Human Rights Committee, Bill C-36 – Anti-Terrorism Act* (October 18, 2001), cited at http://www2.parl.gc.ca/HousePublications/Publication.aspx?DocId=652657&Language=E#T1535.
16 Alec Stone Sweet, *Governing with Judges: Constitutional Politics in Europe* (Oxford: Oxford University Press, 2000), 204.
17 Russell, *supra* note 10, 166.
18 Michael Lusztig, "Federalism and Institutional Design: The Perils and Politics of a Triple-E Senate in Canada," *Publius: The Journal of Federalism* 25:1 (1995): 42.
19 Robert C. Vipond, *Liberty and Community: Canadian Federalism and the Failure of the Constitution* (Albany: SUNY Press, 1991), 151-59.
20 *Attorney General of Canada v. Attorney General of Ontario (Employment and Social Insurance Act Reference),* [1937] A.C. 327. *Employment and Social Insurance Act,* cited in Peter H. Russell, Rainer Knopff, and Ted Morton, eds., *Federalism and the Charter: Leading Constitutional Decisions* (Ottawa: Carleton University Press, 1990), 97-100.

21 *Attorney General of Ontario v. Attorney General of Canada (Reference re Abolition of Privy Council Appeals),* [1947] A.C. 128.
22 Peter H. Russell, *Constitutional Odyssey: Can Canadians Become a Sovereign People?* 2nd edition (Toronto: University of Toronto Press, 1993), 88.
23 *Reference re Offshore Mineral Rights of British Columbia,* [1966] S.C.R. 663.
24 *Reference re Anti-Inflation Act,* [1976] 2 S.C.R. 373. *Anti-Inflation Act,* cited in Peter H. Russell, Rainer Knopff, and Ted Morton, eds., *Federalism and the Charter: Leading Constitutional Decisions* (Ottawa: Carleton University Press, 1990), 162-78.
25 *Reference re Legislative Authority of Parliament to Alter or Replace the Senate,* [1980] 1 S.C.R. 54.
26 *Re: Objection to a Resolution to Amend the Constitution (Quebec Veto Reference),* [1982] 2 S.C.R. 793.
27 *Reference re a Resolution to Amend the Constitution,* [1981] 1 S.C.R. 753.
28 James B. Kelly, *Governing with the Charter: Legislative and Judicial Activism and Framers' Intent* (Vancouver: UBC Press, 2005), 3-20.
29 Section 52(1) of the *Constitution Act, 1982* (U.K.), 1982, c. 11, s. 59, cited in Peter W. Hogg, *Constitutional Law of Canada* (Toronto: Carswell, 2000), 1147.
30 *Constitution Act, 1867* (U.K.), 30 & 31 Vict., c. 3, reprinted in R.S.C. 1985, App. II, No. 5.
31 Section 24(1) of the *Constitution Act, 1982,* cited in Hogg, *supra* note 29, 1133.
32 Christopher P. Manfredi, "Institutional Design and the Politics of Constitutional Modification: Understanding Amendment Failure in the United States and Canada," *Law and Society Review* 31:1 (1997): 114.
33 *R. v. Swain,* [1990] 1 S.C.R. 933 at 934. *Criminal Code,* R.S.C. 1985, c. C-46, s. 264.
34 *Winko v. B.C. (Forensic Psychiatric Institute),* [1999] 2 S.C.R. 625 at 686.
35 Kent Roach, *The Supreme Court on Trial: Judicial Activism or Democratic Dialogue* (Toronto: Irwin Law, 2001), 152.
36 The equality rights provision in the *Canadian Charter of Rights and Freedoms* reads as follows:

> 15. (1) Every individual is equal before and under the law and has the right to the equal protection and equal benefit of the law without discrimination and, in particular, without discrimination based on race, national or ethnic origin, colour, religion, sex, age or mental or physical disability.

37 Kelly, *supra* note 28, 98.
38 *Egan v. Canada,* [1995] 2 S.C.R. 513 at para. 5.
39 *Andrews v. Law Society of British Columbia,* [1989] 1 S.C.R. 143.
40 *Miron v. Trudel,* [1995] 2 S.C.R. 418.
41 *Corbiere v. Canada,* [1999] 2 S.C.R. 203.
42 F.L. Morton and Rainer Knopff, *The Charter Revolution and the Court Party* (Peterborough: Broadview Press, 2000), 45.
43 *Reference re B.C. Motor Vehicle Act,* [1985] 2 S.C.R. 486.
44 Ibid., para. 53.
45 *Reference re ss. 193 and 195.1(1)(c) of the Criminal Code,* [1990] 1 S.C.R. 1123 at 1181 [*Reference re ss. 193 and 195.1(1)(c)*].
46 *R. v. Keegstra,* [1990] 3 S.C.R. 697.
47 *Reference re ss. 193 and 195.1(1)(c), supra* note 45.
48 *RJR-MacDonald Inc. v. Canada,* [1995] 3 S.C.R 199 [*RJR-MacDonald*].
49 *R. v. Sharpe,* [2001] 1 S.C.R. 45.
50 *Tobacco Products Control Act,* S.C. 1988, c. 20.
51 *RJR-MacDonald, supra* note 49, 310-11 (Laforest J.).
52 Ibid., 242 (McLachlin J.).
53 Roach, *supra* note 35, 152.
54 Kelly, *supra* note 28, 175.
55 *Vriend v. Alberta,* [1998] 1 S.C.R. 493 [*Vriend*].
56 Ibid., para. 179 (Iacobucci J.). *Individual's Rights Protection Act,* R.S.A 1980.
57 *Vriend, supra* note 55, para. 178 (Iacobucci J.).
58 Roach, *supra* note 35, 226.

59   Grant Huscroft, "Constitutionalism from the Top Down," *Osgoode Hall Law Journal* 45:1 (2007): 98-99.
60   Peter H. Russell, Special Joint Committee of the Senate and the House of Commons on the Constitution of Canada Hearings (January 8, 1981), 34:148.
61   Hon. Irwin Cotler, Minister of Justice, Legislative Committee on Bill C-38, *Evidence*, 38th Parl., 1st Sess., No. 2 (May 11, 2005), 2.
62   Ibid., 5.
63   Vallinder, *supra* note 12, 93.
64   Bill C-36, *An Act to Amend the Criminal Code, the Official Secrets Act, the Canada Evidence Act, the Proceeds of Crime (Money Laundering) Act and Other Acts*, Standing Committee on Justice and Human Rights, 37th Parl., 1st Sess. (October 18, 2001), http://cmte.parl.gc.ca/cmte/CommitteePublication.aspx?SourceId=45196&Lang=1&PARLSES=371&JNT=0&COM=222.
65   Kelly, *supra* note 28, 222-57.
66   *Department of Justice Act*, R.S., 1985, c. J-2 at s. 4.1(1), cited at http://laws.justice.gc.ca/en/showdoc/cs/j-2///en?page=1.
67   Honourable Brian Dickson, "The Canadian Charter of Rights and Freedoms: Dawn of a New Era?" *Review of Constitutional Studies* 2 (1994): 5 and 12.
68   Alan C. Cairns, *Charter versus Federalism: The Dilemmas of Constitutional Change* (Montreal and Kingston: McGill-Queen's University Press, 1992), 7.
69   Charles R. Epp, *The Rights Revolution: Lawyers, Activists, and Supreme Courts in Comparative Perspective* (Chicago: University of Chicago Press, 1998), 11.
70   Ian Brodie, *Friends of the Court: The Privileging of Interest Group Litigants in Canada* (Albany: SUNY Press, 2002), 100.
71   *Mahé v. Alberta*, [1990] 1 S.C.R. 342.
72   Christopher P. Manfredi, *Judicial Power and the Charter*, 2nd edition (Don Mills: Oxford University Press, 2001), 167.
73   Alexandra Dobrowolsky, *The Politics of Pragmatism: Women, Representation, and Constitutionalism in Canada* (Don Mills: Oxford University Press, 2000), 43. *Bliss v. Canada (Attorney General)*, [1979] 1 S.C.R. 183; and *Attorney-General of Canada v. Lavell*, [1974] S.C.R. 1349.
74   Penney Kowe, *The Taking of 28: Women Challenge the Constitution* (Toronto: Women's Press, 1983).
75   Christopher P. Manfredi, *Feminist Activism in the Supreme Court of Canada: Legal Mobilization and the Women's Legal Education and Action Fund* (Vancouver: UBC Press, 2004), 63.
76   Miriam Smith, "Framing Same-Sex Marriage in Canada and the United States: *Goodridge, Halpern* and the National Boundaries of Political Discourse," *Social and Legal Studies* 16:1 (2007): 6-7.
77   *Multani v. Commission scolaire Marguerite-Bourgeoys*, [2006] 1 S.C.R. 256.
78   Ibid., para. 40.
79   Andrew Petter, "Legalise This: The *Chartering* of Canadian Politics," in this volume.
80   Peter H. Russell, "Bold Statescraft, Questionable Jurisprudence," in Banting and Simeon, *supra* note 6, 210-38.
81   *Reference re a Resolution to Amend the Constitution*, [1981] 1 S.C.R. 753; *Reference re Amendment to the Canadian Constitution*, [1982] 2 S.C.R. 791; and *Reference re Secession of Quebec*, [1998] 2 S.C.R. 217.
82   Rainer Knopff, Dennis Baker, and Sylvia LeRoy, "Courting Controversy: Strategic Judicial Decision Making," in this volume.
83   *Sauvé v. Canada (Chief Electoral Officer)*, [1993] 2 S.C.R. 438; and *Sauvé v. Canada (Chief Electoral Officer)*, [2002] 3 S.C.R. 519.
84   *Canada Elections Act*, R.S.C. *1985, c. E-2, S. 51(e)*.
85   Christopher P. Manfredi and Antonia Maioni, "Judicializing Health Policy: Unexpected Lessons and an Inconvenient Truth," in this volume.
86   *Chaoulli v. Québec*, [2005] 1 S.C.R. 791. *Charter of Human Rights and Freedoms*, R.S.Q. c. C-12.
87   Manfredi and Maioni, *supra* note 85.
88   *Anti-Terrorism Act*, S.C. 2001, c. 41.
89   *Official Languages Act*, R.S.C. 1985, c. 31.
90   *Mahé v. Alberta*, [1990] 1 S.C.R. 342.

91 *Halpern v. Canada (Attorney General)*, [2003] O.J. No. 2268 (Ont. C.A.); and *Barbeau/EGALE v. Canada (Attorney General)*, 2003 BCCA 251 (B.C. C.A.).
92 Sujit Choudhry, "Bills of Rights as Instruments of Nation Building in Multinational States: The Canadian *Charter* and Quebec Nationalism," in this volume.
93 Kiera L. Ladner and Michael McCrossan, "The Road Not Taken: Aboriginal Rights after the Reimagining of the Canadian Constitutional Order," in this volume.
94 Ibid.
95 Peter H. Russell, "The Political Purposes of the Canadian Charter of Rights and Freedoms," *Canadian Bar Review* 61 (1983): 31.
96 Peter H. Russell, "The *Charter* and Canadian Democracy," in this volume.
97 Ibid.

Part 1: Governance and Institutions

2

Legalise This:
The *Chartering* of Canadian Politics
Andrew Petter

I fought the law and the law won.
– Sonny Curtis

In the period immediately following the enactment of the *Canadian Charter of Rights and Freedoms*,[1] a number of academic commentators predicted that a major impact of the *Charter* would be to legalise politics in Canada.[2] In my twenty-five years of experience with the *Charter* – as a government lawyer, as a constitutional law professor, and as a provincial cabinet minister – I have become ever more aware of how prescient these commentators were.[3] Since the *Charter* came into force in 1982, issues of rights in Canada have increasingly become identified and understood as being legal rather than political in nature. This development, which reflects a global trend in favour of legalising public affairs, has been encouraged by politicians as much as by lawyers and has produced two spheres of public discourse: a sphere of justice and rights that has become the primary domain of lawyers and courts and a sphere of policy and interests that remains the principal preserve of politicians and legislatures. Moreover, there can be no question as to which sphere dominates in the event of conflict. For all of the talk of "dialogue" between courts and legislatures, those who speak in the language of justice and rights have a huge rhetorical and political advantage over those who speak in the language of policy and interests.

The legalisation of politics has increased the stature and authority of lawyers and legal discourse within Canadian society and has diminished the importance and influence of politicians and democratic engagement. This shift can be seen most clearly in the context of *Charter* litigation where contentious issues of public policy, such as abortion, unemployment insurance, regulation of commercial advertising, Medicare, Sunday closing of retail stores, same-sex marriage, obscenity laws, judicial salaries, collective bargaining, the powers of customs officials, and even cruise missile testing, have become subjects of legal argument and judicial decision making.[4] However, legal politics within the courts are only the tip of a much larger iceberg – one that shows no signs of diminishing due to global warming. The judicial arena is just one of many forums in which law and/or lawyers direct political debate and shape public policy in the name of upholding *Charter* rights. Indeed, it is no exaggeration to say that such influence has become pervasive within Canadian government and civil society. In the remainder of this chapter, I will draw upon my experiences and those of others to explore some of the ways in which this influence has manifested itself.

The Legalisation of Government Policy Making

As will be evident to those who have been engaged in public policy processes both before and after 1982, the *Charter* has significantly altered the way in which governments in Canada go about making decisions. The federal Department of Justice "now routinely reviews new legislation for potential Charter violations, and recommends to the responsible minister or parliamentary committee whether such limitations may be 'reasonable' and sustained under Section 1 analysis."[5] In addition, existing legislation is reviewed to ensure its consistency with new *Charter* decisions. Comparable legislative review procedures also exist in all provincial governments. Such processes, as Matthew Hennigar has observed, "[do] not occur within a legal vacuum, but typically [involve] bureaucratic actors attempting to gauge the courts' likely response to legislation, based on existing case law. To this extent, there is usually, if not always, an external judicial influence on internal legislative-executive discussions on constitutional rights."[6]

In addition to reviewing new and existing legislation to ensure its consistency with the *Charter*, government lawyers regularly incorporate their understanding of *Charter* requirements in the day-to-day guidance they give government employees, in the legal opinions they issue to ministries, in the advice they provide to the Attorney General, and in the decisions they make during the processes of legislative drafting. In these various ways, government lawyers, and the court decisions upon which they rely, exert huge influence on public policies without those policies ever being tested in court.[7] The extent of this influence is amplified by two related factors. The first is that government lawyers tend to be risk averse in their approach to the *Charter*. This means that, on the margins, they are more inclined to advise that a law or practice violates the *Charter* than that it does not. The reason for this is simple: a government lawyer is much more likely to be criticised for being wrong in predicting that a law or practice complies with the *Charter* than in predicting that it does not. This likelihood is in part because the latter advice, if heeded, will never get tested in court. Moreover, even if advice of a *Charter* violation is ignored, government officials are not prone to being displeased because a law or practice that they were told was unconstitutional survives *Charter* challenge. On the contrary, they are likely to be delighted, as I was as Minister of Forests when a government lawyer successfully defended the ministry's handling of a forest tenure from a constitutional challenge that he had originally advised could not be defended. When the decision came down, I penned him a congratulatory note (though I refrained from doing so a second time when the decision was upheld on appeal). The second factor that amplifies the influence of policy advice provided in the form of *Charter* opinions is the reverence accorded such advice by public servants who are not lawyers. Given their lack of familiarity with the law and the legal system, non-lawyers within government are frequently intimidated by legal opinions, particularly those that speak of possible violations of constitutional rights. Thus, government officials generally go out of their way to accommodate such opinions in their decision-making processes.[8] As a result, *Charter* issues seldom reach the ministerial level, and, when they do, cabinet ministers themselves are disinclined to assume the political risk of proceeding with a policy that they are told is likely to violate the *Charter*.

In one of the rare instances where a cabinet of which I was a member decided to proceed with a policy in the face of an adverse *Charter* opinion, the decision was taken only because the policy in question – the imposition of strict spending limits on third parties in provincial election campaigns – was seen by ministers as being central to both the government's mission and to its ability to compete fairly in the next election. Even then, the decision to proceed might have gone the other way had I and other lawyers in cabinet not challenged the certitude of the legal opinion and persuaded the Attorney General to seek further legal advice on the matter from outside counsel (a course generally not welcomed by lawyers within ministries of the attorney general – or anywhere else for that matter).[9]

An exception to the tendency of cabinet ministers to heed legal advice relating to the *Charter* sometimes arises with respect to legal opinions advising that new policies are required. While cabinet ministers are loath to run the political risk of proceeding with government policies that the courts are likely to strike down under the *Charter*, the political calculus tends to be quite different with respect to policies that the *Charter* is said to require, particularly if those policies are controversial or do not accord with government priorities. In these situations, ministers may find it convenient to avoid incurring the political costs associated with implementing such policies by deferring their decisions and leaving the issues to be resolved by the courts. The British Columbia cabinet of which I was a member, for example, decided not to act on legal advice recommending that it introduce legislation giving francophone parents greater control over their children's French language educational programs, preferring to wait until there was a court decision requiring it to do so.

Perhaps the most obvious example of politicians hiding behind the courts to avoid dealing with a contentious political issue raised by the *Charter* is the federal Liberals' handling of the same-sex marriage controversy.[10] In the years between 2000 and 2003, the government avoided dealing with this issue simply by saying that it was before the courts. Finally, after the British Columbia and Ontario Courts of Appeal determined that the *Charter* required civil rights of marriage to be extended to same-sex couples, and further appeal became politically unpalatable, Prime Minister Jean Chrétien announced that his government would propose legislation to recognize the union of same-sex couples across Canada. However, rather than bringing this legislation directly to Parliament for a vote, where it would have divided the Liberal caucus and created a difficult political situation in advance of a federal election, the government referred the draft bill to the Supreme Court of Canada to seek the Court's opinion concerning its constitutionality.[11] The Court reference provided a pretext for the government to delay parliamentary debate on the legislation for a further nineteen months, thereby diffusing the issue for a period that extended past the election. Moreover, when the Supreme Court of Canada finally issued its judgment supporting the constitutionality of same-sex marriage legislation, the government was able to rely upon that ruling to justify introducing such legislation in Parliament. In sum, by seeking a constitutional reference, the government succeeded both in delaying and diffusing a contentious political issue and in garnering constitutional legitimacy for its decision.

The Role of Attorneys General in Legalising Politics

Not surprisingly, the *Charter* has greatly enhanced the powers of attorneys general who, as chief law officers of the Crown, can use it to influence public policy. Such influence is frequently used without consulting cabinet and almost always without consulting the legislature. The most obvious example of this influence relates to decisions concerning the conduct of *Charter* litigation, such as which arguments to make in court and which cases to appeal. Although these decisions can have a profound impact upon government powers and legislation, final say over them resides with attorneys general rather than with cabinets or legislatures. Within the federal government, for example, decisions concerning appeals to the Supreme Court of Canada are the responsibility of the Attorney General of Canada and turn on an assessment of whether "the public interest *requires* an appeal."[12] The Attorney General (or sometimes the Deputy Attorney General) bases this decision upon advice received from the National Litigation Committee, which is composed of a number of senior Department of Justice lawyers.[13] It is true that decisions concerning the conduct of *Charter* litigation at both the federal and provincial levels often involve attorneys general or their legal officers taking advice from other government officials. Government lawyers, for example, will commonly seek instructions from client ministries concerning whether, and on what basis, to defend a ministry policy that is attacked in court, as happened in relation to the forest tenure that became the subject of a constitutional challenge when I was Minister of Forests.

Similarly, attorneys general will sometimes seek advice from their cabinet colleagues and/or the premier or prime minister on civil litigation decisions affecting major public policy, such as whether to appeal a ruling striking down significant legislation. The federal Attorney General's decision not to appeal appellate court rulings striking down the common-law prohibition on same-sex marriage, for example, was discussed at the cabinet level and was ultimately announced by the Prime Minister.[14] As Attorney General of British Columbia, I spoke with both the Premier and cabinet before deciding not to appeal a trial court decision striking down the third-party election spending restrictions that were enacted following the cabinet deliberations referred to earlier in this chapter.[15] While my decision to forgo the appeal was influenced by legal considerations (particularly the existence of a case from another province that raised the same issue and was likely to reach the Supreme Court of Canada first), the political dimensions of the case were such that I did not feel comfortable making a final determination without first consulting the political executive.

While attorneys general and their law officers sometimes make decisions concerning *Charter* litigation in consultation with others in the executive branch, there are two things that need to be noted in evaluating the significance of these decisions on the legalisation of politics. The first is that such decisions are ultimately an attorney general's to make (although an attorney general would be foolish not to take seriously the advice given by cabinet on a highly contentious political issue such as same-sex marriage or election spending).[16] The second is that, regardless of the influence exerted on such decisions by other members of the executive branch, the decisions themselves remain artefacts of a legal process that involves the use of the *Charter* to shape public policy without legislative deliberation or oversight.

This process is well illustrated by the reaction of the Attorney General of Canada to the 1988 decision of the Federal Court in *Schachter v. Canada*.[17] The trial judge in this case held that a provision of the *Unemployment Insurance Act* providing fifteen weeks of parental leave benefits to adoptive parents contravened the guarantee of equality rights in section 15(1) of the *Charter* by not extending equivalent benefits to biological parents.[18] The Attorney General decided not to appeal this aspect of the decision, thereby leaving Parliament under a constitutional obligation to provide equal benefits to both groups of parents.[19] This obligation was addressed the following year when the Minister of Employment and Immigration tabled Bill C-21, which proposed to provide parental leave benefits to all parents for ten weeks.[20] This proposal represented a major alteration in the statutory scheme, both by reducing benefits for adoptive parents and by granting new benefits to biological parents. Moreover, given the much larger numbers of biological parents, it required a substantial expenditure of public funds not previously authorized by Parliament.

The frustration felt by Members of Parliament (MPs) concerning the constitutional constraints placed upon them by the trial court decision in *Schachter* is evident from the remarks of Jean-Pierre Blackburn, MP, during committee debate on Bill C-21: "When we, as members of Parliament, want to introduce amendments, we feel there is always something hanging over our heads: namely the famous rule that our amendment may run counter to the Charter. I find this rather disturbing. It is like a form of blackmail. As soon as a member tries to move an amendment, he or she is told that it may not be in keeping with the Charter. This fear prevents us from working in the interest of all Canadians."[21] This same frustration seems to have been shared by then Minister of Employment and Immigration, Barbara McDougall, who, during that same committee debate, stated in relation to requests to restore the benefits being taken away from adoptive parents: "I am very sensitive to the situation of adoptive parents. We gave considerable thought to this problem when the Bill was being drafted. The problem still exist. [*sic*] In fact, there are two problems. There is the problem of the Charter of Rights and Freedoms, and that regarding the situation of natural parents and adoptive parents. In addition, the system is open and much more costly. We are trying to find a solution. Before my appearance here today, I had not found a solution. I am sorry, but that is simply the case."[22] What the Minister did not say was that the option of seeking to preserve Parliament's ability to provide differential benefits for adoptive parents by appealing the trial judge's ruling had been taken away by the Attorney General of Canada who, whether he consulted cabinet (as seems likely) or not, made the decision to accept this limitation on legislative powers without ever consulting Parliament.

Some attorneys general have gone even further in using their authority over *Charter* litigation to defeat legislative powers. Ian Scott, acting as Attorney General of Ontario, saw no problem conceding in court that certain legislative provisions violated the *Charter*.[23] In *Re Blainey and Ontario Hockey Association et al.*, he joined with the plaintiff in submitting that the *Ontario Human Rights Code* was unconstitutional in exempting sports organisations from its prohibition on sexual discrimination.[24] Similarly, in *Paul and Wright v. The Minister of Consumer and Commercial Relations*, he conceded that the *Vital Statistics Act* was unconstitutional in requiring a child to be given the father's surname.[25] In the latter case at least, he took this stance after having introduced an amendment in the legislature that would have changed the law, but which had not yet been enacted. In the former case, however, he argued against the constitutionality of the provision without having tabled amending legislation, and, even more incredibly, he maintained this position in the Ontario Court of Appeal even after the impugned provision had been upheld by the trial judge.[26]

The *Charter* sometimes gives attorneys general the opportunity to challenge the constitutionality of laws outside provincial jurisdiction. As Attorney General of British Columbia, I asked the Director of Vital Statistics to withhold his decision to deny a marriage licence to a lesbian couple while I sought a court declaration that the federal common-law prohibition on same-sex marriage was unconstitutional. While I took this decision in the knowledge that the court action did not threaten provincial powers, and having sought and obtained the support of the Premier, there can be no question that it had profound political ramifications and was controversial amongst provincial legislators (including some in my own party).

The Legalisation of Political Advocacy and Discourse

Just as the *Charter* has changed the way in which governments make policy, it has also altered the way in which organised groups practise political advocacy.[27] Prior to the enactment of the *Charter*, the use of the courts to influence public policy by such groups was "exceptional." Since the enactment of the *Charter*, however, there has been a "transformation" through which interest group litigation has become "an established form of collective action" for all categories of organised interests.[28] Canadian feminists, for example, have committed huge amounts of time and energy to pursuing their political objectives through legal mobilisation, guided in large measure by lawyers working with the Women's Legal Education and Action Fund.[29] Groups, such as unions, corporations, civil libertarians, social conservatives, gay and lesbian rights organisations, market libertarians, religious bodies, anti-poverty advocates, and professional associations, have likewise invested heavily in *Charter* litigation. Moreover, given that the *Charter* is an instrument that can cut many ways, these groups have frequently found it necessary to participate in *Charter* cases to defend, as well as advance, their interests.

The inevitable consequence of the shift to litigation as a mechanism for political advocacy has been to increase the influence of law and lawyers within such organised groups.[30] This trend further feeds the tendency of such groups to look to courts rather than legislatures and governments to address their concerns. The overall impact, as Michael Mandel demonstrated in his examination of the court challenge brought against cruise missile testing by Operation Dismantle, is to downplay, or even demobilise, other forms of political action.[31] This is partly because litigation consumes huge amounts of time and money that cannot then be devoted to public education, lobbying, and other grassroots initiatives. It is also because the legal forms and forums in which *Charter* issues are argued makes them less comprehensible and accessible to the public and drains them of their political meaning.

This process is exacerbated by the nature of the discourse that such litigation produces in the media and popular press. Lawyers and law professors, whose opinions and oratory prior to the *Charter* were confined mostly to courtrooms and classrooms, are now regularly asked to share publicly their constitutional views on any and all political issues. These views are invariably packaged as their legal understanding of how the issues in question ought best to be addressed by the courts under the *Charter*. When commenting on court judgments, such commentary is usually comprised of *ex-post facto* legal explanations of how and why a court reached a particular decision, with muted, if any, criticism of the outcome. This posture is hardly surprising, given that judges are regarded as the ultimate authorities on constitutional interpretation. Even lawyers and groups who lose a *Charter* case will generally try to find something positive to say about the court's judgment, if only to justify their efforts to their clients, their supporters, or themselves. Thus, when Operation Dismantle's *Charter* claim against cruise missile testing was unanimously dismissed by the Supreme Court of Canada, the group characterized the decision as "a victory for the strength of the Charter and the civil rights and liberties of Canadians" because it recognized a judicial power to review cabinet decisions.[32] Similarly, when a majority of the Supreme Court of Canada rejected Louise Gosselin's claim that cuts to her social assistance payments violated her *Charter* rights, the *Charter* Committee on Poverty Issues, which had intervened in support of her claim, issued a press release in which one of its members welcomed the views of the dissenting judges and expressed relief "that the majority accepted the possibility the Charter will be found in a future case to protect the right to adequate food, clothing and housing."[33]

The legalisation of political discourse generated by the *Charter* is not confined to political advocacy groups and constitutional pundits. Politicians regularly invoke the *Charter* to explain, criticise, and debate public policy. Cabinet ministers welcome opportunities to rely on the *Charter* to support legislative measures or government actions, particularly where they are politically controversial. Thus, when introducing the legislation giving British Columbia francophone parents greater control over their children's French language educational programs, the first words from the Minister of Education's mouth were: "This bill will enable francophones living in British Columbia to have management and control of their children's francophone educational program, as provided for in Canada's Charter of Rights and Freedoms. Courts have interpreted section 23 of the Charter as requiring that francophone parents have management and control of francophone education, and this legislation is designed to provide that management and control through the Francophone Education Authority."[34] In the same vein, I should confess that my public explanation as Attorney General for seeking a court order declaring the common-law prohibition on same-sex marriage to be unconstitutional relied in large part upon a legal opinion that had been prepared by my Ministry and that I released to the media.

Opposition Members of the Legislative Assembly (MLAs) also commonly invoke the *Charter* to strengthen or legitimise their criticisms of government measures, as they did in British Columbia when challenging the introduction of laws prohibiting the publication of hate propaganda[35] and placing protective zones around abortion clinics (prohibiting harassment of people using or providing abortion services).[36] By invoking the *Charter*, these MLAs were able to give their criticisms a patina of constitutional legitimacy that made them less likely to offend the ethnic communities and the women that these measures were designed to protect.

The flip side of such *Charter*-based criticism is *Charter*-based justification, through which ministers and others defend a particular measure by relying upon the legal opinion that the measure complies with the *Charter*. This technique, which Kent Roach refers to as "Charter-proofing," was used extensively by the federal government when defending anti-terrorism legislation in the early part of this decade.[37] By claiming that the legislation had been reviewed and found by government lawyers to be consistent with the *Charter*, the government sought to conflate the question of whether the legislation was politically justifiable with the issue of whether it was constitutionally acceptable.

Politicians have also taken to using *Charter* discourse to try to manufacture political issues. Perhaps the most blatant example of this was Prime Minister Paul Martin's surprise promise during a leaders' debate in the 2006 federal election campaign to repeal the notwithstanding clause in section 33 of the *Charter*.[38] Martin clearly hoped that the ploy would create a wedge issue between himself and Conservative leader Stephen Harper, thereby diverting public attention from political difficulties he and his party were experiencing. As it turned out, the manoeuvre was too blatant and was widely interpreted as a disingenuous act of political desperation. This assessment was reinforced by the fact that Martin had previously vowed to invoke the notwithstanding clause, if necessary, to prevent courts from imposing same-sex marriage on religious organisations.[39]

Legalisation in Action – A Top Three List

I have thus far discussed with examples some of the ways in which the legalisation of politics in Canada has manifested itself under the *Charter*, including the explosion of *Charter* litigation in the courts; the increased influence of lawyers within government; the enhanced powers of Attorney Generals; and the legalisation of political advocacy and discourse. I will now focus on three instances that demonstrate the degree to which Canadian politics has become legalised in recent years. At a time when *Charter* enthusiasts have been assembling their "top ten" lists of court cases to mark the twenty-fifth anniversary of the *Charter*, I offer the following as my "top three" list of political legalisms, presented in ascending order of audacity.

Number 3: Canada Takes the *Charter* to the United Nations

As a signatory to the *International Covenant on Economic, Social and Cultural Rights (ICESCR)*, Canada is required to report periodically to the Committee on Economic, Social and Cultural Rights on what it is doing to fulfil its obligations under the *ICESCR*.[40] In the 1990s, as Canadian governments were embarking on major cutbacks to social programs, Canada turned to the *Charter* as evidence that it was meeting its *ICESCR* commitments. In its 1993 report to the Committee, for example, the Canadian delegation referenced the *Charter*'s capacity to encompass economic and social rights and the Supreme Court of Canada's use of the *ICESCR* in its interpretation of the *Charter*: "The Committee was informed that the *Charter of Rights and Freedoms* guarantees, in section 7, the right to security of the person and, in section 15, the equal benefit and protection of the law. It notes with satisfaction that Canadian courts have applied these provisions to cover certain economic and social rights, and that the Supreme Court of Canada has, on occasion, turned to the International Covenant on Economic, Social and Cultural Rights for guidance as to the meaning of provisions of the *Charter*."[41]

Five years later, when the 1998 report was due, the *Canada Assistance Plan (CAP)* had been replaced with a block transfer that gave provinces greater flexibility with respect to social programs. [42] This change posed a major problem for the Canadian delegation, as *CAP* had been highlighted in previous reports as a key instrument through which Canada was fulfilling its *ICESCR* obligations: "The Government informed the Committee in its 1993 report that *CAP* set national standards for social welfare, required that work by welfare recipients be freely chosen, guaranteed the right to an adequate standard of living, and facilitated court challenges to federally-funded provincial social assistance programmes which did not meet the standards prescribed in the *Act*."[43] Faced with the embarrassment of having to justify *CAP*'s elimination, the Canadian delegation again trotted out the *Charter* as evidence of Canada's continuing commitment to meeting its obligations under the *ICESCR*. According to its report, "the Canadian Charter of Rights and Freedoms plays a similar role at the domestic level regarding the protection of economic, social and cultural rights to that of the International Covenant on Civil and Political Rights at the international level."[44] The delegation went on to say that section 7 of the *Charter* "may be interpreted to include the rights protected under the Covenant" and that the Supreme Court of Canada "has also held section 7 as guaranteeing that people are not to be deprived of basic necessities." It noted further that the "Government of Canada is bound by these interpretations."[45]

These efforts to use the *Charter* to demonstrate Canada's continuing commitment to its obligations under the *ICESCR* are disturbing for a number of reasons. First, they rely on selective and strained interpretations of *Charter* jurisprudence. Second, these same interpretations have been strongly opposed by Canadian governments in domestic courts. Third, it is not an isolated example. Canada has used the same tactic in relation to the *Convention on the Rights of the Child*, insisting in 1995 that *Convention* rights were subject to *Charter* protection, while arguing the opposite in court a few years later.[46] At a more fundamental level, these practices are disturbing because they show how the *Charter* can be used to legalise even international politics, allowing Canadian delegations to invoke legal interpretations of abstract constitutional rights as a substitute for real evidence of substantive social progress and as a smokescreen for political failings.

Number 2: Senators Take Their Report to the Supreme Court of Canada
In 2002, the Standing Senate Committee on Social Affairs, Science and Technology, chaired by Senator Michael Kirby, released its report on Canada's health care system.[47] The report recommended that governments establish a "health care guarantee" that would oblige them to provide patients with timely access to medically necessary health care within public or private health delivery systems. According to the report, failure to provide patients such a guarantee, while preventing them from purchasing medically necessary services, would violate their rights to life and security under section 7 of the *Charter*. The Kirby report was seen as a contender to the report of the Royal Commission on the Future of Health Care, also released in 2002 by Commissioner Roy Romanow.[48] The Romanow report placed greater emphasis on the need to maintain a single-payer model of health care insurance and called for sweeping changes and a "health covenant" to ensure the sustainability of a universally accessible, publicly funded health care system.

In 2003, Kirby and nine other Senators on his committee sought leave in their official capacity to make arguments as interveners before the Supreme Court of Canada in *Chaoulli v. Quebec (Attorney General)*, which involved a *Charter* challenge to Quebec legislation prohibiting the sale of private health insurance in the province for core medical services.[49] Their application was contested by the respondent Attorney General of Canada on a number of grounds, including that it would create "a whole new forum for political discussion incongruent with the proper functioning and role of Parliament by allowing a particular group of parliamentarians holding a particular point of view a second forum to make their case, without the balance of divergent legislators' views; it would also open the door to Senators or members of the House of Commons opposed to the views of their colleagues to also seek to intervene in order to put forward ... their own point of view."[50] The Court finessed these objections by granting intervener status to the Senators in their individual capacities, whereupon they proceeded to file arguments based on their report in support of the appellants and in opposition to the position of the Government of Canada. In particular, they submitted that, absent a "health care guarantee," the prohibition on private health insurance violated patients' rights under section 7 of the *Charter*.[51] These arguments ultimately found favour with three of the four majority judges, thereby contributing to the Court's decision to declare the Quebec legislation invalid.

Here we see an example of the legalisation of politics in its purest and most potent form. Members of an unelected Senate Committee, not content to influence public policy through normal parliamentary channels, transform their political recommendations into legal arguments in order to persuade an unelected court to make a constitutional ruling that undermines the policies of both an elected federal government and an elected provincial legislature. Moreover, given its inconsistency with the principles of the *Canada Health Act*, this ruling also served to undermine the policies of an elected House of Commons and of the very Parliament to which those Senators belong.[52]

Number 1: Law Professors Take the *Charter* to Parliament

It used to be that law professors were academic mortals like all others. However, that was before the *Charter*. Now law professors are exalted interpreters of constitutional rights, second only to judges – and a close second at that. Consider the case of the 134 law professors who, in 2005, signed an open letter to then Opposition Leader Stephen Harper. The letter told Harper that, if he opposed proposed government legislation extending the right to marry to same-sex couples and offered amendments to limit the definition of marriage to opposite-sex couples, it would be "legally necessary" for him to use the *Charter*'s notwithstanding clause. "You must be completely honest with Canadians about the unconstitutionality of your proposal," the letter went on to say: "The truth is, there is only one way to accomplish your goal: invoke the notwithstanding clause."[53]

What was extraordinary about this advice was that it came in the wake of a Supreme Court of Canada judgment in which the Court, while holding that same-sex marriage was constitutionally permissible, refused to say whether it was constitutionally *required*. One of the reasons given by the judges for refusing to address this issue was that it "ha[d] the potential to undermine the uniformity that would be achieved by the adoption of the proposed legislation."[54] Yet, as the judgment itself noted, such uniformity would have been undermined only if the Court had concluded that same-sex marriage was *not* constitutionally required.[55] It is apparent, therefore, that the judges believed that the "potential" existed for the Court to reach this result – and the constitutional status of the prohibition on same-sex marriage remained an open question in their minds. Thus, while the law professors claimed to be certain that Harper's position was unconstitutional, the judges of the Supreme Court of Canada clearly signalled that they were not.

What makes the law professors' advice even more troubling is that, at the time the letter was written, Parliament remained the one major federal institution that had not yet been given a chance to consider the issue of same-sex marriage following appellate court judgments holding that it was constitutionally required. The Attorney General had considered the issue and decided not to pursue appeals. The cabinet and the Prime Minister had considered the issue and had decided to prepare draft legislation and refer it to the Supreme Court of Canada. The Supreme Court of Canada had considered the issue and had decided that same-sex marriage legislation was constitutionally permissible (but, as indicated earlier, not that it was constitutionally required). Given that the outcome of these various processes was to propose legislation to Parliament, one might have assumed that Parliament should have been given a meaningful opportunity to debate the legislation. One might particularly have thought that MPs, as the elected representatives of the people, should have been entitled to make their own best judgment on the merits of the legislation – including its constitutional merits. Yet, 134 law professors disagreed, suggesting that those opposed to same-sex marriage were not legally entitled to advance their position in Parliament without first conceding, by invoking the notwithstanding clause, that it contravened the *Charter*.

Now I have long been a supporter of the right of same-sex couples to marry. I was the first Attorney General in the Commonwealth to support such a right both by speaking out politically and by seeking a declaration in court under the *Charter*. I am also a law professor. However, the notion of law professors using their position as constitutional authorities to tell elected MPs that they are legally required to concede a breach of *Charter* rights in respect of a matter that was explicitly left open by the Supreme Court of Canada strikes me as more than a tad presumptuous. When I made this point at *The Charter @ 25* conference hosted by the McGill Institute for the Study of Canada in February 2007, a law professor who had signed the letter suggested to me that I was overreacting. The letter, she said, was simply a political strategy to support same-sex marriage rights. Excuse me? I believe that was my point! One hundred and thirty-four law professors engage in a political strategy by using their status as legal experts to challenge the constitutional capacity of elected MPs to advance a policy with which those professors disagree. Sounds like a pretty compelling example of legalised politics to me.

Conclusion

The legalisation of politics foreseen by some commentators at the time of the *Charter*'s enactment has become well established in Canada over the past twenty-five years. This process has increased the influence of lawyers and legal discourse within Canadian society while diminishing that of politicians and democratic engagement. Moreover, such legalisation has not been confined to the judicial arena: it has had a profound influence on the way political issues are considered and treated within governments, legislatures, and society at large. One aspect of legalised politics that I find especially troubling is the use of the *Charter* by public officials as a means of escaping political responsibility. Having been in government, I understand how tempting it can be to invoke the *Charter* to bolster a political argument or to delay making a decision, and I have succumbed to this temptation myself on occasion. What disturbs me is that such tendencies seem to have become endemic and that politicians and other public officials are turning to the *Charter* with increased regularity to justify or avoid taking positions on contentious issues, to shift political responsibility to the courts, and to try to discredit the political views of others.

I have made no secret of my concern that these developments, combined with other forces, are contributing to an impoverishment of Canadian democracy.[56] It would be a mistake, however, to assume that all legalisation of politics is unnecessary and undesirable. To the extent that societies make defined commitments to values such as due process and the rule of law, it is important that we have lawyers, both inside and outside of government, charged with the responsibility of ensuring that elected and unelected officials adhere to these commitments. My concern for legalised politics, therefore, is not absolute but, rather, is directed at the use of law to address politically contested matters that ought, in my view, to be the subject of democratic engagement and decision making. This is a concern that I hope would be shared by others who espouse the values of democracy, including those who seek to justify judicial review on the basis that it forms part of a "democratic dialogue" with legislatures.[57] It is, after all, not much of a dialogue and hardly democratic if the same legal norms and interpretations are driving decisions at both ends.

Acknowledgments
I am grateful to Judy Fudge, Allan Hutchinson, Maureen Maloney, and Murray Rankin for their helpful comments and suggestions and to Jennifer Bond for her invaluable editorial assistance.

Notes

1 *Canadian Charter of Rights and Freedoms,* Part I of the *Constitution Act, 1982,* being Schedule B to the *Canada Act 1982* (U.K.), 1982, c.11 [*Charter*].

2 See, for example, Peter H. Russell, "The Political Purposes of the Canadian Charter of Rights and Freedoms," *Canadian Bar Review* 61 (1983): 51; H. Glasbeek and M. Mandel, "The Legalisation of Politics in Advanced Capitalism: The Canadian Charter of Rights and Freedoms," *Socialist Studies* 2 (1984): 84; and M. Mandel, *The Charter of Rights and the Legalisation of Politics in Canada* (Toronto: Wall and Simpson, 1989).

3 The author served as an articling student and lawyer with the Constitutional Branch of Saskatchewan Justice from 1982 to 1984; as law professor at Osgoode Hall Law School and the University of Victoria Law School from 1984 to the present; and as a Member of the Legislative Assembly of British Columbia from 1991 to 2001, where he held numerous cabinet portfolios, including Aboriginal Relations, Forests, Health, Finance, Inter-Governmental Relations, Advanced Education, and Attorney General.

4 It is true, of course, that judicial policy making on issues such as abortion and obscenity occurred prior to the *Charter* in the context of common law decision making and statutory interpretation. The judicial policy making that takes place under the *Charter,* however, is qualitatively different in that it is based on a constitutional mandate to give political meaning to open-ended rights and in that the policy-making authority of judges takes precedence over that of elected legislators.

5 Matthew A. Hennigar, "Expanding the 'Dialogue' Debate: Federal Government Responses to Lower Court Charter Decisions," *Canadian Journal of Political Science* 37 (2004): 16.

6 Ibid., 16-17.

7 James B. Kelly, *Governing with the Charter* (Vancouver: UBC Press, 2005), 245-49.

8 Janet L. Hiebert, *Charter Conflicts: What Is Parliament's Role?* (Montreal and Kingston: McGill-Queen's University Press, 2002), 11-12.

9 The resulting legislation was subsequently challenged and struck down by the Supreme Court of British Columbia as being contrary to the guarantee of freedom of expression in section 2(b) of the *Charter: Pacific Press v. British Columbia (Attorney General),* [2000] 5 W.W.R. 219. As explained later in this chapter, this decision was not appealed, but the same issue was later addressed by the Supreme Court of Canada in *Harper v. Canada (Attorney General),* [2004] 1 S.C.R. 827, in which a majority of judges disapproved of the *Pacific Press* decision and held that similar third-party spending restrictions in federal legislation were justified under section 1 of the *Charter.*

10 For a fuller discussion of this issue, see Matthew Hennigar, "Reference re Same-Sex Marriage: Making Sense of the Government's Litigation Strategy," in this volume.

11 *Reference re Same-Sex Marriage,* [2004] 3 S.C.R. 698.

12 Department of Justice Canada, *Federal Prosecution Service Deskbook* (Ottawa: Department of Justice Canada, 2000), Sec. 22.3, [emphasis in original].

13 Matthew A. Hennigar, "Why Does the Federal Government Appeal to the Supreme Court of Canada in Charter of Rights Cases? A Strategic Explanation," *Law and Society Review* 41 (2007): 231.

14 Ibid., 232; and Tonda MacCharles, "It Was an Issue of Rights," *Toronto Star* (October 2, 2004), Foundation Émergence, http://www.emergence.qc.ca/default.aspx?scheme=2484. This may have been done because the decision not to appeal was announced together with the decision to propose legislation recognizing the union of same-sex couples and to refer this legislation to the Supreme Court of Canada. See Canada, *Statement by the Prime Minister on Same Sex Unions* (June 17, 2003), Canada News Centre, http://news.gc.ca/web/view/en/index.jsp?articleid=62559&categoryid=9&do_as=true&view_as=search&df_as=17&mf_as=6&yf_as=2003&dt_as=17&mt_as=6&yt_as=2003&categoryid=9&do_as=true&view_as=content&df_as=17&mf_as=6&yf_as=2003&dt_as=17&mt_as=6&yt_as=2003&.

15 *Pacific Press v. British Columbia (Attorney General),* [2000] 5 W.W.R. 219.

16 Matthew A. Hennigar, "Conceptualizing Attorney General Conduct in Charter Litigation: From Independence to Central Agency," *Canadian Public Administration* 51:2 (2008): 201.

17 *Schachter v. Canada,* [1988] 3 F.C. 515.

18 *Unemployment Insurance Act, 1971,* S.C. 1970-71-72, c. 48, ss. 32 (as amended by R.S.C. 1980-81-82-83, c. 150, s. 4) and 32(1) (as amended by R.S.C. 1980-81-82-83, c. 150, s. 5).

19 The Attorney General did appeal the remedy granted by the Federal Court, which extended the benefits to biological parents rather than strike the section down. This appeal had the effect of prolonging the trial judge's order that the operation of his judgment be suspended pending appeal. See *Schachter v. Canada,* [1992] 2 S.C.R. 679.

20 *An Act to Amend the Unemployment Insurance Act and the Employment and Immigration Department and Commission Act,* S.C. 1990, c. 40, s. 24.

21 Canada, House of Commons, *Minutes of Proceedings and Evidence of the Legislative Committee on Bill C-21,* 34th Parl., No. 12:2 (October 3, 1989) [English translation].

22 Ibid.

23 See Ian Scott, "Law, Policy, and the Role of the Attorney General: Constancy and Change in the 1980s," *University of Toronto Law Journal* 39 (1989): 124-26.

24 *Re Blainey and Ontario Hockey Association et al.* (1985), 52 O.R. (2d) 225 (Ont. H.C.J.); *Ontario Human Rights Code,* R.S.O. 1980, c. 340, s. 2.

25 *Paul and Wright v. The Minister of Consumer and Commercial Relations,* unreported decision of the High Court of Justice of Ontario, December 9, 1985; *Vital Statistics Act,* R.S.O. 1980, c. 525 (as amended by R.S.O. 1981, c. 66, and R.S.O. 1983, c. 34).

26 *Re Blainey and Ontario Hockey Association et al.* (1986), 54 O.R. (2d) 5 (Ont. C.A.).

27 For a comprehensive analysis of interest group use of political advocacy, see Troy Riddell, "Explaining the Impact of Legal Mobilization and Judicial Decisions: Official Minority Language Education Rights outside Quebec," in this volume.

28 Gregory Hein, "Interest Group Litigation and Canadian Democracy," in P. Howe and P. Russell, eds., *Judicial Power and Canadian Democracy* (Montreal and Kingston: McGill-Queen's University Press, 2001), 222.

29 See Christopher P. Manfredi, *Feminist Activism in the Supreme Court of Canada: Legal Mobilization and the Women's Legal Education and Action Fund* (Vancouver: UBC Press, 2004); and Gwen Brodsky and Shelagh Day, *Canadian Charter Equality Rights for Women: One Step Forward or Two Steps Back?* (Ottawa: Canadian Advisory Council on the Status of Women, 1989).

30 See Miriam Smith, *Lesbian and Gay Rights in Canada: Social Movements and Equality Seeking, 1971-95* (Toronto: University of Toronto Press, 1999).

31 *Operation Dismantle v. The Queen,* [1985] 1 S.C.R. 441, cited in M. Mandel, *The Charter of Rights and the Legalization of Politics in Canada,* revised edition (Toronto: Thompson Educational Publishing, 1994), 74-81.

32 Ibid., 78; *Toronto Star* (May 9, 1985), A1.

33 *Gosselin v. Quebec (Attorney General),* [2002] 4 S.C.R. 429, cited in Bonnie Morton, *Charter Committee on Poverty Issues,* "Gosselin Decision from Supreme Court," press release (December 19, 2002), http://dawn.thot.net/gosselin1.html.

34 British Columbia, Legislative Assembly, *Hansard,* 6 (June 18, 1997) at 4588 (Hon. P. Ramsey).

35 *Human Rights Amendment Act,* R.S.B.C. 1993, c. 27.

36 *Access to Abortion Services Act,* R.S.B.C. 1996, c. 1.

37 Kent Roach, "The Dangers of a Charter-Proof and Crime-Based Response to Terrorism," in Ronald Daniels, Patrick Macklem, and Kent Roach, eds., *The Security of Freedom: Essays on Canada's Anti-Terrorism Bill* (Toronto: University of Toronto Press, 2001), 131.

38 "Martin Wraps Campaign in Constitutional Pledge," *CBC News* (January 10, 2006), cbc.ca, http://www.cbc.ca/news/story/2006/01/09/elxn-debates-look.html.

39 Janice Tibbetts, "Martin Won't Force Gay Marriages on Churches," *CanWest News Service* (December 19, 2003), Canada.com, http://www.canada.com/national/features/samesexmarriage/story.html?id=ee4d2e69-d040-4e5f-8830-0cb2bb7d8bbd.

40 Much of the information in this section is drawn with permission from Shauna Labman, "Charter Maybes = Starving Babies?" (2002) [unpublished]. *International Covenant on Economic, Social and Cultural Rights* (1976), 993 U.N.T.S. 3, [1976] C.T.S. 46.

41 United Nations Economic and Social Council, Committee on Economic, Social and Cultural Rights, *Consideration of Reports Submitted by States Parties Under Articles 16 and 17 of the Covenant: Concluding Observations of the Committee on Economic Social and Cultural Rights (Canada),* Geneva, Doc. E/C 12/1993/5 (June 10, 1993) at para 93.

42 *Canada Assistance Plan,* R.S.C. 1985, c. C-1.

43 United Nations Economic and Social Council, Committee on Economic, Social and Cultural Rights, *supra* note 41, at para 19.

44 *Implementation of the International Covenant on Economic, Social and Cultural Rights,* Third Periodic Report: Canada, Doc. E/1994/104/Add.17 (January 20, 1998), at para. 8.

45 *Review of Canada's Third Report on the Implementation of the International Covenant on Economic, Social and Cultural Rights: Responses to the Supplementary Questions Emitted by the United Nations Committee on Economic, Social and Cultural Rights,* Doc. E/C/12/Q/CAN/1 (November 1998) on *Canada's Third Report on the International Covenant on Economic, Social and Cultural Rights,* Doc. E/1994//104/Add.17 (1994) at Question 53.

46 C. Scott, "Canada's International Human Rights Obligations and Disadvantaged Members of Society: Finally into the Spotlight?" *Constitutional Forum* 10:4 (1999): 107. *Convention on the Rights of the Child,* G.A. res. 44/25, annex, 44 U.N. GAOR Supp. (No. 49) at 167, U.N. Doc. A/44/49 (1989), entered into force Sept. 2 1990.

47 Canada, Standing Senate Committee on Social Affairs, Science and Technology, *The Health of Canadians – The Federal Role,* vol. 6 (October 2002), http://www.parl.gc.ca/37/2/parlbus/commbus/senate/com-e/SOCI-E/rep-e/repoct02vol6-e.htm.

48 Canada, Royal Commission on the Future of Health Care in Canada, *Building on Values: The Future of Health Care in Canada,* Final Report, http://www.hc-sc.gc.ca/english/care/romanow/hcc0086.html.

49 *Chaoulli v. Quebec (Attorney General),* [2005] 1 S.C.R. 791.

50 Ibid., Response of the Attorney General of Canada to the Motion for Leave to Intervene of Senator Kirby et al., 3, http://www.healthcoalition.ca/int-6.pdf.

51 Ibid., Factum of the Interveners Senator Michael Kirby et al. (March 12, 2002), http://www.law.utoronto.ca/healthlaw/docs/chaoulli/Factum_Senate.pdf.

52 *Canada Health Act,* R.S.C. 1985, c. C-6.

53 Open letter from Canadian law professors to Stephen Harper (January 25, 2005), http://www.law.utoronto.ca/samesexletter.html.

54 *Reference re Same-Sex Marriage,* [2004] 3 S.C.R. 698 at para. 69.

55 Ibid., para. 70.

56 For discussion of some of the other factors contributing to an impoverished Canadian democracy and what might be done to address them, see Andrew Petter, "Look Who's Talking Now: Dialogue Theory and the Return to Democracy," in Richard W. Bauman and Tsvi Kahana, eds., *The Least Examined Branch: The Role of Legislatures in the Constitutional State* (New York: Cambridge University Press, 2006), 519.

57 See, for example, Peter W. Hogg and Allison A. Bushell, "The *Charter* Dialogue between Courts and Legislatures (or Perhaps the *Charter of Rights* Isn't Such a Bad Thing after All)," *Osgoode Hall Law Journal* 35 (1997): 75; and Kent Roach, *The Supreme Court on Trial: Judicial Activism or Democratic Dialogue* (Toronto: Irwin Law, 2001).

3
Rationalizing Judicial Power: The Mischief of Dialogue Theory

Grant Huscroft

The *Canadian Charter of Rights and Freedoms* has become the dominant feature of the Canadian Constitution. Canadians have embraced the idea of rights, and it is difficult to discuss anything of importance these days without the *Charter* being raised. As rights have come to dominate Canadian political discourse, the power of the Supreme Court of Canada has grown enormously. The Court is the self-styled "guardian of the constitution," and the other branches of government have acquiesced in their claims to the mantle.[1] Just over twenty-five years into the life of the *Charter*, the Court's opinion – more accurately, the opinion of a majority of the Court's justices – is the *only* thing that seems to matter. The *Charter* is the Court's to interpret, so much so that for many there is no distinction between the Court and the *Charter* itself – the *Charter*'s vaguely worded rights and freedoms are supposed to mean whatever the Court says they do.

Canadians have come to assume that their elected representatives – the same ones who wrote and entrenched the *Charter* – are the enemy of rights and freedoms, while the Court is their champion. It follows that interpretation of the *Charter* outside the Court must be illegitimate. Indeed, the notion that politicians should contest the meaning of the *Charter* (that is, the Court's interpretation of the *Charter*) is perceived as a radical idea, if not an affront to the rule of law itself. It is assumed that rights are meaningful only if they are entrenched in legal form and that legal rights are only meaningful in the hands of the Court.

Dialogue theory offers a means of rationalizing this world of judicial interpretive supremacy. In their 1997 article that outlined the theory, Peter Hogg and Allison Bushell concluded that judicial review was not a problem for democracy. Canada, they insisted, has a weak form of judicial review in which the Supreme Court of Canada does not have the last word.[2] This conclusion suited the Court, which embraced the dialogue metaphor as a means of answering its critics.

I am all in favour of a dialogue between the Supreme Court of Canada and the other branches of Canadian government about the meaning of the *Charter*, in which the Court would respect and be influenced by the legislature's interpretation of the *Charter*.[3] But this is not the sort of dialogue that dialogue theorists have in mind. They specifically reject the idea of coordinate interpretation, portending interpretive anarchy, tyranny of the majority, and a host of other disasters if the legislature is permitted to disagree with the judicial interpretation of the *Charter*. The "dialogue" they have in mind is one in which the Court is free to interpret the *Charter* as it will, with the legislature required to adopt the Court's interpretation and act within such parameters as the Court allows. This is not a dialogue. It is top-down constitutionalism, and it is a poor way in which to run a constitutional democracy.[4]

I begin with a brief review of dialogue theory before moving on to consider the role dialogue theorists ascribe to the Supreme Court of Canada. The features of the *Charter* that are said to promote dialogue are discussed, and the example of tobacco advertising regulation is considered. I argue that dialogue theory presents a misleading picture of the impact of judicial review under the *Charter*. Judicial supremacy in interpreting the *Charter* – a key premise of dialogue theory – renders meaningful dialogue impossible.

The Nature of Dialogue Theory

The purpose of dialogue theory was to challenge the counter-majoritarian difficulty, or what Hogg and Bushell call the anti-majoritarian objection to the legitimacy of judicial review – the notion that the power of the Court to strike down a democratically enacted law is undemocratic because "it thwarts the will of representatives of the actual people of the here and now."[5] Hogg and Bushell begin from the premise that "judges have a great deal of discretion in 'interpreting' the law of the constitution, and the process of interpretation inevitably remakes the constitution into the likeness favoured by the judges."[6] This premise cedes much ground to critics of judicial review and judicial power. It is especially problematic in light of the large number of cases in which the Supreme Court of Canada has invalidated legislation in the first twenty-five years of the *Charter*. As Peter Hogg has written in another context, "Canada is a tolerant, sophisticated, liberal society with a flourishing democracy. For so many of its laws to be found in conflict with the Charter guarantees can only be explained by activism on the part of the Supreme Court of Canada."[7]

One would expect an argument for checks on judicial power to follow or perhaps an argument for judicial restraint. Instead, Hogg and Bushell argue that the large number of cases in which legislation has been declared unconstitutional is of little moment. The *Charter*, they say, includes a number of features that leave ample room for legislatures to respond to judicial decisions.

The cornerstone of dialogue theory is Hogg and Bushell's survey of the aftermath of decisions of the Supreme Court of Canada. They found that, as of 1997, new legislation was passed following 53 of 66 cases in which the Court declared legislation unconstitutional. Updating their survey to 2007, they found that new legislation was passed following 14 of 23 such cases.[8] The suggestion is that it does not matter how the Court interprets the *Charter*, since the Court need not have the last word.

What Dialogue Theory Does – and Doesn't Do

The meaning of the dialogue metaphor is more modest than might be supposed. As Peter Hogg, Allison Bushell-Thornton, and Wade Wright acknowledge in their 2007 retrospective, "all we meant by the dialogue metaphor was that the court decisions in Charter cases usually left room for a legislative response, and usually received a legislative response."[9] Dialogue theory does not offer a normative justification for judicial review,[10] nor does it offer a theory of constitutional interpretation or otherwise assist courts in interpreting the *Charter*.[11] Hogg and Bushell claimed that dialogue theory resolves the counter-majoritarian difficulty, but this claim was soon retracted.[12]

Hogg, Bushell-Thornton, and Wright make the more limited claim that their findings "certainly made the anti-majoritarian objection difficult to sustain,"[13] but even this weaker claim is not justified. It is impossible to assess the impact of judicial review simply by reference to aggregate legislative responses. The influence of judicial decisions striking down legislation extends far beyond the circumstances of particular legislation. Judicial decisions influence the legislative agenda and, hence, the political processes in ways that cannot be measured empirically. The Court may dissuade, if not preclude, legislators from legislating, or it may in effect dictate the terms of a permissible legislative response, and dialogue theory has nothing to say about either outcome. In general, dialogue theory is not concerned with qualitative outcomes. It is satisfied so long as *any* legislative response follows a judicial decision striking down legislation, even if this response is the simple act of repealing the impugned legislation.

Dialogue theory really has little to offer the study of judicial review. Its main function is to rationalize judicial supremacy over the interpretation of the *Charter*, and it does so by exaggerating the power of the democratic branch of government to respond to judicial decisions.

Judicial Supremacy and Its Place in Dialogue Theory

If there was any doubt about how dialogue theory regards judicial decisions, Hogg, Bushell-Thornton, and Wright make things clear: "Our position is that final authority to interpret the Charter rests properly with the judiciary (or, to put it differently, that judicial interpretation of the Charter is authoritative)."[14] This is judicial supremacy, and it is proffered in answer to claims that the other branches of government are also legitimate interpreters of the *Charter*. No claim is made that the judiciary always gets it right; on the contrary, Hogg, Bushell-Thornton, and Wright admit that judicial mistakes happen. Given their premise about judicial interpretive discretion ("judges have a great deal of discretion in 'interpreting' the law of the constitution, and the process of interpretation inevitably remakes the constitution into the likeness favoured by the judges"[15]), one would expect that the case for judicial interpretive supremacy would be difficult to defend. But defend it they do. They do not limit judicial supremacy to the outcome of particular cases, as proponents of coordinate interpretation would concede is appropriate. They insist on judicial supremacy in interpreting the Charter *per se*.

Consider what judicial interpretive supremacy entails. The Supreme Court of Canada has enormous discretion in deciding whether, and how, to exercise its power to interpret the *Charter*:

- the Court hears cases by leave and so chooses whether or not to intervene in the previous settlement of a matter by the lower courts;
- the Court decides who will be permitted to litigate and has one of the most liberalized standing regimes in the world;
- the Court decides who will be permitted to intervene in litigation and the basis on which they will be allowed to participate;
- the Court hears reference questions, which it may supplement or even refuse to answer at its discretion, and accords precedential value to its advice;
- the Court may decide to answer moot or hypothetical questions;
- the Court may decide to provide answers in *obiter dicta* going well beyond what is required in order to resolve the case before it;
- the Court may modify statutes by "reading-down" particular provisions or "reading-in" others;
- the Court may "strike down" legislation or choose to suspend a declaration of unconstitutionality in order to allow a legislative response;
- the Court may "suggest" how alternative legislation should be drafted;
- and so on.

These are some of the more common examples of the Court's discretionary power where the *Charter* is concerned. Unlike the United States Supreme Court, the Supreme Court of Canada is not constrained by a "case or controversy" requirement,[16] and the "passive virtues" – various means by which the United States Supreme Court avoids or limits the extent of constitutional adjudication – have no place in *Charter* jurisprudence.[17] The Court is, in short, self-defining of the role it plays in the Canadian constitutional order. Once it decides to deal with a matter under the *Charter*, all that is left for the legislature is whatever the Court chooses to allow.

It is important to emphasize this point because the Court need not allow any room for the legislature, or room in any meaningful sense. The Court may preclude a legislative response by holding that legislation does not pursue an end sufficiently important to warrant the establishment of any limits on a right. Alternatively, the Court may leave room for a legislative response but dictate the terms of that response. For example, it may set a timetable for the passage of new legislation by suspending a declaration of unconstitutionality from six to eighteen months rather than giving its decisions immediate effect. More importantly, it may direct the legislature in terms of the policy choices it will permit.[18] In this way, the Court exercises considerable control over the political dynamic.

Judicial decisions interpreting the *Charter* are never politically neutral in their effect, whatever the Court may intend. They create powerful incentives and disincentives to political action that dialogue theory ignores. In order to pass replacement legislation, a government must revisit an issue that had long since been settled. Even assuming that the government can make room on the legislative agenda, perhaps by displacing other legislative priorities, the passage of new legislation following a *Charter* decision involves the expenditure of political capital. It is difficult to legislate at the best of times – even for a majority government – and it may be impossible to do so in the face of new political realities created by the Court's decision. Parliament's inability to pass new legislation regulating abortion following the decision in *R v. Morgentaler* (striking down the *Criminal Code* therapeutic abortion regime) is the classic example in this regard.[19]

The Irrelevance of Formal Response Mechanisms

Constitutions are designed to be difficult to amend, and the Canadian Constitution is no exception.[20] Amendment of the *Constitution Act, 1982,* to overturn a judicial interpretation of the *Charter* is unlikely, to say the least, but dialogue theory suggests that the structure of the *Charter* facilitates legislative responses that render amendment unnecessary. In their original dialogue article, Hogg and Bushell refer to the room legislatures have to limit rights under section 1, even after a judicial decision striking down legislation: "With appropriate recitals in the legislation, and with appropriate evidence available if necessary to support the legislative choice, one can usually be confident that a carefully drafted "second attempt" will be upheld against any future Charter challenges."[21]

But even if a legislature manages to pass replacement legislation, there is no guarantee that it will be found to be constitutional.[22] The *Court* ultimately decides what is reasonable where section 1 is concerned, and this decision depends on how deferential it chooses to be on judicial review. As *Sauvé v. Canada (Chief Electoral Officer)* demonstrates, confidence that a carefully drafted second attempt will be upheld may be misplaced.[23] In that case,

Parliament's good faith attempt to limit prisoners' voting rights – legislation passed following the Supreme Court of Canada's decision striking down a blanket ban on prisoners' voting – was struck down by a deeply divided Court. Writing for the five-justice majority, Chief Justice McLachlin asserted that Parliament is not entitled to deference when it revises legislation following a judicial decision. On the contrary, she repudiated Parliament's attempt to limit the right to vote and, more important, its second attempt at legislating: "The healthy and important promotion of a dialogue between the legislature and the courts should not be debased to a rule of 'if at first you don't succeed, try, try again.'"[24]

According to dialogue theory, however, legislatures have another option. Section 33 of the *Charter* allows legislation to be passed notwithstanding certain *Charter* rights and freedoms. This provision, it is said, "changes the balance of power between the judicial and legislative branches."[25] According to Hogg, "[s]o long as the last word remains with the competent legislative body, there can be no acute or longstanding conflict between the judicial and legislative branches, and much of the American debate over the legitimacy of judicial review is rendered irrelevant."[26] The notwithstanding clause appears to be significant indeed, so much so that its very existence has been lamented by those who fear that it undermines the *Charter* itself.[27] In practice, however, the notwithstanding clause is irrelevant for a number of reasons. It is subject to a number of inherent limitations that are usually underplayed if not ignored:

1 *The notwithstanding clause does not apply to everything in the* Charter.
   The notwithstanding clause applies to sections 2 and 7-15 of the *Charter*. This covers the main rights and freedoms – fundamental freedoms, legal rights, and equality rights – but it leaves out significant provisions. The notwithstanding clause does not apply, for example, to section 3, meaning that the Court's narrow decision in *Sauvé* is the last word on prisoners' voting rights. Nor does the notwithstanding clause apply to mobility rights (section 6), official language rights (sections 16-22), minority language education rights (section 23), judicial enforcement of the *Charter* (section 24), or any of the provisions listed under the "General" heading (sections 25-31).[28]

2 *The notwithstanding clause can only be invoked for five years at a time.*
   A notwithstanding declaration in legislation operates for only a five-year term, subject to legislative renewal. In effect, section 33 provides a five-year respite from judicial supremacy in regard to the interpretation of the relevant rights and freedoms. In order for Parliament or a provincial legislature to prevail over the Court's interpretation of the *Charter* permanently, it must revisit the issue every five years and pass new legislation. The default position is judicial supremacy.

3   *The notwithstanding clause applies only prospectively.*
The notwithstanding clause applies only prospectively.[29] As a result, the efficacy of a notwithstanding declaration may depend on judicial willingness to facilitate its use. This, in turn, depends on something that is arguably extra-constitutional: the Court's willingness to suspend declarations of unconstitutionality in order to allow time for the notwithstanding clause to be invoked.[30]

These limitations on the use of the notwithstanding clause help explain why it is used so rarely: it offers little, and, what is more, the political price that must be paid for its use is high. That is so because the wording of the notwithstanding clause suggests that its purpose is to allow legislatures to opt out of *Charter* rights and freedoms rather than simply to overturn particular judicial interpretations of them.[31] If it is difficult for legislatures to be seen to be disagreeing with the Supreme Court of Canada at the best of times, conflation of the *Charter* and the decisions of the Court interpreting the *Charter* render disagreement with judicial decisions nearly impossible. Thus, the very provision that was required in order to secure the agreement to entrench the *Charter* in the Constitution of Canada has become irrelevant. There have been no significant uses of the notwithstanding clause outside of Quebec, which is obviously a special case in view of that province's opposition to the patriation of the Constitution in 1982. More telling, there has been only one use of the notwithstanding clause to overturn a judicial decision, again in Quebec.[32] Successive prime ministers and premiers in most provinces have disavowed the use of the clause.

This should come as a considerable embarrassment for dialogue theory, which depends on the existence of the notwithstanding clause. The notwithstanding clause is said to separate judicial review in Canada from judicial review in the United States, which dialogue theorists portray as "strong-form" and almost different in kind. Hogg, Bushell-Thornton, and Wright have no doubt that the notwithstanding clause would have been used if such a clause existed in the United States and are sure that it will be used in Canada:

Make no mistake about it: if conflict between the judicial and legislative branches in Canada ever approached the intensity and duration of the conflict that occurred in the United States during the Lochner era (1905-37) or during, and just after, the Warren Court (1953-73) (and that continues to this day with respect to abortion), the current reluctance by Canadian politicians to use the override would disappear.[33]

Of course, they cannot know any of this, let alone be certain. This is rhetoric, and it betrays the flimsiness of the notion that the existence of section 33 legitimizes judicial review. In truth, the notwithstanding clause may be more useful to the Court than to Canadian legislatures. It absolves the Court from responsibility for its decisions, since the Court can insist that the notwithstanding clause is available if the legislature cannot live with its decisions. Indeed, some proponents of dialogue theory rely on the existence of the notwithstanding clause in advocating expansive interpretation of the *Charter*. As Kent Roach puts it, "[t]he fact that their decisions under the Charter can be revised or reversed by the legislature suggests that judges can afford to err on the side of more robust approaches to judicial review."[34]

Despite the importance of the notwithstanding clause to their theory, I expect that proponents of dialogue theory would abhor the use of the notwithstanding clause in practice. Judicial supremacy over the *Charter* is, for them, not simply a description of our constitutional order; it is a normative preference. Given the standard objections dialogue theorists raise in opposition to coordinate interpretation – concerns about tyranny of the legislative majority and the inappropriateness of legislatures being judge in their own cause, and so on[35] – it is ironic that their defence of the democratic legitimacy of judicial review under the *Charter* should depend on a provision that, in theory at least, allows majoritarian outcomes on questions of individual rights.

Canada Has a Strong Form of Judicial Review

Despite all of the evidence to the contrary, dialogue theorists insist that Canada has a weak form of judicial review as compared to the United States.[36] Indeed, it is a point of pride for many constitutional scholars to distinguish judicial review under the *Charter* from judicial review under the American *Bill of Rights*, the paradigmatic model of strong-form judicial review, as though Canadians cleverly avoided the worst aspects of American constitutionalism.[37] This is an embarrassing conceit that depends upon a mischaracterization of the nature of judicial review in the United States and an exaggeration of the features of the *Charter* that are supposed to facilitate dialogue. The difference between judicial review under the *Charter* and the American *Bill of Rights* is more a matter of form than substance. American constitutional law is replete with detailed and sophisticated tests that the courts have established to determine the parameters of the rights protected by the American *Bill of Rights*. The difference is that American courts do not limit rights pursuant to a single provision such as section 1. Instead, the idea of limits is inherent in the rights themselves. As Mark Tushnet explains,

in the United States the Supreme Court *defines* the rights in question by referring to the justifications the government has for its action. Social interests are accommodated in the process of defining constitutional rights, and no right exists to be infringed if the government's justifications are good enough. In that sense only are rights in the United States absolute: Because government justifications have been taken into account at step one, nothing remains to be done by taking a second step."[38]

Consider the sophisticated analysis that goes on in free speech cases under the First Amendment, in which different types of speech are afforded varying degrees of protection. The United States Supreme Court's test for the regulation of commercial expression, established in *Central Hudson Gas and Electric Corp. v. Public Service Commission*,[39] is virtually identical to the approach to limiting rights the Supreme Court of Canada established several years later in *R. v. Oakes*.[40] That different results obtain in freedom of expression cases in Canada and the United States is a reflection of different historical and cultural influences rather than weak or strong constitutional methodology.[41]

There is nothing weak about judicial review in Canada. The power to strike down democratically enacted legislation under the *Charter* sets us apart from parliamentary democracies such as New Zealand,[42] the United Kingdom,[43] and Australia.[44] All of these countries have adopted bills of rights since the *Charter* was passed, whether at the national or state level, but none of them followed Canada's example in adopting a constitutionally entrenched bill of rights that confers the power to strike down legislation on the courts. Courts are limited to declaring inconsistency or reading down a statute in the event that they consider that it unjustifiably infringes rights. If there is such a thing as weak form judicial review,[45] it exists in these countries. Not only do these countries limit the power of their courts, but their bills of rights are subject to amendment pursuant to the ordinary political processes.[46]

Dialogue Theory in Action: Regulating Tobacco Advertising

Canada's experience with the regulation of tobacco advertising demonstrates how misleading dialogue theory can be. The story begins with the *Tobacco Products Control Act*, federal legislation regulating the advertising, promotion, and labelling of tobacco products.[47] Among other things, the legislation prohibited tobacco advertising and required product labels on tobacco products to include unattributed health warnings. Unconstitutional legislation, one would suppose, in light of the dangers posed by tobacco products, but judicial decisions that permit corporations to exercise *Charter* rights and establish expansive conceptions of freedom of expression have made it clear that tobacco companies have a constitutional right to advertise.[48] Thus, the main issue in *RJR-MacDonald Inc. v. Canada (Attorney General)* was whether or not the advertising prohibition and health warning requirement could be justified as a reasonable limit on freedom of expression.[49]

By a five-to-four majority, the Court held that the government had failed to justify the infringements on the tobacco companies' freedom of expression,[50] and the advertising ban and unattributed product warning requirement were struck down. At the same time, however, the majority of the Court essentially told Parliament what sorts of limits on tobacco advertising it would allow. As then Justice McLachlin wrote,

> The government had before it a variety of less intrusive measures when it enacted the total ban on advertising, including: a partial ban which would allow information and brand preference advertising; a ban on lifestyle advertising only; measures such as those in Quebec's Consumer Protection Act, R.S.Q., c. P-40.1, to prohibit advertising aimed at children and adolescents; and labelling requirements only (which Health and Welfare believed would be preferable to an advertising ban: A.J. Liston's testimony). In my view, any of these alternatives would be a reasonable impairment of the right to free expression, given the important objective and the legislative context.[51]

Following the decision in *RJR-MacDonald*, Parliament passed new legislation that followed the majority's guidelines. The *Tobacco Act* allows information and brand-preference advertising but forbids lifestyle advertising and promotion, advertising that appeals to young persons, and false or misleading advertising or promotion.[52] It also includes a requirement that health warnings attributed to the Minister of Health occupy 50 percent of the package area.

The Court's unanimous decision in *Canada (Attorney General) v. JTI-Macdonald Corp.*, upholding the constitutionality of the legislative response to *RJR-MacDonald*, comes as no surprise.[53] Although the Court insists that replacement legislation is not entitled to deference, it could not be seen to preclude Parliament's attempt to regulate tobacco, especially given that Parliament had followed the majority's directions from *RJR-MacDonald*. Chief Justice McLachlin's opinion lauds Parliament's conduct in the matter, suggesting that it took greater care in drafting the replacement legislation than it did in drafting the original legislation: "In general, the new scheme was more restrained and nuanced than its predecessor. It represented a genuine attempt by Parliament to craft controls on advertising and promotion that would meet its objectives as well as the concerns expressed by the majority of this Court in *RJR*."[54]

The patronizing attitude on display here is troubling. So too is the suggestion that things have changed since *RJR-MacDonald* was decided. Chief Justice McLachlin refers to "new scientific insights into the nature of tobacco addiction and its consequences" and notes the trial judge's finding that "tobacco is now irrefutably accepted as highly addictive and as imposing huge personal and social costs,"[55] but nothing is new about any of this. Nor is it correct to say that the international context has changed since *RJR-MacDonald*. Chief Justice McLachlin points to the World Health Organization's *Framework Convention on Tobacco Control*, ratified by Canada in 2004, which commits signatories to a comprehensive ban on tobacco advertising, promotion, and sponsorship.[56] As Justice La Forest pointed out in dissent in *RJR-MacDonald*, however, many democratic countries prohibited tobacco advertising in 1995. And why an international agreement entered into by the government to *limit* what the Court regards as a fundamental right should be relevant in any event is not explained.[57] Nevertheless, Chief Justice McLachlin insists that "*RJR* was grounded in a different historical context and based on different findings supported by a different record at a different time. The *Tobacco Act* must be assessed in light of the knowledge, social conditions and regulatory environment revealed by the evidence presented in this case."[58] The notion that the *Charter of Rights and Freedoms* – our highest commitment to the protection of civil and political rights – precludes Parliament from banning the advertisement of a highly addictive carcinogen is as absurd now as it was when *RJR-MacDonald* was decided. Nothing in the *Charter* compelled that decision, as the deeply divided Court that decided the case demonstrates. This is the context in which dialogue theory must be assessed.

In their original dialogue article, Hogg and Bushell describe the passage of new legislation following *RJR-MacDonald* as a dialogue success:

> The common elements of these cases are: (1) the law impaired a Charter right; (2) the law pursued an important purpose; and (3) the law was more restrictive of the Charter right than was necessary to accomplish the purpose. In each case, the invalidity of the law could be corrected by the enactment of a new law that was more respectful of the Charter right while still substantially accomplishing the important purpose. The form of the new law would have to take account of the way in which the Court analyzed the least restrictive means standard of section 1 justification. Dialogue seems an apt description of the relationship between courts and legislative bodies. Certainly, it is hard to claim that an unelected court is thwarting the wishes of the people. In each case, the democratic process has been influenced by the reviewing court, but it has not been stultified.[59]

This is not how I would characterize things. As far as I can tell, faced with an erroneous decision, Parliament simply legislated in accordance with the parameters that the Court's majority decision allowed. The Court did not just *influence* the democratic process; it dictated the content of constitutionally permissible legislation. The constitutionality of the new legislation had to be upheld in view of the Court's "guidelines" from *RJR-MacDonald*, and it was. There is a second, more fundamental, problem. It is a mistake to assume that Parliament's replacement legislation substantially accomplishes the same important purpose as the legislation struck down in *RJR-MacDonald*, but this is what dialogue theory does. Dialogue theory makes no attempt to assess things qualitatively. It simply identifies legislative responses – whatever they may be. The regulation of tobacco advertising demonstrates dialogue in action simply because there was a legislative response to the Supreme Court of Canada's decision striking down the original legislation.

Now, the fact that legislatures pass replacement legislation demonstrates only that there was a need for legislation in the first place. It does not follow that the replacement legislation is a good substitute for the original legislation, let alone a perfect one. So dangerous is tobacco that Parliament chose to ban tobacco advertising. At the end of the day, however, all we have are advertising restrictions. Dialogue proponents owe it to us to explain why this is a good outcome, rather than simply blaming the government for the way in which *RJR-MacDonald* was litigated or Parliament for not using the "dialogic tools" at its disposal.[60] In the face of this sort of example, it will not do to insist that *Charter* decisions "usually operate at the margins of legislative policy, affecting issues of process, enforcement, and standards."[61]

Conclusion

I suspect that many proponents of dialogue theory would prefer that important decisions be made by the Supreme Court of Canada rather than Canadian legislatures. They cannot bring themselves to admit this essentially elitist position, however, because democracy has a greater hold on the public imagination than judicial review. For all of its imperfections, democracy affords a voice to the people who are governed, and for their part, the people rightly expect that they should be involved in making the decisions that concern them.

This explains the public's apparently contradictory views when it comes to the *Charter*. The *Charter* is overwhelmingly popular; nevertheless, a majority of the public want judges to be elected.[62] Dialogue theory offers a convenient rationalization – a way of downplaying, if not denying, the very judicial power dialogue proponents prefer. The dialogue metaphor has come in handy for the Court in this regard and may well continue to do so in future. Beyond this, however, dialogue theory has little to offer Canadian constitutional law. The need to legitimize judicial review remains. It did not end with the decision to adopt the *Charter*, as some have insisted.[63] On the contrary, it began with that decision and is an ongoing need.

Acknowledgments

I am grateful to James Kelly, Antonia Maioni, and Christopher Manfredi for their invitation to participate in *The Charter @ 25*. James Allan, Bradley Miller, Andrew Petter, and Paul Rishworth read this chapter in draft and provided helpful comments. Thanks also to Ronan Lougheed and Meghan Butler, who provided research and editorial support.

Notes

1 *Hunter v. Southam Inc.*, [1984] 2 S.C.R. 145 at 155 (Dickson J.).
2 Peter W. Hogg and Allison A. Bushell, "The *Charter* Dialogue between Courts and Legislatures (Or Perhaps the *Charter of Rights* Isn't Such a Bad Thing after All)," *Osgoode Hall Law Journal* 35 (1997): 75.
3 See Jeremy Waldron, "Some Models of Dialogue between Judges and Legislators," in Grant Huscroft and Ian Brodie, eds., *Constitutionalism in the Charter Era* (Toronto: LexisNexis Butterworths, 2004), 7.
4 See Grant Huscroft, "Constitutionalism from the Top Down," *Osgoode Hall Law Journal* 45 (2007): 91. See also Andrew Petter's critique, "Taking Dialogue Theory Much Too Seriously (Or Perhaps *Charter* Dialogue Isn't Such a Good Thing after All)," *Osgoode Hall Law Journal* 45 (2007): 147.
5 Alexander Bickel described the idea that judicial review is a counter-majoritarian force as an "ineluctable reality ... [J]udicial review is a deviant institution in the American democracy." Alexander Bickel, *The Least Dangerous Branch: The Supreme Court at the Bar of Politics* (Indianapolis: Bobbs-Merrill, 1962), 16-18.
6 Hogg and Bushell, *supra* note 2, 77.
7 Peter W. Hogg, "Canada: From Privy Council to Supreme Court," in Jeffrey Goldsworthy, ed., *Interpreting Constitutions: A Comparative Study* (New York: Oxford University Press, 2006), 88.
8 Peter W. Hogg, Allison A. Bushell-Thornton, and Wade K. Wright, "*Charter* Dialogue Revisited – Or 'Much Ado about Metaphors,'" *Osgoode Hall Law Journal* 45 (2007): 51.
9 Ibid., 4.
10 Many have pointed this out. See, for example, Andrew Petter, "Twenty Years of *Charter* Justification: From Liberal Legalism to Dubious Dialogue," *University of New Brunswick Law Journal* 52 (2003): 187. Hogg, Bushell-Thornton, and Wright acknowledge that "the notion of dialogue we proposed in '*Charter* Dialogue' was descriptive rather than normative but add "[w]e have since come to appreciate that the notion of dialogue may also have some limited normative content, and we have also come to appreciate that dialogue may influence courts as well as legislatures – something we did not anticipate in 1997." Hogg, Bushell-Thornton, and Wright, *supra* note 8, 26.
11 Recall that Hogg and Bushell began from the premise that "judges have a great deal of discretion in 'interpreting' the law of the constitution, and the process of interpretation inevitably remakes the constitution into the likeness favoured by the judges." Hogg and Bushell, *supra* note 2, 77.
12 Ibid., 105: "[T]he critique of the *Charter* based on democratic legitimacy cannot be sustained." This claim was retracted subsequently ("We perhaps went too far in suggesting that our study was 'an answer' to the anti-majoritarian objection to judicial review"). Hogg, Bushell-Thornton, and Wright, *supra* note 8, 4. Hogg retracted the claim in "Discovering Dialogue," in Huscroft and Brodie, *supra* note 3, 5.
13 Hogg, Bushell-Thornton, and Wright, *supra* note 8, 4. Criticism of dialogue theory is voluminous. See, for example, Christopher Manfredi and James Kelly, "Six Degrees of Dialogue: A Response to Hogg and Bushell," *Osgoode Hall Law Journal* 37 (1999): 513; Christopher Manfredi, "The Life of a Metaphor: Dialogue in the Supreme Court, 1998-2003," in Huscroft and Brodie, *supra* note 3, 105; and Waldron, *supra* note 3, 5.
14 Hogg, Bushell-Thornton, and Wright, *supra* note 8, 31.
15 Hogg and Bushell, *supra* note 2, 77.
16 United States Constitution, Art. III, s. 2., authorizes the United States Supreme Court to hear "cases" and "controversies," which are understood as meaning actual rather than

hypothetical matters, although this is subject to exceptions. See Laurence H. Tribe, *American Constitutional Law*, 3rd edition (Mincola, NY: Foundation Press, 2000) at chapter 3.7

17 Bickel, *supra* note 5, ch. 4. Interestingly, in another context, Hogg has noted many of these points himself in describing a "pattern of activism" in the Court's practice. See Hogg, *supra* note 7, 71-72.

18 See, for example, *Canada (Attorney General) v. JTI-MacDonald*, [2007] 2 S.C.R. 610, discussed later in this chapter.

19 *R. v. Morgentaler*, [1988] 1 S.C.R. 30. In *Morgentaler*, a majority of the Court struck down the Criminal Code regime for infringing section 7 but left room for Parliament to regulate abortion under the criminal law. See Huscroft, *supra* note 4, 98-99.

20 This difficulty is usually cited by Canadian courts in support of a broad interpretation of *Charter* rights rather than a more modest interpretation, even though broad interpretation may give rise to the desire to amend the Constitution. See Huscroft, "A Constitutional 'Work in Progress'? The *Charter* and the Limits of Progressive Interpretation," in Huscroft and Brodie, *supra* note 3, 413.

21 Hogg and Bushell, *supra* note 2, 85.

22 Hogg and Bushell acknowledged as much in a footnote that undermines their point in the text. See ibid., note 32.

23 *Sauvé v. Canada (Chief Electoral Officer)*, [2002] 3 S.C.R. 519.

24 Ibid., 538. See Christopher P. Manfredi, "The Day the Dialogue Died: A Comment on *Sauvé v. Canada*," *Osgoode Hall Law Journal* 45 (2007): 105. Hogg once argued that the Court should defer to replacement legislation. Hogg, *supra* note 12, 12. However, he retracted this argument in Hogg, Bushell-Thornton, and Wright, *supra* note 8, 47-48. Chief Justice McLachlin endorses the Hogg, Bushell-Thornton, and Wright position in *Canada (Attorney General) v. JTI-MacDonald*, [2007] 2 S.C.R. 610 at para. 11: "The mere fact that the legislation represents Parliament's response to a decision of this Court does not militate for or against deference."

25 Peter W. Hogg, Allison A. Bushell-Thornton, and Wade K. Wright, "A Reply on '*Charter* Dialogue Revisited,'" *Osgoode Hall Law Journal* 45 (2007): 200.

26 Peter W. Hogg, *Constitutional Law of Canada* (Toronto: Carswell, 1997), chapter 36.8.

27 Commentators as diverse as former Prime Minister Brian Mulroney (describing the agreement to include the notwithstanding clause as "a surrender of rights ... total and abject") and US Supreme Court Justice William Brennan (describing the danger that the clause would be abused as "far graver than the likely harm from [the] omission [of such a clause]") have lamented the inclusion of the notwithstanding clause. See *House of Commons Debates*, No. 1 (April 6, 1989) at 153 (Right Hon. Brian Mulroney) and William Brennan, "Why Have a Bill of Rights?" *Oxford Journal of Legal Studies* 9 (1989): 437.

28 As Bradley Miller pointed out to me, litigants have sometimes urged the Court to decide cases under section 27 rather than section 15 in order to insulate the Court's decision from the possibility – however remote – that the notwithstanding clause might be invoked.

29 *Ford v. Quebec (Attorney General)*, [1988] 2 S.C.R. 712 at para. 36.

30 The suspended declaration draws on rule of law-inspired arguments from cases such as *Re Manitoba French Language Rights*, [1985] 1 S.C.R. 721, in which suspension avoided the egregious consequences that would have followed from the conclusion that the entire Manitoba statute book was unconstitutional because it was not translated into French. In *Schachter v. Canada*, [1992] 2 S.C.R. 679, Justice Lamer said that a suspended declaration of unconstitutionality would be preferable if striking down the impugned legislation would pose a danger to the public, threaten the rule of law, or deprive some of benefits where unconstitutionality sprang from the under-inclusiveness of the legislation. The limits on the availability of the suspension have proven inconvenient, however, and courts have been much more generous in granting the suspension than could have been anticipated. See Sujit Choudhry and Kent Roach, "Putting the Past Behind Us? Prospective Judicial and Legislative Constitutional Remedies," *Supreme Court Law Review* 21 (2003): 205; and Bruce Ryder, "Suspending the *Charter*," *Supreme Court Law Review* 21 (2003): 267.

31 See Jeremy Waldron, *supra* note 3, 7. It is significant that the notwithstanding clause is commonly referred to as the "*Charter* override."

32 *Ford v. Quebec (Attorney General)*, [1988] 2 S.C.R. 712.
33 Hogg, Bushell-Thornton, and Wright, *supra* note 25, 201. "The existence of a legislative override for Congress and the state legislatures would have changed everything. It would certainly have been used on each of the issues mentioned above." This claim extends to everything from the New Deal legislation to school desegregation, prayer in schools, criminal procedural protection, flag-burning, and abortion (Ibid., 200).
34 Kent Roach, "Dialogic Judicial Review and Its Critics," in Huscroft and Brodie, *supra* note 3, 71-72.
35 All of these standard objections have been dispatched by Jeremy Waldron. See Waldron, "The Core of the Case against Judicial Review," *Yale Law Journal* 115 (2006): 1346, 1395-1401.
36 Hogg, Bushell-Thornton, and Wright make this claim throughout *"Charter* Dialogue Revisited," *supra* note 8.
37 Kent Roach, *The Supreme Court on Trial: Judicial Activism or Democratic Dialogue* (Toronto: Irwin Law, 2001), 29-33, 290, critically reviewed by Mark Tushnet, "Judicial Activism or Restraint in a Section 33 World," *University of Toronto Law Journal* 53 (2003): 89; and James Allan, "The Author Doth Protest Too Much, Methinks," *New Zealand Universities Law Review* 20 (2003): 519. See also Justice McLachlin, "Charter Myths," *UBC Law Review* 33 (1999): 23 at para. 15: "[T]he absolute terms in which the American rights are cast probably encourages the courts to interpret them as absolutely as possible. The court starts from the position that the rights are absolute and cuts them down only to the minimum extent required, in order to reconcile them with other rights or imperative collective interests."
38 Mark Tushnet makes these remarks in noting that Kent Roach "has been misled by an earlier generation's debates about the proper approach to interpreting the US Bill of Rights." See Tushnet, *supra* note 37, 92.
39 *Hudson Gas and Electric Corp. v. Public Service Commission*, 447 U.S. 557 (1980).
40 *R. v. Oakes*, [1986] 1. S.C.R. 103. Hogg makes this point in *Constitutional Law of Canada*, ch. 35.1.
41 Grant Huscroft, "The Constitutional and Cultural Underpinnings of Freedom of Expression: Lessons from the United States and Canada," *University of Queensland Law Journal* 25 (2006): 181.
42 The *New Zealand Bill of Rights Act 1990*, 1990 (N.Z.), 1990/109. The original proposal to adopt this bill of rights in entrenched form, with judicial power to strike down legislation, was rejected decisively and the *New Zealand Bill of Rights Act* was passed in ordinary statute form. See Paul Rishworth, Grant Huscroft, Scott Optican, and Richard Mahoney, *The New Zealand Bill of Rights* (Melbourne: Oxford University Press, 2003), 1-24.
43 *Human Rights Act, 1998,* (U.K.), 1998, c. 42.
44 There is no federal bill of rights in Australia, but there is one at the state level (Victoria's *Charter of Human Rights and Responsibilities 2006* (Vic.)) and one in the Australian Capital Territory (*Human Rights Act 2004* (A.C.T.)).
45 Here I note my agreement with Mark Tushnet, James Allan, and others that judicial review inevitably becomes strong, no matter how ostensibly weak it appears. Experience under the UK *Human Rights Act* makes this point – declarations of inconsistency are invariably accepted by the legislature. See Francesca Klug and Keir Starmer, "Standing Back from the Human Rights Act: How Effective Is It Five Years On?" *Public Law* [2005]: 721. An analogous point can be made about the Supreme Court of Canada's power on reference questions. The Court's power is advisory, but its "advice" is accepted invariably.
46 Hogg, Bushell-Thornton, and Wright concede that judicial review in Canada is stronger than in these countries, but they reiterate that "we have no doubt that Canada's judicial review is weaker than that in the United States." See Hogg, Bushell-Thornton, and Wright, *supra* note 25, 199.
47 *Tobacco Products Control Act*, S.C. 1988, c. 20.
48 See, for example, *Irwin Toy Ltd. v. Quebec (Attorney General)*, [1989] 1 S.C.R. 927.
49 *RJR-MacDonald Inc. v. Canada (Attorney General)*, [1995] 3 S.C.R. 199 [*RJR-MacDonald*].
50 Justices McLachlin and Iacobucci expressed concern that the government had not disclosed all of the information in its possession about alternatives to an advertising ban. Justice La

Forest, dissenting, acknowledged that the government's conduct was problematic but considered that there was overwhelming evidence before the Court that the infringement was reasonable.

51 *RJR-MacDonald, supra* note 49, para. 164.

52 *Tobacco Act,* S.C. 1997, c. 13.

53 *Canada (Attorney General) v. JTI-Macdonald Corp.,* [2007] 2 S.C.R. 610 [*JTI-Macdonald*].

54 Ibid., para. 7.

55 Ibid., para. 9.

56 *Framework Convention on Tobacco Control,* 2302 U.N.T.S. 229.

57 International authority is usually cited in support of arguments to expand rather than contract the scope of rights. See James Allan and Grant Huscroft, "Constitutional Rights Coming Home to Roost? Rights Internationalism in American Courts," *San Diego Law Review* 43 (2006): 1-59.

58 *JTI-Macdonald, supra* note 53, para. 11.

59 Hogg and Bushell, *supra* note 2, 87.

60 Roach, *supra* note 37, 184-87.

61 Hogg, Bushell-Thornton, and Wright, *supra* note 8, 39. Dialogue proponents know better, and when the Court reaches a decision they cannot abide, they may acknowledge the problem. Thus, Kent Roach's opposition to the Supreme Court of Canada's decision in *Chaoulli v. Quebec (Attorney General),* [2005] 1 S.C.R. 791, leads him to support the "passive virtues" he once repudiated. See Kent Roach, "Sharpening the Dialogue Debate: The Next Decade of Scholarship," *Osgoode Hall Law Journal* 45 (2007): 183-85.

62 This is demonstrated in two recent polls. In 2007, a Strategic Counsel poll asked: "Do Canadians support or oppose the idea of judges being elected to serve at certain levels of court?" Of those that responded, 63 percent indicated their support. See "A Report to *The Globe and Mail* and CTV on the *Canadian Charter of Rights and Freedoms,*" http://www. thestrategiccounsel.com/our_news/polls/2007-03-21%20GMCTV %20CharterofRights %20Mar%2010-13.pdf. This result is consistent with an earlier Environics poll commissioned on the twentieth anniversary of the *Charter,* which asked: "Do you think that Supreme Court Justices should be appointed by the federal government or elected by the public?" Of those that responded, 68 percent favoured election. See "Canada's *Charter of Rights and Freedoms* Seen as Having Positive Impact on Rights and Is Growing Symbol of Canadian Indentity," http://www.acs-aec.ca/oldsite/Polls/Poll1.pdf.

63 See, for example, *Re B.C. Motor Vehicle Act,* [1985] 2 S.C.R. 486 at para. 15 (Lamer J.). Responding to an argument about judicial power, he asserted:

> This is an argument which was heard countless times prior to the entrenchment of the Charter but which has in truth, for better or for worse, been settled by the very coming into force of the Constitution Act, 1982. It ought not to be forgotten that the historic decision to entrench the Charter in our Constitution was taken not by the courts but by the elected representatives of the people of Canada. It was those representatives who extended the scope of constitutional adjudication and entrusted the courts with this new and onerous responsibility. Adjudication under the Charter must be approached free of any lingering doubts as to its legitimacy.

The answer to Justice Lamer is that although the *Charter* established judicial review, it did not mandate any particular approach to it. The Court decides how it exercises its power and, ultimately, the extent to which concerns about the legitimacy of judicial review arise. See Huscroft, *supra* note 20, 413.

4
Courting Controversy: Strategic Judicial Decision Making

Rainer Knopff, Dennis Baker, and Sylvia LeRoy

Although the *Canadian Charter of Rights and Freedoms*, abstractly considered, has become the symbol of Canadian identity that Pierre Elliott Trudeau hoped for, the judges who apply it frequently "court controversy" as they take sides in disagreements about the practical implications of the document's lofty generalities.[1] To the extent that the *Charter* represented a "flight from politics," in other words, it was a flight not from politics altogether but, rather, from parliamentary to judicial politics. Politics, of course, is a realm of strategic behaviour, and politicians clad in robes are no less inclined to act strategically than their unrobed counterparts. Judges "realize that their ability to achieve their goals depends on a consideration of the preferences of others, of the choices they expect others to make, and of the institutional context in which they act."[2] The "others" whose preferences a judge strategically considers include the general public and other institutions of government (whose cooperation is often needed if judgments are to be effectively implemented). Strategic judges must also consider the views of their judicial colleagues. Lower court judges need the support of colleagues further up the judicial hierarchy. Appellate court judges can achieve their policy goals only as part of a majority coalition of the court itself. In short, judges act strategically with respect to both external and internal audiences.[3] Such strategic judicial decision making at the constitutional level has a long history. Indeed, it was a prominent feature of *Marbury v. Madison*, the celebrated 1803 US decision that launched the modern practice of judicial review.[4] In Canada, too, as we shall see, there are prominent early examples of rhetorically strategic judgments. While Canada's *Constitution Act, 1982*, including the *Charter*, has provided important new opportunities for strategic judicial behaviour, these are best understood against the backdrop of the longer tradition.[5]

This chapter explores strategic judicial rhetoric with respect to both external and internal audiences. With respect to external audiences, we set the stage and context with some early American and Canadian examples and then explore the strategic dimensions of a series of three cases – *Reference re a Resolution to Amend the Constitution* (*Patriation Reference*), *Reference re Amendment to the Canadian Constitution* (*Quebec Veto Reference*), and *Reference re Secession of Quebec* (*Quebec Secession Reference*) – which raised high-stakes federalism controversies about the establishment and consequences of the *Constitution Act, 1982*.[6] With respect to internal audiences, we explore strategic coalition building that occurred among the judges of the Supreme Court of Canada in two *Charter* cases – the first and second decisions of *Sauvé v. Canada (Chief Electoral Officer)* (*Sauvé I* and *II*) – dealing with prisoners voting rights.[7]

Whether it is directed to external or internal audiences, strategic judicial behaviour often manifests itself in carefully calculated jurisprudential rhetoric. Rhetoric is the art of persuasion, and sometimes persuasion requires advancing reasons and arguments that are more publicly acceptable than those that convince the rhetorician. In other words, rhetoric may sometimes require silence about the real reasons, or at least substantial additional reasons, for a particular conclusion. Thus, strategic political calculations underlying the jurisprudential surface must often be inferred. Compelling inference is possible because legal and political logics are not always in alignment, meaning that legal coherence must often be sacrificed to political goals or vice versa. As several observers have noted, political calculation is often the most plausible explanation for jurisprudence that is legally anomalous.[8]

Strategic Rhetoric and External Audiences

Certainly, political calculation with respect to external audiences is often the only way to explain anomalous jurisprudence in many cases that have posed controversial issues for significant audiences external to the Court. Before moving to cases that concern the *Constitution Act, 1982*, we set the stage with a discussion of two earlier cases. Although our focus in this chapter is Canadian cases, we begin with an American example, the first and archetypical instance of modern judicial review. *Marbury v. Madison* arose out of the bitter partisan politics of the election of 1800 and its immediate aftermath. The defeated and outgoing federalist administration of John Adams used its "lame duck" period to appoint federalist supporters to the judiciary.[9] In the rush of making these "midnight appointments," however, John Marshall, Adams' secretary of state, failed to deliver the commission of one William Marbury. Marbury appealed to the Supreme Court of the United States, now headed by the same John Marshall (whose own midnight appointment had been fully consummated). Marbury asked the court for a writ of mandamus, ordering James Madison, secretary of state in Jefferson's newly elected Republican administration, to turn over the signed and sealed commission.

Chief Justice Marshall was in a difficult situation. The Jeffersonians had made it clear that not only would they ignore a writ of mandamus, but they would also impeach Marshall if he ordered one. Clearly, such action would possibly harm the still fragile authority of the Supreme Court of the United States and would end Marshall's own judicial career. However, backing down in the face of obvious political pressure would not enhance the court's prestige either, and it would be politically unpalatable to the federalist bench. The court seemed caught between two equally bad alternatives.

Although there seemed to be no obvious avenue of escape, John Marshall, Houdini-like, found one. As Robert McCloskey has famously put it, "[t]he decision is a masterwork of indirection, a brilliant example of Marshall's capacity to sidestep danger while seeming to court it, to advance in one direction while his opponents are looking in another."[10] Marshall escaped confrontation by denying that the Supreme Court of the United States could issue the requested writ in the first instance – that is, as part of its "original," rather than its "appellate," jurisdiction. Section 13 of the *Judiciary Act*, which purported to grant the court this power, had unconstitutionally added to the court's "original jurisdiction" and was thus null and void.[11] With breathtaking audacity, Marshall claimed the still novel power of striking down national legislation in the very course – indeed, as the principal means – of avoiding an open confrontation with the Jefferson administration. While denying his court's power to issue a writ of mandamus, he simultaneously established the far greater power of judicial review.[12] The Republicans, in no position to object to Marshall's reasons for coming to the very bottom-line conclusion they wanted, were left strategically stranded, and the court's authority and legitimacy, far from being eroded, were enhanced. In short, Marshall "appear[ed] to absorb a short-term defeat in exchange for a long-term victory."[13]

The obvious conclusion that Marshall's jurisprudence was *politically* rhetorical is strengthened by the fact that it was legally questionable. Section 13 of the *Judiciary Act* did not clearly give the Supreme Court of the United States original jurisdiction over the writ of mandamus.[14] In other words, Marshall could easily have turned Marbury away because the *Judiciary Act* did *not* provide original jurisdiction, rather, because it had *unconstitutionally* provided it. The confrontation between the court and the Jeffersonians would have been similarly avoided, but the opportunity to claim the power of judicial review in this case would have been lost. And even if section 13 had given the court original jurisdiction over mandamus, it was far from clear that the Constitution prevented Congress from adding to the explicitly enumerated matters of original jurisdiction.[15] As Alexander Bickel has said, quoting Justice Learned Hand, the opinion "will not bear scrutiny."[16] That is, it will not bear scrutiny from a strictly legal point of view. Politically, it makes perfect sense.

If the very origins of the judicial enforcement of constitutional law display questionable or surprising jurisprudence in the service of obviously political rhetoric, it should come as no surprise to find the example repeated in the subsequent history of judicial review. Certainly, jurisprudence as political rhetoric has been a regular occurrence in Canada, both before and after the *Charter's* advent in 1982. One example from the pre-*Charter* era must suffice. While it is no *Marbury v. Madison*, the 1938 Alberta Press case certainly contains surprising jurisprudence that cannot easily be explained except by reference to political context.[17] In this case, three of the six participating judges provided the first official articulation of the constitutional doctrine of an implied bill of rights. They did so in a surprising *obiter dictum*. It was *obiter* because the Supreme Court of Canada unanimously found the legislation unconstitutional on federalist grounds. It was surprising because, as Carl Baar notes, "[t]he Court had no record of support for civil liberties."[18] Indeed, Justice Lyman Duff, who penned the main implied bill of rights opinion and who has since become famous as the principal judicial author of this doctrine, "had written opinions in previous years that reflected the anti-oriental sentiments of the Canadian west coast."[19] Political context best accounts for this otherwise inexplicable new departure by Duff and two of his colleagues. The legislation in question infringed upon the freedom of the press, and there was widespread national opinion that jurisdictional division of powers issues should not obscure this central freedom. The Liberal government in Ottawa could have achieved a direct defence of freedom of the press by disallowing the legislation on this basis. However, Ottawa had already disallowed some Alberta legislation and was cautioned by the Alberta Liberals against overusing this heavy-handed device. Thus, Ottawa resorted to a reference case, but its factum strongly urged the Court to transcend federalism considerations and decide on civil libertarian grounds.[20] In this context, says Baar, "it was both politically safe and politically heroic for the Supreme Court to defend civil liberties," and three of the judges did so.[21]

In a federal system, one way of being "politically safe" when high controversy divides contending governments is to split the difference between them, even if this tactic requires some fancy rhetorical footwork involving jurisprudential inconsistencies.[22] This is what happened in the 1981 *Patriation Reference*, which concerned the constitutional validity of the federal government's proposal to have Britain enact its proposed charter of rights and new constitutional amendment procedures without significant provincial consent. The dissenting provinces argued that there was a convention of provincial consent for the kinds of changes contemplated by Ottawa's patriation package and that this convention had crystallized into binding constitutional law. The Trudeau government argued that no such convention existed and that, even if it did, it was legally unenforceable. In Ottawa's view, conventions, which were established and changed politically, were not appropriately defined, never mind enforced, by a court of law. All nine Supreme Court of Canada judges accepted the distinction between law and convention, agreeing that the courts could not enforce the latter. Nevertheless, just as John Marshall had illogically addressed the merits of the mandamus claim in *Marbury* despite disavowing jurisdiction, so a majority of the Supreme Court in the *Patriation Reference* refused to let their inability to enforce conventions stand in the way either of defining a convention of provincial consent or of emphasizing that conventions of this stature were often constitutionally more weighty than technical constitutional law. Moreover, while recognizing that political agreement was the test of convention, the court defined the convention in terms advocated by only one province. Seven of the eight dissenting provinces insisted on a convention of *unanimous* provincial consent, and only Saskatchewan suggested the definition that was ultimately adopted by the Court, namely *substantial* provincial consent.

Although the jurisprudence of the *Patriation Reference* was clearly questionable, the political consequences have been described as "bold statescraft."[23] In effect, the questionable jurisprudence was necessary in order to give each side half a loaf and thereby moderate the conflict. Ottawa was told that it could *legally* proceed with its plan of unilateral amendment but that in doing so it would violate a key constitutional convention. The latter finding provided important ammunition to opponents of the scheme and clearly made Ottawa more cautious. On the other hand, while the provinces emerged with a convention on their side, they were told that it was legally unenforceable. Given the popularity of the proposed charter of rights, the provinces understood that too much obstructionism would turn the public against them and embolden Ottawa to use its legal prerogative to go it alone. Thus, the dissenting provinces also became more cautious. However questionable the jurisprudence may have been, in other words, it significantly altered the distribution of symbolic legal resources so as to bring previously recalcitrant opponents back to the bargaining table.[24] The result was the agreement of Ottawa and nine provinces to a revised patriation package, which soon became part of Canada's Constitution. Significantly, Quebec was the only province to withhold its agreement.

Predictably, Quebec immediately launched another courtroom challenge to the *Patriation* package. The so-called 1982 *Quebec Veto Reference* probed the meaning of the newly declared convention of substantial consent. Was it simply a numerical concept or a qualitative one that took into account cultural duality and thus required the consent of Quebec? That is, could provincial consent to the patriation project be sufficiently substantial if Quebec, representing one of Canada's founding nations, was excluded? If not, the project was unconstitutional despite the agreement of all of the other Canadian governments.[25]

The *Patriation Reference* had relied on British constitutionalist Sir Ivor Jenning's tripartite test for the existence of a convention. It asked: "[F]irst: what are the precedents; secondly, did the actors in the precedents believe they were bound by a rule; and thirdly, is there a reason for the rule? A single precedent with a good reason may be enough to establish the rule."[26] In the *Quebec Veto Reference*, the Court uncovered neither the precedents nor the rationale because it decided that the second part of the test – acceptance or recognition – had not been met. Acceptance could only be proven through explicit statements of the conventional rule by relevant actors, and none had been brought to the Court's attention. Since such explicitly articulated recognition was absolutely essential to the existence of a convention, moreover, its absence was sufficient to dispose of the case.

Once again, the jurisprudence is highly questionable. Marc Gold demonstrates that the very authorities invoked by the Court in support of its conclusion can just as easily – indeed, more plausibly – be read to show that recognition is not essential and can, in any case, be tacitly established.[27] Moreover, the Court's insistence on explicit articulation cannot be squared with how it arrived at the convention of substantial consent in the *Patriation Reference*.[28] Finally, even if one accepts that explicit articulation is essential, the Court's refusal to comment on either precedent or rationale is difficult to reconcile with its enthusiasm in other cases for addressing more issues than strictly necessary. The Court usually justifies the tackling of unnecessary issues by stressing their inherent importance. Surely, its reason for avoiding the precedents and rationale relevant to the conventional issues in the *Quebec Veto Reference* cannot be their inherent unimportance!

The Court was obviously straining at this point, and, once again, political context provides the reason: "Had the Court discussed precedents, it would have had to come to grips with the fact that all previous constitutional amendments had been passed with the consent of Quebec and that no amendments (prior to patriation) had been pursued over the objections of Quebec."[29] The precedential part of the test, in other words, clearly favoured Quebec. Similarly, Quebec had strong arguments in support of cultural dualism as the rationale or principle that ought to inform the convention.[30] It is hard not to conclude that the Court created the questionable test of explicit articulation precisely in order to defeat Quebec's claim by more easily sidestepping the issues of precedent and rationale.

And defeating Quebec's claim is pretty much what the Court *had* to do. The new constitutional dispensation was in force by the time the *Quebec Veto Reference* reached the Court. The *Quebec Veto Reference*, by challenging the very legitimacy and authority of Canada's constitutional regime, reflected what Mark Walters has called the "pathology of legal systems."[31] In such circumstances, courts tend to rally to the defence of the order from which their own authority derives. It is difficult, in other words, to conceive of the Court retroactively invalidating new and popular constitutional documents, especially since that would serve to undo what the Court's "bold statescraft" in the *Patriation Reference* had helped broker. Once again, we meet jurisprudence that cannot be understood except by reference to political calculation.

As usual, however, the political calculation must be inferred – the surface of the judgment goes to great lengths to hide it. In a unanimous opinion – itself a tip-off of careful political and rhetorical calculation – the Court proceeds as though its jurisprudence flowed inescapably from authority, when it clearly did not. Conclusions were misleadingly presented "as if no choice was open to the Court."[32] This legal formalism was a "judicial defence mechanism" that allowed the Court "to decide the case against Quebec, while writing reasons for judgment that obscured the responsibility of the Court for the decision reached."[33] Upon inspection, in other words, even the most legalistic style of reasoning (perhaps *especially* this form of reasoning) reveals itself as political rhetoric.

The "pathology of legal systems" that is evident in the *Quebec Veto Reference* had reached the boiling point in the 1998 *Quebec Secession Reference*. Just as Ottawa in 1980-81 had claimed the right to undertake major constitutional restructuring unilaterally, without provincial consent, so Quebec now insisted on the right to a unilateral declaration of independence – in effect, the right to break up the country without the consent or participation of the rest of Canada.[34] Quebec contended, moreover, that Canadian courts could not rule on the legitimacy of a unilateral declaration of independence.[35] For Quebec, this was a political matter, not a legal one, and Premier Lucien Bouchard made it clear that he had no intention of respecting or abiding by a Supreme Court of Canada ruling. The Court's decision, he announced, "will be a political ruling and will be null and void and we will ignore it."[36] Consistent with this logic, Quebec refused to participate in the reference case, and the court had to assign a stand in (an *amicus curiae*) to argue on behalf of the province. Clearly, the Bouchard government was in no mood to listen to the kind of legal formalism employed in the *Quebec Veto Reference*. If the constitutional order was to be protected, and the Court's own legitimacy preserved, a very different rhetorical approach was called for.

The Court rose to the occasion. Speaking to a Harvard audience in April 1998, Justice Claire L'Heureux-Dubé hinted at its approach. The judgment, she said, must be presented in clear, lay language in order to prevent politicians from twisting the verdict to other ends, since Canadians should weigh the implications of the opinion themselves.[37] And, indeed, the opinion – once again unanimous – is remarkable for its lack of technical legalese. It reads more like a treatise on political principle than a legal document. Ultimately, the conclusion of this analysis of principle is that a clear affirmative answer to a clear question on secession would trigger a duty to negotiate on the part of the rest of Canada.

By this point, no one will be surprised to learn that this conclusion is jurisprudentially suspect. In the *Patriation Reference*, the Court had implausibly supported a convention of "substantial consent" suggested by only one of the parties. In the *Quebec Secession Reference*, the duty to negotiate had been proposed by none of the parties.[38] In effect, the Court had pulled it "out of rarefied air."[39]

Nor should anyone be surprised to discover that "bold statescraft" rested on the foundation of this questionable jurisprudence. As in the *Patriation Reference*, "what was necessary was a judgment which would both respect the constitutional division of functions between the judiciary and executive and, at the same time, put pressure on the political actors to compromise."[40] The invented duty to negotiate achieved this end, and it did so through the now tried and true strategy of "splitting the difference." Quebec, which had been poised to reject the judgment – indeed, to use it to whip up secessionist sentiment in the province – now embraced the decision as underlining its own long-term position that the rest of Canada would indeed come to the table after a successful referendum on separation.[41] On the other hand, Ottawa took comfort in the fact that the duty to negotiate depended on a clear answer to a clear question – concepts that it claimed a role in clarifying. The decision left plenty to argue about, but it contained attractive legal resources for the various players, who rushed to claim them.[42] The Court's own legitimacy was no longer at stake, and, for a time at least, the extreme claims leading up to the decision were moderated. As Robert Young has said, the judgment "tossed the extremists out of court, and tilted the political playing field on both sides toward moderation and civility rather than polarization."[43]

Internal Coalition Building and the Strategic Waiting Game under the *Charter*: *Sauvé I* and *Sauvé II*

We now turn to the strategic dimensions of internal coalition building, using as our case study two successive cases on prisoners' voting rights involving section 3 of the *Charter*: *Sauvé I* (1993), which invalidated a blanket disqualification of all prisoner voting, and *Sauvé II* (2002), which struck down any kind of prisoner disqualification whatsoever. As in the case of strategic interaction with external audiences, internal coalition building is often reflected in carefully crafted compromises in the logic and rhetoric of the judicial opinion. We detect such strategic compromises in *Sauvé I*.

At first glance, *Sauvé I* seems a poor candidate for strategic or any other kind of analysis. In an unusually terse opinion, the judgment offers only the virtually unelaborated conclusion that a blanket disqualification of all prisoner voting violated the *Charter*'s section 3 right to vote and was unreasonable under section 1 of the *Charter*, leaving open the question of whether a more finely tuned disqualification might pass constitutional muster. Nine years later, in *Sauvé II*, however, several of the same judges disagreed so vehemently about whether any kind of prisoner disqualification could be justified that their earlier unanimity must have been strategically constructed. Working back from the more fulsome evidence of *Sauvé II*, it is possible to infer the strategic calculations underlying the carefully crafted brevity of *Sauvé I*. Our analysis confirms James Gibson's view that judicial decision making is a "function of what [judges] prefer to do, tempered by what they think they ought to do, but constrained by what they perceive is feasible to do."[44] We show that neither side on the substantive question could achieve a clear majority in 1993, perhaps because at least some of the judges were motivated not only by results-oriented policy considerations but also by scruples concerning proper judicial procedure – by what they thought "they ought to do." As a consequence, the most "feasible" outcome was a strategic waiting game, in which both sides of the substantive policy debate gambled that the inevitable turnover of their colleagues would turn the tide in their favour. The extreme brevity of *Sauvé I* is explained by this delaying strategy, but, despite this brevity, it is possible also to discern a key rhetorical compromise in the decision's only substantive sentence, which is carefully designed to reflect the preferences of each policy camp while keeping both options open.

Sauvé I Minimalism

The *Sauvé* decisions apply section 3 of the *Charter*. Section 3 ensures that "[e]very citizen of Canada has the right to vote in an election of members of the House of Commons." At first blush, section 3 appears to require very little interpretation: if one is a citizen, one is entitled to a vote. Such an approach would, however, overturn even the most benign and generally accepted restrictions on the franchise, such as age restrictions and residency requirements. Fortunately, section 1 of the *Charter* provides for the establishment of reasonable limits on rights, including section 3, so long as they are "demonstrably justified in a free and democratic society." While age and modest residency requirements have met this section 1 standard,[45] several other exclusions in the federal election law have failed to pass constitutional muster: mentally incompetent citizens (*Canadian Disability Rights Council v. The Queen*); federally appointed judges (*Muldoon v. Canada*); and citizens absent from Canada (*Re Hoogbruin and Attorney General of British Columbia*).[46] The *Sauvé* cases test whether another class of citizens, prisoners, may be constitutionally denied the vote.

Sauvé I arose under a provision of the *Canada Elections Act* that imposed a blanket voting disqualification on anyone incarcerated for any reason on voting day.[47] The following is the sum total of the Supreme Court of Canada's substantive opinion in the case, with the key sentence emphasized: "The Attorney General of Canada has properly conceded that s. 51(*e*) of the *Canada Elections Act*, R.S.C., 1985, c. E-2, contravenes s. 3 of the *Canadian Charter of Rights and Freedoms* but submits that s. 51(*e*) is saved under s. 1 of the *Charter*. We do not agree. *In our view, s. 51(e) is drawn too broadly and fails to meet the proportionality test, particularly the minimal impairment component of the test, as expressed in the s. 1 jurisprudence of the Court.*" By the time the Court rendered this decision, the law had been revised to disqualify only those imprisoned for terms of two years or more – that is, only "more serious" offenders.[48] Clearly, the brief *Sauvé I* opinion gave no indication of what the judges thought of this new law, and there was certainly no reason for them to address issues that were not directly raised by the blanket disqualification that had triggered the case. Nevertheless, there are many examples of the Court addressing issues not directly before them or giving hints about pending related issues, and the Court's decision to say so little on a significant constitutional issue is curious.[49] Indeed, the extreme and unusual brevity of the opinion is obviously studied in its determination to steer clear of any hints whatsoever.

Table 4.1 sets the decision in the context of the broader options available to the Court. Option 1 – upholding the blanket disqualification – was clearly rejected by all of the judges and needs no further discussion. Under option 2, the Court would have invalidated the blanket disqualification but given a relatively clear indication that the new law's disqualification of those sentenced to two years or more was permissible. If the Court had thought that the two-year criterion was too low, they might have suggested a longer alternative, such as the ten-year criterion proposed by the Lortie Commission,[50] which is option 3 in the table. Under option 5, the Court would have struck down the law in a manner that precluded any other kind of disqualification. The Court did none of these things, unanimously agreeing to duck most of the issues with the minimalist opinion represented by option 4.

Table 4.1

Supreme Court options in *Sauvé I*

1 Uphold blanket disqualification

2 Invalidate blanket disqualification but uphold new 2-year limit

3 Invalidate both blanket disqualification and new 2-year limit, suggesting a longer limit (e.g., Lortie: 10 yrs.)

4 Invalidate blanket disqualification on proportionality grounds without further comment
   (*actual* Sauvé I *decision: 9-0*)

5 Invalidate all prisoner disqualifications

Strategic Delay

We know from *Sauvé II* that the minimalist fourth option in *Sauvé I* papered over an intense disagreement on the substantive issues. Table 4.2 shows that three of the *Sauvé I* judges (Justices Claire L'Heureux-Dubé, Charles Gonthier, and John Major) followed option 2 nine years later when they voted to uphold the two-year criterion. Similarly, two of the *Sauvé I* judges (Justices Beverley McLachlin and Frank Iacobucci) voted for option 5 in 2002. Four of the *Sauvé I* judges (Justices Antonio Lamer, Gerard La Forest, John Sopinka, and Peter Cory) left the Court before *Sauvé II*, so we lack knowledge of where they stood in this dispute at the time of *Sauvé I*.

It is possible, of course, that the two groups of *Sauvé I* alumni had simply not made up their minds in 1993, but, given how fervently and intransigently they supported their preferences in 2002, it seems unlikely that all of them were previously uncommitted. It is much more plausible that disagreement was equally intense in 1993 but that the committed judges chose not to make their quarrel fully public at that time because neither side could achieve a majority coalition (for reasons we shall explore later in this chapter) – in effect, that they were biding their time, hoping to find their preferred majority in a future case.

Table 4.3 shows why option 4's minimalism was the only rationally available choice for both substantive camps, assuming neither could achieve a majority. The "conservatives" on this issue preferred option 2 but might have been induced to compromise on a threshold that was higher than two years if a majority could have been found for option 3. This option would at least have preserved the principle of a constitutionally legitimate form of disqualification. With no majority possible for either option 2 or 3, they would have been prepared to accept the compromise of minimalism under

Table 4.2

Preferences of *Sauvé I* judges based on *Sauvé II* opinions (2002)*

1 Uphold blanket disqualification

2 Invalidate blanket disqualification but uphold new 2-year limit
   L'Heureux-Dubé, Gonthier, Major (3)

3 Invalidate both blanket disqualification and new 2-year limit, suggesting
   a longer limit (e.g., Lortie: 10 yrs.)

4 Invalidate blanket disqualification on proportionality grounds without
   further comment
   (actual Sauvé I *decision: 9-0)*

5 Invalidate all prisoner disqualifications
   McLachlin, Iacobucci (2)

*   Four unknowns (left Court between *Sauvé I* and *Sauvé II*): Lamer, La Forest, Sopinka, and Cory.

Table 4.3

Strategy in *Sauvé I*: biding time *with no majority possible*

	Conservative Win-set	Liberal Win-set
1 Uphold blanket disqualification		
2 Invalidate blanket disqualification but uphold new 2-year limit *L'Heureux-Dubé, Gonthier, Major (3)*	•	
3 Invalidate both blanket disqualification and new 2-year limit, suggesting a longer limit (e.g., Lortie: 10 yrs.)	•	
4 Invalidate blanket disqualification on proportionality grounds without further comment *(actual* Sauvé I *decision: 9-0)*	•	•
5 Invalidate all prisoner disqualifications *McLachlin, Iacobucci (2)*		•

---

option 4. Their win-set in the spatial array of alternatives, in other words, extends from option 2 through option 4.[51] For the option 5 "liberals," on the other hand, only option 4 would have been an acceptable alternative in the absence of a majority able to implement their preference. Their principled opposition to any kind of disqualification would have to be sacrificed were they to compromise on the higher threshold of option 3. The liberals' win-set, in short, includes only options 4 and 5. Assuming no substantive majority on either side, the two win-sets overlap only on the evasive minimalism of option 4, making this the only rational result in *Sauvé I*. The result reflects the fact that "a court opinion that is inconsistent with a justice's policy preferences may be more detrimental to the justice's policy goals than no opinion"[52] or a minimalist one.[53]

Strategic Rhetoric
While *Sauvé I* clearly represents a disagreement-disguising minimalism, it does not hide the disagreement altogether. Although it is clear that the justices did not make their disagreement fully public in 1993, one can with the benefit of hindsight see the outline of their quarrel in the central substantive sentence of Sauvé *I*: "In our view, s. 51(*e*) is drawn too broadly and fails to meet the proportionality test, particularly the minimal impairment component of the test, as expressed in the s. 1 jurisprudence of the Court."[54] This seemingly straightforward sentence is actually a finely balanced rhetorical compromise. To see this compromise, we need to remind ourselves of the components of section 1 analysis as set out in *R. v. Oakes*.[55] In order for a

prima facie infringement of a *Charter* right to be "demonstrably justified as a reasonable limit" under section 1, it must have a "pressing and substantial" purpose and the legislative means must be "proportional" to that purpose. If there is no pressing purpose, no further analysis is necessary, and the law is struck down as an unreasonable limit. If there is a pressing purpose, the legislative means can be proportional to that purpose only if they are rationally connected to it. That is, they must actually achieve the pressing purpose. If they do not, again the analysis ends and the law is struck down. Even if the law actually achieves the pressing purpose, however, it may still be disproportional because it infringes the right more than necessary to achieve the purpose. Why kill flies with a sledgehammer when a flyswatter will do? This is the minimal impairment component of the proportionality test. Finally, even legislative means that are rationally connected to the purpose and meet the minimal impairment criterion must show that the gains in achieving the compelling purposes outweigh the cost in lost rights.

In sum, the *Oakes* test proceeds through an ordered progression – from pressing purpose to rational connection to minimal impairment to cost-benefit balancing – with the analysis reaching each subsequent stage only if the legislation passes the previous one. In most cases, laws pass the pressing purpose and rational connection tests, and the analysis focuses on the minimal impairment issue, which is why it has become popular to speak of an inter-institutional policy dialogue between courts and legislatures.[56] Striking a law down on minimal impairment grounds, in other words, implies that it would be possible to achieve the goal with more finely tuned legislation, thus inviting the legislature, as the Court's dialogic interlocutor, to respond with a new law.[57] Needless to say, such dialogue is not possible if a law lacks a sufficiently pressing purpose or if the imaginable legislative means are not rationally connected to such a purpose.

With this in mind, consider the option 2 group in the *Sauvé* decisions – that is, the group that upheld the two-year criterion in 2002 and likely had the same preference in 1993. This group clearly sees the blanket disqualification as failing the minimal impairment component of the section 1 analysis but thinks that the more carefully crafted two-year criterion for disqualification meets that test. In their view, "[t]his case is another episode in the continuing dialogue between courts and legislatures on the issue of prisoner voting ... Parliament responded to [the 1993] judicial advice by enacting legislation aimed at accomplishing part of its objectives while complying with the Charter."[58] In other words, the option 2 group sees the earlier blanket disqualification as failing only the minimal impairment component of the *Oakes* proportionality analysis, meaning that it passed both the pressing purpose and rational connection tests.

The option 5 group, by contrast, believes that no prisoner disqualification can pass constitutional muster, meaning that no amount of fine-tuning to achieve minimal impairment will suffice. Accordingly, they see no room for inter-institutional dialogue: "The healthy and important promotion of a dialogue between the legislature and the courts should not be debased to a rule of 'if at first you don't succeed, try, try again.'"[59] This statement can only mean that a prisoner disqualification of any kind fails to pass either the pressing purpose or rational connection aspects of the *Oakes* test. In *Sauvé I*, almost half of Richard Sauvé's factum (fifteen of the thirty-two pages) argues that there is no pressing and substantial purpose,[60] and, in *Sauvé II*, the option 5 group shows that it is strongly tempted by this view, noting the "thin basis" of the law's objective and maintaining that "[q]uite simply, the government has failed to identify particular problems that require denying the right to vote."[61] This group could not have made this clear in *Sauvé I*, however, without clearly exposing the policy disagreement that all of the judges were eager to disguise. They would instead have contented themselves with an indication that the law infringed the proportionality test. In doing so, of course, they created a path dependency that prevented a *Sauvé II* invalidation explicitly on the grounds of pressing purpose, however much they may have been tempted to do so. Thus, while their *Sauvé II* opinion casts doubt on the law's pressing purpose, it ultimately rests its case on rational connection grounds.

However, the option 5 group could not afford to make its views on rational connection public in *Sauvé I* either, for such a move would have also brought into the open their intention to foreclose the kind of dialogue that their option 2 opponents wanted to keep open. The option 5 group in *Sauvé I* would thus have favoured a simple indication that the proportionality test had been infringed, without specifying which prong of the test was at stake. They would no doubt have preferred the key sentence in *Sauvé I* to stop after its first clause: "[S.] 51(*e*) is drawn too broadly and fails to meet the proportionality test." For similar reasons, the option 2 group would likely have preferred the sentence to say only that "s. 51(e) fails to meet the minimal impairment component of the proportionality test." The fact that the sentence includes both clauses – "[S.] 51(*e*) ... fails to meet the proportionality test, particularly the minimal impairment component of the test" – clearly represents a strategic compromise. Had a majority agreed that only "minimal impairment" was at issue, a more extensive opinion would likely have emerged, making the option of further dialogue quite clear. Had a majority agreed that "rational connection" was violated, that again would likely have been made clear in a more extensive opinion, saving nine years of additional litigation.[62]

Explaining the Lack of a Substantive Majority
Clearly, *Sauvé I* is best understood as a strategic response to the lack of a majority on either side of the substantive policy issue. However, this conclusion

Figure 4.1

The coalition puzzle

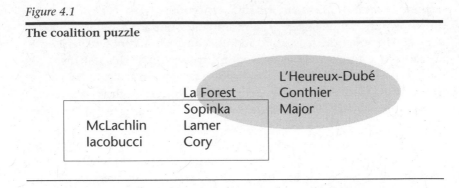

begs the question of why a majority did not exist. Consider the puzzle posed in Figure 4.1. The column on the left contains the two known *Sauvé I* liberals, while the column on the right displays the three known conservatives. The central column contains the four *Sauvé I* judges that were no longer on the Court when Sauvé *II* was decided in 2002. The known liberals would have needed to attract three of these four potential votes to form a majority (represented by the hypothetical boxed group) in *Sauvé I*. If they had fallen short by just one, that may have left two judges to join a conservative majority of five (represented by the hypothetical circled group). There are two possible reasons that neither side was able to gain a majority on the substantive policy issue. First, there may have been some judges who had genuinely not made up their minds and wanted to buy time. Second, a cross-cutting issue might have outweighed the central issue in the minds of some judges.

In fact, there was a cross-cutting issue related to the middle clause in Gibson's earlier-quoted statement that judicial decision making is a "function of what [judges] prefer to do, *tempered by what they think they ought to do,* but constrained by what they perceive is feasible to do." It may well be that some judges in the Court had scruples about the propriety of reaching the substantive policy issue. The judicial process is suffused with rules enjoining judges from deciding more than they have to in any particular case. The rules of standing limit the right to raise issues for judicial decision to those who have been directly affected by a law.[63] One cannot launch the legal challenge of a censorship law, for example, just because it offends one's libertarian sensibilities. One must wait until one has been hauled into court for violating the law. Similarly, courts need not decide issues that have become moot because of the death of the litigant or settlement of the issue. The same logic means that courts should limit their decision making to only those issues actually posed by the parties, the facts of the case, or the law under which the case arose. These rules have all become increasingly honoured in the breach, with courts treating them as more and more discretionary (which is to say less and less rule-like). Standing is more likely to be granted to litigants not directly affected by a law and to moot issues more likely to be decided.[64] Similarly, issues and laws not directly raised by the factual context or by the parties are often addressed.[65] Nevertheless, these traditional rules of judicial propriety still persist and can affect decisional outcomes.

In *Sauvé I*, the law actually brought before the courts by the original litigation was the previous blanket voting disqualification for anyone incarcerated on voting day. Here, traditional principles of judicial propriety would counsel precisely the minimalism of option 4 that the Court adopted, namely a narrow invalidation of the blanket disqualification as an unreasonable limit on the right to vote, leaving the question of the other kinds of limits to another day and another case. It seems likely that this option was chosen strategically rather than sincerely by the most policy-committed judges involved in the case. Given the disdain, almost revulsion, that Justices McLachlin and Iacobucci expressed for the very idea of a prisoner disqualification, it is hard to imagine them depriving prisoners of the centrally important democratic right to vote for almost another decade if they did not have to. Similarly, the *Sauvé I* conservatives displayed such staunch support for the principle of disqualification in 2002 that at least some of them would have been strongly inclined to dispel uncertainty about its constitutional *bona fides* in 1993, had they been able to do so.

Had all of the judges been policy committed to this extent, a majority would have formed and strategic minimalism would have been unnecessary. It may have been made strategically necessary for the policy-committed judges because some of their colleagues had simply not made up their minds on the central issue and preferred a minimalist decision in the meantime. Of course, the inclination of such "policy-uncommitted" judges to opt for minimalism would also reflect strategic calculation – the need to buy time – rather than a sincere attachment to the propriety principle. It is possible, however, that one or more judges were sincerely devoted to the rules of judicial propriety, perhaps to the extent that they outweighed strong policy commitments on the issue. This possibility is well represented in the literature. Cornell Clayton, for example, reports how Hermann C. Pritchett long ago "developed an intervening variable between a justice's policy preferences and a justice's votes in cases, which he called 'judicial role conception.'"[66] The plausibility of this intervening variable having a sincere effect on the *Sauvé I* decision varies directly with the extent to which any of the judges involved had a consistent record of supporting judicial propriety principles in a principled manner. Such a suggestion clearly points to an area that deserves further research.

Reading back from *Sauvé II* to *Sauvé I* reveals two camps of judges with strong and opposed preferences on the substantive issue of prisoners' voting rights. It seems likely that at least some of the judges in *Sauvé I* were also

Table 4.4

Who won the waiting game? (Or where did the newcomers go in *Sauvé II*?)

1   Uphold blanket disqualification

2   Invalidate blanket disqualification but uphold new 2-year limit
    L'Heureux-Dubé, Gonthier, Major + Bastarache *(4)*

3   Invalidate both blanket disqualification and new 2-year limit, suggesting
    a longer limit (e.g., Lortie: 10 yrs.)

4   Invalidate blanket disqualification on proportionality grounds without
    further comment

5   Invalidate all prisoner disqualifications
    McLachlin, Iacobucci + Binnie, Arbour, LeBel *(5)*

sufficiently motivated by what they thought "they ought to do" – in this case, deciding no more than necessary to resolve the concrete issue originally brought before them – to prevent a majority from forming on the substantive issue, thereby causing the more intensely policy-committed judges to "feel constrained by what [was] feasible to do." The latter found it most "feasible" to play a strategic waiting game, delaying a substantive decision in the hope of a more certain majority on their side in the future. As Table 4.4 shows, the "liberals" won this strategic gamble, attracting three of the four newcomers to the Court to form a narrow five-judge majority in favour of an outright ban on prisoner voting disqualifications.

Conclusion
Judicial decision making, Gibson aptly states, is a "function of what [judges] prefer to do, tempered by what they think they ought to do, but constrained by what they perceive is feasible to do."[67] Simply put, judges are strategic actors. Among other things, this means that judicial claims to follow precedent are sometimes suspect. Yet, there is one precedent – set right at the beginning in *Marbury v. Madison* – that judges often follow in cases arousing high levels of controversy. It is a political, as much as a legal, precedent, namely the construction of legal judgments with an eye to the external and/or internal political context. Time and again, purely legal considerations fail to explain judgments. In fact, the legal surface is often perplexing in its own terms and can be satisfactorily explained only in terms of unacknowledged political calculation with respect to external or internal audiences. Jurisprudence as political rhetoric must usually be inferred, but the inference is often inescapable. Whether John Marshall has equals in the "capacity to sidestep danger while seeming to court it, to advance in one direction while his opponents are looking in another," is an open question.[68] He certainly has

followers, including in Canada. Canadian judges have always "courted controversy" strategically. The advent of *Charter* politics has brought them a rich new field in which to continue this tradition.

Notes

1 *Canadian Charter of Rights and Freedoms,* Part 1 of the *Constitution Act, 1982,* being Schedule B to the *Canada Act 1982* (U.K.), 1982, c. 11.
2 Lee Epstein and Jack Knight, *The Choices Justices Make* (Washington, DC: CQ Press, 1998), 10.
3 Carl Baar, "Using Process Theory to Explain Judicial Decision Making," *Canadian Journal of Law and Society* 1 (1986): 57-79.
4 *Marbury v. Madison,* 5 U.S. (Cranch) 137 (1803).
5 *Constitution Act, 1982* (U.K.), 1982, c. 11, s. 59.
6 *Reference re a Resolution to Amend the Constitution,* [1981] 1 S.C.R. 753; *Reference re Amendment to the Canadian Constitution,* [1982] 2 S.C.R. 791; and *Reference re Secession of Quebec,* [1998] 2 S.C.R. 217.
7 *Sauvé v. Canada (Chief Electoral Officer),* [1993] 2 S.C.R. 438 [*Sauvé I*]; and *Sauvé v. Canada (Chief Electoral Officer),* [2002] 3 S.C.R. 519 [*Sauvé II*].
8 For example, Peter H. Russell, "The Anti-Inflation Case: Anatomy of a Constitutional Decision," *Canadian Public Administration* 10 (1977): 395-416; Peter H. Russell, "Bold Statescraft, Questionable Jurisprudence," in Keith G. Banting and Richard Simeon, eds., *And No One Cheered: Federalism, Democracy and the Constitution Act* (Toronto: Methuen, 1983); Richard A. Posner, *Breaking the Deadlock: The 2000 Election, the Constitution, and the Courts* (Princeton, NJ: Princeton University Press, 2001), 175.
9 Robert G. McCloskey, *The American Supreme Court* (Chicago: University of Chicago Press, 1960), 38.
10 Ibid., 40.
11 *Judiciary Act of 1789,* 1 Stat 73.
12 Robert Lowry Clinton argues that Marshall's power of review is not as far-reaching as modern legal scholars suggest. According to Clinton, Marshall's decision means that federal courts are "entitled to invalidate acts of the coordinate branches of government only when to allow such acts to stand would violate constitutional restrictions on judicial power, not on legislative or executive power." Robert Lowry Clinton, *Marbury v. Madison and Judicial Review* (Lawrence: University of Kansas Press, 1989), 1.
13 Louis Fisher, *Constitutional Dialogues: Interpretation as Political Process* (Princeton: Princeton University Press, 1988), 55.
14 Christopher P. Manfredi, *Judicial Power and the Charter: Canada and the Paradox of Liberal Constitutionalism,* 2nd edition (Don Mills, ON: Oxford University Press, 2001), 10.
15 Ibid., 10; and Fisher, *supra* note 13, 56.
16 Alexander M. Bickel, *The Least Dangerous Branch: The Supreme Court at the Bar of Politics* (Indianapolis: Bobbs-Merrill, 1962), 2.
17 *Reference re Alberta Statutes,* [1938] S.C.R. 100.
18 Baar, *supra* note 3, 73.
19 Ibid.
20 Federalism cases were typically decided based on the "exhaustion theory," which asserted that "no point of internal self-government was withheld from Canada." See Peter H. Russell, "The Political Role of the Supreme Court of Canada in Its First Century," *Canadian Bar Review* 53 (1975): 585, n. 24.
21 Baar, *supra* note 3, 74.
22 Russell, *supra* note 8, 374.
23 Ibid., 210-38.
24 See Peter H. Russell, "The Supreme Court and Federal-Provincial Relations: The Political Use of Legal Resources," in R.D. Olling and M.W. Westmacott, eds., *Perspectives on Canadian Federalism* (Scarborough, ON: Prentice-Hall, 1988), 94. Elsewhere, Russell has commented

that "[f]or the Trudeau government it amounted to a legal green light but a political red light." Peter H. Russell, *Constitutional Odyssey: Can Canadians Become a Sovereign People?* 2nd edition (Toronto: University of Toronto Press, 1993), 119.

25 Gil Rémillard, "Legality, Legitimacy and the Supreme Court," in Banting and Simeon, *supra* note 8, 199.

26 Quoted in Russell, *supra* note 24, 128.

27 Marc E. Gold, "The Mask of Objectivity: Politics and Rhetoric in the Supreme Court of Canada," *Supreme Court Law Review* 7 (1985): 455. See also David M. Thomas, *Whistling Past the Graveyard: Constitutional Abeyances, Québec, and the Future of Canada* (Toronto and New York: Oxford University Press, 1997), 10, n. 39.

28 Gold, *supra* note 27, 477.

29 Ibid., 489.

30 Russell, *supra* note 24, 129.

31 Mark D. Walters, "Nationalism and the Pathology of Legal Systems: Considering the Quebec Secession Reference and Its Lessons for the United Kingdom," *Modern Law Review* 62:3 (1999): 371.

32 Gold, *supra* note 27, 487.

33 Ibid., 484 and 504. See also Russell, *supra* note 20, 592. The same can be said for the re-strained approach to *Bill of Rights* jurisprudence.

34 Warren Newman has described this as "a revolution that dared not speak its name." Warren J. Newman and York University, *The Quebec Secession Reference: The Rule of Law and the Position of the Attorney General of Canada* (Toronto: York University, 1999), 7. See also Patrick Monahan, "The Public Policy Role of the Supreme Court of Canada in the Secession Reference," *National Journal of Constitutional Law* 11:2 (1999): 71.

35 Mary Dawson, "Reflections on the Opinion of the Supreme Court of Canada in the Quebec Secession Reference," *National Journal of Constitutional Law* 11:2 (1999): 11.

36 Cited in H. Wade MacLauchlin, "Accounting for Democracy and the Rule of Law in the Quebec Secession Reference," *Canadian Bar Review* 76 (1997): 156.

37 Cited in Bruce Wallace, "Moment of Decision," *Maclean's* 111:34 (1998): 12.

38 Monahan, *supra* note 34, 103.

39 John D. Whyte, "The Secession Reference and Constitutional Paradox," in David Schneiderman, ed., *The Quebec Decision: Perspectives on the Supreme Court Ruling on Secession* (Toronto: J. Lorimer, 1999), 133; and Peter W. Hogg, "The Duty to Negotiate," *Canada Watch* 7:1-2 (1999), http://www.yorku.ca/robarts/projects/canada-watch/html/vol_7_1-2/hogg.html.

40 G.J. Brandt, "Judicial Mediation of Political Disputes: The Patriation Reference," *University of Western Ontario Law Review* 20 (1982), 124.

41 "Ruling Legitimizes Sovereignty Drive, PQ Leaders Say," *Globe and Mail* (August 21, 1998).

42 Chris Cobb, "Natives Put Positive Spin on Court Ruling," *Kingston Whig-Standard* (August 21, 1998).

43 Robert Young, "A Most Politic Judgment," in David Schneiderman, ed., *The Quebec Decision: Perspectives on the Supreme Court Ruling on Secession* (Toronto: J. Lorimer, 1999), 112. See also Monahan, *supra* note 34, 67.

44 "From Simplicity to Complexity: The Development of Theory in the Study of Judicial Behavior," *Political Behavior* 5:1 (1983): 9.

45 Age: *Fitzgerald v. Alberta*, 2004 ABCA 184. Residency: *Re Yukon Residency Requirement*, [1986] 27 D.L.R. (4th) 146 (Y. C.A.); *Arnold v. Ontario*, [1987] 61 O.R. (2d) 481 (H.C.); *Haig v. Canada*, [1993] 2 S.C.R. 995 at para. 1029 (*obiter*). See Peter W. Hogg, *Constitutional Law of Canada*, 4th edition (Scarborough, ON: Carswell, 1997), 42-43.

46 *Canadian Disability Rights Council v. R*, [1988] 3 F.C. 622 (F.C.T.D.); *Muldoon v. Canada*, [1988] 3 F.C. 628 (F.C.T.D.); and *Re Hoogbruin and Attorney General of British Columbia* (1985), 24 D.L.R. (4th) 718 (B.C. C.A.). See, generally, Hogg, *supra* note 45, 42-43.

47 *Canada Elections Act*, R.S.C. 1985, c. E-2, s. 51e.

48 *Canada Elections Act*, S.C. 1993, c. 19, amending s. 51 and adding s. 51.1.

49 Compare the *Sauvé* decisions' silence on the new law to the treatment of amendments to the Criminal Code in *R. v. Heywood*, [1994] 3 S.C.R. 761 at 799 (Cory J.). In *Heywood*, the majority (Cory, Lamer, Iacobucci, La Forest and Major JJ.) explicitly recognized changes to

the vagrancy/loitering provisions enacted after the Court of Appeal's decision in *Heywood* and the Supreme Court of Canada hearing. The majority did not go so far as to affirm the constitutionality of the amendments, but they did suggest that the more narrowly tailored revisions addressed the overbreadth problems that the Court had with the law before it (at para. 800). In fact, the majority used the existence of the new law as confirmation that the earlier law was indeed overly broad (at 801).

50 Canada, Royal Commission on Electoral Reform and Party Financing, *Reforming Electoral Democracy: Final Report*, vol. 1 (Ottawa: Royal Commission on Electoral Reform and Party Financing, 1991).

51 A win-set is defined as the set of all possible arrangements that could achieve majority support from the participants if a measure was simply voted up or down. For a discussion in the context of multi-level games, see Robert D. Putnam, "Diplomacy and Domestic Politics: The Logic of Two-Level Games," *International Organization* 42:3 (1988): 437.

52 Forrest Maltzman, James F. Spriggs, and Paul J. Wahlbeck, "Strategy and Judicial Choice: New Institutionalist Approaches to Supreme Court Decision-Making," in Cornell W. Clayton and Howard Gillman, eds., *Supreme Court Decision-Making: New Institutionalist Approaches* (Chicago: University of Chicago Press, 1999), 53.

53 Cass R. Sunstein, *One Case at a Time: Judicial Minimalism on the Supreme Court* (Cambridge, MA: Harvard University Press, 1999).

54 *Sauvé I, supra* note 7, 438.

55 *R. v. Oakes*, [1986] 1 S.C.R. 103 at paras. 138-39.

56 Peter W. Hogg and Allison A. Bushell, "Charter Dialogue between Courts and Legislatures (Or Perhaps the Charter of Rights Isn't Such a Bad Thing after All)," *Osgoode Hall Law Journal* 35:1 (1997): 529.

57 F.L. Morton, "Dialogue or Monologue?" in Paul Howe and Peter H. Russell, eds., *Judicial Power and Canadian Democracy* (Montreal: Insitute for Research on Public Policy, 2000), 112.

58 *Sauvé II, supra* note 7, para. 104 (Gonthier J. quoting with approval Linden J. in the Court of Appeal).

59 Ibid., para. 17 (McLachlin C.J.)

60 Ibid., "Factum of the Respondent Richard Sauvé." By contrast, the minimal impairment portion of the factum is one paragraph. Sauvé, facing life imprisonment, had obvious reasons for preferring the insufficient objective argument to any discussion of minimal impairment.

61 *Sauvé II, supra* note 7, para. 26 (McLachlin C.J.).

62 *Sauvé I, supra* note 54.

63 *Canadian Council of Churches v. Canada (Minister of Employment and Immigration)*, [1992] 1 S.C.R. 236.

64 *R. v. Smith*, [2004] 1 S.C.R. 385 (narrow exceptions where the death of the accused does not make a case moot); *Borowski v. Canada (Attorney General)*, [1989] 1 S.C.R. 342 (public interest may warrant a grant of standing and the deciding of a moot case); and *Doucet-Boudreau v. Nova Scotia (Minister of Education)*, [2003] 3 S.C.R. 3 (need for judicial guidance as reason for hearing moot case).

65 *R. v. Smith*, [1987] 1 S.C.R. 1045.

66 Cornell W. Clayton and Howard Gillman, *Supreme Court Decision-Making: New Institutionalist Approaches* (Chicago: University of Chicago Press, 1999), 23.

67 Gibson, *supra* note 44, 9.

68 McCloskey, *supra* note 9, 38.

5

Legislative Activism and Parliamentary Bills of Rights: Institutional Lessons for Canada

James B. Kelly

The relationship between the Supreme Court of Canada and Parliament has received a significant amount of attention, due, in part, to dialogue theory attributed to the *Canadian Charter of Rights and Freedoms*.[1] While *Charter* dialogue does exist, it is almost exclusively between the Supreme Court of Canada and the Cabinet – a direct result of an underdeveloped parliamentary role in critically assessing the constitutional merits of legislation introduced into the House of Commons by the political executive. Indeed, after more than twenty-five years, a highly institutionalized *Charter* scrutiny is conducted during the pre-introduction stages of policy development by the Department of Justice on behalf of the federal Cabinet.[2] However, the institutionalization of post-introduction parliamentary scrutiny has not emerged in Canada, despite dialogue theory suggesting that there is an important role for parliamentarians outside of Cabinet. As a result, an imbalance exists within the legislative response to the *Charter*, which misrepresents the complexity of *Charter* dialogue *within* Parliament and its dominance by the Cabinet through the machinery of government.

The only significant reform involving the interpretation of the *Charter* involves the appointment of judges to the Supreme Court of Canada, which is modelled loosely on the process in the United States. In certain respects, this process demonstrates a fundamental limitation in the *Charter* debate, as its theoretical benchmark continues to be the United States and the concern with judicial power.[3] While important limitations exist in the parliamentary approach to the *Charter* after more than twenty-five years,[4] it is a mistake to assume that the most significant limitation of the *Charter* is its interpretation by the justices of the Supreme Court of Canada. In this chapter, the imbalance within legislative activism resulting from executive dominance will be explored in the context of *Charter* dialogue. Instead of drawing upon the example of the United States, this chapter will argue that important lessons can be found in the experience of Westminster democracies that have grafted bills of rights onto parliamentary structures, such as New Zealand.[5]

Since the drafters of the *New Zealand Bill of Rights Act 1990* (NZBORA) were influenced by the Canadian *Charter* and rights-based dialogue figures prominently in this Westminster democracy, New Zealand represents a more suitable case for improving *Charter* dialogue within the Canadian parliamentary setting.[6] Although New Zealand is a unitary system with a unicameral parliament, it provides important lessons for Canada and other parliamentary democracies with bills of rights because of the institutional similarities and the historical linkages derived from common experiences as former British colonies.

The imbalance within legislative activism is significant within the context of the *Charter* debate and the debilitating effect on democratic institutions suggested by the critics of judicial activism.[7] The emergence of an institutionalized *Charter*-vetting process within the legislative process has offset the implications of judicial activism and ensured that the parliamentary arena remains the centre of public policy. Thus, the "democratic deficit" associated with judicial review involving the *Charter* is overstated. However, where the argument for democratic deficit has merit is within the parliamentary arena and the political response to the *Charter* that has further marginalized parliamentarians outside of the Cabinet. The political response is decidedly cabinet centred, and *Charter* dialogue within the parliamentary setting is an exercise overwhelmingly within the machinery of government in support of the Cabinet's legislative agenda to the general exclusion of the House of Commons and the Senate.

This chapter considers the implications of *Charter* dialogue for the growing democratic deficit between parliamentarians and the Cabinet and is divided into three sections. The first section focuses on the nature of constitutional dialogue in Canada and the deficiencies that have emerged as a result of a cabinet-centred discourse. The second section considers the example of New Zealand and the emergence of a more balanced parliamentary dialogue on rights and freedoms. The final section advocates the adoption of important New Zealand practices that are argued to facilitate a robust and balanced dialogue on rights within Parliament and between parliamentarians.

Constitutional Dialogue and the *Charter*

The United States and Canada are generally argued to be excellent comparative cases in judicial politics, as both are federations with entrenched constitutions that provide the judiciary with the ability to invalidate government action when it is inconsistent with protected rights and freedoms. While there are important reasons to analyze the Canadian *Charter* in relation to the United States *Bill of Rights*, that comparison overlooks the significant differences between parliamentary and presidential systems and distinctive approaches to bills of rights adopted by Westminster systems.[8] Indeed, analyses of the "parliamentary bill of rights" in recent scholarship suggest that more appropriate comparisons are New Zealand, the United Kingdom, and Australia because of their institutional congruence as Westminster parliamentary democracies.[9] Specifically, this model has attempted to limit judicial supremacy by providing Parliament with mechanisms to temporarily override judicial decisions, such as the Canadian *Charter's* notwithstanding clause or, alternatively, limiting the judiciary to non-binding "declarations of incompatibility" under the United Kingdom's *Human Rights Act, 1998,* and similar provisions in the Australian state of Victoria's *Charter of Human Rights and Responsibilities 2006.*[10]

The introduction of bills of rights by Canada and New Zealand demonstrate the ability of Westminster systems to retain the principles of parliamentary democracy while adding the benefits of bills of rights through institutional dialogue. Such developments have occurred despite notable institutional differences, as Canada is a federation with a bicameral Parliament and New Zealand is a unitary system with a unicameral Parliament. Both examples of the "parliamentary model" emphasize the development of a constitutional dialogue involving rights and freedoms in two institutional settings: first, the parliamentary arena and, second, the judicial arena.[11] Although these Westminster democracies have notable differences in their approach to the Commonwealth or parliamentary model of bills of rights,[12] they attempt to ensure that the protection of rights is fundamentally a parliamentary responsibility, though to varying degrees, complemented by judicial review.[13]

A significant difference between Canada and New Zealand involves the status of the bill of rights and whether it constitutes higher law. While the Canadian *Charter* is an entrenched document that is supreme law, the *NZBORA* is a statutory document. As a result of the different status of the bill of rights in each nation, the judiciary has a different role as well. Only the Canadian *Charter* allows for judicial invalidation of legislation as unconstitutional because of the supreme law status of the *Charter.* In the case of New Zealand, the judiciary cannot make declarations of unconstitutionality but must, where possible, provide an interpretation that is consistent with the bill of rights.[14] There are very limited judicial remedies available for rights violations under the *NZBORA,* as compared to the Canadian *Charter,* and the first public pronouncement on the consistency of legislation is the responsibility of the attorney general under section 7 of the *NZBORA.* Perhaps more significantly, Parliament can pass legislation into law that is identified by the attorney general to be in breach of the *NZBORA.* However, the value of the *NZBORA* is argued to be the development of a rights culture within the legislative process, and the reduced judicial function is not considered detrimental to the robustness of rights dialogue.[15]

Despite the passage of the *Charter* by the Parliament of Canada, the political responsibility for this document quickly became the domain of the Cabinet with little participation by those parliamentarians outside of the executive. Three factors account for the ability of the Cabinet to govern with the *Charter* from the centre: the emergence of the Department of Justice as a central agency within the machinery of government; the deficiencies of the *Charter*-certification process under section 4.1(1) of the *Department of Justice Act* and the status of the minister of justice; and, finally, the limited resources available for parliamentarians to engage in a rights-based scrutiny of the Cabinet's legislative agenda.[16] While the emergence of a highly institutionalized vetting process has offset the implications of judicial power under the *Charter*, it has resulted in a scrutiny process that contains few parliamentary constraints on the Cabinet's legislative agenda.[17] In this respect, judicial review by the Department of Justice on behalf of Cabinet represents one of the only effective and functional checks on the *Charter* certification process.

The Department of Justice as a Central Agency

The principal institutional response to the *Charter* has transformed the Department of Justice into a central agency within the machinery of government. This transformation is a result of the Department of Justice's monopoly over *Charter* vetting during the pre-introduction stages of policy development within the bureaucratic arena as well as of changes to the Memoranda from Cabinet that require line departments to seek a *Charter* opinion by the Department of Justice before draft legislation is submitted to the Privy Council Office.[18] Further, all departmental legal personnel, with the exception of the Department of Foreign Affairs, are employees of the Department of Justice. In regard to the *Charter*, the Department of Justice has sole responsibility for two functions. First, the Department of Justice provides legal advice to client departments regarding the constitutionality of policy proposals and whether the legislative objectives are consistent with the *Charter*. Second, through the attorney general's branch, the Department of Justice is responsible for all constitutional and civil litigation involving the Canadian government.

The provision of *Charter* advice to client departments is advanced by the Department of Justice's unique organizational structure. While there is a central office where the Human Rights Law Section is located, the provision of legal advice at the departmental level is provided by seconded crown lawyers within organizational structures that are referred to as legal service units. Legal service units remain the responsibility of the Department of Justice but are involved in the development of policy from a legal perspective with client departments. Since the introduction of the *Charter* and the development of a rights culture within government, legal service units have been used by the Department of Justice, on behalf of the Cabinet, to perform a substantive review of legislation for its *Charter* implications.[19]

Charter scrutiny at the departmental level does not simply involve the legal service units but also involves the Department of Justice, just as the legal service units rely on the Human Rights Law Section within the Department of Justice to ensure that *Charter* values receive adequate attention in the design of legislation. Further, once the line department in consultation with its legal service unit drafts a memorandum to Cabinet, the Department of Justice provides advice to the Privy Council Office regarding the attempts taken to ensure that the proposed policy is constitutional or, at a minimum, a reasonable limitation on a *Charter* right. Once the Cabinet approves the policy and the Parliament of Canada passes it into law, the Department of Justice has the final responsibility for drafting the act into law. This relationship has transformed the Department of Justice into a powerful central agency, possibly the most powerful within the federal government, save for the Department of Finance. This amount of power, in itself, is cause for concern since the Canadian constitutional dialogue is generally the domain of those with a legal background and is monopolized by the Department of Justice before legislation is introduced into the House of Commons.

While important institutional reforms have been implemented to ensure that legislation is subjected to an extensive *Charter* scrutiny, it has clearly strengthened the Cabinet in the parliamentary arena. Indeed, the development of a rights culture within the government has not challenged executive control but has strengthened it because *Charter* vetting by the Department of Justice can ensure that the policy choices of the Cabinet may survive scrutiny by the courts. Further, the limited resources available to parliamentarians to scrutinize the Cabinet's legislative agenda is problematic as it prevents the emergence of a balanced dialogue on the *Charter* among members of the House of Commons. The imbalance within legislative activism in Canada is evident in *A Guide to the Making of Federal Acts and Regulations*, which was produced by the Department of Justice to aid departments in the development of legislation. *Charter* certification by the minister of justice to the House of Commons is outlined in the guide, but there is no role for Parliament, independent of the *Charter* vetting performed by the Department of Justice, to challenge the *Charter* certification of the minister of justice.[20] This situation reinforces Frank's position that "[w]hile the executive took additional measures in pre-vetting to ensure that legislation met the new standards imposed by the charter, parliament did not, itself, add additional procedures or mechanisms to review bills from a rights perspective, as it has with the joint committee on statutory instruments."[21] Certification by the minister of justice is based on the review performed by the Department of Justice and demonstrates that legislative activism is dominated by the political executive through its control of the machinery of government.[22] The parliamentary response to *Charter* review, therefore, has simply strengthened the Cabinet as a result of the *Charter* review performed by the Department of Justice.

The Minister of Justice, Constitutionalism, and the
Charter Certification Process

The minister of justice is required under section 4.1(1) of the *Department of Justice Act* to inform Parliament if the Cabinet introduces legislation into the House of Commons that the minister concludes is unconstitutional.[23] There are a number of practical difficulties with section 4.1(1) that undermine the reporting function as a constraint on the Cabinet's legislative agenda and that limit the effectiveness of this reporting duty to Parliament. The most serious limitation with section 4.1(1) is that it has not been formalized as part of the legislative process required before a bill is introduced into the House of Commons. While the minister of justice is required to certify that a bill is constitutional, he or she is not required to provide the substantive reasons that a particular bill is considered compliant with the Canadian *Charter*.[24]

This lack of transparency is a significant resource that allows the Cabinet to govern with the *Charter* from the centre and to ensure that bureaucratic scrutiny cannot be effectively challenged at the parliamentary committee stage. Under section 4.1(1), the minister of justice is only required to inform Parliament when a bill is considered unconstitutional, as a violation of the *Charter*. While this appears to be an important power that serves as an internal check on the Cabinet, in reality, it is compromised by the principle of cabinet solidarity that undermines the independence of the attorney general in relation to *Charter* certification and, finally, adds to the complexity of *Charter* compatibility and its contestable nature.

Under the *Department of Justice Act*, the minister of justice is also the attorney general of Canada and, therefore, the highest independent legal officer of the Crown. This would suggest that the minister of justice has the necessary independence to report to Parliament when the Cabinet has introduced legislation that, in the opinion of the minister of justice, breaches the *Charter*. However, such a decision would require the minister of justice, functioning as the attorney general, to violate cabinet solidarity and provide a negative assessment of legislation agreed to by the Cabinet. The tension between partisanship as the minister of justice and the principle of legal independence as attorney general is difficult, if not impossible, to reconcile within a single parliamentarian and partially explains why section 4.1(1) has never been used. An important check exists on the Cabinet and its legislative agenda in relation to the *Charter*, but it is rendered unworkable by the principle of responsible government that is at the heart of parliamentary democracy – if the minister of justice disagreed with a cabinet decision because of its implication for the *Charter*, he or she would be required to resign from Cabinet before the legislation was presented to the House of Commons, rendering the reporting duty to Parliament ineffective.

The futile nature of the certification process is the result of the complexity of constitutionalism, as the assessment of consistency by the minister of justice can be based on three distinct understandings of the *Charter*. First, the bill is considered constitutional because it does not infringe a protected right or freedom. Second, the legislation violates a protected right but is considered by the minister of justice to be a reasonable limit under section 1 of the *Charter* and thus constitutional. Finally, the legislation violates the *Charter*, is considered by the Department of Justice to be an unreasonable limitation, but is determined by the Cabinet, on the advice of the minister of justice, to be a reasonable limitation. Concluding that a violation is a reasonable limitation is a highly discretionary decision of the minister of justice, which may be challenged by the members of parliament. However, the present reporting duty undermines robust *Charter* dialogue on the merits of the Cabinet's legislative agenda because the minister of justice is only required to report that a bill is unconstitutional. In Parliament, robust debate would likely centre on the defence of reasonable limitations because it is an inherently contestable constitutional justification. Indeed, this process has led to robust disagreement by the Supreme Court of Canada, which has rejected the defence of reasonable limitations in forty cases in which federal statutes have been invalidated as inconsistent with the *Charter*.[25]

The limitations in the reporting duty of the minister of justice are illustrated in Bill C-27, *An Act to Amend the Criminal Code (Dangerous Offenders and Recognizance to Keep the Peace)*, which was introduced in 2006 and granted royal assent in 2008.[26] Bill C-27 changes the process for designating individuals as dangerous offenders in three important respects. First, the bill provides that the Crown must seek dangerous offender status for an individual previously convicted of two serious personal injury offences or sexual offences. Second, the bill removes the judiciary's discretion to order a dangerous offender assessment, and, finally, the bill creates a reverse-onus provision that requires the accused to demonstrate that a lesser designation is warranted. By its introduction, Bill C-27 is considered by the Conservative government to be constitutional. It is debatable whether this bill is in fact constitutional because it will be decided by section 1 of the *Charter*. Thus, it limits judicial discretion and is a violation of section 11.d (judicial independence), it infringes the right to be presumed innocent, and it brings in a reverse-onus provision that the Supreme Court of Canada has been reluctant to accept as being consistent with the *Charter*'s legal rights guarantees. This bill can only be viewed as constitutional because the government considers it a reasonable limitation on protected rights. In an important sense, Bill C-27 demonstrates the hollowness of the minister of justice's reporting duty to

Parliament. It is simply a procedural requirement that cannot serve as the basis of a robust legislative-executive dialogue at the select committee stage because only the Cabinet has access to the substantive reasons that a bill is considered constitutional.

This is in stark contrast to the practice in New Zealand, where the former attorney general Margaret Wilson established the practice of making available to the select committees of the House of Representatives the advice on all bills prepared by the Ministry of Justice and the Crown Law Office.[27] As a result, because of the transparent nature of the reporting duty there is a greater ability of parliamentarians to challenge the attorney general's assessment of legislative compliance with the *NZBORA* and to dispute the assessment of whether a rights violation is a reasonable limitation.[28] This has had an important educative effect in so far as the constitutional discourse considers both rights and limitations, which has not generally occurred in Canada despite the longer history of the Canadian *Charter*. The significance of full disclosure is that it provides parliamentarians, at the select committee stage, with an opportunity to debate the merits of the policy and to fully scrutinize the government's justification when a bill must be defended as a reasonable limitation on a protected right or freedom.[29]

Parliament and Constitutional Scrutiny
While there are notable examples of parliamentary committees engaging in *Charter* scrutiny, such as with the *Anti-Terrorism Act*, there is little evidence of the certification of the minister of justice being successfully challenged or thoroughly scrutinized at the committee stage.[30] Unlike the United Kingdom, which engaged in both parliamentary and bureaucratic reform to ensure that the introduction of the *Human Rights Act, 1998,* did not result in a loss of policy autonomy for the British Parliament, or the Australian state of Victoria, which introduced a *Charter of Human Rights and Responsibilities* in July 2006, the Canadian response has generally been one-dimensional within the bureaucratic arena in support of the Cabinet's legislative agenda. The British Parliament created the Joint Committee on Human Rights in 2001 with an explicit mandate to engage in parliamentary scrutiny of legislation from a rights perspective.[31] In Victoria, the Scrutiny of Bills Committee has been given responsibility for evaluating statements of compatibility issued when bills are introduced into Parliament.[32] However, no standing committee or standing senate committee of the Parliament of Canada has been given such a mandate, and parliamentary scrutiny has been displaced by executive certification, by the minister of justice to the House of Commons, that proposed legislation is constitutional.[33]

In addition to this institutional absence, the apparatus supporting parliamentary committees pales in comparison to the machinery of government supporting the Cabinet. The Office of the Law Clerk and Parliamentary

Counsel provides support for all twenty-two standing committees of the House of Commons and has a staff of eleven lawyers.[34] The Human Rights Law Section at the Department of Justice has a staff of twenty-two lawyers, and the legal service unit at Health Canada is comprised of fifty-nine lawyers.[35] This support compounds the lack of clarity in the reporting function under section 4.1(1) as parliamentarians outside of the executive have limited resources to engage in substantive scrutiny of the Cabinet's claim that legislation is consistent with the *Charter*. Second, the composition of parliamentary committees and the issue of partisanship results in scrutiny becoming the responsibility of opposition parties, as government members are constrained by party discipline and reluctant to challenge the Cabinet's position that legislation complies with the *Charter*.

The overall impact of the institutional imbalance between the Cabinet and parliamentarians is to insulate bureaucratic scrutiny from parliamentary scrutiny and to produce a cabinet-centred discourse on the *Charter* within the parliamentary setting. While this discourse is not without merit, as only forty federal statutes have been invalidated by the Supreme Court of Canada (1982-2007), and very few statutes enacted since the institutionalization of rights vetting in 1990 have been declared unconstitutional,[36] it has contributed to the decline of Parliament as an institution and furthered the democratic deficit within political institutions because it complicates an essential role of parliamentarians – the political and constitutional scrutiny of the Cabinet's legislative agenda.[37]

New Zealand and the Collaborative Model

Although the Canadian *Charter* is a stronger document than its New Zealand counterpart, based on its entrenched status and the ability of judges to invalidate unconstitutional legislation, the two documents have had the same impact on the development of legislation. Indeed, it is not the status of the document that has improved the quality of legislation but, rather, the bureaucratic and parliamentary commitment to designing principled legislation.[38] This was the justification offered by New Zealand's minister of justice Geoffrey Palmer during the introduction of a draft bill of rights in 1985.[39] Palmer presented a critique of the judicial-centred approach to understanding the value of a bill of rights, arguing that the bureaucratic and parliamentary response would ensure the value of a bill of rights, despite its status as ordinary legislation.

In New Zealand, the changes to the machinery of government and the introduction of rights-vetting processes are very similar to those of Canada. Vetting the *NZBORA* is the responsibility of the departmental legal advisors, who are not employees of the Ministry of Justice or the Crown Law Office but, rather, are employees of the ministries in which they reside.[40] The concern expressed by Palmer, that this decentralized approach would result in inconsistent legal advice, has recently been addressed by the Bill of Rights Unit at the Ministry of Justice and by the creation of guidelines for the development of legislation consistent with the *NZBORA*.[41] In many respects, these guidelines are New Zealand's equivalent of the *Charter* checklists, which are maintained by the Human Rights Law Section at the Department of Justice in an attempt to ensure consistent advice by legal service units seconded to line departments.

There are, however, a number of important institutional differences that may result in a more balanced constitutional dialogue in New Zealand. Unlike in Canada, where the minister of justice is also the attorney general and the Department of Justice houses both bureaucratic organizations, in New Zealand there exists a Ministry of Justice *and* a Crown Law Office, which are headed by a minister of justice and an attorney general, respectively. These two government departments are responsible for legal issues – the Ministry of Justice administers legal policy, while the Crown Law Office has the responsibility for litigation. Further, the Ministry of Justice is responsible for vetting all non-justice bills, and the Crown Law Office is responsible for vetting bills proposed by the Ministry of Justice that need to be consistent with the *NZBORA*.[42] Unlike in Canada, where the minister of justice certifies that a draft bill is consistent with the *Charter*, the sponsoring minister in New Zealand is required by the Cabinet handbook to certify compliance with the *NZBORA* before a bill is added to the government's legislative agenda.[43]

In New Zealand, drafting instructions by the sponsoring department are not sent to the Ministry of Justice for the purpose of preparing legislation but, rather, to the Parliamentary Counsel Office, which has the responsibility for drafting all government bills. During the development of legislation, the established practice is that departmental legal advisors contact the Bill of Rights Unit at the Ministry of Justice throughout a policy exercise to ensure that any issues with the *NZBORA* are adequately addressed. This is an important practice, as it aids the Parliamentary Counsel's office in drafting legislation that complies with the *NZBORA*. Although departments are not required to consult the Ministry of Justice, this practice has emerged largely because the Ministry of Justice must vet all non-justice bills for their relationship with the *NZBORA* before draft legislation can be presented to the House of Representatives.[44] A similar practice has also been developed between the Ministry of Justice and the Crown Law Office in regard to justice bills. Indeed, the Ministry of Justice and the Crown Law Office must present assessments of proposed legislation to the attorney general, who is required under section 7 of the *NZBORA* to report to Parliament any bill that appears to violate rights and freedoms.[45]

The significance of *BORA* vetting is the remarkable similarity it has to Charter vetting in Canada, despite the different status of the documents. Grant Huscroft has remarked that "[a] country's commitment to the idea of human rights is more important than the legal form that commitment takes."[46] Both Canada and New Zealand engage in institutionalized rights vetting to ensure that legislation, when introduced into Parliament, is consistent with rights commitments or, at the very least, a reasonable limitation. While there are important institutional differences in the structure of legal advice and the government departments providing this advice, it is difficult to contend that bureaucratic scrutiny in Canada is superior to that of New Zealand, despite the superior status of the Canadian *Charter*.[47]

The point of departure for legislative scrutiny in Canada and New Zealand involves the issue of parliamentary scrutiny and the nature of constitutional dialogue that occurs during the post-introduction phase of the legislative process. In New Zealand, the attorney general – not the minister of justice – has the responsibility under section 7 of the *NZBORA* to report to Parliament when a bill appears to be inconsistent with rights or freedoms.[48] This procedure has resulted in thirty-nine section 7 reports being issued by the attorney general between 1991 and 2007, and twenty-one have involved government bills. In an important sense, the New Zealand practice of having separate parliamentarians serve as minister of justice and attorney general has reduced the tension between partisanship and legality that has undermined the reporting function in Canada. The attorney general has a different relationship to the Cabinet as an independent legal officer responsible for guarding the public interest.[49] While the Canadian minister of justice does possess attorney general independence, it has been limited to prosecutorial freedom and has yet to emerge in the context of the *Charter* through section 4.1(1) of the *Department of Justice Act*.

Under section 7, the attorney general provides an opinion to Parliament that legislation violates the *NZBORA* and provides a justification, based on pre-introduction scrutiny, as to why the legislation in question does not constitute a minimal impairment on a right or freedom. However, this is simply an opinion presented by the attorney general, which Parliament has the discretion to accept and, therefore, to remove the proposed bill from the parliamentary agenda or to dispute the attorney general's section 7 report and proceed to send the bill to select committees for further investigation.[50] Further, a section 7 report does not prevent a bill from being passed by Parliament but requires the Cabinet to justify introducing a bill indentified by the attorney general as being inconsistent with rights.

Although the dialogue metaphor was developed in Canada, a more balanced version occurs in New Zealand because of significant advancements in parliamentary scrutiny involving rights and the willingness of the House of Representatives to challenge the attorney general's assessment of the relationship between proposed legislation and the *NZBORA*. Michael Taggart has suggested that "[o]n the negative side is the undignified sight – as has occurred in New Zealand – of the House disregarding or rejecting the view of the Attorney General on inconsistency."[51] However, as Carolyn Archer and Gaze Burt suggest, the rejection of a section 7 report by Parliament may indicate that "the House has taken a different view of the law. Section 7 is designed to give Parliament the final say, but also to ensure that it 'acts publicly with its eyes open.' It requires that inconsistent provisions are identified and reported to the House so that any inconsistencies subsequently enacted, are the result of an informed, conscious choice by Parliament."[52] When the attorney general's advice has been challenged, it has generally involved the issue of reasonable limitations and not the *prima facia* infringement of a protected right.[53]

In effect, there are two dimensions to constitutional review and dialogue in New Zealand: first, whether a right has been violated, which the attorney general is well placed to perform with the assistance of the Crown Law Office and Ministry of Justice, and, second, how the reasonable limitations are to be assessed when the legislation infringes a right. The first level of scrutiny is clearly a legal task, and the attorney general's advice should rarely, if ever, be rejected in this regard. However, the consideration of reasonableness is a policy function that should not be monopolized by the attorney general since Parliament and the select committees are well placed to determine whether the proposed policy is both pressing and substantial and can be demonstrably justified to support the rights violation despite the attorney general's assessment.

In certain respects, the explanation for this balanced constitutional discourse relates to the political objectives behind the *NZBORA* at the time of its enactment. Geoffrey Palmer did not defend the proposed bill of rights as an instrument of national unity, as Pierre Trudeau did with the Canadian *Charter*, but, rather, as an institutional mechanism to check the political executive in a unicameral parliamentary setting.[54] In this sense, it was part of a wider rethinking of institutional arrangements designed to reinvigorate Parliament as an institution and to compensate for the absence of adequate checks on prime ministerial government that became increasingly problematic during the tenure of New Zealand's prime minister Robert Muldoon (1975-84).[55]

Until 2003, the attorney general only presented *NZBORA* vets to Parliament when a bill was considered in violation of the act. In 2002, the attorney general's assessment that the Climate Change Response Bill did not violate the *NZBORA* was challenged by expert witnesses during its review by the Foreign Affairs, Defence, and Trade Select Committee.[56] During its report on the bill, the select committee articulated the importance of a balanced dialogue between the attorney general and the committee system, which could only take place if all vets prepared by the Ministry of Justice and the Crown Law Office, and not simply section 7 reports by the attorney general, were made available once legislation was introduced into the House of Representatives: "Without the benefit of the Attorney General's advice or the time to utilize independent advice for the Bill of Rights Act, we are in an impossible position to refute submitters' claims that the bill is not compliant with the Bill of Rights Act."[57] The committee's report presented the attorney general with a dilemma: to refuse to release *NZBORA* vets to select committees and potentially undermine pre-introduction scrutiny by the Ministry of Justice and the Crown Law Office or to release the vets and engage in a collaborative relationship with select committees through a transparent and public discourse on constitutionality.[58]

In response, the attorney general announced in 2003 that all vets produced by the Ministry of Justice and Crown Law Office would be made available to the select committees and general public by posting them on the Ministry of Justice's website.[59] The provision of *NZBORA* vets by the Ministry of Justice and Crown Law Office allows select committees to review the *NZBORA* analysis prepared for the attorney general and, in regard to legislation that violates rights, to determine whether policy instruments chosen to advance a legislative objective are demonstrably justified. By focusing on the justification for the policy instrument chosen, the transparent process of legislative activism in New Zealand can ensure that it is both legalistic and parliamentarian and that it is a collaborative exercise between the attorney general and the members of select committees.

The Next Twenty-Five Years

In the remainder of this chapter, institutional reforms in the bureaucratic and parliamentary arenas that are needed to address the problem of executive supremacy under the Canadian *Charter* are considered. At the present time, the attempts at reform have focused on the appointment process of justices for the Supreme Court of Canada, which began under former prime minister Paul Martin.[60] This reform is misguided in a number of respects, least of which is the perpetuation of the judicially centred view of the *Charter* and the assumption that Canadian democracy can be improved by changing the appointment of justices to the Court. A concern is that this is a reform borrowed from the American experience, where the public vetting of judges is viewed as democratic and necessary to ensure the integrity of the legislative process. This is the wrong comparative framework since the Canadian *Charter* is a constitutional document embedded with the principles of Westminster democracy. It is argued, instead, that reform of the bureaucratic and parliamentary approaches to rights scrutiny provide a better opportunity to improve constitutional dialogue on rights and freedoms. Perhaps more importantly, the reforms are non-constitutional and simply require a political commitment from the prime minister to govern with the *Charter* in a new way that includes parliamentarians outside of the Cabinet.

There Should Be a Separate Department of Justice and Attorney General's Department

One of the benefits of centralized *Charter* scrutiny in Canada is that it has resulted in the provision of consistent constitutional advice, and the institutional structure of the Department of Justice with legal service units at the department level has allowed an assessment of legislative proposals to begin early in the development of policy. This structure has provided an important set of checks and balances within the legislative process, whereby the policy objectives of client departments are checked by the Department of Justice for their *Charter* consistency, and a series of checks occur within the Department of Justice on the advice provided by legal service units, such as the Human Rights Laws Section. This is an important aspect of ensuring that legislative objectives are consistent with entrenched rights, but it is a task that should not be monopolized by the Department of Justice.

Between 1982 and 2007, the acts administered by the Department of Justice accounted for 53 percent of the cases (twenty-one out of forty) in which the Supreme Court of Canada invalidated statutory provisions as being inconsistent with the *Charter*. Such decisions potentially occur because statutes that the Department of Justice is responsible for, such as the *Criminal Code*, the *Extradition Act*, and the *Privacy Act*, are not subjected to the same type of *Charter* scrutiny that exists for non-Justice bills.[61] While the legislative objectives of client departments are subjected to external review by the Department of Justice, no comparable exercise occurs when the legislation in question is proposed by the Department of Justice – it is simply an internal review performed by the department on its own statutes. In effect, the Department of Justice certifies to the minister of justice that its legislation is consistent with the *Charter*, and, in turn, the minister of justice certifies to Parliament that all legislation is constitutional.

To address this issue, an important innovation from the New Zealand experience should be adopted in Canada. The Department of Justice and the attorney general of Canada should be reorganized into a Department of Justice, with the responsibility for legal policy and the vetting of non-Justice bills, and a Department of the Attorney General, which would have the responsibility for litigation and the vetting of Justice bills for their *Charter* consistency. Since the proposed Department of the Attorney General would be responsible for defending challenged legislation in the courts, and since most challenges involve legislation proposed by the Department of Justice, the presence of legal counsel from a Department of the Attorney General would be a significant resource to draw upon when challenged legislation is defended as a reasonable limitation on a *Charter* right. More practically, the present benefits of legislation proposed by client departments being subjected to an external and independent review by the Department of Justice and the attorney general would be replicated in regard to legislation proposed by the Department of Justice through an external review by a Department of the Attorney General.

There Should Be a Minister of Justice and an Attorney General in Cabinet

At the present time, the minister of justice is also the attorney general for Canada, and this practice should be abolished because of the potential conflict between the two roles. This deficiency was identified during the proceedings of the Standing Senate Committee on Legal and Constitutional Affairs when amendments to the *Extradition Act* were argued to be unconstitutional because of the absence of formal checks on the discretion exercised by the minister of justice in cases involving the extradition of Canadians to foreign jurisdictions. While the standing senate committee was unable to convince the minister of justice of the constitutional problems with the *Extradition Act*, the Supreme Court of Canada nonetheless reduced the discretion available to the minister of justice in *United States v. Burns*.[62]

A more practical problem exists within the *Charter* and the *Department of Justice Act* as the minister of justice has the responsibility under section 4.1(1) to report any inconsistency between legislation and the *Charter* to the House of Commons. This reporting duty has never been used by the minister of justice, whereas a similar responsibility under section 7 of the *NZBORA* has seen the attorney general make thirty-nine reports to Parliament since 1990, stating that bills are inconsistent, and twenty-one have involved government bills. An explanation for the use of this important power in New Zealand and its absence in Canada is the lack of an independent attorney general in the Canadian context. Although the attorney general is a member of Cabinet in New Zealand, he or she is viewed as a non-political member of Cabinet with the responsibility for maintaining the rule of law, which includes the *NZBORA*.[63] Since the attorney general is required to report inconsistencies between proposed legislation and the *NZBORA*, and has been willing to exercise this responsibility, the statutory nature of the *Bill of Rights* has not reduced its effectiveness. Indeed, Attorney General Margaret Wilson stated that a potential section 7 report normally results in the sponsoring minister amending the bill to ensure its consistency with the *NZBORA*, and the limited use of section 7 is explained by the Cabinet's response to a potential declaration of inconsistency.[64]

In Canada, an attorney general should be created with an equivalent role that now exists under section 4.1(1) of the *Department of Justice Act*. Thus, the reporting duty would be the responsibility of the attorney general as legal officer and not the minister of justice as cabinet minister. Further, section 4.1(1) should be amended to require the attorney general to provide a substantive statement to Parliament regarding the constitutionality of bills introduced to the House of Commons. For instance, the reporting duty would require the attorney general to disclose whether a bill is found to be constitutional by recourse to section 1 and the rationale for determining the limitations to be reasonable in a free and democratic society.[65] By redefining the minister of justice as the political spokesperson on legal issues within the Cabinet and the attorney general as the Cabinet's legal advisor with a mandate to protect the rule of law and not the interests of the government, the partisan characteristics of statutes invalidated by the Supreme Court of Canada, such as in *Dunmore v. Ontario (Attorney General)* and the rights of agricultural workers being revoked in Ontario during the Harris Conservative government's "common sense revolution" or the restrictions on campaign financing under the *Canada Elections Act* in *Figueroa v. Canada (Attorney General)* can be addressed.[66] This would add an important check on the dominance of the Cabinet in the policy process and provide an independent legal assessment of the constitutionality of government legislation, neither of which exists at the present time. The independence of the attorney general could be enhanced by establishing the practice that this member of cabinet be selected from the Senate to ensure that an outstanding jurist could be appointed as the chief law officer of Canada.

A *Charter* Scrutiny Committee Should Be Established in Parliament
The creation of a Department of the Attorney General would challenge the Department of Justice's monopoly on *Charter* advice within the bureaucratic arena, but it would not address executive supremacy. A *Charter* Scrutiny Committee should be established in Parliament with a mandate to review legislation and to assess the certifications by the minister of justice and the attorney general that legislation is consistent with the *Charter*. The benefit of such a committee is that it would allow parliamentarians to participate in assessing the constitutionality of proposed legislation and when such legislation is considered to violate the *Charter*, and it could also provide an important legislative record to demonstrate the reasonableness of the infringement if a statute is found to violate the *Charter* by a court. Laws that are passed with minimal parliamentary debate provide the Supreme Court of Canada with the political and policy space to substitute its judgment for legislative intention. Further, limits on rights that have been clearly articulated present hurdles and narrow the discretion of judges in interpreting the policy choices of Parliament. A *Charter* Scrutiny Committee would be able to call the sponsoring ministers and their officials before it to seek elaborations on why a particular course of action was chosen, what the considered

alternatives were, and why the chosen approach was considered the least restrictive on a *Charter* right. Moreover, a *Charter* Scrutiny Committee would convey an important message, namely, that rights are not only the responsibility of courts or the Cabinet but are also a parliamentary responsibility that is taken seriously.

Within the present Parliament of Canada, a joint committee of the Senate and the House of Commons, in which the government does not possess a majority, would be ideal to ensure effective and substantive scrutiny of bills for their relationship to the *Charter*. In Australia, this is the responsibility of the Senate Scrutiny of Bills Committee, where the absence of a government majority on the committee and an opposition member as chair has led to a close scrutiny of legislation from a rights perspective, despite the absence of a bill of rights.[67] In Canada, a scrutiny committee within the House of Commons may suffer from partisanship, which would undermine its effectiveness, whereas a joint committee with equal membership, and chaired by the opposition, may neutralize partisanship to the advantage of substantive review. This has been the experience in the United Kingdom, and the Joint Committee of the Senate and the House of Commons can serve as a model for Canada until an elected Senate assumes this role.[68]

One of the difficulties facing parliamentary committees at the present time is the lack of documentation provided, on the basis of which the minister of justice can certify that legislation is consistent with the *Charter*. Recently, the attorney general of New Zealand has established the practice of posting on the website of the Ministry of Justice the constitutional advice on all proposed bills provided by the Crown Law Office and the Ministry of Justice. This practice should be adopted in Canada as it would facilitate an institutional dialogue between the *Charter* Scrutiny Committee and the sponsoring department and its minister on the constitutional merits of the proposed legislation. More importantly, it would facilitate a parliament-centred approach to *Charter* certification and address executive supremacy in this process. Finally, the *Charter* Scrutiny Committee should be provided with sufficient legal personnel to engage in a substantive review of the certification presented by the attorney general to Parliament.

Conclusion

The first twenty-five years of the *Charter* has seen an important political response to the need to govern in a culture of rights. The institutionalization of *Charter* vetting within the machinery of government ensures that the government's legislative agenda is designed in response to the constitutional commitments that the *Charter* embodies. In this respect, the parliamentary response to the *Charter* has ensured an appropriate relationship between the Supreme Court of Canada and Parliament, and the claims of a democratic deficit arising from judicial activism have been overstated. While the need for a reformed appointment process is evident, it is not the most pressing change needed to address the deficiencies of the parliamentary response to the *Charter*. Since the political response has been centred within the machinery of government, parliamentarians outside of the Cabinet do not engage the *Charter* in a substantive way during the legislative process. This is the democratic deficit associated with the *Charter*, which will not be addressed by a new appointment process to the Supreme Court of Canada.

The link between parliamentary reform and the *Charter* needs to be significantly strengthened for a balanced *Charter* dialogue to occur within the parliamentary arena. Indeed, the invalidation of statutes by the Supreme Court of Canada as being inconsistent with the *Charter* may be an indication of the weaknesses of the minister of justice's reporting duty and the inability of those members outside of the executive to engage in parliamentary scrutiny from a rights perspective. In effect, judicial activism can challenge executive certification because the judicial process requires the Cabinet to disclose the rationale behind its legislative agenda in a transparent way, which the present certification process to Parliament does not require of the Cabinet in regard to the question of constitutionality. The need for a transparent disclosure process can be modelled on the commonwealth experience of parliamentary democracies that have adopted bills of rights, such as New Zealand, the United Kingdom, and the Australian state of Victoria. However, if institutional reforms continue to be adopted from the United States, the present limitations of *Charter* dialogue will not be addressed. Reform is to be found, therefore, in the Commonwealth and not in the compound republic to the south.

Acknowledgments

I would like to thank Grant Huscroft, who provided comments on an earlier version of this chapter.

Notes

1 Peter Hogg and Allison Bushell, "The Charter Dialogue between Courts and Legislatures (Or Perhaps the Charter Hasn't Been Such a Bad Thing after All)," *Osgoode Hall Law Journal* 35 (1997): 75-124. *Canadian Charter of Rights and Freedoms*, Part 1 of the *Constitution Act, 1982*, being Schedule B to the *Canada Act 1982* (U.K.), 1982, c. 11.
2 This process also occurs at the provincial level. See James B. Kelly, *Governing with the Charter* (Vancouver: UBC Press, 2005), 209-20.
3 Kent Roach, *The Supreme Court on Trial: Judicial Activism or Democratic Dialogue* (Toronto: Irwin Law, 2001), 95.
4 Kelly, *supra* note 2, 222-25.
5 Janet L. Hiebert, "Interpreting a Bill of Rights: The Importance of Legislative Rights Review," *British Journal of Political Science* 35 (2005): 240-45.
6 *New Zealand Bill of Rights Act 1990*, 1990 (N.Z.), 1990/109.
7 F.L. Morton and Rainer Knopff, *The Charter Revolution and the Court Party* (Peterborough: Broadview Press, 2000), 33-58.

8 *Bill of Rights.*
9 Janet L. Hiebert, "Parliamentary Bills of Rights: An Alternative Model?" *Modern Law Review* 69 (2006): 7-9; Carolyn Evans and Simon Evans, *Australian Bills of Rights* (Melbourne: Buttersworth, 2008); Julie Debeljak, "Rights Protection without Judicial Supremacy: A Review of the Canadian and British Models of Bills of Rights," *Melbourne University Law Review* 26 (2002): 286-324.
10 *Human Rights Act, 1998,* (U.K.), 1998, c. 42; and *Charter of Human Rights and Responsibilities 2006* (Vic.).
11 Jeremy Webber, "Institutional Dialogue between Courts and Legislatures in the Definition of Fundamental Rights: Lessons from Canada and Elsewhere," in Wojciech Sadurkski, ed., *Constitutional Justice, East and West* (The Hague: Kluwer Law, 2002), 65-66.
12 Stephen Gardbaum, "The New Commonwealth Model of Constitutionalism," *American Journal of Comparative Law* 49 (2001): 708-10.
13 Grant Huscroft, "Protecting Rights and Parliamentary Sovereignty: New Zealand's Experience with a Charter-Inspired, Statutory Bill of Rights," *Windsor Yearbook of Access to Law* 21 (2002): 111-12.
14 Paul Rishworth, Grant Huscroft, Scott Optican, and Richard Mahoney, *The New Zealand Bill of Rights* (Wellington: Oxford University Press, 2003), 116.
15 Janet McLean, "Legislative Invalidation, Human Rights Protection and Section 4 of the New Zealand Bill of Rights Act," *New Zealand Law Review* (2001): 447.
16 *Department of Justice Act,* R.S.C. 1985, c. J-2.
17 Donald J. Savoie, *Governing from the Centre: The Concentration of Power in Canadian Politics* (Toronto: University of Toronto Press, 1999), 7-8.
18 James B. Kelly, "Governing with the Charter of Rights and Freedoms," *Supreme Court Law Review* 21 (2003): 299-337.
19 James B. Kelly, "Bureaucratic Activism and the Charter of Rights and Freedoms: The Department of Justice and Its Entry into the Centre of Government," *Canadian Public Administration* 42 (1999): 486-90.
20 Department of Justice, *A Guide to the Making of Federal Acts and Regulations,* http://www.tbs-sct.gc.ca/asd-dmps/db/gmfa_s-eng.asp, ch. 2 – Principles and Policies, 2.
21 C.E.S. Franks, "Parliament, Intergovernmental Relations, and National Unity" (Kingston: Institute of Intergovernmental Relations, 1999), 8.
22 Janet L. Hiebert, "New Constitutional Ideas: Can Parliamentary Models Resist Judicial Dominance when Interpreting Rights?" *Texas Law Review* 82 (2004): 1971.
23 Kelly, *supra* note 19, 497.
24 Interview with Senator Serge Joyal, Standing Senate Committee on Legal and Constitutional Affairs, October 22, 2002, Ottawa.
25 Kent Roach, "Not Just the Government's Lawyer: The Attorney General as Defender of the Rule of Law," *Queen's Law Journal* 31 (2006): 601-2.
26 Bill C-27, *An Act to Amend the Criminal Code (Dangerous Offenders and Recognizance to Keep the Peace),* 39th Parl., 1st Sess., October 17, 2006. The provisions dealing with dangerous offenders were passed into law as part of Bill C-2, *An Act to Amend the Criminal Code and to Make Consequential Amendments to Other Acts.* 39th Parl., 1st Sess., February 28, 2008.
27 Interview with Honourable Margaret Wilson, attorney general of New Zealand, May 12, 2004, Wellington, New Zealand. The advice provided by the Ministry of Justice and Crown Law Office to the attorney general of New Zealand is available at http://www.justice.govt.nz.
28 Huscroft, *supra* note 13, 111-14.
29 Interview with Justice and Electoral Select Committee: Tim Barnett and Russell Fairbrother, New Zealand Parliament, Wellington, New Zealand (May 5-6, 2004).
30 *Anti-Terrorism Act,* S.C. 2001, c. 41.
31 David Kinley, "Parliamentary Scrutiny of Human Rights: A Duty Neglected?" in Philip Alston, ed., *Promoting Human Rights through Bills of Rights* (Oxford: Oxford University Press, 1999), 158-84.
32 George Williams, "The Victorian *Charter of Human Rights and Responsibilities*: Origins and Scope," *Melbourne University Law Review* 30 (2006): 898-903.

33   Department of Justice Canada, *A Guide to the Making of Federal Acts and Regulations*, http://www.tbs-sct.gc.ca/asd-dmps/db/gmfa_s-eng.asp.
34   Interview with Robert Walsh, Law Clerk and Parliamentary Counsel, Office of the Law Clerk and Parliamentary Counsel, House of Commons, Ottawa (July 24, 2007).
35   These figures are current as of July 21, 2007. See http://direct.srv.gc.ca/cgi-bin/direct500/XEou%3dLS-SJ%2cou%3dHC-SC %2cou%3dHC-SC%2co%3dGC%2cc%3dCA.
36   Kelly, *supra* note 2, 148-49.
37   Peter Aucoin and Laurie Turnbull, "The Democratic Deficit: Paul Martin and Parliamentary Reform," *Canadian Public Administration* 46 (2003): 436-40.
38   McLean, *supra* note 15, 448.
39   *A Bill of Rights for New Zealand: A White Paper* (1985), AJHR A.6.
40   Geoffrey Palmer, "The Provision of Legal Services to Government," *Victoria University of Wellington Law Review* 31 (2000): 69.
41   *The Guidelines on the New Zealand Bill of Rights Act 1990: A Guide to the Rights and Freedoms in the Bill of Rights Act for the Public Sector* (Wellington: Ministry of Justice, 2004).
42   New Zealand, Department of the Prime Minister and Cabinet, *Cabinet Manual 2001*, http://www.dpmc.govt.nz/cabinet/manual/index.html.
43   Huscroft, *supra* note 13, 121.
44   Interview with the departmental officials at the Ministry of Justice, Wellington, New Zealand (May 4, 2004); and Interview with Parliamentary Counsel Office, Wellington, New Zealand (May 12, 2004).
45   Paul Fitzgerald, "Section 7 of the New Zealand Bill of Rights Act 1990: A Very Practical Power or Well Intentioned Nonsense?" *Victoria University of Wellington Law Review* 22 (1992): 137.
46   Huscroft, *supra* note 13, 127.
47   Ibid., 123.
48   Fitzgerald, *supra* note 45, 136.
49   J.L.J. Edwards, "The Attorney General and the Charter of Rights," in Robert J. Sharpe, ed., *Charter Litigation* (Toronto: University of Toronto Press, 1987), 46-48.
50   Carolyn Archer and Gaze Burt, "Section 7 of the Bill of Rights Act," *New Zealand Law Journal* (August 2004): 321.
51   Michael Taggart, "Tugging on Superman's Cape: Lessons from Experience with the New Zealand Bill of Rights Act 1990," *Public Law* (1998): 272.
52   Archer and Burt, *supra* note 50, 321.
53   Grant Huscroft, "Impact of the Bill of Rights on Policy Development," in Paul Rishworth and Grant Huscroft, eds., *The Bill of Rights: Getting the Basics Right* (Auckland: New Zealand Law Society Seminar, 2001), 68.
54   Geoffrey Palmer and Matthew Palmer, *Bridled Power*, 4th edition (Wellington: Oxford University Press, 2004), 319-24.
55   *A Bill of Rights for New Zealand: A White Paper*, *supra* note 39, 27.
56   Climate Change Response Bill, as reported by the Foreign Affairs, Defence and Trade Committee, http://www.parliament.govt.nz/en-NZ/SC/Reports/0/e/f/0ef8d4136814159a2d5709715ff24fe.htm.
57   Ibid., 14.
58   Philip A. Joseph, "Parliament, the Courts and the Collaborative Enterprise," *King's College Law Journal* 15 (2004): 328.
59   Ministry of Justice, New Zealand, http://www.justice.govt.nz/bill-of-rights/.
60   Privy Council Office, *Ethics, Responsibility, Accountability: An Action Plan for Democratic Reform*, http://www.pco-bcp.gc.ca/default.asp?Language=E&Page=Publications&doc=dr-rd/dr-rd_e.htm.
61   *Criminal Code*, R.S.C. 1985, c. C-46, s. 264; *Extradition Act*.
62   *United States v. Burns*, [2001] 1 S.C.R. 283.
63   The Honourable Paul East, "The Role of the Attorney General," in Philip A. Joseph, ed., *Essays on the Constitution* (Wellington: Brooker's 1995), 189-95.
64   Interview with Attorney General Margaret Wilson, Wellington, New Zealand (May 12, 2004).

65 Roach, *supra* note 25, 625-26.
66 *Dunmore v. Ontario (Attorney General),* [2001] 3 S.C.R. 1016; *Figueroa v. Canada (Attorney General),* [2003] 1 S.C.R. 912; and *Canada Elections Act,* R.S.C. 1985.
67 Meg Russell, *Reforming the House of Lords: Lessons from Overseas* (Oxford: Oxford University Press, 2000), 133; and Janet L. Hiebert, "A Hybrid-Approach to Protect Rights? An Argument in Favour of Supplementing Canadian Judicial Review with Australia's Model of Parliamentary Scrutiny," *Federal Law Review* 26 (1998): 125-30.
68 David Feldman, "Parliamentary Scrutiny of Legislation and Human Rights," *Public Law* (2002): 327-28.

6

Compromise and the Notwithstanding Clause: Why the Dominant Narrative Distorts Our Understanding

Janet L. Hiebert

No section of the *Canadian Charter of Rights and Freedoms* has generated as wide-ranging opinion on its merits as the notwithstanding clause, which allows provincial and federal legislatures to pre-empt judicial review or set aside the effects of a judicial decision on most sections of the *Charter* for renewable five-year periods.[1] The clause has become so unpopular that some perceive it to be largely irrelevant, if not rendered unconstitutional by convention. Politicians are reluctant to openly contemplate its use, never mind invoke this power, even to protect impugned social policies for which they are strongly committed. At one level, public and political disdain for a clause so infrequently used during the past twenty-five years is perplexing, particularly as the *Charter* was not placed on the constitutional agenda in response to strong public demand to alter either of Canada's constitutional principles – the finality of parliamentary judgment for legislation or the accommodation of provincial-based differences as authorized by federalism. Although a small contingent of supporters long pressed for a bill of rights to redress concerns about unchecked political powers, particularly the post-war powers of federal governments,[2] the decision to pursue a constitutionally entrenched bill of rights was largely an elite-driven project that quickly gained strong public support. This chapter asks two questions. First, to what extent is Canada's disdain for the notwithstanding clause a legacy of our failure to disentangle different notions of "compromise" as they relate to its origins and function? Second, does Canada's constitutional myopia contribute to the legitimacy deficit of this power in so far as we tend toward an insular vision of constitutionalism, unchallenged by comparative experiences?

Claims that the notwithstanding clause was the product of compromise reflect at least three different meanings of compromise that distort and muddy debate: *compromise as political necessity*, because political circumstances compelled the political negotiators in the *Charter* project to settle for an arrangement that they would not have accepted had they sufficient political resources to maintain their preferred position; *compromise of principles*, because section 33 is said to be inconsistent with a core principle of legal constitutionalism, which authorizes legal adjudication of disagreements about rights principles; and *compromise of competing constitutional ideas*, because this power helped establish a new equilibrium in inter-institutional powers between the primary (and rival) constitutional models prevalent at the time. Movement exists across some of these categories. Some believe that although the notwithstanding clause may have been necessary to secure political agreement, it was a deal-breaker that undermined the purpose and integrity of the *Charter* because compromise is considered neither consistent nor desirable with a new emphasis on legal adjudication. Others view the genesis of the notwithstanding clause as a political act to broker a political compromise but one with salutary benefits for striking a new constitutional equilibrium between juridical and political views of constitutionalism.

Debate about the notwithstanding clause has lacked clarity over what the participants are criticizing or supporting when they refer to compromise or whether compromise is considered regrettable or desirable in constitutional politics. This lack of clarity has reinforced the popular perception that the notwithstanding clause lacks redeeming value (it was not born of any grand theory but of pragmatism) and contradicts the purposes of the *Charter* (legal adjudication of claims that governments have improperly transgressed rights). Debate has focused mostly on the first and second uses of compromise. The dominant narrative emphasizes both this power's pragmatic origins and its supposed tension with the legal rights project many associate with the *Charter*. However, with notable exceptions,[3] insufficient attention has been paid to the third understanding of compromise. This chapter will argue that although the origins of this clause were clearly inspired by political necessity, the third notion of compromise is also a persuasive interpretation of the ideas behind this power.

This chapter will examine these different notions of compromise and how they have structured the political debates about the legitimacy of the notwithstanding clause. It will focus specifically on the political concerns of Allan Blakeney, one of the premiers most opposed to a constitutional bill of rights. The reason for focusing on Blakeney, apart from the fact that he was among the most articulate of those politicians critical of a bill of rights, was that he struggled against conceiving of a bill of rights in a manner that portrayed the legislature as the inherent or exclusive threat to rights. In trying to resist conventional wisdom in this way, he played an important role in advocating and supporting some of the important elements in the *Charter* that recognize a legitimate role for government to promote and protect policies that are believed to facilitate rights, even when these differ from judicial interpretations.

Understanding Constitutional Compromise

The first use of compromise focuses on its instrumental value in brokering a political agreement for constitutional reforms between federal and provincial leaders that resulted in the *Constitution Act, 1982*. In the wake of the Supreme Court of Canada's clever ruling in *Reference re Amendment of the Constitution of Canada*,[4] which managed to convey victory and loss for each side on the constitutionality of unilateral patriation, an immense political pressure arose to seek a compromise. The first ministers reconvened November 2, 1981 for one more round of negotiations, characterized by a "mixed mood of grudging necessity, persistent mistrust, and modest hope."[5] At this stage, an alliance of premiers of the eight dissenting provinces opposed the federal proposals. As is widely known, a resolution to bridge the two opposing groups was worked out late in the process. Ottawa would accept the provincial government's preferred amending formula, but without fiscal compensation for opting out, and seven of the eight opposing provinces would accept the *Charter*, but with a notwithstanding clause that would apply to fundamental freedoms and legal and equality rights.

However, this political resolution would suffer two legitimacy problems, both with serious, persistent political consequences. One was the widespread perception, primarily although not exclusively within Quebec, that this agreement violated constitutional justice in its treatment of Quebec, owing to Quebec's strongly held belief that constitutional changes should not adversely impact one of the original partners of the federation without its explicit consent. Quebec representatives were not part of the negotiating team that worked out this resolution, and when presented with this "*fait accompli*" the next day, Premier René Lévesque refused to sign the constitutional accord. The legitimacy of the notwithstanding clause would also suffer because of its "deal-breaking" connotations. Jamie Cameron aptly captures the cynicism associated with the origins of the clause in her suggestion that its genesis "can hardly be described as aspirational."[6] The demand for the clause was a "pawn," not an "idea," in the entrenchment process. Howard Leeson, less skeptical about the virtue of the notwithstanding clause, argues that the version of the notwithstanding clause that was ultimately enacted "had more to do with the raw politics of bargaining and chance phone calls late at night than with reasoned debate about what might constitute a rational compromise between democracy and constitutional law."[7]

The second use – compromise of principle – considers the notwithstanding clause to be inconsistent with a robust and coherent legal-based rights project. This view is heavily influenced by assumptions that a legal form of constitutionalism requires not only judicial review but also judicial finality. According to this interpretation, a bill of rights authorizing judicial review conveys a commitment to rights as the criterion for determining the legitimacy of state actions; reflects an agreement to use legal adjudication to resolve disagreements about whether rights have been respected by state actors; and, finally, does not accept the legitimacy of legislative revision to constitutional interpretations through ordinary legislative means. Thus, according to these assumptions, a legal-adjudicative approach to constitutionalism recognizes the exclusive authority of judges to determine the meaning and scope of rights unless the political community engages in the extraordinary effort to formally amend the Constitution and therefore alters the commitments for which the state is obliged. Thus, the problem with the notwithstanding clause is that it allows political considerations to displace judicial determinations of constitutional meaning and obligations through ordinary legislative means.

A legal view of constitutionalism was espoused by Pierre Trudeau, who never accepted the merits of the notwithstanding clause. Trudeau saw its inclusion as being inconsistent with the purpose of the *Charter*. As he stated, its inclusion "violated my sense of justice: it seemed wrong that any province could decide to suspend any part of the Charter, even if the suspension was only temporary."[8] Trudeau considered the notwithstanding clause to be inconsistent with legal constitutionalism and equated the meaning of *Charter* rights with judicial decisions. This view is espoused by many legal scholars who consider the notwithstanding clause to be inherently incompatible with Canada's new constitutional order, which privileges legal adjudication over political resolution. Consider, for example, John Whyte's skepticism about the value of the notwithstanding clause: "[O]nce the advantages of constitutional interpretation were accepted, as a general matter, it is not easy to see why the framers of the 1982 *Constitution* then saw political judgment to be a preferred form of political accommodation in each and every instance in which political interests wished to suspend the operation of legalism."[9] While Whyte believes that it is perfectly legitimate for a political community to determine its constitutional principles, he also believes that it is fundamentally inconsistent, and of little intrinsic value, to decide upon a legal form of constitutionalism and then choose to allow political judgment to prevail, even if only occasionally.

A third use of compromise considers the notwithstanding clause in terms of contributing to a new constitutional equilibrium – one rooted neither in Canada's Westminster heritage of parliamentary supremacy, altered to fit a federal state, nor based on judicial supremacy for interpreting constitutional norms, as characterized by American constitutionalism (at least as it has evolved). At the time of the entrenchment debate in Canada, conventional wisdom portrayed the relevant constitutional models as conforming to one of two rival paths, one emphasizing a more political brand of constitutionalism, the other stressing a more juridical form. The first path was equated with parliamentary supremacy and rejected the idea of construing political debates as legal disagreements that would require judicial participation in their resolution. The second path included the codification of rights in a manner different from what Canada had attempted with the 1960 *Canadian Bill of Rights*, with rights forming part of the higher law and with judges empowered to interpret rights and determine the appropriate remedies for their breach.[10] This second path, influenced by American-style judicial review, treated judicial review as being synonymous with judicial supremacy and assumed that the constitution, including its commitment to rights, could only be considered a superior form of law if it could not be amended through ordinary legislative means.

The notwithstanding clause is significant because it represented the final attempt by those provincial premiers critical of the proposed *Charter* to envisage a different constitutional model from either of these traditional rival approaches. However, before this argument can be made, it is important to first consider the reservations of those who opposed the idea of having to reject the political form of constitutionalism for the more juridical form. From the time a bill of rights was placed on the constitutional agenda in the late 1960s, many of the provincial premiers adopted a two-track strategy in their negotiations, with their positions freely moving back and forth between the two. For different reasons, most preferred not to have a constitutional bill of rights at all and used the language of parliamentary supremacy to oppose this proposal for a radical change to constitutional principles. Thus, one track was their categorical rejection of a constitutional bill of rights and an insistence that the idea be distinguished from other more "pressing" constitutional amendments, such as changes affecting the division of powers, reform of the Senate, changes to the appointment procedure for the Supreme Court of Canada, and the inclusion of a constitutional clause dealing with regional economic disparities.[11]

The second track was both more strategic and imaginative. Assuming a bill of rights was to be adopted as one element in a larger package of constitutional changes, would it be possible to restrict the scope of judicial review in the event that judicial interpretation of rights fundamentally undermined social policy objectives to which political leaders were strongly committed? Could these *Charter* skeptics conceive of a way to ensure that the proposed *Charter* would evolve differently from the way conventional wisdom anticipated? The intention of this second track was to resist a project that interpreted rights, and government's relations to them, solely in negative terms – freedom from interference – in which the government was assumed the principal threat to rights. Constitutional values and their accommodation were understood by some of the premiers in more expansive terms than the negative liberties that were historically associated with judicial interpretations of a bill of rights. Several premiers believed that the parliamentary system had evolved in a manner that provided a healthy balance between rights, security, and other public values and were worried that judicial review of a bill of rights could undermine this balance. Thus, their concern was that rights "should be expressed in a form which will reflect their development in our laws over the years; any new expression of them must be applied so as not to diminish any existing right recognized by law or usage."[12] Yet, for at least one of the premiers, Blakeney, the concern was that judicial review might undermine more progressive views on what rights entail.

Although a majority of the premiers supported measures to limit the effects of judicial review, most did not elaborate on their reasons for this support or on their criticism of the bill of rights as it was proposed, other than stating confidence in Canadian political development and rejecting the prudence of undermining or repealing the principle of parliamentary supremacy. Sterling Lyon was one of the staunchest defenders of retaining the principle of parliamentary supremacy. However, Blakeney's explanation differed from Lyon's. While he also supported the retention of parliamentary supremacy, Blakeney's arguments against a bill of rights were implicitly, if not explicitly, based on rights. His reasons for resisting a bill of rights warrant reassessing conventional wisdom that political opposition to the *Charter* was influenced solely by concerns for retaining power rather than by a genuine interest in rights.[13]

Blakeney was committed to protecting human rights. Yet, he did not equate these rights solely with the kinds of negative interpretations associated with bills of rights. His concern with a constitutional bill of rights for Canada was that courts would be too conservative in their interpretation of rights and may hinder progressive legislation such as affirmative action programs or policies intended to redistribute power and wealth. Blakeney's support for the notwithstanding clause arose in part from his idea that parliamentary judgment should not be considered inherently inconsistent with a human rights project just because it might differ from judicial interpretation. His opposition to the *Charter*, and his attempt to restrict the scope of judicial review should the *Charter* be adopted, represent a nascent and underdeveloped attempt to imagine a different constitutional option. He was prepared to accept judicial review of legislation but only if the bill of rights also recognized a valid parliamentary role for judgments about rights.

Preserving this opportunity for parliamentary disagreement with judicial interpretations of rights was important to Blakeney for at least three reasons. First, Blakeney did not consider American or Canadian judicial records to be impressive in terms of respecting policies that, as a social democrat, he believed were necessary for equality. His skepticism was greatly influenced by the struggle between Franklin Roosevelt's attempt to enact New Deal legislation and judicial review in the United States, which reflected *laissez faire* assumptions about the conditions for liberty. This focus on negative liberty, he worried, would not be any less a problem for Canada because the

Charter was "inspired by 18th-century" assumptions that "the only dangerous source of power was the government."[14] Thus, Blakeney considered the
proposed *Charter* to be a serious threat to progressive governance. If adopted,
conservative judicial decisions could frustrate progressive and substantive
views of equality.[15]

A second reason Blakeney considered it important that a bill of rights
retain the political capacity to disagree with judicial decisions was his appreciation for the contestable nature of rights claims. He was troubled that
if a bill of rights was adopted, this lack of determinacy in how rights guide
or constrain state actions could lead to judicial interpretations that favoured
business and property interests and thus could thwart legislative objectives
inspired by uses of the state to redress inequalities.[16] This concern about
judicial discretion when assigning meaning to constitutional language was
also influenced by Blakeney's critical assessment of judicial review of division
of powers claims, involving two natural resource decisions affecting Saskatchewan – *CIGOL v. Saskatchewan* and *Amax Potash Ltd. v. Government of
Saskatchewan* – which reinforced his concern that legal language is malleable
and can be interpreted in a way unsympathetic to progressive causes.[17]

His third reason for resisting a constitutional bill of rights arose from differences he perceived in the mission and function of a parliamentary system,
where the political process is engaged in an ongoing project of accommodat-
ing interests, as contrasted with the mission and function of courts. Blakeney
considered a virtue of parliamentary supremacy to be its recognition of a
reasoned process of adjustment and change. He saw the political decision-
making process as a fluid one – capable, through ongoing discussion, of
shaping, mediating, and changing the way issues are framed and what decisions are reached. In contrast, judicial review allows rights to be marshalled
in a way that vetoes or trumps the possibility for an ongoing process of
mediation and accommodation. In his view, principles upon which rights
claims are based "should not be divorced from who interprets them and
decides on how they interact with other principles."[18] These perceived differences contributed to his skepticism about a bill of rights. They also influenced his determination to ensure that, in the event that a constitutional
bill of rights was accepted, judicial review would be moderated. This would
be achieved, either by allowing the possibility for parliament to contribute
to decisions about the scope of rights through a limitation clause structured
to encourage judicial respect for political decisions or, failing that, to overturn
judicial decisions where this judicial respect may not occur.[19]

Judicial Review and the Choice of Constitutional Instruments

Blakeney's concerns that judicial review might frustrate social policies intended to address human rights meant that he considered the project of
constructing an appropriate bill of rights to be more complicated than

proponents of the *Charter* had suggested. It required a structure to give legal recognition to the different institutional roles necessary to protecting and monitoring the accommodation of codified (and mostly negative) rights with the positive conditions he equated with non-enumerated values of substantive equality and social justice. In other words, it was not enough to simply talk about the benefits of a bill of rights. One had to imagine the institutional setting in which a bill of rights functions. Although Blakeney and his fellow *Charter* skeptics were not successful in preventing the adoption of the *Charter*, it does not mean that their concerns about judicial power were ignored in the *Charter*'s final design. The *Charter* reflects the attempt to conceive of an alternative constitutional model that is not solely concerned with protecting negative rights from governmental interference. This concept is recognized in four different ways, including the recognition that affirmative action is consistent with equality; the absence of property rights; a broad general limitation clause; and the notwithstanding clause.

One way to recognize a positive role for government to interpret rights is found in the affirmative action section for equality rights in section 15(2) of the *Charter*. Saskatchewan supported arguments by women's groups to include this clause.[20] It reflects the idea that substantive equality may require legislative actions to redress inequalities. Section 15(2) in the *Charter* is a conscious attempt to direct courts away from interpreting equality in a manner that is automatically suspicious of government-sponsored distinctions in social policy. As such, it reflects a core reason that Blakeney was so reticent about judicial review – his fear that a conservative court might interpret rights in a manner that restricts a legislature from introducing policies intended to ameliorate inequalities and vulnerabilities.[21]

A second way to guard against the *Charter* evolving in a manner that treats government as an inherent threat to human rights was the explicit decision not to include property rights. This was an essential condition of Blakeney's support for the *Charter* as well as for then national leader Ed Broadbent. The concern for these New Democratic Party leaders was that judicial interpretations of property rights could hinder government policy designed to provide broad social and economic benefits or to address environmental concerns.

A third way was the inclusion of a general limitation clause. From the outset, all provincial premiers indicated that any bill of rights they supported would have to include broadly constructed limits on rights. The clear intent of a general limitation clause was to encourage judicial sensitivity to a broad set of non-enumerated values that governments may subsequently claim justify restrictions upon negative rights.[22] The first attempt to define the general limitation clause, the failed *Victoria Charter* of 1971, conceived of limits on rights in much broader terms than would ultimately be adopted in the final Canadian *Charter* of 1982. When constitutional change was again on the national agenda in 1980, the proposed *Charter* included a broadly constructed limitation clause with a deliberate overture to the provinces. It would now subject rights to "such reasonable limits as are generally accepted in a free and democratic society with a parliamentary system of government." This wording had been chosen intentionally to address the provincial reticence about a *Charter*.[23]

Although federal *Charter* supporters had tacitly accepted provincial demands for a broadly constructed limitation clause for almost a decade, this willingness abruptly changed in 1980 following a hostile reception to this version of the limitation clause during the joint parliamentary committee hearings on the proposed *Charter*. Federal political leaders were admonished for their refusal to make a hard choice in terms of which political project they wished to promote – did they intend to retain parliamentary supremacy or did they wish to adopt judicial supremacy. As Stanley Cohen argued before the parliamentary hearings on the proposed *Charter* in 1980, "[t]o the extent that you want to have equilibrium between a charter regime and parliamentary supremacy, you must accept the fact that, once you introduce a charter regime, parliamentary supremacy is modified for ever to that extent. That is a plain legal and political fact, and you cannot have the best of both worlds, except in an emergency."[24]

Ottawa responded to criticism by re-wording the proposed limitation clause. Removed was the reference to a "parliamentary system of government," which had been an intentional reminder of the principle of parliamentary supremacy. As amended, the clause would now require limits to be "prescribed by law" rather than "generally accepted" and would also change the onus for persuading courts about whether rights had been unconstitutionally restricted, from litigants having to establish the unreasonableness of legislation to governments having to demonstrate the reasonableness of any restriction. Yet, despite these changes, the limitation clause still serves the purposes envisaged by the premiers (albeit, with less force than they may have wished). Its reference to the values of a free and democratic society, as the normative context for justifying restrictions on rights, is sufficiently broad to allow Parliament and the provincial legislatures to defend a wide range of non-enumerated values that are important to justifying restrictions on rights, providing these are reasonable and meet the judicial standards of proportionality.

The fourth, and most controversial, manifestation of the attempt to construct an alternative model is the inclusion of the notwithstanding clause.[25] Both Blakeney and Alberta premier Peter Lougheed had earlier raised the possibility of the notwithstanding clause as a condition for accepting the *Charter*.[26] For Blakeney, the notwithstanding clause would guard against the *Charter* evolving in a manner that excluded a parliamentary role in defining the scope of protected rights. The notwithstanding clause, in other words, was not thought of to negate rights but, rather, to allow for a more expansive understanding of human rights, in which Parliament, as well as the judiciary, would be responsible for their articulation and protection.[27]

The idea of including a notwithstanding clause became more important to Blakeney and other premiers after the earlier-described changes were made to the limitation clause. By the time of the final round of negotiations in November 1981, the premiers were not confident that they could continue their first strategy of opposing a *Charter* and, instead, felt they might have to emphasize their second strategy: to place limits on unqualified judicial power to interpret the *Charter*. By November 1981, the premiers were now on the defensive in arguing against a *Charter*, and many were reluctantly reconciled to its adoption. However, they wanted to ensure some way to preserve the political capacity to dissent from judicial interpretations. The notwithstanding clause was a last resort to give effect to an alternative rights framework emphasizing values other than negative liberty. Although it would operate differently from the limitation clause, in an important sense, these clauses were conceptually similar. Both clauses addressed the provinces' concerns about using a bill of rights to resolve disagreements between citizens and states without a full appreciation for the legislative concerns and objectives that underlie legislation. As Blakeney put it,

> I could certainly go along with entrenching and with a non obstante clause, because basically the courts are good places to decide individual cases of human rights issues, but bad places to decide broad social policies in the guise of deciding issues of human rights. Therefore what we need is some basis whereby the legislatures can override if, in the course of deciding an issue about a single citizen, they have made a decision which affects broad public policy. I had thought that the resolution before [The Joint Parliamentary Committee] was not too bad in that regard, because it has Section 1 which is a kind of non obstante clause in advance ... [T]he suggestion of deleting section 1 raise[s] all my apprehensions, because we are then left with a very large number of judgments to be made by judges.[28]

Failure to Defend the Notwithstanding Clause

Although critics of the notwithstanding clause are often quick to characterize its intent in terms of "overriding" rights, this interpretation is not warranted. Critics are correct in their apprehensions that this power could be used to disagree with judicial interpretations of rights. Yet, they are unfair if they assume that its advocates considered this power to be inconsistent with the idea of respecting fundamental rights. Two persistent questions continued to trouble some of the provincial premiers: who interprets rights and are constitutional values confined to the enumerated provisions in the *Charter*? As Hugh Segal suggests, from the vantage point of reflecting on Ontario's important role of urging Ottawa to accept the *Charter* with a notwithstanding clause, the premiers neither intended nor anticipated that the notwithstanding clause would be an instrument to "gut" or "undermine" the protection of rights. They firmly believed its role was integral to the protection of rights; albeit defined in ways that may differ from judicial interpretations.[29]

Three issues explain the failure of political supporters of this clause to challenge the perception that the notwithstanding clause was intended to override or "compromise" rights. The first issue concerned the historical timing of this innovation. In the absence of the kind of constitutional experimentation that has subsequently occurred (see discussion below), there was no context for defending the idea of construing constitutional options as an equilibrium between competing models. The language of parliamentary sovereignty became inseparable from the premiers' argument for the institutionalization of mechanisms to allow for legislative revision to judicial decisions. However, this language of parliamentary supremacy, when juxtaposed against claims that equated rights protection with judicial review, reinforced the perception that those premiers who opposed the *Charter* were more interested in power than in rights. Just as it was difficult to appear to be arguing against the *Charter* (provincial concerns with other constitutional issues resulted in disparaging comments that they were willing to trade "fish for rights"), it was also difficult to argue for a version of a rights project that was inconsistent with the constitutional discourse of the day.

Second, most premiers opposing the *Charter* poorly articulated their objections. Their defence of parliamentary supremacy seemed neither intellectually interesting nor politically progressive in the face of a well-orchestrated federal strategy to promote the Charter through the use of "bold promises" that equated the *Charter* with "forever guaranteeing" Canadians' rights.[30] Blakeney was an exception. But even his explanation had little resonance. Although Blakeney's resistance to the *Charter* was often grounded in an explicit defence of rights, it was a defence that conferred rights-respecting qualities to Parliament and, as such, was inconsistent with the more common view that rights are protected by insulating them from political decision making. Blakeney, in essence, was arguing that rights have to be restricted (in the sense of disagreeing with judicial decisions) in order for them to be protected (by Parliament). Third, the timing of the decision to include the notwithstanding clause hindered thoughtful debate about how the notwithstanding clause would affect political or judicial behaviour. The clause attracted little discussion, during the actual entrenchment debate, about how it would affect a rights project that gave the courts an important interpretive and adjudicative role.

The tight time frame for scrutiny, much of which focused on the touchy issue of whether or not it would apply to minority education language rights, helps explain why so little attention was paid to this new clause. As Blakeney has since suggested, the atmosphere and context of negotiating complex issues of constitutional reform is simply not conducive for ideal constitution making.[31] Yet, in hindsight, it is unfortunate that the provinces' decade-long attempt to craft a limitation clause to recognize their view that fundamental values extended beyond the specified rights in the *Charter* did not encourage them to frame the language for the notwithstanding clause to reflect a similar aspiration. Arguably, the notwithstanding clause would not have suffered as serious a legitimacy deficit if, rather than language indicating that legislation would operate "notwithstanding" a specific Charter provision, it instead referred to political disagreements with judicial interpretations of the *Charter* or, more specifically, to political disagreements with judicial interpretations of what comprises a reasonable limit in section 1 of the *Charter*.[32]

The tight time frame for debate also explains why the notwithstanding clause included an element unanticipated by some. Everyone understood this power could be used to set aside judicial rulings. However, not everyone recognized that it could also be used to pre-empt judicial review.[33] Tom Axworthy, who served as principal secretary to Pierre Trudeau during the entrenchment debate, suggests that not only had the pre-emptive capacity not been anticipated, but, had there been more time to discuss this power, the pre-emptive possibility would have been identified and the clause would almost certainly have been re-worded to preclude this ability.[34] Yet, others reject the idea that a pre-emptive element was not anticipated. Blakeney has suggested that at the time the notwithstanding clause was negotiated, he envisaged that it could be used both in a pre-emptive and reactive manner. From his perspective, if a government anticipates that the court would likely find the legislation unconstitutional, it may want to apply the power pre-emptively in order to ensure stability and certainty in the operation of its legislation.[35]

Subsequent federal commentary on the clause has not helped in terms of its legitimacy. For example, a federal Department of Justice press release posted online for several years (but now removed) characterized the notwithstanding clause as an "escape clause" at the behest of a majority of the provincial premiers, so that they could "make some laws as if the *Charter* doesn't exist."[36] The political attacks on the notwithstanding clause by successive prime ministers reinforced the image of the notwithstanding clause as having been inspired by the power-hungry demands of the premiers. Trudeau subsequently argued that provincial premiers should give up this power, suggesting that the protection of rights would be strengthened by deleting this power and chastised political supporters of the Meech Lake Accord for their failure to remove the clause as part of the bargaining process with the provinces.[37] Then prime minister Brian Mulroney's retaliation did little to elevate the status of the notwithstanding clause. He blamed Trudeau for agreeing to a power that so gutted rights that the *Charter* was "not worth the paper it is written on."[38] So powerful is political repudiation of the notwithstanding clause that Paul Martin thought he could salvage a faltering election campaign by pledging, during a televised political leaders' debate, that if elected his government would remove the constitutional power of a federal government to invoke the notwithstanding clause.[39]

Continued Disdain – A Legacy of Canada's Constitutional Myopia?

The dominant narrative on compromise and the notwithstanding clause emphasizes its deal-breaking aspects. In earlier works, I also accepted this pragmatic explanation.[40] So what has changed? Why revisit this dominant narrative of the origins of this clause? What has changed is that constitutional developments elsewhere cast a fresh light on the ideas and concerns that animated some of the premiers' arguments for the notwithstanding clause. More specifically, comparative research exposes the shortcomings of focusing on the notwithstanding clause in isolation from the broader ideas and debates associated with giving shape to a new form of rights instrument. In discussing these ideas and debates, the intent is not to refute the pragmatic element of the notwithstanding clause, as the price of the premiers' consent for a *Charter* they would otherwise have preferred not to adopt. Instead, it is to question the assumption that this compromise is inconsistent with ideas about protecting rights, even in a model that is premised on legal adjudication.

Much of the Canadian commentary on the notwithstanding clause treats it as a uniquely Canadian constitutional phenomenon. It is evaluated primarily in terms of the immediate events that led up to its negotiation in the *Charter*. Yet, this treatment of the origins of this power as a unique and singular moment in Canada's constitutional development fails to recognize the much larger project that was at play. This project was concerned with how to mitigate the consequences of judicial review for the protection and recognition of rights and other fundamental values. For Blakeney, the issue was not whether rights should be protected but, rather, how the Charter would affect judicial and political outcomes within the Canadian context? This attempt to imagine a different constitutional option than existed at the time has been subsequently mirrored elsewhere. Research on comparative constitutional developments in other parliamentary systems reveals a similar intent to resist the idea that judicial opinion should be considered the sole authority for interpreting and resolving rights-based disagreements. And as in Canada, these concerns have influenced the structure and design of the bills of rights subsequently adopted. The primary difference is that time and familiarity have allowed other political leaders to consciously and unapologetically pursue a hybrid rights instrument.[41]

The emergence of a new form of rights instrument in other parliamentary jurisdictions has not gone unnoticed.[42] These jurisdictions have introduced judicial review but in a manner that does not give courts the full authority normally associated with a bill of rights, such as remedy-granting powers of invalidating legislation. Instead, they introduce a limited form of judicial review, with some systems also introducing mechanisms that would put pressure on Parliaments to revisit the legislative objectives should the judiciary rule that these are incompatible with protected rights. What is common in these jurisdictions (New Zealand, the United Kingdom, and one Australian district and state) is that political leaders have rejected the necessity of having to make a stark choice between parliamentary supremacy and a bill of rights that recognizes courts as their exclusive interpreter. In essence, political participants in these debates have sought to imagine a hybrid of British and American principles – a way to introduce judicial review without surrendering political dominion over decisions about the reconciliation of judicially interpreted rights with legislatively defined rights and values. As such, this alternative, hybrid model challenges earlier assumptions associated with parliamentary supremacy where rights did not function as discrete standards against which parliamentary actions would be judged and where courts had no explicit role to pronounce on the merits of legislation from a rights perspective. At the same time, this model does not adhere to the central assumption associated with conventional views about a bill of rights – that a bill of rights not only requires judicial review but also treats courts as having the exclusive authority for determining the meaning of rights and the remedies that are appropriate where rights are infringed.

Research on these developments suggests the need to revisit the political arguments of those skeptical about introducing the *Charter* and to consider the extent to which these concerns affected the *Charter*'s structure. The notwithstanding clause was one of four ways to modify the emphasis of negative liberty and exclusive reliance on judicial resolutions for societal and political disagreements involving claims of rights. However, its significance extends well beyond the *Charter*. It helped provide an impetus for this new form of rights instrument to emerge. What the notwithstanding clause introduced to the realm of constitutional ideas (even if not fully appreciated in Canada) was the possibility of bridging what traditionally had been thought of as competing and opposing models of constitutionalism.[43] For parliamentary systems, it challenged the presumption that a bill of rights is incompatible with the idea of Parliament retaining final judgment about the merits of legislative decisions. It did this because it encouraged the reassessment of the scope and role of judicial review. Judicial review could be distinguished from judicial supremacy. This reassessment was important because it dismantled a fundamental obstacle for introducing a rights regime within a Westminster-based parliamentary system. It meant that the introduction of judicial review need not result in judicial monism – a fundamental requirement for any political system whose Constitution recognizes Parliament as having the final authority for determining the constitutional merits of duly enacted legislation.

Other parliamentary systems have not replicated the notwithstanding clause in their bills of rights[44] (which is not required when courts lack an express power to disallow legislation). However, the idea that it represents underscores the larger idea that exposure to judicial review will exert significant (although not binding) influence on subsequent political behaviour where legislation has been called into question. Some will remain skeptical about preserving a legislative capacity to disagree with the judicial interpretations of rights. Yet, this skepticism misses the fundamental point of the exercise – rejecting the necessity of having to choose a legal form of adjudication over a political form. What has to be recognized is that the development of, and reflection on, constitutional ideas since 1982 have led many to reject the premise that constitutional options must comply with one of two mutually exclusive approaches, as if the choice is between choosing to protect rights or choosing to protect power. Instead, the attempt has been to imagine a model that increases the sensitivity given to rights, which is associated with using the language of rights and by empowering courts to play an important interpretive role, while also recognizing that the force of these judgments will change how political actors interpret their roles and responsibilities. The objective of the traditional court-centred model and this newer hybrid approach is the same, namely to give prominence to rights as critical standards for evaluating the legitimacy of state actions. But what is different is the way a final judgment is reached and how the remedies are determined. Under this hybrid approach, judicial review is conceived as the penultimate, rather than the final, authority on whether legislation appropriately accommodates rights.[45] It is a model that some commentators have tentatively suggested introduces a valuable "compromise that combines the best features of both the traditional models, by conferring on courts constitutional responsibility to review the consistency of legislation with protected rights, while preserving the authority of legislatures to have the last word."[46]

Conclusions

The notwithstanding clause has had difficulty shedding the pragmatic view of compromise for which it has been so firmly cast. To many Canadians, this clause arose simply to broker an agreement between the provinces and Ottawa to accept the *Charter*. As such, its origins are widely assumed to have been devoid of any intrinsic value, and its presence presumed to have compromised the essential purpose of a bill of rights. This chapter questioned the exclusivity of this dominant narrative about the notwithstanding clause. Two arguments have been made. The first is that most assessments of the notwithstanding clause fail to recognize and distinguish between important differences in how compromise is interpreted. Although there was a pragmatic element in the decision to adopt the notwithstanding clause, it does not diminish the relevance of the third interpretation of compromise – of trying to establish a compromise between competing constitutional principles. The dominant narrative on the notwithstanding clause pays insufficient regard to the persistent concerns of those who were genuinely troubled by the prospects of Canada adopting an American-style bill of rights and who tried to navigate an alternative course between the existing regime, with no explicit constitutional framework for rights, and the adoption of a system that gave courts an authoritative role for interpreting rights without recognition of any explicit opportunity for legitimate political dissent. The fact that the premiers did not persuade Canadians that the notwithstanding clause is a legitimate component of constitutionalism is not particularly surprising. The power of this dominant narrative is reinforced by the paucity of recorded debate at the time of entrenchment on the consequences or merits of including a notwithstanding clause, by the absence of an accepted framework for imagining or assessing constitutional options other than parliamentary or judicial supremacy, and by continued political statements impugning the value of the *Charter* because of its inclusion.

The second argument is that Canada's constitutional myopia reinforces the idea that the notwithstanding clause was simply born out of pragmatism and that it contradicts the basic idea of a bill of rights. Our insistence that the notwithstanding clause is a constitutional novelty and our general disinterest or lack of familiarity with other constitutional modes reinforces the dominance of this traditional narrative. To the extent that we look beyond our own borders, our gaze is generally limited to the United States, where the notwithstanding clause clearly contradicts the essence of American constitutional principles: that the constitution is the supreme law, its meaning is determined solely by the judiciary, and that the force of constitutional law is compromised if judicial decisions can be revised or set aside through ordinary legislative means.

However, familiarity with constitutional developments elsewhere reveals that the ideas represented by the notwithstanding clause are not particularly unique. It also suggests that the premiers' advocacy of this power need not be viewed as being inconsistent with a rights-respecting project. Assumptions that the notwithstanding clause is inherently inconsistent with a rights project should be re-examined or suspended until more is known about the political and judicial impact of constitutional innovations that have implicitly built upon the ideas it embodies – of imagining a method to introduce greater sensitivity to rights by articulating rights and authorizing judicial review without surrendering all political capacity to determine how rights should guide or constrain legislative decisions.

Acknowledgments
I wish to acknowledge the helpful comments and suggestions made in conversations about the ideas in this chapter with Richard Simeon, Mark Tushnet, Tsvi Kahana, Andrew Lister, Marc-Antoine Adam, Emmett MacFarlane, Jeremy Clarke, and participants in the Queen's politics/law brown bag meetings. Any errors or omissions in my argument are my responsibility.

Notes
1 *Canadian Charter of Rights and Freedoms,* Part 1 of the *Constitution Act, 1982,* being Schedule B to the *Canada Act 1982* (U.K.), 1982, c. 11.
2 See Christopher MacLennan, *Toward the Charter* (Montreal and Kingston: McGill-Queen's University Press, 2003).
3 Paul Weiler, "Rights and Justice in a Democracy: A New Canadian Version," *University of Michigan Journal of Law Reform* 18 (1984): 51-92; Peter H. Russell, "Standing Up for Notwithstanding," *Alberta Law Review* 29 (1991): 293-309; Christopher P. Manfredi, *Judicial Power and the Charter,* 2nd edition (Don Mills, ON: Oxford University Press, 2001); Mary Ann Glendon, *Rights Talk: The Impoverishment of Political Discourse* (New York: Free Press, 1993); Janet L. Hiebert, *Charter Conflicts: What Is Parliament's Role?* (Montreal and Kingston: McGill-Queen's University Press, 2002); and Kent Roach, *The Supreme Court on Trial: Judicial Activism or Democratic Dialogue?* (Toronto: Irwin Law, 2001).
4 *Reference re Amendment of the Constitution of Canada,* [1981] 1 S.C.R. 753.
5 Roy Romanow, John Whyte, and Howard Leeson, *Canada ... Notwithstanding: The Making of the Constitution 1976-1982* (Toronto: Carswell, 1984), 193.
6 Jamie Cameron, "The Charter's Legislative Override: Feat or Figment of the Constitutional Imagination?" in Grant Huscroft and Ian Brodie, eds., *Constitutionalism in the Charter Era* (Toronto: LexisNexis Butterworths, 2004), 141.
7 Howard Leeson, "Section 33: The Notwithstanding Clause – A Paper Tiger?" in Paul Howe and Peter H. Russell, eds., *Judicial Power and Canadian Democracy* (Montreal and Kingston: McGill-Queen's University Press, 2001), 298.
8 Pierre Trudeau, *Memoirs* (Toronto: McClelland and Stewart, 1995), 327.
9 John D. Whyte, "On Not Standing for Notwithstanding," *Alberta Law Review* 28 (1990): 347-57.
10 *Canadian Bill of Rights,* S.C. 1960, c. 44.
11 Canadian Inter-Governmental Conference Secretariat, *The Constitutional Review 1968-1971: Secretary's Report* (Ottawa: Information Canada, 1972), 68-72.
12 W.A.C. Bennett, Premier of British Columbia, "Opening Statement of the Province of British Columbia to the Constitutional Conference," Federal-Provincial Constitutional Conference of First Ministers on the Constitution, Ottawa (February 10-12, 1969), 7-8.
13 I have formed the following view from reading the speeches and statements made during the entrenchment debates, others' written accounts of the process (primarily Romanow, Whyte, and Leeson, *supra* note 5), and interviews with some of the public officials who worked with the premiers and were privy to their concerns.
14 "Judges: Canada's New Aristocracy – An Interview with Allan Blakeney," *Inroads* 18 (winter-spring 2006): 32.
15 Dennis Gruending, *Promises to Keep: A Political Biography of Allan Blakeney* (Saskatoon: Western Producer Prairie Books, 1990), 96.
16 "Judges: Canada's New Aristocracy," *supra* note 14, 31.
17 Author's interpretation was influenced by ongoing conversations with John Whyte (January and February 2007) and a telephone interview with Allan Blakeney (February 21, 2007).

CIGOL v. Saskatchewan, [1978] 2 S.C.R. 545; and *Amax Potash Ltd. v. Government of Saskatchewan,* [1977] 2 S.C.R. 576.

18 "Judges: Canada's New Aristocracy," *supra* note 14, 40.

19 This interpretation of Blakeney's view on the problems of judicial review was influenced by a series of telephone conversations with John Whyte in January and February 2007.

20 Information obtained from the author's interview with Allan Blakeney (February 21, 2007) and with Howard Leeson, former Saskatchewan deputy minister of intergovernmental relations (February 8, 2007).

21 Author's interview with Howard Leeson (February 8, 2007).

22 Janet L. Hiebert, *Limiting Rights: The Dilemma of Judicial Review* (Montreal and Kingston: McGill-Queen's University Press, 1996), 10-31.

23 *Canadian Charter of Rights and Freedoms,* revised discussion draft, September 3, 1980, Federal-Provincial Conference of First Ministers on the Constitution, Ottawa (September 8-12, 1980).

24 Stanley Cohen, Special Joint Committee of the Senate and of the House of Commons on the Constitution, *Hearings,* October 28, 1980, 7:86.

25 Federal strategists had earlier considered the notwithstanding clause as a way of increasing provincial support for the *Charter* but eventually chose to focus on a broadly constructed limitation clause, which they considered as the "lesser of two evils." This information was obtained through interviews by the author with federal officials involved with the entrenchment process in Ottawa (November 1987).

26 Tom Axworthy, "Sword of Damocles or Paper Tiger: Canada's Continuing Debate over the Notwithstanding Clause," paper presented to the Festschrift Konference "Recreating Canada" in honour of Paul Weiler, Harvard University, Cambridge, MA (November 3-4, 2006), 8.

27 Author's interview with Allan Blakeney (February 21, 2007); and author's interview with Hugh Segal (February 5, 2007).

28 Allan Blakeney, Special Joint Committee of the Senate and of the House of Commons on the Constitution, *Hearings,* December 19, 1980, 30:39.

29 Author's interview with Hugh Segal (February 5, 2007).

30 *House of Commons Debates,* (October 15, 1980) at 3704 (Yvon Pinard).

31 Author's interview with Allan Blakeney (February 21, 2007).

32 Christopher Manfredi has recommended a similar amendment to the wording. Christopher P. Manfredi, *Judicial Power and the Charter,* 2nd edition (Don Mills, ON: Oxford University Press 2001), 191-93.

33 Author's interview with Tom Axworthy (January 12, 2007).

34 Ibid.

35 Author's interview with Allan Blakeney (February 21, 2007).

36 This is no longer on the website for the Department of Justice, but it was there for at least three years. "Section 33: The Notwithstanding Clause – An Escape Clause for Provincial Governments," http://canada.justice.gc.ca/en/justice2000/s33back.html.

37 Pierre Trudeau, *Evidence of the Special Joint Committee of the Senate and of the House of Commons the 1987 Constitutional Accord,* August 27, 1987, 14:139-40.

38 *House of Commons Debates,* (April 6, 1989) at 153 (Brian Mulroney).

39 "Martin Wraps Campaign in Constitutional Pledge," CBC, January 10, 2006, http://www.cbc.ca/news/story/2006/01/09/elxn-debates-look.html.

40 Janet L. Hiebert, "Is It Too Late to Rehabilitate Canada's Notwithstanding Clause?" in Huscroft and Brodie, 172.

41 For more discussion on the adaptation of this idea elsewhere, see Janet L. Hiebert, "Parliamentary Bills of Rights: An Alternative Model?" *Modern Law Review* 69:1 (2006): 7-28; Hiebert, "New Constitutional Ideas: But Can New Parliamentary Models Resist Judicial Dominance When Interpreting Rights?" *Texas Law Review* 82 (2004): 1963-87.

42 Stephen Gardbaum, "The New Commonwealth Model of Constitutionalism," *American Journal of Comparative Law* 49 (2001): 707; Mark Tushnet, "New Forms of Judicial Review and the Persistence of Rights – and Democracy – Based Worries," *Wake Forest Law Review* 38 (2003): 813; and Michael J. Perry, "Protecting Human Rights in a Democracy: What Role for the Courts?" *Wake Forest Law Review* 38 (2003): 635.

43 Stephen Gardbaum also makes this argument. Gardbaum, *supra* note 42, 707.

44 An exception is Victoria's *Charter of Human Rights and Responsibilities 2006* (Vic.).
45 While the notwithstanding clause has been interpreted elsewhere in this manner, it is important to remember that in Canada it does not allow for legislative judgment to replace judicial opinion on the meaning of *Charter* rights. It only allows for temporary revisions or alterations to that meaning.
46 Jeffrey Goldsworthy, "Homogenizing Constitutions," *Oxford Journal of Legal Studies* 23 (1990): 483-84.

Part 2: Policy Making and the Courts

7
Judicializing Health Policy: Unexpected Lessons and an Inconvenient Truth

Christopher P. Manfredi and Antonia Maioni

The Supreme Court of Canada is, and always has been, a policy-making institution. Moreover, it makes policy not as an accidental byproduct of adjudicating legal disputes but, rather, by explicitly determining which legal rules will produce the most socially beneficial results. Over the past quarter-century, the *Canadian Charter of Rights and Freedoms* has increased the opportunity for judicial policy-making in this sense by expanding the range of social and political issues subject to the Court's jurisdiction.[1] Nowhere is this more evident than in the use of rights-based *Charter* litigation as an instrument of health policy reform in Canada.[2] Physician supply management, medical practice regulation, hospital restructuring, and the regulation and provision of specific treatment and services are among the key issues litigated under the *Charter* before various courts. The Supreme Court of Canada itself has affected health care policy by nullifying the federal abortion law, modifying professional advertising regulations, upholding the criminal prohibition against assisted suicide, and establishing a constitutional right to sign language interpretation in the provision of health care services.[3]

The issues decided in these cases were, of course, important for the administration of health policy. However, in 2005, the Court decided a case that challenged the very existence of publicly provided health care by seeking to dismantle the public monopoly over the provision of core medical services. In *Chaoulli v. Québec,* a sharply divided Court held that, where waiting periods exceed reasonable standards, Quebec could not prohibit private insurance coverage for core services provided through the public health care system.[4] In addition to its obvious substantive importance, *Chaoulli* stands out in two ways. First, the Court reversed the unanimous judgments of the lower appellate and trial courts. Second, and arguably more importantly, the reversal was based not so much on differences of legal interpretation (although such differences played a role) as it was on different interpretations of the empirical evidence. Indeed, the judgments in *Chaoulli* were the public manifestation of a debate within the Court about evidence unavailable to, and therefore untested by, the lower courts about whether limiting access to private insurance is a legitimate means of protecting collective access to public health care.

In our view, *Chaoulli* represents both an end and a beginning. On the one hand, it is a logical consequence of the way in which judicial policy-making has evolved during the *Charter*'s first quarter-century. On the other hand, it lays the foundation for an even more aggressive judicial role in policy-making, especially in the health care field, during the *Charter*'s next quarter-century. In the remainder of this chapter, we explore this Janus-like quality of *Chaoulli* in three phases. First, we provide a fairly extensive description of the litigation that led to this result. Second, we explore how *Chaoulli* might be understood as logically emanating from previous developments. Finally, we speculate about *Chaoulli*'s future impact on both the role of Canadian courts and health care policy.

Creating a Right to Private Health Insurance

> Access to a waiting list is not access to health care.[5]
> – Chief Justice Beverley McLachlin and Justice John Major

In 1994, sixty-one-year-old George Zeliotis began experiencing hip problems, leading him to consult a variety of medical specialists. His general practitioner referred him to an orthopaedic specialist in 1995, and he had surgery on his left hip. In 1997, after some delay, he had surgery on his right hip. During his year-long wait in 1996, Zeliotis investigated whether he could pay privately for surgery and learned that the terms of Quebec's health care laws prohibited him both from obtaining insurance that would pay for surgery in a private facility and from paying directly for services provided by a physician in a public hospital. He pleaded his case with administrators, politicians, and the local media without success.

Although Zeliotis' condition and waiting time for surgery was the catalyst for litigation, the most visible protagonist in the legal battle became Dr. Jacques Chaoulli. Trained in France and Quebec, Chaoulli received his licence to practise medicine in Quebec in 1986. Then, as now, physicians had to practise outside "over-serviced" urban areas, such as greater Montreal, or receive lower reimbursement rates for their services. Chaoulli decided to return to Montreal after only two years. He soon became well known in medical circles through his attempts to set up a home-based, twenty-four-hour practice for doctors making house calls in Montreal's south shore region. After intense lobbying and the subsequent refusal of the Regional Health Board to recognize his practice in 1996, Chaoulli began a hunger strike to draw attention to the situation. The strike lasted three weeks, and, at that point, Chaoulli decided to become a "non-participating" doctor in the Quebec health care system.[6]

As in every province, Quebec physicians may "opt out" of the public system and bill patients directly for services rendered. However, as Chaoulli soon discovered, the disincentives for opting out are substantial. Under the terms of Quebec's health care laws, patients may not seek reimbursement from the public system if they consult non-participating doctors. In addition, such doctors may not provide private services in publicly funded hospitals.[7] From 1996 to 1998, Chaoulli attempted to gain permission, from both Quebec officials and the federal Ministry of Health, to create a private hospital. After this initiative failed, Chaoulli returned to the public system and worked as a general practitioner in a walk-in clinic.

Although Chaoulli was never Zeliotis' physician, they effectively combined resources for a legal challenge before the Quebec Superior Court in 1997. Together, they claimed that Article 15 of the Quebec *Health Insurance Act*, which prohibits private insurers from covering publicly funded services, and Article 11 of the Quebec *Hospital Insurance Act*, which prevents non-participating physicians from contracting for services in publicly funded hospitals, were unconstitutional under the terms of the Canadian *Charter*.[8] Chaoulli represented himself in the initial trial, claiming that he had a "duty" to provide services, and he called upon several high-profile critics of public health care to testify on his behalf. Zeliotis, who stated that his personal goal was to ensure that any future surgery would not be "delayed again," retained the services of Philippe Trudel, of Trudel and Johnston.[9] The Montreal law firm, which specializes in constitutional litigation, consumer protection, and health and medical liability, was also associated with a high-profile class action suit, in the late 1990s, against the tobacco industry on behalf of Quebec smokers and ex-smokers who became addicted to nicotine.[10]

Trial and Appellate Court Proceedings

Trial proceedings in *Chaoulli v. Québec* began in December 1997 and continued for four weeks before Justice Ginette Piché in the Quebec Superior Court. At trial, the basic question was whether the combination of waiting times for health care services in the public system and restrictions on private insurance for publicly provided services constituted a violation of the rights to life, liberty, and security of the person enshrined in section 7 of the Canadian *Charter*. Chaoulli's testimony emphasized the mental anguish caused to him as a victim of an allegedly discriminatory law that prohibited him from practising his profession as a "non-participating" doctor outside the public system, and he further portrayed Quebec's health care monopoly as infused with "Marxist-Leninist" theories of egalitarian ideology. His testimony was so intense that the judge commented on his "tireless" efforts.[11]

Zeliotis' counsel, meanwhile, focused on how Article 11 of the *Hospital Insur-ance Act* and Article 15 of the *Health Insurance Act* were contrary to the *Charter* under section 7 and section 15 as they prohibited non-participating Quebec doctors from using public hospital facilities and Quebec residents from using their own financial resources to insure themselves for private care.[12]

The court heard testimony from various medical specialists. Two expressed concern with the problems of access to timely care in orthopaedic surgery and cataract surgery, which could seriously reduce the quality of life of pa-tients as well as be potentially fatal. Another argued that there could not be any reasonable delay for cancer patients. Although all of the physicians expressed frustration with the health care system in Quebec, there was no consensus that the system should be changed in the way in which the plain-tiffs were demanding.[13] The highest profile witness was undoubtedly Claude Castonguay, the provincial minister of health and social services during the early 1970s, who was considered to be the "father of medicare" in Quebec. He claimed that, while he still agreed with the objective of the 1970 law to ensure equal access to health care, the province's strained financial situation and growing elderly population meant that new solutions and partnerships had to be created in the health care system. Nevertheless, he disagreed with the remedy suggested by the plaintiffs in the case.[14] The court also heard the opinions of several experts in the health care sector, who provided historical and comparative perspectives on the Quebec health care system:

- Dr. Fernand Turcotte, a professor of medicine at Laval University, who reminded the court of the historical impetus for public health care and the relationship between access to health care and socio-economic status;[15]
- Dr. Howard Bergman, director of geriatrics at the Jewish General Hospital in Montreal, who agreed that patients were unsettled by the rapid changes in the health care system but deplored privatization (the "healthy" versus the "wealthy") as a solution;[16]
- Dr. Charles Wright, a British Columbia surgeon, who commented on the administrative efficiency of the single-payer system in Canada;
- Jean-Louis Denis, a professor of health system organization at the Univer-sity of Montreal, who pointed out that rationing is explicit in every health care system, either through need, as in Quebec, or through the ability to pay, as in the United States;[17]
- Theodore Marmor, a professor of public policy at Yale University, who was asked about the likely impact of a parallel private system in Canada and his opinion was that the "undesirable side effects" would include decreased support for the public system and increased costs of care and administra-tion;[18] and
- Dr. Edwin Coffey, a retired obstetrician/gynaecologist and research associ-ate for the Montreal Economic Institute, a conservative think-tank that

advocates privatization of health care in Canada, who provided a lengthy testimony deploring the "ideological and politically driven myths" in health care.[19]

Justice Piché delivered her judgment on February 25, 2000. Unlike Justice Marion Allan in British Columbia, who reacted sympathetically to the claims of the autistic children and their parents, Justice Piché was critical of the plaintiffs in *Chaoulli*.[20] She began her summary by remarking: "Let's say it from the start: in light of Mr. Zeliotis' testimony and an examination of his medical record, it is apparent that he did not really suffer all of the misfortune and delay that he claims in his deposition."[21] As for Chaoulli, she questioned his motivation, pointed to contradictions in his testimony, and deplored his use of the court for a personal "crusade" against the Quebec health care system.[22] Although she conceded that the court had to take into account all sides of the expert testimony, she concluded that Coffey was very much alone in his heavy-handed criticism of the shortcomings of the Quebec health care system.[23]

Justice Piché's central legal analysis concerned the claims relating to the right to life, liberty, and security of the person under section 7 of the *Charter*.[24] She concluded that access to health care is indeed a right since "without access to the health care system, it would be illusory to believe that the rights to life and security are respected,"[25] but she also pointed out that there exists no right to determine the "provenance" (or source) of that care.[26] On the question of whether the existing limits on private insurance coverage were in violation of these same rights, she affirmed that these restrictions could limit an individual's timely access to care but that such limitations would only contravene life, liberty, and security of the person if the public system could not guarantee access to similar care. The justice was careful to point out that, although these limitations existed and could be a "threat," they did not conflict with the principles of fundamental justice and, therefore, could not be considered to be in contravention of section 7 of the *Charter*.[27]

In effect, she argued that, although Quebec's health care laws constrained economic rights, this prevention of "discrimination based on one's ability to pay does not violate the values of the charter."[28] Justice Piché referred to expert testimony that compared the efficiency and access to care offered by public and private health care systems and cited at length Theodore Marmor's description of the negative impact of a parallel system of private insurance on the viability of the public system.[29] Her decision was interpreted as a strong defence of the existing health care legislation's restrictions on private insurance and private care. Although recognizing a right to receive health care, her decision did not recognize a right to receive privately contracted services.

Justice Piché concluded her analysis by observing that, while the health care system in Quebec was based on sound principles, there was evidently need for some change. However, she declared that this question was political rather than legal. In effect, Justice Piché argued that health care reform was the responsibility of legislators, not judges: "[T]he Court notes that solutions to problems of the health care system are not to be found on the legal side."[30] Chaoulli and Zeliotis were convinced, however, that by losing the battle they "had a chance to win the war" because Justice Piché had agreed that the limitations on private insurance could constitute a violation of the *Charter* under section 7.[31] They appealed to the Quebec Court of Appeal in November 2001. Chaoulli changed his tactics slightly by arguing that the "excessive" limitations on private delivery and insurance in Quebec's health care legislation could be remedied by allowing less restrictive regulations based on European models. This strategy was designed to show that parallel private systems did not necessarily jeopardize the public system, as had been argued by experts in the trial proceedings on the basis of US experience.

The appellate court delivered its judgment on April 22, 2002. The three justices upheld Justice Piché's decision in its entirety. Justice Jacques Delisle made an important contribution in emphasizing the broadened definition of the right to access to care and agreed with the Superior Court that, although the health care legislation constituted a *prima facie* limitation of section 7 rights, this limitation was not inconsistent with principles of fundamental justice. He also argued that, while the right to enter into a private contract is prohibited by Quebec's health care legislation, this remains an economic right and not "fundamental to the life of the person" and, furthermore, that the violation of section 7 rights had to be immediate and real, which was not evident in the case at hand.[32] Justice Delisle also took the position that the *Charter* was not an instrument to remedy "societal choices" in the public domain. In other words, as Justice Piché had argued, the courts cannot be expected to meddle too far in the realm of legislative responsibility.

An Unexpected Reversal

A full year after oral arguments in *Chaoulli*, a divided Supreme Court of Canada – seven justices rendered three separate judgments – invalidated Quebec's prohibition against private insurance for publicly provided services by a one-vote margin. According to Justice Marie Deschamps, the existence of lengthy waiting lists for certain surgical procedures affected the rights to life and personal inviolability protected under section 1 of the Quebec *Charter of Human Rights and Freedoms* (which has quasi-constitutional status) in a way that could not be justified under section 9.1 of the same document (which operates similarly to section 1 of the Canadian *Charter*).[33] Justice

Deschamps rejected both the alleged micro- and macro-level consequences of eliminating the public monopoly on health care provision. She indicated that "no study produced or discussed" at trial supported the conclusion that the availability of private insurance would have perverse consequences on individual behaviour in the system,[34] nor did she find adequate evidence that private insurance would lead to increased costs or a general deterioration of the public system.[35] To the contrary, she cited the experience of other countries in the Organisation for Economic Co-operation and Development as evidence that "a number of measures are available ... to protect the integrity of Quebec's health care plan" even with private insurance.[36] In choosing to base her decision on the Quebec, rather than the Canadian, *Charter*, Justice Deschamps departed significantly from the issues that engaged the attention of the judges below her as well as of the parties before the Court. None of the lower court judgments had discussed the Quebec *Charter*, and none of the twelve constitutional questions formulated by Justice John Major for the Court on August 15, 2003 dealt with the Quebec *Charter*. Moreover, contrary to the impression given by Justice Deschamps, only four brief paragraphs of Zeliotis' factum raised arguments based on the Quebec *Charter*.[37]

Chief Justice Beverley McLachlin, with Justices John Major and Michel Bastarache, concurred with Justice Deschamps' Quebec *Charter* analysis but went further in declaring that the prohibition was also invalid under section 7 of the Canadian *Charter*. According to the chief justice, "access to a waiting list is not access to health care," so that "prohibiting health insurance that would permit ordinary Canadians to access health care, in circumstances where the government is failing to deliver health care in a reasonable manner, thereby increasing the risk of complications and death, interferes with life and security of the person as protected by s. 7 of the *Charter*."[38] Moreover, she found the prohibition "arbitrary" and therefore contrary to the principles of fundamental justice.[39]

Like Justice Piché in the trial court, Justices Ian Binnie and Louis LeBel, writing in dissent with Justice Morris Fish, argued that the question at issue in *Chaoulli* was not one that could "be resolved as a matter of law by judges."[40] In their view, there is no "constitutionally manageable standard" for determining what constitutes "reasonable" access to health care services.[41] Moreover, even if such standards did exist, the dissenting justices saw no reason, either as a matter of fact or law, to reverse the lower court decisions. On the factual question, they accepted the lower court finding that broad access to private insurance would promote a two-tier health care system that "would likely have a negative impact on the integrity, functioning and viability of the public system."[42] On the legal issue, although recognizing that the meaning of section 7 of the Canadian *Charter* had been expanded, they noted that this challenge did not "arise out of an adjudicative context or one involving the administration of justice."[43] Therefore, it did not engage even a broad interpretation of section 7.

Although the trial court proceedings in *Chaoulli* engaged live expert testimony on both sides of the question, the Supreme Court of Canada's decisions effectively reflected a dispute over the relative merits of two reports that presented the results of exhaustive studies of the state of health care in Canada. The Commission on the Future of Health Care in Canada (known as the Romanow Commission, after its director, former Saskatchewan New Democratic Party premier Roy Romanow) published a vigorous defence of public health care against privatization, and its recommendations had been widely acclaimed by public interest groups. The Senate Standing Committee on Social Affairs, Science and Technology (known as the Kirby Committee, after its chairman, the Conservative senator Michael Kirby) also produced a six-volume report that, while supportive of the public health care system, suggested that there might be a better mix of public and private delivery of health care.[44]

As it turned out, the Kirby report swayed the majority of the justices, with the two majority judgments referencing it thirteen times (as compared to two references to the Romanow report). The chief justice summarized the Kirby report's findings in ten short paragraphs, leading her to conclude that access to private insurance for core services would improve individual health care outcomes without adversely affecting collective access to public health care.[45] This empirical conclusion played a central role in her legal judgment that Quebec's statute was an unconstitutionally arbitrary denial of section 7 rights. To put the Court's decision starkly, four justices preferred Kirby; three preferred Romanow; and the statutory provision fell.

An Inconvenient Truth

The outcome in *Chaoulli* shocked Court watchers and health policy experts alike. In retrospect, however, it was entirely consistent with doctrinal developments over the *Charter*'s first twenty-five years. For example, the Supreme Court of Canada has progressively abandoned largely categorical rules of standing and mootness in favour of entirely discretionary criteria for the application of these doctrines. This was an important move in the expansion of judicial power because the traditional purpose of these doctrines has been to exclude certain questions from judicial review on the grounds that there are fixed limits to adjudicative decision-making capacity.[46] It is arguable that, under traditional categorical rules, neither Zeliotis nor Chaoulli would have had standing to challenge the Quebec law.[47] Moreover, Zeliotis' claim would have been moot under traditional rules since he had received the hip replacement surgery that he was seeking. Nevertheless, even the *Chaoulli* dissenters conceded that the two men could be given a type of "public interest standing" to challenge the law, simply because they were Quebec citizens raising serious questions about Quebec's health plan that might not otherwise be brought before a court.[48] Yet, the principle underlying the traditional doctrines of standing and mootness is precisely that some questions are unsuitable for judicial resolution, no matter how serious.

Chaoulli is also the logical consequence of the Court's acceptance of substantive judicial review under section 7. Such a review occurred in *B.C. Motor Vehicle Reference* in 1985, when Justice Antonio Lamer held that a "broad, purposive analysis" of section 7 required that the "principles of fundamental justice" not be constrained by any meaning that the *Charter*'s drafters might have attached to them. To interpret section 7 according to its intended meaning, Justice Lamer argued, would cause *Charter* rights to be "frozen in time to the moment of adoption with little or no possibility of growth, development and adjustment to changing societal needs."[49] "If the newly planted 'living tree' which is the Charter is to have the possibility of growth and adjustment over time," he continued, "care must be taken to ensure that historical materials ... do not stunt its growth."[50] The practical consequence of this approach was to attach a substantive meaning to the principles of fundamental justice, which the *Charter*'s framers had sought to avoid precisely because it had allowed the Supreme Court of the United States to declare laws unconstitutional because they "arbitrarily" interfered with protected rights.[51] It is hardly surprising, then, that Chief Justice McLachlin was able to invoke the substantive principle of "arbitrariness" to invalidate Quebec's prohibition against private health insurance two decades later.

Chaoulli also demonstrated the Court's inability to overcome systemic barriers to the use of extrinsic evidence. These barriers arise from the difference between deciding particular cases – the particular strength of the adversarial system – and formulating general policies.[52] The strength of the adversarial system is its capacity to sort through historical facts about past events that transpired between disputing parties in order to implement retrospective remedies that will restore each party to the status it enjoyed prior to the dispute. By contrast, general policy formation requires the analysis of complex social facts about the relationship between ongoing phenomena in order to regulate those relationships prospectively. The Court has faced tremendous difficulty in adapting the strengths of the adversarial system to the demands of policy-making, even in cases involving the administration of justice where judicial expertise is presumptively high.[53]

This difficulty was clear in *Chaoulli*. At issue was the relationship between two indisputable facts: waiting lists exist for certain services in the Quebec health care system, and Quebec law prohibits private insurance for services provided by the public system. If there is any advantage to exploring issues like this through litigation, it is that concrete cases may reveal how a law actually operates. In this case, however, not even the historical facts of the two complaints shed light on the relationship between waiting lists and the prohibition against private insurance. There was no evidence that Zeliotis himself would have been better off without the prohibition or even that he had not received "health care services" that were "reasonable as to both quality and timeliness."[54] Chaoulli's complaint was not really even about waiting lists but, rather, about his philosophical opposition to state interference with the freedom to practise medicine as he wished. Zeliotis had no evidence of actual harm (thus no standing) but only a plausible and sympathetic section 7 claim, and Chaoulli had standing by virtue of receiving administrative penalties but an implausible and unpalatable section 7 claim (freedom of contract).

It was the absence of concrete evidence about the relationship between waiting lists and private insurance in Quebec in the facts of the particular case that led the Court to focus on the Kirby and Romanow reports. However, the Court's attempt to use these reports to overcome the systemic barriers to social fact-finding in the adversarial system was characteristically unsuccessful because the reports became part of the decision-making process only during the final stages of the proceedings. Both the Romanow Commission and Kirby Committee issued their final reports in 2002, approximately four years after the trial proceedings in *Chaoulli* and two years after Justice Piché's appellate court decision. Consequently, to the extent that the adversarial process can provide an effective critical review of competing social facts, the Court did not even have the benefit of this process for the two reports. Its only opportunity to subject them to external assessment came during a four-hour hearing.

Judicial Power and Health Care after *Chaoulli*

> The courts are therefore the last line of defence for citizens.[55]
> – Justice Marie Dechamps

What might *Chaouilli* foreshadow about the next twenty-five years, both in terms of judicial power and health care policy? One important point to note is that *Chaoulli* brought an end to the seamless co-existence of two national symbols cherished by Canadians: publicly funded health care and the *Charter*. The principal short-term victim of this aspect of *Chaoulli* was the federal Liberal Party, which had presented itself as the founder and principal defender of both. We suggest that this newly opened and unresolved conflict between policy icons will reverberate politically for some time.

Chaoulli also tells us that the next twenty-five years will probably see an expansion of private health care in Canada, both as a result of concrete policy responses to its holding and the emergence of new litigation to exploit and expand this holding. Quebec, of course, was the first province obliged to adjust its health policy framework in the aftermath of *Chaoulli*. The Quebec government's response to *Chaoulli* was immediate, but its legislative response took several months to craft and refine. Hours after the ruling, the premier, along with the minister of health, Philippe Couillard, and the minister of inter-governmental affairs, Benoît Pelletier, held a press conference reiterating Quebec's jurisdictional responsibilities in health care. Within weeks, the *procureur général du Québec* (Quebec's attorney general) had filed a deposition with the Supreme Court of Canada asking for a stay of eighteen months in order to allow the government enough time to analyze and respond to the decision. Although Chaoulli and Zelitois returned to the courts in an attempt to argue against this delay, the Supreme Court of Canada finally accorded a stay of twelve months to the Quebec government.

The political stakes for the government of Premier Jean Charest, which was suffering in public opinion polls, were great. The Liberal Party had to preserve its federalist leanings while still proving its ability to protect Quebecers' collective rights to public health care. At the same time, however, the essence of the *Chaoulli* ruling echoed many of the attempts of the provincial government to "re-engineer" the state in Quebec, although these had not been successful to that point. And just weeks after the legal decision, Charest's hand-picked working group on the continuity of the health care system, led by Bank of Montreal president Jacques Ménard, cited the *Chaoulli* decision in proposing to extend the reach and numbers of private clinics in Quebec and to "set guidelines for the private sector's involvement in the delivery of health care services."[56]

As the battle lines formed in preparation for the public consultations on both the Ménard report and the *Chaoulli* decision, the Quebec government had to engineer a finely tuned policy response. There were, in effect, several options. One was to maintain the prohibition against private insurance, declaring that it applies despite section 52 of the Quebec *Charter* and notwithstanding section 33 of the Canadian *Charter*. Another option was to remove the absolute prohibition against private insurance and replace it with some form of limited or highly regulated access.

In February 2006, after several months of extensive internal research, the Quebec government finally made public its recommendations for changes to the health insurance laws that would respond to the Supreme Court of Canada ruling. The essential message was that while the government recognized that something would have to be done to ensure access to surgeries such as those at issue in the *Chaoulli* ruling, it would not open up the entire health care system to private insurance nor would it allow physicians to receive both public and private payment. This message was confirmed when Bill 33 was introduced into the National Assembly, just before the one-year anniversary of the *Chaoulli* decision. After months of public hearings and considerable pressure from defenders and detractors of the public system, the new legislation reaffirmed a commitment to public health care but, at the same time, used the *Chaoulli* ruling to present a larger reform plan for guaranteeing access to specialized health care services and to widen the scope of public-private partnerships in the Quebec health care sector.

The legislation opened the provision of core services in the Quebec health care system to private insurance but only in three specific areas: hip, knee, and cataract surgery. It also went further in introducing a wait time guarantee in these areas, akin to what the federal Conservative Party had promised in the January 2006 election. At the same time, it retained the "wall" between physicians who remain in the public system and those who opt out of it completely. However, the legislation also added measures that were other priorities of the Liberal government in Quebec – for example, the eventual extension of private insurance to "other procedures" and the introduction of a new instrument for the provision of services through the establishment of "affiliated medical clinics" through public-private partnerships.

Bill 33 passed late in the fall session of 2006, but it had not yet been fully implemented even by mid-2007, and its effects had yet to have a meaningful impact on the health care system. In the meantime, health care entrepreneurs, including Chaoulli himself, had attempted to use the prospects of Bill 33 to offer private surgeries and accelerated access to certain types of care. The Charest government, in a minority situation after a setback in the polls in March 2007, remained careful in responding to such initiatives. In the May budget, the finance minister, Monique Jerome-Forget, announced that Claude Castonguay, the former minister of health who designed Quebec's original public health insurance plan, would lead a task force to find new ways to finance health care and suggest a greater role for the private sector as well as to examine how the *Canada Health Act* might have to be amended to accommodate such a role.[57] Castonguay, who has lobbied for user fees in the past and has publicly denounced the *Canada Health Act* as a major hindrance to viable health reform, presented his report in December 2008.

Alberta and Ontario are the first provinces to face *Chaoulli*-inspired test case litigation. In both provinces, the Canadian Constitution Foundation (CCF) – an individual rights-oriented public interest litigation group – have recruited plaintiffs to extend *Chaoulli*'s reach both geographically and legally. The Alberta case involves a fifty-seven-year-old man who, like George Zeliotis, faced difficulty in obtaining hip surgery. The Alberta government refused to provide William Murray with a form of surgery that was less invasive than full hip surgery, causing him to bear the full cost of the procedure. In Ontario, the CCF has recruited two patients who allege that they had to undergo brain tumour surgery in the United States after failing to receive timely care from the public system and being prohibited from obtaining private care within the province. In both cases, the objective is to solidify and extend the *Charter* principles articulated by the chief justice and her two colleagues. If successful, the cases will undoubtedly move Canada closer to the vision of health care articulated in the Kirby report.

The most important potential legacy of *Chaoulli*, however, is found in Justice Deschamps justification for judicial intervention in the matter. "Courts," Justice Deschamps argued, "have all the necessary tools ... to find a solution to the problem of waiting lists" and respond to "the urgency of taking concrete action" in the face of a "situation that continues to deteriorate." Governments "cannot choose to do nothing," and, when they do, "courts are the last line of defence for citizens."[58] The notion that courts are the last line of defence for citizens generally, rather than for particularly vulnerable groups, goes well beyond the principal modern justification for rights-based judicial review. This justification stems from the Supreme Court of the United States' decision in *United States v. Carolene Products* in 1938, in which the court indicated that legislation affecting "discrete and insular minorities" would be subject to "more searching judicial inquiry" than economic regulation.[59] Since this decision, such groups have been seen as requiring special judicial protection because they have been targets of discrimination and excluded from political participation.

The policy negated in *Chaoulli*, however, was one of general applicability that presumably reflected a choice made by the very citizens whom Justice Deschamps sought to protect by ruling in favour of Zeliotis and Chaoulli. Democratic theory would suggest that those citizens are best positioned to reverse this choice if they determine that it no longer serves their interests. By defining judicial review as the *last line of defence for citizens*, Justice Deschamps effectively invited anyone dissatisfied with the outcome of a policy debate to seek a different result in the courts. This anticipates a far more active role for judicial review in the policy process.

Conclusion

Much ink has been spilled over the past quarter-century in debating the *Charter*'s impact on judicial power and public policy. Wherever one stands in this debate, *Chaoulli* makes clear that the *Charter* has become – unexpectedly to some, inevitably to others – an important tool for policy change in the health care field. Although the desire of Canadians, frustrated by perceived bureaucratic and legislative inaction, to seek health care solutions from the courts is understandable, the benefits and costs of this path to policy change merit closer attention. The obvious benefit is that courts can order governments to act more quickly and forcefully than can citizens. It is easy to sympathize with parents of autistic children, who are unable to access affordably a potentially effective treatment because of government budgetary decisions. Jacques Chaoulli's desire for a private alternative to the Quebec health care system's waiting lists is equally understandable. From seeking the provision of specific services to claiming more timely access to health care, Canadians increasingly see litigation as more effective than lobbying.

Yet, litigation is not without disadvantages. First, the articulation of policy demands in the form of constitutional rights can exclude alternative policy choices from consideration. Second, the adversarial nature of litigation is best suited to resolving concrete disputes between two parties by imposing retrospective remedies. Complex policy issues – such as health care – involve multiple stakeholders, constantly changing facts and evidence, and predictive assessments of the future impact of decisions. Finally, rights-based litigation, particularly at the Supreme Court of Canada level, by definition imposes national solutions on inherently local problems. These solutions can ignore differences among provinces and suppress the provincial experimentation necessary to find innovative approaches to policy problems.

This is particularly problematic in health care, which is the largest single expenditure item in provincial government budgets. The use of rights-based litigation invites the courts to become an influential player in the health policy field and to impose a new set of constraints on provincial policy-makers already burdened by difficult choices in the allocation of public resources to health care and other fiscal responsibilities. It also forces political authorities to undertake piecemeal solutions rather than to engage in a more coordinated policy process that would take into account not only individual preferences but also the larger question of the public interest. Canadian health care faces a multitude of complex challenges. As we begin the *Charter*'s next twenty-five years, we need to give more careful consideration to the contribution that courts can make in meeting these challenges before embracing litigation as an instrument of reform in health care policy.

Notes

1 *Canadian Charter of Rights and Freedoms,* Part 1 of the *Constitution Act, 1982,* being Schedule B to the *Canada Act 1982* (U.K.), 1982, c. 11.

2 Martha Jackman, "The Regulation of Private Health Care under the Canada Health Act and the *Canadian* Charter," *Constitutional Forum* 6:2 (1995): 54-60; Martha Jackman, "The Right to Participate in Health Care and Health Resource Allocation Decisions under Section 7 of the *Canadian Charter," Health Law Review* 4 (1995-1996): 3; André Braen, *Health and the Distribution of Powers in Canada,* Discussion Paper no. 2, Commission on the Future of Health Care in Canada (2002); Martha Jackman, *The Implications of Section 7 of the Charter for Health Care Spending in Canada,* Discussion Paper no. 31, Commission on the Future of Health Care in Canada (2002); Donna Greschner, *How Will the Charter of Rights and Freedoms and Evolving Jurisprudence Affect Health Care Costs,* Discussion Paper no. 20, Commission on the Future of Health Care in Canada (2002); and Christopher Manfredi and Antonia Maioni, "Courts and Health Policy: Judicial Policy Making and Publicly Funded Health Care in Canada," *Journal of Health Politics, Policy and Law* 27 (2002): 211.

3 *Morgentaler, Smoling and Scott v. R.,* [1988] 1 S.C.R. 30 (abortion); *Rocket v. Royal College of Dental Surgeons of Ontario,* [1990] 2 S.C.R. 232 (professional advertising); *Rodriguez v. British Columbia,* [1993] 3 S.C.R. 519 (assisted suicide); and *Eldridge v. British Columbia,* [1997] 3 S.C.R. 624 (sign language interpretation).

4   *Chaoulli v. Québec*, [2005] 1 S.C.R. 791 [*Chaoulli 2005*].
5   Ibid., para. 123.
6   B. Sibbald, "In Your Face: A New Wave of Militant Doctors Lashes Out," *Canadian Medical Association Journal* 158 (1998): 1505-9.
7   Colleen Flood and Tom Archibald, "The Illegality of Private Health Care in Canada," *Canadian Medical Association Journal* 164 (2001): 825-30.
8   *Health Insurance Act*, R.S.Q., c. A-29; and *Hospital Insurance Act*, R.S.Q., c. A-28.
9   Susan Pinker, "The Chaoulli Case: One-Tier Medicine Goes on Trial in Quebec," *Canadian Medical Association Journal* 161 (1999): 1305-6.
10 Josée Hamelin, "L'industrie freine les recours collectifs québécois," *Info-tabac* 46 (aout 2003): 5.
11 Susan Pinker, "'Why Does Such a Big Issue Rest on the Shoulders of Two Citizens?' FP Asks after Losing Private Medicine Battle," *Canadian Medical Association Journal* 162 (2000): 1348.
12 *Chaoulli and Zeliotis v. Québec*, [2000] R.J.Q. 786 at para. 5 [*Chaoulli 2000*].
13 Ibid., para. 10-11.
14 Ibid., para. 12.
15 Ibid., para. 16-18.
16 Ibid., para. 18-20.
17 Ibid., para. 20-24.
18 Ibid., para. 24-28.
19 Ibid., para. 29. Coffey and Chaoulli later co-authored a text on "universal private choice," see Edwin Coffey and Jacques Chaoulli, *Universal Private Choice: Medicare Plus* (Montreal: Montreal Economic Institute, 2001).
20 *Auton et al. v. Attorney-General of British Columbia*, 2000 B.C.S.C. 1142.
21 *Chaoulli 2000*, *supra* note 12, para. 6 (author's translation).
22 Ibid., para. 7-9.
23 Ibid., para. 29.
24 Martha Jackman, "Misdiagnosis or Cure? Charter Review of the Health Care System," in Colleen Flood, ed., *The Frontiers of Fairness: Who Decides What Is in and out of Medicare* (Toronto: University of Toronto Press, 2005).
25 *Chaoulli 2000*, *supra* note 12, para. 223.
26 Ibid., para. 227.
27 Ibid., para. 310.
28 Pinker, *supra* note 11, 1348.
29 Cited in Jackman, *supra* note 2, 6.
30 *Chaoulli 2000*, *supra* note 12, para. 315.
31 Pinker, *supra* note 11, 1348.
32 *Chaoulli and Zeliotis v. Québec*, [2002] R.J.Q. 1205 at paras. 23-29.
33 *Charter of Human Rights and Freedoms*, R.S.Q., c. C-12.
34 *Chaoulli 2005*, *supra* note 4, para. 62.
35 Ibid., para. 66.
36 Ibid., para. 84.
37 Ibid., para. 12.
38 Ibid., paras. 123-24.
39 Ibid., para. 153.
40 Ibid., para. 161.
41 Ibid., para. 163.
42 Ibid., para. 181.
43 Ibid., para. 195.
44 Commission on the Future of Health Care in Canada, *Building on Values: The Future of Health Care in Canada – Final Report* (Ottawa: The Commission, 2002) (Romanow); Canada. Senate. *The Health of Canadians: The Federal Role – Final Report of the Standing Senate Committee on Social Affairs, Science and Technology* (Ottawa: The Senate, 2002) (Kirby).
45 Ibid., paras. 140-49.
46 *United States v. Richardson*, 418 U.S. 166 at 188 (1974) (Powell, J., concurring).

47   For a similar criticism of the Court's decision to grant standing, see Kent Roach, "The Courts and Medicare: Too Much or Too Little Judicial Activism?" in Colleen M. Flood, Kent Roach, and Lorne Sossin, eds., *Access to Care, Access to Justice* (Toronto: University of Toronto Press, 2005), 184-204.
48   *Chaoulli 2005, supra* note 4, para. 188.
49   *Reference re B.C. Motor Vehicle Act,* [1985] 2 S.C.R. 486.
50   Ibid., 554-55.
51   *Lochner v. New York,* 198 U.S. 45 (1905).
52   Donald Horowitz, *The Courts and Social Policy* (Washington: Brookings Institution, 1976), 45 and 47.
53   Christopher P. Manfredi, *Judicial Power and the Charter: Canada and the Paradox of Liberal Constitutionalism,* 2nd edition (Don Mills, ON: Oxford University Press, 2001), 159-60.
54   *Chaoulli 2005, supra* note 4, para. 158.
55   Ibid., para. 96.
56   Jacques Ménard, *Pour sortir de l'impasse: la solidarité entre nos generations* (Quebec: Ministère des services sociaux et de santé, 2005).
57   *Canada Health Act,* R.S.C. 1985, c. C-6.
58   *Chaoulli 2005, supra* note 4, paras. 96-97.
59   The phrase comes from *United States v. Carolene Products,* 304 U.S. 144 (1938).

8
National Security and the *Charter*
Kent Roach

National security law spans traditional divides between criminal and administrative law and includes the exercise of prerogative powers related to foreign relations. It raises contested issues concerning equality, privacy, state secrecy, and compliance with international norms and instruments as well as the role of legal rights in restraining state prosecutions of those suspected of committing serious crimes such as terrorism. Canada's response to the attacks of 9/11 in New York City has intensified concerns about both national security and respect for the *Canadian Charter of Rights and Freedoms*.[1] There was also considerable engagement between national security and the *Charter* before 9/11, and a number of early *Charter* decisions established important themes that remain with us today. As will be seen, these early cases established several important principles. The courts rejected blind deference to the state's national security activities and allowed even the most unpopular litigants to make claims to the independent courts that their rights were being infringed by the state's national security activities. *Charter* considerations have restrained legislative action in the name of national security and forced Parliament to consider rights issues that it otherwise might have neglected or ignored. These are major virtues of the *Charter* that have the potential to temper and improve national security policy-making.

There are, however, some vices in the degree to which the *Charter* has influenced the development of national security policy. At times, there has been a focus on "*Charter*-proofing" national security legislation, as opposed to determining whether the policy is effective and workable.[2] Although the Supreme Court of Canada, in its landmark decision *Operation Dismantle v. R.*, reminded us that the consistency of a policy with the *Charter* should not be confused with its wisdom, this lesson has not always been respected. Another vice is that the limits of *Charter* litigation in restraining secret executive action in the national security field have not always been recognized. For example, the activities of Canada's security intelligence agencies have rarely been the subject of *Charter* litigation, and their effective review depends more on the vigour of independent review bodies than on the courts.

The first part of this chapter will examine the impact of the *Charter* on prerogative powers concerned with national security. My focus will be on the Supreme Court of Canada's landmark decision in 1985, *Operation Dismantle*, which applied the *Charter* to all of the activities of the Canadian government.[3] Although the Court found no *Charter* violation in this case, *Operation Dismantle* has far-reaching implications that extend to the Court's decision that Canadian participation in the interrogation of Omar Khadr at Guantanamo Bay violated the *Charter*.[4]

The second part of this chapter will explore how the national security context has influenced the Court's approach to investigative powers, including investigative hearings into terrorism. In the *Hunter v. Southam* decision of 1984, the Supreme Court of Canada restrained criminal law investigative powers by articulating a general requirement for warrants issued by judges on the basis of probable cause that a search would reveal evidence about a crime.[5] Significantly, however, the Court left open the possibility that different standards might apply with respect to national security.

The third part examines how *Charter* concerns in both legislatures and courts have shaped the contours of various criminal laws in the national security area. Following the 1985 *Reference re B.C. Motor Vehicle Act,* in which the Supreme Court of Canada ruled that the *Charter* applied to the substance of penal laws,[6] recent decisions have demonstrated that the *Charter* has played an important role with respect to fault requirements for terrorism offences, the definition of terrorist activities, and an oft-criticized offence of the possession of official secrets. The Court's decision in *R. v. Stinchcombe* revolutionized the criminal justice system by providing the accused with a *Charter* right to disclosure of the Crown's case.[7] Even before this decision, however, broad disclosure requirements severely affected a number of terrorism prosecutions. The breadth of our disclosure requirements, coupled with Canada's unique and awkward structure to obtain non-disclosure orders to protect secrets, raises issues about the viability of terrorism prosecutions in Canada that are in part, but only in part, related to the *Charter*.

The fourth section will examine how the *Charter* continues to influence the use of immigration law for national security reasons. In no small part because of the difficulties of criminal prosecutions, Canada has made robust use of immigration law as anti-terrorism law. However, this development must be placed in the context of Justice Bertha Wilson's decision in *Singh v. Canada,* which affirmed that non-citizens in Canada would enjoy the fundamental justice protections of section 7 of the *Charter*.[8] There is a line from *Singh* to the Court's subsequent decision in *Charkaoui* that the security certificate regime violated the *Charter* because it provided no adversarial challenge to the intelligence used by the government to hold and deport non-citizens suspected of involvement with terrorism.[9] *Singh* also played a role in the Court's decision that it would generally violate the *Charter* to deport a person to face torture.[10] The remainder of this chapter will contain a preliminary assessment of the positive and negative effects of the *Charter* on national security policy-making.

The *Charter* and Prerogative National Security Powers

In 1985, the Supreme Court of Canada decided an improbable case brought by a peace group, Operation Dismantle, who alleged that the government's decision to allow the United States to test cruise missiles in northern Canada violated section 7 of the *Charter* because it increased the risk of nuclear war with the Soviet Union and made Canada a more likely target for nuclear attack. The Cold War context of the case seems old-fashioned today, but the allegation that Canada was co-operating with aggressive American security policies has a certain contemporary ring. The federal government moved to strike the peace group's claim in part on the basis that prerogative powers of commanding armed forces were not subject to the *Charter* and that the questions raised by the case were not justiciable. There was some support for this position in American constitutional law and pre-*Charter* jurisprudence. Nevertheless, the Supreme Court of Canada decisively rejected such arguments, even while it unanimously held that the case should not be allowed to proceed because the peace group's claim could not be proven.

In a decision that demonstrated her fearless concern for principle and fairness, Justice Wilson dismissed arguments that the Court was intruding on political questions and stressed that the issue for judges was not the wisdom of the government's policy but, rather, their duty to determine whether the government had infringed the *Charter*. She argued that a person conscripted into the Canadian Forces during a war would find the *Charter's* protections to be "somewhat illusory ... if the validity of his challenge is to be determined by the executive."[11] At the same time, Justice Wilson recognized that the government could defend a policy of conscription under section 1 of the *Charter* – the reasonable limits clause. In a foreshadowing of lawless post-9/11 rendition practices, however, she suggested that it would be more difficult to defend "press gang" policies that targeted particular groups without even the benefit of enabling legislation. Writing for the majority, Chief Justice Brian Dickson agreed with Justice Wilson that cabinet decisions are reviewable for their consistency with the *Charter*: "I have no doubt that the executive branch of the Canadian government is duty bound to act in accordance with the dictates of the *Charter*. Specifically, the cabinet has a duty to act in a manner consistent with the right to life, liberty and security of the person and the right not to be deprived thereof except in accordance with the principles of fundamental justice."[12]

In a series of cases illustrated by *R. v. Cook*, the Court made clear that while the *Charter* does not apply to the actions of foreign governments even when they act in co-operation with Canadian officials, it does apply to the actions of Canadian officials even when they act in foreign countries.[13] These decisions, combined with *Operation Dismantle*, had far-reaching implications. In short, Canadian officials took the *Charter* with them when they went abroad. For instance, Justice Konrad von Finkenstein of the Federal Court granted an interlocutory injunction in 2005 prohibiting Canadian officials from questioning Omar Khadr, a Canadian detained by the United States in Guantanamo Bay, Cuba. The judge examined evidence that Omar Khadr, who is alleged at the age of fifteen to have killed an American soldier in a battle on the Afhganistan/Pakistan border, was questioned by Canadian officials for law enforcement and intelligence purposes, that conditions at Guantanamo fell below *Charter* standards, and that the information collected by Canadian Security Intellegence Service (CSIS) was shared with the Royal Canadian Mounted Police (RCMP) and American officials without undertakings or caveats restricting its subsequent use. In his decision, the judge restrained Canadian officials from questioning Khadr except for consular assistance purposes.[14]

The granting of this injunction demonstrates the important role of the independent judiciary in protecting the rights of the unpopular. A subsequent decision affirmed that Canadian officials owed Khadr a duty of disclosure with respect to the information that they had obtained in interviews with him in Guantanamo Bay in 2003 and had subsequently handed over to American officials.[15] This decision was affirmed in 2008 by the Supreme Court of Canada in *Canada (Justice) v. Khadr*. The Court held that "s. 7 imposes a duty on Canada to provide disclosure of material in its possession arising from its participation in the foreign process that is contrary to international law and jeopardizes the liberty of a Canadian citizen."[16] Omar Khadr's rights under section 7 of the *Charter* were violated because "the regime providing for the detention and trial of Mr. Khadr at the time of the CSIS interviews constituted a clear violation of fundamental human rights protected by international law."[17] In reaching this conclusion, the Court relied on decisions made by the Supreme Court of the United States in 2004 and 2006, which held that the Guantanamo Bay procedure violated the right to *habeas corpus* and the *Geneva Conventions*.[18] Although critics of judicial review are fond of arguing that judges should not trump legislatures with respect to reasonable disagreements about rights, this case demonstrates how courts under the *Charter* can restrain executive action that is not explicitly authorized by law and that infringes the rights of the most unpopular. As the late Justice Wilson reminded us, the *Charter*, as well as the rule of law, prohibits "press gang" tactics even in the pursuit of worthy causes such as national security.[19]

Omar Khadr's brother, Abdurahman Khadr, was also apprehended in Afghanistan and held in Guantanamo Bay but later released. Based on an assertion of prerogative powers, the minister of foreign affairs denied him a passport. As a reviewing judge described the situation, Abdurahman Khadr "is a member of a family, many of whom are openly supporters of al-Qaeda. The principal reason for denying the passport – in the interests of national security – was based on concern about Canada-U.S. relations and public disapproval for issuing a passport to a member of such an infamous family. National security was not a ground for denial of a passport listed in the *Canadian Passport Order* at the time."[20] The judge, however, found that the minister's prerogative power was subject to the *Charter* as well as to the common-law doctrine of legitimate expectations. He quashed the minister's decision and instructed that the passport application be dealt with according to the law at the time of the original application. Justice Phelan stressed that while "the interests of the protection of national security and the very legitimate public interest in countering terrorism and other threats" were pressing, "a nation which has as a core principle that of the rule of law, must still adhere to the very legal principles that it seeks to protect."[21]

The government responded with regulations allowing passports to be denied on broad grounds relating to national security, but these were held to constitute an unjustified violation of the right of citizens to leave Canada under section 6 of the *Charter*. The court was concerned that the vagueness of the term *national security* meant that the limit on rights imposed by the law was not prescribed by law and could not effectively be challenged.[22] These decisions are consistent with the *Operation Dismantle* principle that all government action is subject to the *Charter*. They are also consistent with the idea that the *Charter* reinforces traditional rule of law values, including the need for specific and precise legislation to authorize and govern deprivations of rights.

The earlier-mentioned cases suggest that the *Charter* should apply to the actions of Canadian troops abroad. Even before recent concerns were raised about the treatment of detainees transferred to Afghanistan forces, it was reported that the Canadian Forces handed off detainees to the Americans, whereupon some were subsequently transferred to Guantanamo Bay.[23] Given that the Supreme Court of Canada ruled in *Cook* that the *Charter* applied to the actions of Canadian police officers acting in a foreign country, so long as application of the *Charter* was not inconsistent with the sovereignty of the foreign country, it is likely that the *Charter* would have applied to the independent actions of the Canadian Forces in Afghanistan.[24] The fact that the potential mistreatment of captives might be inflicted by others does not seem to be a viable *Charter* defence, given the Court's decisions that the *Charter* generally prohibits extradition or deportation when the death penalty or torture will be inflicted by foreign powers.[25]

R. v. Hape in 2007, however, suggests that the *Charter* will generally no longer apply to Canadian officials when they act abroad.[26] The majority's concerns about extraterritorial application and enforcement of the *Charter* are, in my view, inflated and exaggerated. The Canadian Forces, like other officials of the Canadian state, would surely follow the law as articulated by Canadian courts, even if Afghanistan did not consent to the application of the *Charter* as is required under the majority's decision in *Hape*. Requiring the Canadian Forces to abide by the *Charter* while in Afghanistan is not a serious infringement on Afghan sovereignty. Although some accommodation has to be made for the foreign context, the locus of enforcement of the *Charter* with respect to Canadian officials is Canada and not the foreign state. *Hape* represents a regrettable retreat from the sound first principles articulated in *Operation Dismantle* and *Cook,* which restrained Canadian officials from questioning Omar Khadr in Guantanamo. The Federal Court has already applied *Hape* to dismiss a *Charter* challenge to Canadian actions in transferring detainees to Afghan authorities largely on the basis that the Afghan authorities had not consented to the application of the *Charter*.[27] *Hape* is at odds with the spirit of *Operation Dismantle* and may represent the rise of a *de facto* doctrine of political questions that refuses to apply the *Charter* to the increasing foreign activities of Canadian police, military, and security intelligence officials, at least when they do not breach international law or participate in a process that violates international law.

The Supreme Court of Canada's subsequent unanimous decision that Omar Khadr's rights under section 7 of the *Charter* were violated by the non-disclosure of records of interviews between him and the Canadian officials at Guantanamo Bay, which were subsequently passed on to American authorities, demonstrates that the *Charter* can still apply extraterritorially, but only when Canadian conduct breaches its international obligations. The Court's decision is both curious and limited because of its reliance on findings of the Supreme Court of the United States for the proposition that Canada breached its international obligations when it interviewed Omar Khadr in 2003 when there was no judicial review of detentions or hearing process used in Guantanamo Bay in contravention of the *Geneva Conventions*. The Court also did not find that the interviews conducted by CSIS officials in Guantanamo Bay violated the *Charter*. The ruling was limited to disclosure of the records of the interviews in order "to mitigate the effect of Canada's participation by passing on the product of the interviews to U.S. authorities."[28] The Court also seemed to limit the *Charter* obligation to Canadian citizens even though section 7 applies to all persons.[29] Finally, the government retains the right to argue that harms of disclosure to national security and international relations outweigh the harms of non-disclosure before information could be disclosed to Omar Khadr.[30] The impact of the

Khadr decision on the Afghan detainee cases remains to be seen. The focus in these cases will not be whether the actions of Canadian officials were contrary to the *Charter* but, rather, whether they violated Canada's international law obligations. If they do violate Canada's international law obligations, then the Court's decisions in *Hape* and *Khadr* suggest that the *Charter* can now provide a remedy under domestic law for breaches of international law.

The *Charter* and Investigative Powers

Although the Court's decision in *Operation Dismantle* affirmed that the *Charter* would apply to the national security activities of Canadian governments, it did not mean that *Charter* standards would not take into account the importance of national security interests or the complex international context in which national security powers are exercised. In *Hunter*, Justice Dickson applied a generous and purposive approach to section 8 of the *Charter* to protect reasonable expectations of privacy. This purpose would be best secured by requiring the state to obtain a warrant from an independent judge on the basis of a probable cause to believe that a crime had been committed and that the search would reveal evidence of the crime. *Hunter* was the start of a legal rights revolution that transformed many parts of the criminal justice system by requiring the state to respect rights at the pre-trial, trial, and punishment stages of the criminal process.[31] At the same time, however, Justice Dickson also suggested in *Hunter* that different due process standards might apply when "state security is involved."[32] Much subsequent and future *Charter* litigation in the national security area has involved, and will involve, fleshing out the difference that the national security context makes when interpreting *Charter* standards.

Three years after *Hunter,* the Federal Court of Appeal held in *R. v. Atwal* that CSIS' warrant scheme complied with the *Charter* even though it allowed judges to grant electronic surveillance warrants on the basis of reasonable grounds that they were necessary to investigate threats to the security of Canada and not on probable grounds related to crime. The majority decision stressed the distinct preventive role of security intelligence and the role of the judge in applying objective standards before granting the warrant. The minority stressed the breadth of the investigative powers and the lack of any requirement that the electronic surveillance would likely find evidence that confirmed threats to national security.[33] This decision remains the leading precedent, in part because it is rare to use CSIS wiretaps as evidence in court.

The 2001 *Anti-Terrorism Act (ATA)* expanded the investigative powers of the state in several ways, including amendments that allow the minister of defence to authorize the Communications Security Establishment (CSE),

Canada's signals intelligence agency, to intercept communications from the global information infrastructure for the sole purpose of collecting intelligence about a foreign individual, state, organization, or terrorist group that is related to international affairs, defence, or security.[34] Such authorizations apply to conversations with a connection to Canada, but they must include satisfactory measures to protect the privacy of Canadians. In some ways, the Canadian law authorizes warrantless spying in a manner that has resulted in considerable controversy in the United States when it was revealed that the National Security Agency was intercepting communications involving Americans. The CSE amendments may be ripe for a *Charter* challenge to the extent that they might produce evidence through a warrantless search that might be used in Canadian proceedings.[35] That said, there is a distinct reluctance to attempt to use intelligence as evidence, and this fact limits the role of the *Charter* and the courts in ensuring the legality of the work of Canada's security intelligence agencies.

The *Charter* has played an important role in shaping new police powers in the *ATA* in so far as preventive arrest provisions were patterned on existing peace bond provisions that had been upheld under the *Charter*.[36] Indeed, even though the power to detain a person for up to seventy-two hours on the basis of reasonable suspicion has now expired, it is still possible to obtain year-long peace bonds on the basis of reasonable fears that a person will commit a terrorism offence.[37] Investigative hearings were also introduced as a new power, but, consistent with *Charter* standards, they were subject to the right to counsel and use and derivative use immunity of any statements or evidence compelled from the target. The constitutionality of investigative hearings were tested during the trial of two men charged but acquitted in the 1985 bombing of Air India. A majority of the Supreme Court of Canada rejected arguments that investigative hearings violated the *Charter* but extended the derivative use immunity provisions to apply not only to criminal proceedings but also to immigration and extradition proceedings.[38] In the companion case *Re Vancouver Sun*, the Court held that a sweeping publication ban was overbroad and that investigative hearings would, as judicial proceedings, be subject to a rebuttable presumption that they be conducted in open court.[39]

The decisions in these cases suggest that there are limits to the Court's willingness to make accommodations. It rejected the idea that the legislation was justified by "national security" and warned that "courts must not fall prey to the rhetorical urgency of a perceived emergency or an altered security paradigm."[40] It recognized that while the need to prevent and prosecute terrorism "necessarily changes the context in which the rule of law must operate, it does not call for the abdication of law."[41] To this end, the Court went beyond the legislation by extending the immunity provisions to encompass immigration and extradition proceedings. It stressed the role of the judge at the investigative hearing and held that the rebuttable open court principle must accompany the judge into the courtroom. Indeed, these safeguards added by the Court may have made investigative hearings less attractive to terrorism investigators.

In any event, investigative hearings, along with preventive arrests, expired after a five-year sunset provision when the minority Conservative government was unable to gain parliamentary support for their extension. Although the Court upheld investigative hearings as being consistent with the *Charter*, dialogue with Parliament continued.[42] Indeed, the repeal of investigative hearings and preventive arrests hearkens back to a pre-*Charter* period in which Parliament repealed capital punishment even though the Supreme Court of Canada ruled that it was consistent with the *Canadian Bill of Rights*.[43] The Court has made clear that the *Charter* will apply to the national security activities of the state while, at the same time, indicating some willingness to accommodate the national security context. However, Parliament has had, for the time being, the last word on the expiry of investigative hearings and preventive arrests. The dialogue, this time within Parliament, continues as the government has introduced a bill to re-enact preventive arrests and investigative hearings, albeit one that does not on its face contain the *Charter* immunity and open court safeguards read in by the Court.[44]

The *Charter* and the Substantive Criminal Law

In *Reference Re B.C. Motor Vehicle*, the Court refused to be bound by the framer's intent that section 7 of the *Charter* only provided procedural protections. The Court held that the *Charter* authorized it to strike down legislation that was fundamentally unfair.[45] In subsequent cases, the Court has held that it could require fault standards and strike down laws that were vague and overbroad under the *Charter*. Although the Court has been quite cautious in applying these standards to the criminal law, they have had a significant impact in shaping substantive law in the national security area.

While Canada has opted in the *ATA* for a broad definition of terrorist activities and an expansive range of crimes, consideration of the *Charter* may explain why Parliament has generally required the Crown to prove that the accused either knew about, or intended to be involved in, terrorism. In possible recognition that the courts might hold terrorism to be a crime, which, because of its stigma and punishment requires proof of subjective fault, none of the new terrorism offences have employed objective fault levels or reverse onuses as found in some anti-terrorism laws of other democracies. At the same time, Canadian subjective fault requirements have been qualified in an attempt to ensure that the prosecution does not have to prove that the accused knew the specific nature of the planned terrorist activity.[46] The recent convictions of a young offender in Toronto and Momin Khawaja illustrate the breadth of these new terrorism offences.

Although Canada followed the British example of distinguishing terrorism from ordinary crime by requiring the Crown to establish a political or religious motive for terrorist crimes, Canada added an interpretative clause that "the expression of a political, religious or ideological thought, belief or opinion" would not constitute a terrorist activity "unless it constitutes an act or omission that satisfies the criteria" of the broad definition of terrorist activities.[47] This attempt to accommodate *Charter* values did not stave off a successful constitutional challenge. The first accused charged under the *ATA* in 2004, Mohammad Momin Khawaja, brought multiple *Charter* challenges to the substance of the act. Justice Douglas Rutherford of the Ontario Superior Court of Justice held that the offences were neither vague nor overbroad on the basis that "a good lawyer can almost always create a hypothetical circumstance that might arguably be caught within the reach of a provision and that arguably should not be caught" and that such cases should be left to "case-by-case determination ... with a view to avoiding absurd results."[48] Justice Rutherford also rejected arguments that qualifications of subjective fault in terrorism offences violated the *Charter*. He seemed to concede that terrorism offences may require subjective fault but then held that "I see nothing wrong in asking, indeed expecting law-abiding citizens to avoid any knowing activity that aids, supports or advances terrorist activity or a group engaged in such activity."[49]

Justice Rutherford did accept one *Charter* challenge. He required the Crown to prove that the fact that the accused had committed terrorism offences for a political, religious, or ideological purpose constituted an unjustified violation of freedom of expression, association, and religion under section 2 of the *Charter*. He concluded that such a requirement "will chill freedom, protected speech, religion, thought, belief, expression and association, and therefore, democratic life; and will promote fear and suspicion of targeted political or religious groups, and will result in racial or ethnic profiling by governmental authorities at many levels."[50] The focus of Justice Rutherford's concern was the effect of the political or religious motive requirement on third parties. This is not a hypothetical concern, given that the Arar Commission had found that the RCMP had passed on inaccurate information to the Americans, branding both Maher Arar and his wife Monia Mazigh as "Islamic extremists associated with al Qaeda."[51]

The Crown was unable to justify the political or religious motive required under section 1 of the *Charter* despite the interpretative clause stating that political or religious opinion would not generally constitute a terrorist activity. Admissions of *Charter* vulnerabilities may only make judges more assertive of the role, affirmed in *Operation Dismantle*, of deciding whether legislation unreasonably violates *Charter* rights. Justice Rutherford was influenced by the fact that others, including the Supreme Court of Canada in *Suresh v. Canada*, were able to define terrorism without reference to a political or religious motive.[52] At the same time, however, Justice Rutherford's limited remedy of striking down and severing the political and religious motive requirement may not be adequate because the broad Canadian definition applies to all violent acts intended to compel persons (as well as governments and international organizations) to act. Indeed, the remaining overbreadth problems in the definition of terrorist activities await further judicial or legislative pruning.

The *ATA* re-named and expanded the *Official Secrets Act* so that passing secrets to terrorist groups would be treated as a serious offence. Parliament, however, omitted to revise the oft-criticized offence of communicating or receiving any "secret official" information. In *R. v. O'Neill*, a case involving a reporter writing on Arar, this antiquated and poorly drafted offence was struck down on multiple substantive *Charter* grounds. The lack of any definition or classification system for secret official information rendered the offence overbroad and vague. There was no fault requirement, and the broad offence constituted a disproportionate limitation on freedom of expression.[53] Although the federal government defended the *ATA* in 2001 on the basis that it was consistent with the *Charter*, the ultimate determination of its constitutionality can only be made by the courts.

The *O'Neill* case is not without its ironies. The judge found that there was an abuse of process because the RCMP conducted its infamous search of the reporter's home and office in order to obtain information about who leaked false and damaging information about Maher Arar to her. Although this decision removes an old and overbroad offence, it comes at the cost of crime control since it makes it very unlikely that those who leaked information about Arar will be held to account. The Arar affair suggests that the government may claim secrecy to protect itself from embarrassment, while those with access to secret information may leak secrets when it is in their interest to do so. While the Supreme Court of Canada has recognized that Canada, as a net importer of intelligence, must take special care to protect secrets from disclosure,[54] this goal is in considerable tension with the objective of the fair prosecution of terrorist crimes.

The *Charter* and Terrorism Prosecutions
In *R. v. Stinchcombe*, the Supreme Court of Canada constitutionalized a broad right of the accused to the disclosure of relevant information in the Crown's possession. Indeed, disclosure requirements produced problems for Canadian terrorism prosecutions long before *Stinchcombe* as there may be compelling reasons not to disclose secret information obtained from foreign and domestic security intelligence agencies and vulnerable informants. At the same time, there may be compelling reasons to disclose such information in order to allow the accused to make full answer and defence and to ensure that innocent people are not convicted because of their associations with terrorists

or their extreme political and religious beliefs. These issues of disclosure and non-disclosure create very difficult dilemmas for prosecutors, defence lawyers, and judges.

In 1987, the Federal Court of Appeal ordered that an affidavit used to obtain a CSIS wiretap be disclosed to accused men charged with conspiracy to murder a visiting Indian cabinet minister. The Crown sought to introduce the wiretap, and the accused challenged the admissibility of the evidence under the *Charter*. The Court of Appeal overturned a trial judge decision that disclosure might reveal CSIS' methods on the basis that "the ends of national security are not tantamount to the ends of justice ... Assuming that its disclosure would not have a cataclysmic impact on our entire social order, it is not the ends of justice that may be subverted by disclosure of the affidavit."[55] A month later, the charges were withdrawn, and the director of CSIS resigned as a result of inaccuracies in the affidavit that was used to obtain the original CSIS warrant. This episode demonstrates that disclosure promotes not only fairness but also transparency and accountability.

Another prosecution of an alleged terrorist conspiracy collapsed in 1987 because of a refusal by the state to disclose a confidential informant who had provided key information to support a *Criminal Code* wiretap warrant.[56] The lead accused, Talwinder Singh Parmar, is widely believed to have been the principal perpetrator of the 1985 Air India bombings that killed 331 people. The trial judge found that the affidavit that was included in support of the wiretap should have been disclosed to allow the accused to challenge the warrant under section 8 of the *Charter* because disclosure was "compatible with the fundamental justice guarantee of s. 7 of the Charter."[57] The judge was sensitive to the "catch-22 position" of the accused, who, under the restrictive wiretap law in force, had to demonstrate fraud or material non-disclosure without having even seen the information that supported the warrant. As the trial court judge stated, even if the disclosure was something of a "fishing expedition" it was "a fishing expedition in what are now constitutionally protected waters."[58]

The approach taken to disclosure in *R. v. Parmar*, however, was not absolute in favouring the accused. Justice Watt recognized that the information could be edited before it was disclosed to protect the identities of confidential police informers, ongoing investigations, intelligence-gathering techniques, and the interests of innocent persons.[59] This approach was subsequently approved by the Supreme Court of Canada and is now codified in the *Criminal Code*. Editing, however, comes with a price. The state has to defend the adequacy of the warrant on the basis of the edited affidavit. Once the identifying information was edited out, the *Parmar* warrant could not be supported. The informer refused to allow his identity to be disclosed, and wiretap evidence illegally obtained without a valid warrant was, at the time, subject to an automatic exclusionary rule under the *Criminal Code*.[60] Thus, these cases raise the pressing question of how broad *Charter* disclosure obligations can co-exist with terrorism prosecutions. The issue of how the accused's rights to disclosure can be reconciled with the state's interests in protecting secret information will be a critical issue in the ongoing Toronto terrorism prosecution.

The main method by which the Crown can seek to avoid having to disclose information in terrorism prosecutions is to claim national security confidentiality over the material. In 1982, when the *Charter* was enacted, the courts had to accept such claims. They were precluded by statute from even examining information over which the Crown claimed national security confidentiality. This procedure was a remnant of the absolute state prerogative that the Supreme Court of Canada decisively rejected in *Operation Dismantle*. In 1982, the *Canada Evidence Act (CEA)* was amended to allow specially designated Federal Court judges to examine whether disclosure of information would harm national security before ordering non-disclosure.[61] Judges were, however, initially reluctant to even examine the information. In 1983, the Federal Court ordered non-disclosure of information in the trial of a former member of the RCMP's Security Service without examining the information that the accused claimed justified his break-in.[62] It also ordered non-disclosure of CSIS surveillance logs, wiretaps, and profiles as well as information about a key informer in a case involving charges of conspiracy to murder a Turkish diplomat, with the Federal Court judge incredibly asserting that "credibility of a witness is not the main issue to be determined even at trial but merely a side issue."[63] The criminal trial went on, and the accused were convicted, but only after the criminal trial judge had made an agonizing decision that a fair trial was still possible without the disclosure of information that no judge had examined.[64] In 1998, however, the Quebec Court of Appeal held that prolonged and systemic non-disclosure by the Crown of key information relating to an informant who participated in discussions of an alleged plot to blow up another Air India plane justified a stay of proceedings.[65]

In 2001, the *CEA* was again amended as part of the *ATA*. Parties were required to notify the attorney general of Canada of plans to introduce sensitive information in the proceedings in order to minimize the inefficiencies caused by the two-court approach to national security confidentiality claims. Specially designated Federal Court judges were allowed to balance the public interest in disclosure against the public interest in non-disclosure and to order partial disclosure and the use of summaries or admissions as a means of reconciling the rights of the accused with the state's interests in secrecy. Mandatory provisions for *in camera* hearings were provided in an attempt to protect state secrets, but the courts have subsequently held that such provisions constitute a disproportionate restriction on freedom of expression compared to the more tailored approach of giving judges the discretion to order closed hearings where necessary.[66]

The ability of the attorney general to make *ex parte* representations to the court about the need for secrecy has also been subject to *Charter* challenge in *Khawaja v. Canada*. In the context of an access to information request in *Ruby v. Canada*, the Supreme Court of Canada upheld *ex parte* representations in part because of recognition that Canada, as a net importer of intelligence, must take special care with secrets received from other countries.[67] In the context of criminal prosecutions, however, such care may threaten the accused's right to a fair trial. Nevertheless, Chief Justice Lutfy rejected Khawaja's challenge and ruled that any unfairness regarding disclosure was compensated by the ability of the Federal Court to appoint a security-cleared "friend of the court" to challenge the government's case for secrecy as well as to reaffirm the ability of the criminal trial judge to stay proceedings if nondisclosure made a fair trial impossible.[68]

Although Khawaja had been detained in 2004 and a trial of alleged co-conspirators was completed in London, United Kingdom, in late April 2007, the Canadian trial was only completed with a conviction in late October 2008. Even if the amendments to the *CEA* are ultimately found to be consistent with the *Charter*, this case demonstrates that Canada's two-court approach to balancing disclosure with secrecy produces significant difficulties and delay in the resolution of criminal charges. The two-court structure is a matter of the wisdom and workability of the legislation. It is not dictated in any way by the *Charter*, although the *Charter* does increase demands for disclosure.

Charter demands for disclosure have added a new dimension to the traditional dilemmas of whether to prosecute and risk disclosure or to decline prosecution in order to keep the secrets of Canada and her allies. A number of terrorism prosecutions have foundered on the requirement to disclose material involving confidential informants. At the same time, *Charter* standards of disclosure and full adversarial challenges play an important role in ensuring that the innocent are not convicted. The risk of wrongful convictions is acute in terrorism cases, and we should not lightly deny the accused full disclosure even if this includes material that Canadian and foreign security agencies would prefer to keep secret.

The *Charter* and Immigration Law

In *Singh*, Justice Wilson rejected arguments in 1985 that the *Charter* claims of non-citizens from India applying for refugee status should be treated on the basis that immigration is a privilege and that any real threat to the immigrants would be caused by the actions of foreign governments not subject to the *Charter*. As in *Operation Dismantle*, she stressed the obligation of the courts to enforce section 7 rights that apply to everyone. Subsequent cases have qualified the approach in *Singh* and have stressed that non-citizens have no right to remain in Canada.[69] Nevertheless, the *Singh* principle that holds that section 7 of the *Charter* binds the Canadian state in its treatment of non-citizens remains. It has become more important in the post-9/11 context in which Canada has used immigration law as anti-terrorism law.

Both before and after 9/11, Canadian officials were attracted to the lower standards of proof in immigration law and the increased provision for secrecy of information when dealing with non-citizens suspected of involvement in terrorism. These lower standards have not generally been evaluated by either the public or the courts in the context that non-citizens were declared by the Supreme Court of Canada to be a discrete and insular minority vulnerable to discrimination[70] or exposed to the dangers of miscarriages of justice in immigration law.[71] Rather, the focus has often been on the idea that non-citizens do not enjoy all of the rights of citizens.[72]

The most controversial immigration law procedure – security certificates – allowed six men suspected of involvement with terrorism to be detained on the basis of certificates signed by the ministers of immigration and public safety. Specially designated judges of the Federal Court reviewed the reasonableness of these certificates, but the government had a statutory right to present intelligence to the judge without the detainee or his lawyer being present. The Supreme Court of Canada in *Charkaoui v. Canada* found that this lack of adversarial challenge violated section 7 of the *Charter*.[73] It held that long-term detention under security certificates could be constitutional provided the affected person had regular judicial reviews of the necessity of detention and the stringency of conditions imposed on release. The Court summarily rejected arguments that the entire process violated the equality rights of non-citizens by arguing that the right to remain in Canada under section 6 of the *Charter* is restricted to citizens. This formalistic approach, however, ignores the vast procedural protections that citizens accused of terrorism offences possess in contrast to non-citizens who are subjected to security certificates.

The Court delayed a declaration of invalidity for a year to enable Parliament to select the precise means of an adversarial challenge to the secret intelligence presented to the court to support the security certificate. The deferential remedy in *Charkaoui* illustrates the reluctance to dictate the terms of a revised security certificate process to the government as well as the possibility of dialogue between courts and legislatures under the *Charter*. The crucial issue to be decided is whether the security-cleared counsel is restricted from communicating with the detainee after having seen the secret information, as in the British special advocate system, or whether the lawyer is allowed to consult with the affected person and demand further disclosure from the government, as was done in the Arar Commission as well as under the Security Intelligence Review Committee procedures previously used to review security certificates. In its reply to *Charkaoui*, Parliament opted for the more limited British special advocate model. The new legislation allows a security-cleared special advocate to examine and challenge the secret information and to challenge the government's claims that the information must be kept secret. The reply legislation also allows the presiding Federal Court judge to authorize the security-cleared special advocate to demand further disclosure or discuss matters with the affected person after having seen the secret information if "necessary to protect the interests of the permanent resident or foreign national."[74]

One of the problems of security certificates is the long period of delay created by their ultimate remedy, which is the deportation of the non-citizen. In its 2002 decision in *Suresh v. Canada*, the Supreme Court of Canada indicated that the courts should generally defer to ministerial determinations of whether there was a substantial risk of torture if the detainee was deported.[75] In the companion case, *Ahani v. Canada*, the Court deferred to ministerial determinations that a person could be deported to Iran without a substantial risk of torture.[76] The Court also held in *Suresh* that while deportation to torture would generally violate the *Charter*, there might be "exceptional circumstances" when such action, even though in breach of international law, could be held to be consistent with the *Charter*.[77] A significant amount of delay involving security certificates has been caused by litigation surrounding whether the return of terrorist suspects to Egypt, Syria, and Algeria would result in torture and whether the exceptional circumstances contemplated by the Court in *Suresh* exist. The courts have so far held that there are no exceptional circumstances that justify deportation to torture.[78]

Canada and the Supreme Court of Canada have received international criticism for contemplating that there might be an exception to the right not to be deported to face torture. Any decision by a court that there would be exceptional circumstances that would justify deportation to torture under the *Charter* would place Canada in clear breach of its international law obligations. The decision by the Court in *Khadr* to provide a *Charter* remedy for Canada's participation in a violation of international law,[79] as well as provisions in the reply legislation to *Charkaoui* that prohibit the use of intelligence obtained by torture or cruel, inhumane, or degrading treatment,[80] suggest that both the Canadian judiciary and Parliament have little appetite to make use of an exception for torture that the Supreme Court of Canada regrettably appeared willing to contemplate in the immediate aftermath of 9/11.

The Limits of *Charter* Litigation

Although *Charter* litigation and its threat can restrain executive and legislative national security action, there are important limitations. The work of the Arar Commission, both with respect to reviewing the actions of Canadian officials who failed Maher Arar and recommending enhanced review mechanisms, underlines the importance of review – and not just litigation – in applying the values of the *Charter* to the often secret national security activities of the state.[81] The *Charter* cannot, however, be used to force governments to ensure that review mechanisms keep pace with intensified and increasingly integrated national security activities. The same is true with respect to the work of Canada's signals intelligence agency, the CSE. Although the issue of whether ministerial authorizations for the CSE intercepts are consistent with the *Charter* is interesting, it is likely to remain hypothetical given the secrecy of the CSE's activities and the reluctance to introduce CSE intercepts in criminal prosecutions. Fortunately, the CSE is subject to review by an independent commissioner to ensure that its activities are legal. A parliamentary committee has recently recommended that the CSE commissioner be given the explicit power to report on violations of the *Charter* and the *Privacy Act*.[82] Interestingly, such a review will likely be more important than any *Charter* litigation that might attempt to challenge the CSE's activities.

Another fundamental limitation of *Charter* litigation is that it does not apply to the actions of foreign governments, even when they act in close co-operation with Canadian officials. In a series of cases, the Supreme Court of Canada has held that the *Charter* does not apply to foreign police officers, even when they act in close co-operation with the Canadian police.[83] The integrated nature of many international terrorism investigations in the post-9/11 era presents a real risk that the Canadian government will contract out dubious work to its allies, and this action would mitigate the restrictions placed on the CSE, CSIS, and the Canadian police in their terrorism investigations. Only strong and independent review bodies that share information and, when necessary, conduct integrated reviews can ensure that such contracting out does not occur. The work of the Arar Commission is particularly relevant, not only with respect to its findings that Canadian officials did not contract out dirty work to the Americans or the Syrians, but also in its recommendations for enhanced review powers. However, the Canadian government has not acted on these recommendations, and this fact presents a danger that the values and restraints of the *Charter* will not be applied to the day-to-day national security activities of Canadian officials.

The Dangers of *Charter*-Proofing

When applying the *Charter* to Cabinet decisions in *Operation Dismantle*, the Supreme Court of Canada stressed that it was not judging the wisdom or effectiveness of the government's policy. Although this argument was made in defence of judicial review, it also has implications for the limits of *Charter* review. While legislatures, and, in particular, the attorney general, have a duty to consider and respect the *Charter* when devising legislation, there are

dangers in relying on a *"Charter*-proofing" strategy as the prime consideration in making security policy.[84] One danger is that the government's claims
may turn out to be wrong. The government's claim that the *ATA* was consistent with the *Charter* have been belied by recent decisions striking down the
religious and political motive requirement as an unjustified violation of
fundamental freedoms and striking down mandatory publication bans as a
disproportionate restriction on freedom of expression.[85]

Another danger is that the government will place more emphasis on
complying with the minimum standards of the *Charter* than on devising
wise and effective security policies.[86] Although *Charter* lawyers within government have an important role to play,[87] they should not dictate policy.
As well, we should not assume that policies that go as far as the *Charter*
allows are necessarily the best or most effective. The government largely
succeeded in *Charter* proofing investigative hearings. At the same time, investigative hearings are blunt and coercive instruments. They can be unfair
if applied to reluctant witnesses from close-knit communities who may
genuinely fear that they will be harmed if they co-operate with authorities
in terrorism investigations. In this respect, they can be a band-aid for the
need for effective source and witness protection. When applied to people
who may turn out to have been involved with terrorism, investigative hearings can be a poor policy response because *Charter* immunity requirements
may make subsequent prosecutions difficult if not impossible. Premature
use of investigative hearing can create broad immunity trails. The fact that
investigative hearings have been found to be consistent with the *Charter*
does not make them a wise or effective instrument of anti-terrorism policy.

The government won its *Charter* battle with respect to investigative hearings but lost the larger war both with respect to the decision not to hold an
investigative hearing in the Air India prosecution and Parliament's decision
in March 2007 not to renew them. New legislation, however, has been
introduced that will restore investigative hearings without examining larger
issues concerning the protection of intimidated witnesses or the practical
effects of the use and derivative use immunity provisions, which will make
it extremely difficult to prosecute a person subject to an investigative hearing should that person turn out to have been involved in terrorism.[88] Similarly, the government has had some successes (and some failures) in making
section 38 of the *CEA* consistent with the *Charter*. Although mandatory
publication bans on all such hearings have been struck down, the courts
have so far upheld the right of the attorney general to make submissions
about secrecy without the defence being present. At the same time, the courts
have indicated that a security cleared "friend of the court" may be appointed
in some cases, a decision that could increase existing delays in terrorism
prosecutions. In addition, under the *Charter*, a criminal trial judge must

retain the right to stay proceedings if a non-disclosure order by the Federal Court makes a fair criminal trial impossible. There is a danger that the government may win its battles over *Charter*-proofing and lose the larger war with respect to the viability of terrorism prosecutions. None of Canada's allies uses the awkward two-court structure to protect information from disclosure. Although it eventually ended in a conviction, the *Khawaja* case was delayed eighteen months by secrecy litigation in the Federal Court. *Charter* compliance, therefore, is a necessary, but not a sufficient, condition for sound security legislation.

Charter litigation also does not address the practice, as found by both the Arar Commission and the Federal Court, of the government making excessive claims of national security confidentiality.[89] Such claims may not violate the *Charter*, but they risk delaying and ending terrorism prosecutions. They also create widespread skepticism, even when governments make legitimate claims of secrecy in situations where disclosure might jeopardize confidential informants and ongoing investigations. The government has been sent back to the drafting table, given the Supreme Court of Canada's decision in *Charkaoui* that the procedure used to introduce secret intelligence in support of security certificates violated section 7 of the *Charter*. It was relatively easy for Parliament to *Charter* proof the security certificate process by providing some adversarial challenge to the government's secret evidence. Yet, again, this approach raises the danger that the government might win its *Charter* battles but lose the larger war. Although security certificates may be temporarily *Charter* proofed by providing for British-style special advocates or other forms of adversarial challenge, real questions remain about the viability of using immigration law as anti-terrorism law. Immigration law cannot touch citizens who are involved with terrorism. Deportation of a terrorist may simply displace the terrorism as well as implicate Canada with countries that have dubious human rights records. It may be more effective to subject suspected terrorists to a fair and public criminal trial rather than give them the publicity victory of detention under security certificates.

The legislative response to *Charkaoui* will not end *Charter* challenges to security certificates. It is only a matter of time before the courts have to confront whether indefinite detention or restrictive house arrest without charge is consistent with the *Charter*.[90] The government's invocation of the *Suresh* exception to allow the detainees to be deported to Syria or Egypt is also a no-win proposition. Even if the government wins the *Charter* battle and establishes exceptional circumstances,[91] it will lose the larger war because deportation to torture is clearly unjust and violates international law. The sustainability of a national security policy under the *Charter* is an important factor in determining whether the policy should be adopted or retained, but it should not be the only factor. Parliament's response to *Charkaoui* does not address the broader problems of using immigration law as anti-terrorism law, particularly with respect to indeterminate detention and the difficulty of deporting terrorist suspects to countries with poor human rights records.[92]

The Benefits of the *Charter*

Despite the limits of *Charter* litigation and the dangers of *Charter* proofing, it would be wrong to end on a negative note. The *Charter* has the virtue of increasing accountability and respect for rights in the state's national security efforts. Despite strong traditions of judicial deference verging on abdication on national security matters, the Supreme Court of Canada has not hesitated to use the *Charter* to review the national security activities of the state. In *Operation Dismantle*, the Court rejected the idea that the national security activities of the state were immune from *Charter* review while also distinguishing whether a particular national security policy is wise from whether it violates the *Charter*. Until *Hape* in 2007, Canadian courts were willing to apply the *Charter* to Canadian officials who acted abroad, and this precedent resulted in an injunction preventing CSIS from questioning Omar Khadr in Guanantamo Bay.[93] The Court's unanimous 2008 decision in *Khadr* demonstrates that even after *Hape*, the Court is prepared to enforce the *Charter* rights of unpopular people, at least when Canadian officials acting abroad participate in violations of international law.[94] As a result of the foundations laid in *Operation Dismantle* by the work of principled and courageous judges such as Justices Wilson and Dickson, Canadian officials have been bound by the *Charter* in all of their national security activities.

The *Charter* has required Parliament to confront rights issues that it would otherwise have ignored or finessed. For instance, the *ATA* would have been less restrained without the *Charter*. Although they were allowed to expire by Parliament, both preventive arrests and investigative hearings were crafted with the *Charter* in mind. *Charter* standards of disclosure and fair trials have played – and will continue to play – an important role in helping to minimize the risk of miscarriages of justice in emotive terrorism cases. The Supreme Court of Canada's recent unanimous decision that Canada had participated in violations of the *Geneva Conventions* and the *Charter* when it interviewed Omar Khadr in Guantanamo Bay in 2003 and passed on information from the interviews to American officials may increase pressure on the Canadian government to address the fairness of his continued detention and pending trial by military commissions in Guantanamo.[95] Finally, the Supreme Court of Canada has required Parliament to address the utter lack of adversarial challenge to the secret intelligence it uses to support security certificates and has generally restrained the Canadian state from deporting people to face torture. Without *Charter* litigation, it is doubtful that Parliament would have seriously considered the rights claims of non-citizens accused of terrorism. Cases such as *Khadr* also demonstrate the important role of the court in reviewing executive action that in the national security area would often be conducted in secrecy and in the absence of explicit legislative authorization.

Conclusion

The benefits of the *Charter* in restraining the national security activities of the state are significant in terms of increasing accountability and respect for the rights of even unpopular people accused of terrorism. At the same time, there is a need for Parliament to ensure that security policies not only comply with the *Charter*, but are also wise and effective. There is also a need for Parliament to empower independent review bodies to apply the *Charter* to the vast array of the state's secret security activities. If, however, Parliament fails to do so, then individuals, including unpopular individuals such as the Khadrs, non-citizens detained under security certificates, and those accused of terrorism offences will still be able to make *Charter* arguments to independent judges. This is the way it should be in a free and democratic society that respects the rule of law.

Acknowledgments

I started work on this article a few months before Justice Bertha Wilson passed away. She was an inspiration as I worked on this article. Indeed, she has been an inspiration for me since I had the great privilege of clerking for her in 1988-89. I respectfully dedicate this chapter to her memory.

Notes

1 *Canadian Charter of Rights and Freedoms,* Part 1 of the *Constitution Act, 1982,* being Schedule B to the *Canada Act 1982* (U.K.), 1982, c. 11.
2 See generally Kent Roach, "The Limits of a Charter-Proof and Crime-Based Approach to Terrorism," in Ronald J. Daniels, Patrick Macklem, and Kent Roach, eds., *The Security of Freedom: Essays on Canada's Anti-Terrorism Bill* (Toronto: University of Toronto Press, 2001), 131-47.
3 *Operation Dismantle v. R.,* [1985] 1 S.C.R. 441 [*Operation Dismantle*].
4 *Canada (Justice) v. Khadr,* 2008 SCC 28 [*Khadr* 2008].
5 *Hunter v. Southam,* [1984] 2 S.C.R. 145.
6 *Reference re B.C. Motor Vehicle Act,* [1985] 2 S.C.R. 486.
7 *R. v. Stinchcombe,* [1991] 3 S.C.R. 326.
8 *Singh v. Canada,* [1985] 1 S.C.R. 177 [*Singh*].
9 *Charkaoui v. Canada,* 2007 SCC 9.
10 *Suresh v. Canada,* [2002] 1 S.C.R. 3 [*Suresh*].
11 *Operation Dismantle, supra* note 3, 473.
12 Ibid., 455.
13 *R. v. Cook,* [1998] 2 S.C.R. 597 [*Cook*].
14 *Khadr v. Canada,* 2005 FC 1076 at para. 44. I thank my colleague Audrey Macklin for her assistance in understanding this case.
15 *Khadr v. Canada,* 2007 FCA 182.
16 *Khadr* 2008, *supra* note 4, para. 31.
17 Ibid., para. 24.
18 *Geneva Conventions,* 12 August 1949, 1125 U.N.T.S. 3.

19   *Operation Dismantle, supra* note 3, 473.
20   *Khadr v. Canada,* 2006 FC 727 at para. 2.
21   Ibid., para. 128.
22   *Kamel v. Canada,* 2008 FC 338. See Craig Forcese, *National Security Law* (Toronto: Irwin Law, 2008), 517-18, as updated at http://www.nationalsecuritylaw.ca.
23   Kent Roach, *September 11: Consequences for Canada* (Montreal and Kingston: McGill-Queen's University Press, 2003), 158-63.
24   *Cook, supra* note 13.
25   *United States of America v. Burns and Rafay,* [2001] 1 S.C.R 283; and *Suresh, supra* note 10.
26   *R. v. Hape,* [2007] S.C.C. 26 [*Hape*].
27   *Amnesty International v. Canada,* 2008 FC 336 at para. 159. The court also rejected an alternative argument that the detainees remained in the effective control of Canadian officials as inconsistent with *Hape, supra* note 26, and its implicit overruling of *Cook, supra* note 13. At the same time, Canadian transfers of prisoners to Afghan authorities were stopped in the midst of public revelations about the conditions of confinement. This demonstrates that sometimes public opposition, as well as the threat of *Charter* litigation, may be effective in changing governmental behaviour. One problem with relying on such political pressures is that so much activity in the national security field remains secret, perhaps because of the overclaiming of secrecy by the government.
28   *Khadr* 2008, *supra* note 4, para. 34.
29   Ibid., paras 22-26 and 31.
30   For a decision balancing the government's secrecy claims based on harms to national security and international relations against Khadr's claims to disclosure, see *Khadr v. Canada,* 2008 FC 807.
31   On these changes, see Kent Roach, *Due Process and Victims' Rights: The New Law and Politics of Criminal Justice* (Toronto: University of Toronto Press, 1999); Jamie Cameron, ed., *The Charter's Impact on the Criminal Justice System* (Toronto: Carswell, 1996); Michael Mandel, *The Charter of Rights and Freedoms and the Legalization of Politics in Canada,* revised edition (Toronto: Thompson, 1994); James B. Kelly, *Governing with the Charter* (Vancouver: UBC Press, 2005); and Jamie Cameron and James Stribopoulous, eds., *The Charter and Criminal Justice: Twenty-Five Years Later* (Toronto: LexisNexis, 2008).
32   *Hunter v. Southam,* [1984] 2 S.C.R. 145 at para. 43.
33   *R. v. Atwal,* [1987] 36 C.C.C. (3d) 161 (Fed. C.A.).
34   *Anti-Terrorism Act,* S.C. 2001, c. 41.
35   Stanley Cohen argues that ministerial authorizations are a restraint on the activities of the Communications Security Establishment and "the norm in the countries of the common law world with which Canada is ordinarily compared." See Stanley Cohen, *Privacy, Crime and Terror* (Toronto: Butterworths, 2005), 231. Nevertheless, intercepts are generally not admissible in proceedings in the United Kingdom and are generally authorized by a judge of the *Foreign Intelligence Surveillance Act* court in the United States.
36   *R. v. Budreo* (1999), 142 C.C.C. (3d) 225 (Ont. C.A.).
37   *Criminal Code,* R.S.C. 1985, c. C-46, s. 810.01.
38   *Application under s. 83.28 of the Criminal Code,* [2004] 2 S.C.R. 248.
39   *Re Vancouver Sun,* [2004] 2 S.C.R. 332.
40   *Application under s. 83.28 of the Criminal Code, supra* note 38, para. 39.
41   Ibid., para. 6.
42   At the same time, the tenor of the parliamentary debate on these issues was very partisan and did not engage the merits. See Kent Roach, "Better Late Than Never? The Canadian Parliamentary Review of the Anti-Terrorism Act," *Choices* 13:5 (2007): 1-38.
43   *Canadian Bill of Rights,* S.C. 1960, c. 44.
44   Bill S-3, *An Act to Amend the Criminal Code (Investigative Hearings and Recognizance with Conditions),* 39th Parl. 2nd Sess., passed by Senate March 6, 2008.
45   *Reference re B.C. Motor Vehicle Act,* [1985] 2 S.C.R. 486.
46   See, for example, *Criminal Code,* s. 83.18(2), 83.19(2), 83.21(2).
47   Ibid., s. 83.01(1.1).
48   *R. v. Khawaja* (2006), 214 C.C.C. (3d) 349 at paras 25-26 (Ont. S.C.).

49 Ibid., para. 34.
50 Ibid., para. 73. See Kent Roach "Terrorism Offences and the Charter: A Comment on *R. v. Khawaja,*" *Canadian Criminal Law Review* 11 (2007): 271.
51 Commission of Inquiry into the Actions of Canadian Officials in Relation to Maher Arar, *Report of the Events Relating to Maher Arar Analysis and Recommendations* (Ottawa: Public Works and Government Services, 2006). The Arar Commission did not find that there was religious profiling, but this conclusion has been disputed by others. Julian Falconer and Sunil Mathai, "The *Anti-Terrorism Act* and the Arar Findings," *National Journal of Constitutional Law* 21 (2006): 49.
52 *Suresh, supra* note 10.
53 *R. v. O'Neill* (2006), 213 C.C.C.(3d) 389 (Ont. Sup. Ct.).
54 *Ruby v. Canada,* [2002] 4 S.C.R. 3 at para. 44.
55 *R. v. Atwal* (1987), 36 C.C.C. (3d) 161 at 190-91 (Fed. C.A.).
56 *Criminal Code,* R.S.C. 1985, c. C-46, s. 264.
57 *R. v. Parmar* (1987), 34 C.C.C. (3d) 260 at 276 (Ont. H.C.).
58 Ibid., 279.
59 Ibid., 281-82.
60 *R. v. Parmar* (1987), 31 C.R.R. 256 (Ont. H.C.) Justice Watt also held that the accused should be able to cross-examine the affiant on the warrant. *R. v. Parmar* (1987), 37 C.C.C. (3d) 300, affd (1990) 53 C.C.C. (3d) 489 (Ont. C.A.).
61 *Canada Evidence Act,* R.S.C. 1985, c. C-5.
62 *Goguen v. Gibson,* [1983] 1 F.C. 872, aff'd [1984] F.C.J. no. 13 (Fed. C.A.).
63 *R. v. Kevork* (1984), 17 C.C.C. (3d) 426 at 434 (F.C.T.D.).
64 *R. v. Kevork* (1985), 27 C.C.C. (3d) 523 at 537 (Ont. H.C.).
65 *R. v. Khela* (1998), 126 C.C.C. (3d) 341 (Qc. C.A.).
66 *Toronto Star v. Canada* 2007 FC 128 (T.D.).
67 *Ruby v. Canada,* [2002] 4 S.C.R. 3.
68 *Khawaja v. Canada* 2007 FC 463, affd 2007 FCA 388 [*Khawaja* 2007]. For a subsequent decision in which a security cleared lawyer was appointed to provide adversarial challenges to the government's claims of secrecy, see *Canada v. Khawaja* 2008 FC 560.
69 *Chiarelli v. Canada,* [1992] 1 S.C.R. 711 [*Chiarelli*]; and *Medovarski v. Canada,* 2005 SCC 51 [*Medovarski*].
70 *Andrews v. Law Society of British Columbia,* [1989] 1 S.C.R. 149.
71 Kent Roach and Gary Trotter, "Miscarriages of Justice in the War against Terrorism," *Penn State Law Review* 109 (2005): 1001-10.
72 *Chiarelli, supra* note 69; and *Medovarski, supra* note 69.
73 *Charkaoui v. Canada,* 2007 SCC 9 [*Charkaoui*].
74 *An Act to Amend the Immigration and Refugee Protection Act,* S.C. 2008, c. 3, s. 85.2(c).
75 *Suresh, supra* note 10.
76 *Ahani v. Canada,* [2002] 1 S.C.R. 72.
77 *Suresh, supra* note 10, para. 78.
78 *Re Jaballah,* 2006 FC 1230 (rejecting the government's argument that exceptional circumstances justify the deportation of a terrorist suspect to Egypt).
79 *Khadr* 2008, *supra* note 4.
80 *Act to Amend the Immigration and Refugee Protection Act, supra* note 74.
81 Commission of Inquiry into the Actions of Canadian Officials in Relation to Maher Arar, *supra* note 51; and *A New Review Mechanism for the RCMP's National Security Activities* (Ottawa: Public Works and Government Services, 2006).
82 *Rights, Limits, Security: A Comprehensive Review of the Anti-Terrorism Act and Related Issues,* Final Report of the Standing Committee on Public Safety and National Security (Ottawa: Parliament of Canada, 2007) at 56. *Privacy Act,* R.S.S. 1978, c. P-24.
83 *Schreiber v. Canada,* [1998] 1 S.C.R. 841; *R. v. Terry,* [1996] 2 S.C.R. 607; and *R. v. Harrer,* [1995] 3 S.C.R. 562.
84 Kent Roach "Not Just the Government's Lawyer: The Attorney General as the Defender of the Rule of Law within Government," *Queens Law Journal* 31 (2006): 598.
85 *R. v. Khawaja* (2006), 214 C.C.C. (3d) 349; and *Toronto Star v. Canada,* 2007 FC 128 (T.D.).

86   Roach, *supra* note 2, 133-35.
87   On the role of the Department of Justice in shaping policy for compliance with the *Charter,* see James B. Kelly, *Governing with the Charter* (Vancouver: UBC Press, 2005).
88   *An Act to Amend the Criminal Code, supra* note 44. See also Kent Roach, "Compelled Self-Incrimination in Terrorism Investigations: A Comparison of Canadian Investigative Hearings and American Grand Juries," *Cardozo Law Review* 30 (2008): 1089.
89   Commission of Inquiry into the Actions of Canadian Officials in Relation to Maher Arar, *supra* note 51, 302-3; *Khawaja* 2007, *supra* note 68, para. 150; and *Canada v. Arar Commission,* 2007 FC 766 at para. 91.
90   The Supreme Court of Canada in *Charkaoui, supra* note 73, approved the releasing of security certificate detainees under house arrest while also stressing they would have a right to periodic reviews of the conditions of their confinement. Shortly after, a man from Egypt with alleged Al Qaeda links, Mahmoud Jaballah, was ordered released subject to over $43,000 being provided in bail, electronic and video monitoring, house arrest with limited exceptions, prohibition on the use of telephone and computers, and consent to the recording of any telephones in the house. *Re Jaballah, supra* note 78. This case raises the question of whether such tight restrictions are sustainable in the long run.
91   The Federal Court has found that the Canadian government has failed to establish exceptional circumstances that would justify deporting Mahmoud Jaballah to Egypt where he would face a substantial risk of torture. *Re Jaballah, supra* note 78, paras 80-83.
92   Kent Roach, "*Charkaoui* and Bill C-3: Some Implications for Anti-Terrorism Policy and Dialogue between Courts and Legislatures," *Supreme Court Law Review* 42 (2008) 281-353.
93   *Hape, supra* note 26. See also Kent Roach, "*R. v. Hape* Creates Charter-Free Zones for Canadian Officials Abroad," *Criminal Law Quarterly* 53 (2007): 1.
94   *Khadr* 2008, *supra* note 4.
95   The Court's ruling could, perhaps, be distinguished on the basis that changes have been made to the legal procedures used at Guantanamo Bay since 2003 when Omar Khadr was interviewed by CSIS officials. The United States Supreme Court has, however, subsequently found in *Boumediene v. Bush,* 553 U.S. (2008), that the legal regime at Guantanamo still violates American domestic constitutional guarantees of habeas corpus.

9
Canadian Language Rights: Liberties, Claims, and the National Conversation
Graham Fraser

Despite the natural tendency to celebrate the twenty-fifth anniversary of the *Canadian Charter of Rights and Freedoms*, it is useful to remember that the patriation of the *British North America Act, 1867, (BNA Act)* and its amendment with a *Charter* occurred over the objections of the Quebec National Assembly.[1] In the context of the *Charter's* anniversary, it is easy to lose sight of the feelings of pain and loss that were felt in Quebec – and not simply among sovereignists. As a former journalist who covered the patriation round of constitutional politics, I know an English-speaking resident of Quebec City at the time – and a strong federalist – who wept watching the April 17, 1982 signing ceremony because of Quebec's absence. Nevertheless, the significance of the *Charter* in the development of language rights cannot be overstated. Indeed, the history of the *Charter* is intimately entwined with the debate over language rights.

F.R. Scott, one of those individuals who spent his career stressing the importance of a *Charter* – and who inspired Pierre Trudeau – was a key member of the Royal Commission on Bilingualism and Biculturalism in the 1960s. He began a 1949 article on human rights and fundamental freedoms with the remarkably clear statement: "To define and protect the rights of individuals is a prime purpose of the constitution in a democratic state."[2] When the *Charter* became part of Canada's constitution in 1982, language rights were enshrined in sections 16 to 23. Since entrenchment, they have sometimes been overshadowed by the focus on equality rights, as expressed in section 15.

In this spirit, this chapter will argue that language rights are equality rights. And the debate over equality rights – the difference between formal equality and substantive equality, for example, or the tension between individual and collective rights – has had a substantial impact on the changing landscape of language rights in Canada and will continue to do so. So what are language rights, anyway? Are they individual rights? Collective rights? What do they actually mean? What is intriguing about language rights as defined in the *Charter* is that they are both a freedom and a right: a kind of personal armour to fend off interference and an engine for social change. In part because of the *Charter*, and the Supreme Court of Canada's decisions on language cases, Canada's language disputes have become part of a contemporary international discussion on language. For, as Phil C.W. Chan wrote, "language is essential to one's identity."[3]

In considering the *Charter*, it is easy to think that rights and freedoms are almost synonyms. Yet, they are not. Rights require a change in behaviour. And language rights are no exception. For most of Canada's first century, language rights were, at best, limited and constrained and, at worst, eliminated. Since 1982, building on a conversation on language that began with the Royal Commission on Bilingualism and Biculturalism, the *Charter* has set off a chain of events that have started a process of restoring language rights, changing the behaviour of governments, and creating a new dynamic for linguistic minorities in Canada. English and French are Canadian languages that belong to all Canadians. The *Charter* has accelerated a process to make this claim a reality.

This chapter will be organized into three sections. The first section explores the nature of language rights and their limited protection before the introduction of the *Charter* in 1982. While the introduction of the *Charter* was a significant event in the protection of language rights, it did not begin the national conversation on language. In fact, the *Charter* was the latest attempt to refine a conversation that began with the joining of Upper and Lower Canada in 1841 and the union of British North America in 1867. The second section explores the development of language rights as a dialogue between Parliament, the provincial legislatures, and the courts since the *Charter*'s introduction and the implications of this dialogue for the *Official Languages Act*.[4] The concluding section reflects on the national conversation twenty-five years after the entrenchment of the *Charter* and ends with a consideration of the Court Challenges Program and its modified reinstatement by the Harper government in June 2008.

Language Guarantees before the *Charter*

In an international and historical context, language has been included in treaties and covenants since the 1516 Treaty of Perpetual Union between the King of France and the Helvetic state and has involved various protections of minority groups to maintain and use their language.[5] However, in many discussions of rights, over the centuries – including language rights – there has been a kind of dualism. Roman law made a distinction between rights *in rem* (rights attached to a place or property rights) and rights *in personam* (rights of the individual). In 1774, during the debate on the *Quebec Act* in the British House of Commons, Edmund Burke referred to two categories of rights: the rights of human conquest and the rights of human nature.[6] In a contemporary context, Peter Jones distinguishes between "claim rights," which are rights that require a duty to be performed, and "liberty rights," which are actions that one is not prohibited from performing.[7] In terms of language rights, linguist Heinz Kloss makes a distinction between "tolerance-oriented" language rights and "promotion-oriented" language rights – a slightly different, more generous version of Burke's dichotomy between rights of conquest and rights of human nature and Jones' categories of liberty rights and claim rights.[8]

Jones' distinction between liberty rights and claim rights is a particularly useful one in looking at language rights, for they are clearly in both categories. F.R. Scott wrote in 1949 that "[a] Bill of Rights, of any kind, is a shield for defence," and language rights represent the protection of a liberty to speak a language.[9] These are passive, protective rights to be, in effect, left alone. However, they are also "claim rights" (or, as Scott put it in the next sentence, "a sword for attack"), which, for Scott, meant the right to be responded to, and provided services, in one's language, by the state.

The *BNA Act* had very limited rights but, as Scott points out, there were more definite protections included for groups – linguistic and religious minorities – than for individuals: "The guarantee for the use of two languages, for instance, and for denominational schools are group freedoms."[10] Indeed, some of the parliamentarians who debated the *BNA Act* realized that even those limited rights would have some long-term effects. During the debate in the New Brunswick House of Assembly in June 1866, Bliss Botsford argued that it should be one language or the other: "Not only is the difference of race to be perpetuated, but they provide for the continuance of two languages in the federal government and federal courts ... Instead of these differences of race and language being abolished or confined to places where they previously existed, we find that this class distinction is to be propagated and engrafted on provinces where it has never been before."[11]

It took a while for substantive language rights to be realized. In the decades following Confederation, language rights in Manitoba, Alberta, Saskatchewan, and Ontario were abolished before there was any thought of their being "propagated and engrafted" where they had never been before. It was not until the years that followed the Second World War – the years during which the *Universal Declaration of Human Rights* at the United Nations was introduced, ratified, and debated – that the idea of a bill of rights began to be seriously considered in Canada.[12] However, while the subject was debated in Parliament, considered in committee, and became the subject of several legal analyses such as Scott's, there was little reference to language rights. There was, however, certainly an awareness of the difference between granting a freedom and acknowledging a right.

Sixty years ago, the Deputy Minister of Justice, F.P. Varcoe, appeared before a parliamentary joint committee that was studying the possibility of a Human Rights Charter and defined what a right is, as compared to a freedom. A freedom, he said, is the benefit or advantage a person derives from the absence of legal duties. A right, Varcoe said, is quite different: "A right, according to this view, connotes a corresponding duty in some other person, or the state towards the person holding the right ... If, for example, a person has the right to education, there is a corresponding duty upon the state to provide it."[13] There was, therefore, a clear statement of what Peter Jones, almost fifty years later, would define as a "liberty right" and a "claim right." Language rights, clearly, are both.

Parliament, beginning in the early 1960s, began to respond to the obvious disparities – political, economic, and social – that existed between English-speaking and French-speaking Canada. In 1962, Créditiste Members of Parliament – many of whom spoke no English – complained that the Parliament of Canada was an overwhelmingly English-speaking institution: the Orders of the Day were in English only, the rules of procedure were in English only, the menus in the parliamentary restaurant were in English only, and the security guards spoke no French. In 1962, in an extraordinary memo, Maurice Lamontagne, then an economic advisor to Lester Pearson (and future member of his cabinet), laid out his recommendations for the next Liberal government. Lamontagne argued that it was up to the Liberal Party to set out – and achieve – three concrete objectives. First, the patriation of the Constitution and, as he added, "it must include a declaration of human rights covering federal and provincial areas." Second, the creation of a national flag and a national anthem that would, he said, leave no doubt about the sovereignty of the country. "Finally, all federal institutions must become bilingual and be the concrete demonstration of our bilingualism," he wrote. "These three objectives will constitute the immediate goals for the next Liberal government. If we want to maintain the integrity of Canada and assure our life together, the federal government must become as soon as possible and as completely as possible the synthesis and the symbol of a truly bicultural Canadianism."[14]

Lamontagne was not the only one thinking in these terms. In his memoirs, Brian Mulroney quotes from a note he wrote to John Diefenbaker in January 1962, in which he recommended, among other things, that Diefenbaker should "let it be known that henceforth bilingualism will be considered as a requisite for advancement into the higher reaches of the civil service."[15] The process was neither as quick nor as complete as Lamontagne had hoped. In fact, it can be argued that a whole series of unanticipated and unintended consequences from political acts has led to the creation of a new dynamic that has, itself, reinforced the nature of the national conversation. Thus, the Front de libération du Québec bombings in the spring of 1963 accelerated the creation of the Royal Commission on Bilingualism and Biculturalism, and General de Gaulle's "Vive le Québec libre!" speech in 1967 and the repercussions laid the groundwork for widespread acceptance of its recommendations. These recommendations led to the *Official Languages Act* in 1969 and the creation of the position of Commissioner of Official Languages in 1970.[16] The Gens de l'Air crisis in the summer of 1976 contributed to the election of the Parti Québécois in November, and this election muted much of the criticism of federal language policy in the rest of Canada. The failure of the Quebec referendum on sovereignty association in 1980 made it possible for Pierre Trudeau to patriate the Constitution with a charter of rights in 1982, and the *Charter* led to the amendment of the *Official Languages Act* in 1988.[17] Indeed, Quebec's use of the notwithstanding clause for its language law in 1989 was a factor in the failure of the Meech Lake Accord in June 1990. Finally, this failure strengthened support for Quebec's sovereignty, but the failure of the Quebec referendum in 1995 resulted in the Supreme Court of Canada's decision in *Reference re Secession of Quebec* and the *Clarity Act*.[18] For almost half a century, the conversation over language and language rights was critical to the constitutional and political evolution of Canada.

In 1963, almost immediately after becoming prime minister, Lester Pearson appointed the Royal Commission on Bilingualism and Biculturalism, which told Canadians in 1965 that Canada was passing through the greatest crisis in its history. The commission addressed the paradox of official bilingualism – a paradox that is still widely misunderstood. An official languages policy does not exist to require everyone to learn two languages – although, obviously, if no one is bilingual the policy cannot succeed. Forty years ago this fall, Pierre Trudeau, then Minister of Justice, laid out the fundamental principles of language rights during a speech to the Canadian Bar Association in September 1967: "While language is the basic instrument for preserving and developing the cultural integrity of a people, the language provisions of the British North America Act are very limited ... I believe that we require a broader definition and more extensive guarantees in the matter of recognition of the two official languages. The right to learn and to use either of the two official languages should be recognized. Without this, we cannot assure every Canadian of an equal opportunity to participate in the political, cultural, economic and social life of this country."[19] There are two extraordinary things about this passage. The first is that Trudeau neatly blurs the definition of language rights, establishing them first as collective rights ("the basic instrument for preserving and developing the cultural integrity of a people") and then describing them as individual rights ("without this, we cannot assure every Canadian of an equal opportunity to participate in the political, cultural, economic and social life of this country"). Second, Trudeau defines language rights quite narrowly as the right to learn and the right to use.

The entire edifice of language rights in Canada that has been created since then – the *Official Languages Act* (1969), the *Charter* (1982), and the amended versions of the act (1988 and 2005) – all rest on those two very simple, but quite sweeping, principles: the right to learn and the right to use. It would take another fifteen years, however, before those rights were enshrined in the *Charter*. As Trudeau said, the language provisions in the *Constitution Act, 1867*, were indeed very limited. Section 133 granted official status to the French and English languages in the Parliament of Canada and the federal courts as well as in the legislature and courts of Quebec. It did not prevent Ontario, Manitoba, Saskatchewan, and Alberta from moving at the beginning of the twentieth century to eliminate French as a language of instruction in schools. According to Robert Leckey, "Section 133 was never intended to create a constitutional framework for language or to establish official languages in Canada formally."[20] However, he added, "Section 133 ... is founded on the moral principle of cultural security and the political objective of national unity. It exemplifies the unwritten constitutional principle of protection of minorities."[21]

When Trudeau delivered this speech to the Canadian Bar Association, he was already working on a White Paper that emerged in January 1968 entitled *A Canadian Charter of Human Rights*. In this document, the rights were clarified slightly, "guaranteeing the right of the individual to deal with agencies of government in either official language" and "guaranteeing the right of the individual to education in institutions using as a medium of instruction the official language of his choice." A lot of detail remained to be filled in, as the white paper acknowledged.[22]

In 1982, the *Charter* consolidated equality and language rights. It also recognized through section 23 that English or French linguistic minority communities of a province have a right to primary and secondary instruction in their language where numbers warrant. Language rights were central to the *Charter* and enshrined in section 16 of that document. Recently, I found out how this entrenchment occurred. Senator Serge Joyal, then a Member of Parliament, was asked by then Prime Minister Pierre Trudeau to be the co-chair of the parliamentary committee examining the *Charter*. He agreed but on the condition that the principles of the *Official Languages Act* be included. The reason, according to Joyal, was due to an experience he had had in 1976. At that time, there was an intensive controversy over the right of French-speaking pilots to speak to French-speaking air controllers in French – what became known as the Gens de l'Air Affair.[23] Joyal took the Department of Transport and Air Canada to court – ultimately unsuccessfully – at his own expense. During the controversy, he was a guest on a popular television program, and the host, Lise Payette (later a Parti Québécois cabinet minister), welcomed him with the words: "Now, our next guest, Serge Joyal – our hero!"

Joyal decided then that a citizen should never have to be a hero to defend his or her language rights.

However, there are other direct lines that can be drawn from certain events to the *Charter*, in particular, from the Royal Commission on Bilingualism and Biculturalism's recommendations. In its first report, the Commissioners were very clear about the federal government's responsibilities: "The administration in Ottawa must be able to communicate adequately with the public in both languages," they wrote. "Federal government offices and Crown corporations across the country must be able to deal with people in either French or English ... everywhere, even in the completely unilingual sections of the country where there is contact with the traveling public, services should be available in both languages as a matter of course."[24] From this recommendation came Part IV of the *Official Languages Act: Communications with and Services to the Public.* This section also became entrenched as section 20 of the *Charter*, which protects the right to communicate with, and the right to receive services from, certain institutions in French or English. As Nicole Vaz and Pierre Foucher argue, "[t]he framers appear to have intended that where government services are destined for members of the public (i.e., persons outside the public service), the service must be made available in the official language of choice of the client."[25] The scope and nature of those rights continue to be matters of debate and litigation. The tension between individuals demanding that their rights be respected and the institutions that are obliged to respond continues to be felt.

Language Rights after Twenty-Five Years of *Charter* Review

When the *Charter* was introduced, I confess that I was a skeptic – for several reasons. First, it was deeply troubling that the *Charter* was introduced over the objections of the Quebec National Assembly, whose continued refusal to sign the Constitution has left a long shadow over Canadian political life for the last quarter-century. Second, the relationship between the courts and Parliament was a concern since I shared the view, expressed most cogently by the late Seymour Martin Lipset in 1990, that the *Charter* would lead to the Americanization of Canada: "Although the principles of parliamentary supremacy and consideration for group rights are retained, the Charter makes Canada a more individualistic and litigious culture, one that will place more stress on the enforcement of personal rights through adversary procedures rather than government adjudication."[26]

My view has changed, particularly with regard to language *and* language rights. The *Charter* has introduced a critical voice, but not the only voice, in a Canadian conversation about language that has gone on for the last forty-five years. Language rights have developed and advanced in Canada over the last quarter-century through an elaborate three-way discussion between Parliament, the provincial legislatures, and the courts.[27] In addition, Parliament has often engaged in its own dialogue, first with the Royal Commission on Bilingualism and Biculturalism and now with the Commissioner of Official Languages. It is a conversation in which the *Charter*, far from Americanizing Canada, has created a new jurisprudence, building on the critical relationship between Canada's English-speaking and French-speaking communities that has defined our past, underpins our present, and will continue to shape our future.

An official languages policy exists for two fundamental reasons: to protect the unilingual and to protect minority language communities. There are four million unilingual French-speaking Canadians in Canada, and one of the key reasons for the *Official Languages Act* to exist is to ensure that they get the same level of service from the federal government as the twenty million unilingual English-speaking Canadians. There are also a million French-speaking Canadians who live in minority communities across Canada, and almost a million English-speaking Canadians living in minority communities in Quebec. These communities deserve not only to survive but also to thrive, and, in 2005, the Parliament of Canada amended the *Official Languages Act* for only the second time to require the government to take positive measures to help these communities develop.

The *Charter* came about as a series of political compromises. Even though the Quebec National Assembly refused to sign the Constitution, section 23 was drawn up in a way that took account of the language debate that had been going on in Quebec. Yet, the fact that compromises occurred as a result of the three-way dialogue between Parliament, provincial legislatures, and the courts has not diluted the nature of those rights. In fact, a series of decisions by the Supreme Court of Canada has laid out, in eloquent terms, the way in which language rights in Canada are to be not merely protective but also transformative. For instance, in *Reference re Manitoba Language Rights* in 1985, a case involving the constitutionality of publishing provincial laws in English, despite the requirement under the *Manitoba Act* that all laws be published in English and French,[28] the Court wrote: "The importance of language rights is grounded in the essential role that language plays in human existence, development and dignity. It is through language that we are able to form concepts; to structure and order the world around us. Language bridges the gap between isolation and community, allowing humans to delineate the rights and duties they hold in respect of one another, and thus to live in society."[29] While the Court found the unilingual publication of Manitoba's laws to be unconstitutional as a violation of section 23 of the *Manitoba Act* and section 133 of the *Constitution Act, 1982*, the laws were allowed to continue in force for a period of five years.

Recognizing that a declaration of unconstitutionality would strike down all provincial laws and create a legal void, the Court provided Manitoba with a five-year period to translate all of its laws into French. While this was an onerous task for Manitoba, since it required the province to translate all of its laws since the province's entry into Confederation in 1870, it illustrates an important aspect of the national conversation involving language rights, namely the general weakness of political mechanisms to enforce constitutional guarantees before 1982. Manitoba had simply abandoned the constitutional requirement that it publish its laws in English and French as well as the strengthened national conversation after 1982 that had resulted from the significant remedies available to the courts under section 24(1) of the *Charter* and section 52 of the *Constitution Act, 1982*.

In *Ford v. Quebec (Attorney General)* in 1988, the Court ruled that sections of the *Charter of the French Language,* which prohibited languages other than French on public signs were a violation of section 2(b) of the *Charter* on freedom of expression.[30] Although this decision did not directly involve language rights, the Supreme Court of Canada commented on the powerful relationship that existed between expression and language:

> Language is so intimately related to the form and content of expression that there cannot be true freedom of expression by means of language if one is prohibited from using the language of one's choice. Language is not merely a means or medium of expression; it colours the content and meaning of expression. It is, as the preamble of the Charter of the French Language itself indicates, a means by which a people may express its cultural identity. It is also the means by which the individual expresses his or her personal identity and sense of individuality.[31]

While the *Charter of the French Language* was invalidated as being inconsistent with the *Charter*, the Quebec National Assembly quickly overturned this decision by invoking section 33 of the *Charter*, the notwithstanding clause. As a result, provisions of Bill 101 would continue in force for five years *notwithstanding* the Court's decision in *Ford*.

This decision should not be taken as evidence of the continued weakness of the national conversation on language rights. Once the use of the notwithstanding clause expired in December 2003, the Quebec government decided against renewing section 33 for a further five years. Instead, the Quebec National Assembly amended the *Charter of the French Language* to conform with *Ford*. As long as French is accorded "marked predominance" on public signs, the *Charter of the French Language* now allows for languages other than French on public signs.[32]

In *R. v. Beaulac,* the Court reversed an earlier decision in *Société des Acadiens v. Association of Parents* that restricted the right to be understood in both official languages in court.[33] In *Société des Acadiens,* the Court narrowed section 19(2) of the *Charter* to simply refer to the right of an individual to use either official language in a court proceeding. This right, according to the majority decision by Justice Jean Beetz, did not extend to the "right to be heard or understood in the language of his choice."[34] This approach to section 19(2) was abandoned by the Court in *Beaulac* according to the reasons presented by Justice Michel Bastarache:

> Language rights must in all cases be interpreted purposively, in a manner consistent with the preservation and development of official language communities in Canada ... To the extent that Société des Acadiens du Nouveau-Brunswick ... stands for a restrictive interpretation of language rights, it is to be rejected. The fear that a liberal interpretation of language rights will make provinces less willing to become involved in the geographical extension of those rights is inconsistent with the requirement that language rights be interpreted as a fundamental tool for the preservation and protection of official language communities where they do apply. It is also useful to re-affirm here that language rights are a particular kind of right, distinct from the principles of fundamental justice. They have a different purpose and a different origin.[35]

Further, the Court itself made it clear that there is no contradiction between individual rights and group rights as far as language is concerned: "The objective of protecting official language minorities, as set out in s. 2 of the Official Languages Act, is realized by the possibility for all members of the minority to exercise independent, individual rights which are justified by the existence of the community. Language rights are not negative rights or passive rights; they can only be enjoyed if the means are provided."[36] In these judgments, and many others, one can see how the Supreme Court of Canada has used the dynamic relationship between liberties and claims and built on the *Official Languages Act* and Quebec's *Charter of the French Language* to strengthen both the liberties and claims that are so interwoven in language rights.

The conversation between judges and parliamentarians has continued over the last twenty-five years. As a result of section 16 in the *Charter*, the *Official Languages Act* was amended and strengthened in 1988, leading the Court to observe that "[t]he 1988 Official Languages Act is not an ordinary statute. It reflects both the Constitution of the country and the social and political compromise out of which it arose ... it belongs to that privileged category of quasi-constitutional legislation which reflects certain basic goals of our society; and must be so interpreted as to advance the broad policy considerations underlying it."[37]

The members of the Supreme Court of Canada not only drew on the *Charter* but also on the *Charter of the French Language*. More recently, in 2005, parliamentarians from every party but the Bloc Québécois voted to strengthen the *Official Languages Act* by giving minority communities the right to legal recourse to ensure that the federal government takes positive measures to help their development. This change in the act was driven by parliamentarians, not the courts or the government. It renders the *Official Languages Act* an even more important lever to improve the status of French and English minority communities in Canada and helps them achieve substantial equality with the majority communities. While the amendment to the *Official Languages Act* was driven by parliamentarians, it was also a response to the jurisprudence of the courts. For instance, in the 2004 Federal Court of Appeal decision in *Forum des maires de la Péninsule acadienne c. Canada (Agence d'inspection des aliments)*, the court referred to Parliament the question of whether Part VII of the act imposed a legally enforceable duty on the federal government.[38] Parliament, in turn, responded by strengthening the *Official Languages Act* and giving minority communities legal recourse to enforce their rights.

In addition to the legislative realm, this dialogue has also played out in the courts, where we have witnessed a constant evolution in the interpretation of the *Charter* and equality and language rights legislation. For example, a major development in the law of equality in Canadian courts was the recognition of the concept of "substantive equality," which was initially understood in the context of challenges based on section 15 of the *Charter*. Substantive equality can be contrasted with the "formal" notion of equality, which asks whether the law treats all individuals the same. Substantive equality, then, recognizes that sameness of individual treatment does not always guarantee equality of result, particularly in cases in which individuals come before the law with different experiences, histories, advantages, and disadvantages. For instance, in *Beaulac,* the Supreme Court of Canada applied the principle of substantive equality to language rights, stating that "equality does not have a lesser meaning in matters of language."[39] Justice Bastarache, writing for the majority, declared that language rights must be given a liberal and purposive interpretation, in a manner consistent with the preservation and development of minority official language communities in Canada.

One of the most important areas in which the Court has acted to shape public policy and public institutions has been in the area of education. The "right to learn" that Pierre Trudeau defined as a key right to be protected was outlined in Section 23 of the *Charter*. At first glance, section 23 seems more limiting than inclusive. In contrast with section 12, which refers to "everyone" and section 15, which applies to "every individual," section 23 is quite specifically limited to "citizens of Canada." Indeed, much of the thrust of the section is focused, in reality, on who cannot attend minority language schools. The "right to learn" is clearly defined as the right to be educated in minority language schools, and there is no defined right of access to second-language learning for children in majority-language communities. The focus of section 23 has to be understood in the context of the political debate in Quebec that preceded the framing of the *Charter*. While Quebec refused to sign the *Constitution Act, 1982*, members of the National Assembly who debated the *Charter* were very aware that successive governments in Quebec – Jean-Jacques Bertrand in 1970 and Robert Bourassa in 1976 – had been defeated over the precise question of who should have access to English language education in Quebec.

Despite this limitation, a series of Supreme Court of Canada decisions have broadened and strengthened minority language education rights in Canada. In *Attorney General (Quebec) v. Quebec Protestant School Boards*, the Court struck down the so-called "Québec clause" in the Quebec language law, which restricted access to English school in Quebec to those whose parents had been educated in English in Quebec.[40] In the decision, the Court quoted Justice Jules Deschênes, who wrote that "[t]he Quebec clause enacted in the Quebec Charter is inconsistent with the Canada clause contained in the federal Charter."[41] Quebec's attempt to argue that restricting English school to those whose parents had been educated in English in Quebec was a reasonable limitation within the meaning of section 1 of the *Charter* was rejected by the Court. In its judgment, the Court made a distinction between a limitation and a denial of a right for the purposes of section 1 analysis. Since the Quebec government was determined to have *denied* access to English education through the Quebec clause, this provision of Bill 101 could not be saved as a reasonable *limitation* on section 23 of the *Charter*.

While *Protestant School Boards* is generally viewed as evidence that the *Charter* does not respect the language regime within Quebec, contemporary examples demonstrate that language policy has been the result of dialogue between Parliament, the Court, and the Quebec National Assembly. Unlike previous challenges to Bill 101 and the restrictions on English education in Quebec, a 2005 decision by the Supreme Court of Canada involved a challenge to Bill 101 from Francophone parents. In *Gosselin (Tutor of) v. Quebec (Attorney General)*, members of the linguistic majority argued that the inability to send their children to the English school system violated the right to equality protected under the Canadian *Charter* and the Quebec *Charter of Human Rights and Freedoms*.[42] The Supreme Court of Canada rejected this claim and upheld the educational regime within Quebec by relying on the testimony of former Justice Minister Jean Chrétien before the Special Joint Committee on the Constitution of Canada in 1981: "We are not determining education for the majority, but for the minorities ... Here, in the charter, we aim to protect the rights of the minority."[43] According to the Court, the challenge to Bill 101 by Francophone parents lacked merit: "The appellants are members of the French language majority in Quebec and, as such, their objective in having their children educated in English simply does not fall within the purpose of s. 23."[44] The decision in *Gosselin* demonstrates sensitivity for the *Charter*, for the rights of linguistic minorities, and for provincial control over education policy. This approach to minority language education policy, therefore, can be characterized as a dialogue of respect between the Supreme Court of Canada and the Quebec National Assembly.

The same day that the Supreme Court of Canada delivered *Gosselin*, it also rendered judgment in *Solski (Tutor of) v. Quebec (Attorney General)*, a case resulting from Quebec's approach to French immersion. Under the *Charter of the French Language*, French immersion was classified as education in French when it occurred outside Quebec and English-language education when it was provided within Quebec.[45] Until the decision in *Solski*, Quebec officials ruled that parents who had been educated in French immersion outside Quebec were unable to send their children to French immersion in Quebec. They had been educated in French, the reasoning was, and so they were not allowed to send their children to French immersion, which is operated by the English-language school system. Similarly, students coming from immersion in other provinces were found not to have taken "the major part" of their education in English and were thus unable to transfer to immersion in Quebec.

In *Solski*, the Supreme Court of Canada defined what constituted the "major part" of a child's education under the *Charter of the French Language*. The Court upheld the constitutionality of the *Charter of the French Language* and the rationale for limiting access to English school as a balancing act between the concerns of the Francophone minority outside Quebec and the English minority inside Quebec.[46] While the Court upheld the *constitutionality* of Bill 101, it found that the *administration* of the "major part" requirement by the Administrative Tribunal of Quebec – the body to which parents apply for approval to have their children educated in English – was inconsistent with section 23 of the *Charter*. Indeed, the Court cautioned against a quantitative approach to the "major part" requirement and reasoned that a qualitative approach would be consistent with section 23 and outlined the following criteria for the Administrative Tribunal of Quebec: how much time was spent in either language in an educational setting, the stage of education when the language of instruction was chosen, the availability of minority language education instruction, and, finally, whether the child experienced any disabilities or difficulties.

The Court also endorsed the common sense position that French immersion, while it provides instruction in French, is for English-speaking students such as Shanning Casimir, who had gone to a French immersion program in Ottawa for grades 1 and 2 and now, upon moving to Montreal, wanted to enrol in an English-language school: "Shanning Casimir was actually receiving education for Anglophones," the judges wrote. "She has a stronger link with the English linguistic community than the French."[47] However, the Court reiterated the need to balance competing interests and recognized the significance of language and education policy for Quebec: "The application of s. 23 is contextual. It must take into account the very real differences between the situations of the minority language community in Quebec and the minority language communities of the territories and the other provinces. The latitude given to the provincial government in drafting legislation regarding education must be broad enough to ensure the protection of the French language while satisfying the purposes of s. 23."[48]

In summary, it is this national conversation and this interaction of liberties and claims, rights and obligations, rights and the delivery of service that have made the language provisions in the *Charter*, as well as in the *Official Languages Act*, so dynamic and transformative. In twenty-five years, this conversation has changed the linguistic landscape of the country. It will continue to do so. The 2005 amendments to the *Official Languages Act* require the federal government and its departments and agencies to take positive measures to address the needs of minority communities and to enhance their vitality. Part VII of the *Official Languages Act* is one of the most potent tools currently available to minority official language communities in achieving substantive equality. It is this dialogue that has made the language rights protections of the *Charter* and the *Official Languages Act* meaningful, dynamic, and transformative for minority language communities in Canada. And it is this dialogue that will be critical in continuing to ensure that the federal government fulfills its obligations to enhance the vitality of these communities.

Conclusion

In 1970, as the work of the Royal Commission on Bilingualism and Biculturalism was coming to an end, F.R. Scott gave the sixth annual Manitoba Law School Foundation lecture and summarized much of the work that the Commissioners had done since 1963. He concluded with a look to the future: "Canadians must approach the language question with two special qualities: realism and goodwill," he said. "Realism means accepting facts. French Canada is a fact, and English Canada is a fact."[49] If Canadian federalism were to survive, he said, bilingualism would have to be sensibly applied. It was one – but not the only one – of the essential conditions for survival. The other essential quality was goodwill – the ability to see pluses as well as minuses, advantages along with difficulties. "To accept bilingualism means a greater respect for human rights, a greater domestic tranquility, and, above all, the development within our country of the richness and creative ability that have made England and France two of the great centers of western civilization," he said. "That it will give Canada a national identity unique in the Americas goes without saying."[50] The words still ring true. The conversation continues.

The Court Challenges Program: A Postscript
In 1978, the federal government responded to complaints about Quebec's *Charter of the French Language* by creating a program to fund court challenges by those who felt that their language rights had been unfairly constrained. In 1985, following the adoption of the *Charter* in 1982, the program was expanded to cover all equality rights. The program funded a number of key language cases, including *Mahé v. Alberta*, which established the right of Francophone minority communities to control French-language schools through their own school boards.[51] Seven years later, in 1992, the Mulroney government cancelled the program. In response, the then Commissioner of Official Languages, Victor Goldbloom, commissioned Richard Goreham to undertake a study of the program.[52] Goreham concluded that a number of issues remained to be clarified in all areas of language rights, that the process of judicial interpretation was incomplete, and that the Court Challenges Program should be maintained.[53] The program was reinstated in 1994, and it provided funding for, among other cases, the translation of expert evidence in *Doucet-Boudreau v. Nova Scotia (Minister of Education)* and *Arsenault-Cameron v. Prince Edward Island*, both of which clarified the nature of minority language education rights.[54]

On September 26, 2006, following an expenditure review, the Harper government eliminated funding for the Court Challenges Program. This cut resulted in 118 complaints being submitted to the Office of the Commissioner of Official Languages, most of which argued that, in eliminating funding for the Court Challenges Program, the government was in breach of its obligations under Part VII of the *Official Languages Act,* which requires the federal government to take positive measures for the growth and development of minority communities. In response to the complaints, the Office of the Commissioner of Official Languages conducted a major investigation and commissioned a study by constitutional lawyer and language rights authority Ingride Roy. The report concluded that, while the government has the right to govern – and review and revise its priorities, policies, and programs – it must respect the law and take into account its legislative commitments, duties, and roles. The investigation found no evidence that the government had given due consideration to the needs and interests of minority language communities in its decision-making process, as it is now required to do under Part VII of the act. The federal government disagreed, arguing that the lack of evidence that it had complied with its obligations did not prove that it was in contravention of the act.

The Fédération des communautés Francophones et acadienne (FCFA) took the government to court, and the Office of the Commissioner of Official Languages was granted intervenor status. In its intervention before the Federal Court on February 25 and 26, 2008, the Office of the Commissioner of Official Languages' legal counsel argued that the government had a two-part duty: the duty not to impede the development of official language minority communities and the duty to take specific measures to enhance their vitality. This implies that each federal institution must be aware of the particular needs and interests of these communities and their specificity. In June 2008, the government reached an out-of-court settlement with the FCFA that resulted in the government agreeing to create a new program to support linguistic rights. The new program will include a mediation component and an element of promotion of language rights as well as funding for court proceedings to focus on linguistic rights under the Constitution of Canada when mediation efforts have failed and a test case is involved. The case was a significant victory for the FCFA and confirmed the continuing need to develop jurisprudence in regard to language rights.

Acknowledgments
An earlier version of this text appeared in *Policy Options* in February 2007. My thanks to the legal staff at the Office of the Commissioner of Official Languages for some of the research into the court decisions cited in this article, to James B. Kelly for his expertise and attentive editing, and to L. Ian MacDonald, editor of *Policy Options*, for permission to re-use some of the same material.

Notes
1 For a description of this debate, see Graham Fraser, *René Lévesque and the Parti Québécois in Power*, 2nd edition (Montreal and Kingston: McGill-Queen's University Press, 2001), 279-320. *Canadian Charter of Rights and Freedoms*, Part 1 of the *Constitution Act, 1982*, being Schedule B to the *Canada Act 1982* (U.K.), 1982, c. 11. *Constitution Act, 1867* (U.K.), 30 and 31 Victoria, c. 3, s. 93.
2 F.R. Scott, "Dominion Jurisdiction over Human Rights and Fundamental Freedoms," *Canadian Bar Review* 27 (1949): 497.
3 Phil C.W. Chan, "Important Decisions of Hong Kong Courts in 2002: Language Rights, Foreign Offenders Sentencing and Immigration and Refugee Law," *Chinese Journal of International Law* 4 (2005): 219.
4 *Official Languages Act*, R.S.C. 1985, c. 31.
5 Fernand de Varennes, "To Speak or Not to Speak: The Rights of Persons Belonging to Linguistic Minorities," working paper prepared for the UN Sub-Committee on the Rights of Minorities (March 21, 1997), http://www.unesco.org/most/ln2pol3.htm.
6 *Quebec Act*, 1774, 14 George III, c.83 (U.K.).
7 Peter Jones, *Rights* (New York: St. Martin's Press, 1994).
8 Heinz Kloss, *The American Bilingual Tradition* (Rowley, MA: Newbury House, 1977), 21-22.
9 Scott, *supra* note 2, 534.
10 Ibid., 511.
11 Cited in Janet Ajzenstat, Paul Romney, Ian Gentles, and William D. Gairdner, eds., *Canada's Founding Debates* (Toronto: Stoddart, 2003), 350.
12 *Universal Declaration of Human Rights*, GA Res. 217(III), UN GAOR, 3d Sess., Supp. No. 13, UN Doc. A/810 (1948), 71.
13 Varcoe cited in Scott, *supra* note 2, 506.

14 Lamontagne's discussion is found in Graham Fraser, *Sorry, I Don't Speak French: Confronting the Canadian Crisis That Won't Go Away* (Toronto: McClelland and Stewart, 2006), 27.

15 Brian Mulroney, *Memoirs* (Toronto: McClelland and Stewart, 2007), 73.

16 *Official Languages Act,* 1969 (17-19 Elizabeth II, c.54).

17 *Official Languages Act,* 1988, c.38.

18 *Reference re Secession of Quebec,* [1998] 2 S.C.R. 217. *Clarity Act,* 2000, c.26.

19 Pierre Elliott Trudeau, *Federalism and the French Canadians* (Toronto: Macmillan of Canada, 1968), 55-56.

20 Robert Leckey, "Bilingualism and Legislation," in Michel Bastarache, ed., *Language Rights in Canada* (Cowansville, QC: Éditions Yvon Blais, 2004), 47.

21 Ibid., 48.

22 Hon. Pierre Elliott Trudeau, *A Canadian Charter of Human Rights* (Ottawa: Queen's Printer, 1968), 25-26.

23 See Sanford Borins, *Language of the Skies: The Bilingual Air Traffic Control Conflict in Canada* (Montreal and Kingston: McGill-Queen's University Press, 1983).

24 *Report of the Royal Commission on Bilingualism and Biculturalism,* Book I: *The Official Language* (Ottawa: The Queen's Printer, 1967), 98.

25 Nicole Vaz and Pierre Foucher, "The Right to Receive Public Services in Either Official Languages," in Bastarache, *supra* note 20, 266.

26 Seymour Martin Lipset, *Continental Divide: The Values and Institutions of the United States and Canada* (New York and London: Routledge, 1990), 225.

27 Peter Hogg and Allison Bushell, "The *Charter* Dialogue between Courts and Legislatures (Or Perhaps the *Charter of Rights* Isn't Such a Bad Thing after All)," *Osgoode Hall Law Journal* 35 (1997): 75-125.

28 Peter H. Russell, Rainer Knopff, and Ted Morton, eds., *Federalism and the Charter* (Ottawa: Carleton University Press, 1990), 626-27.

29 *Reference re Manitoba Language Rights,* [1985] 1 S.C.R. 721 at 744. *Manitoba Act,* 1870, R.S.C.

30 *Charter of the French Language,* R.S.Q. c. C-11.

31 *Ford v. Quebec (Attorney General),* [1988] 2 S.C.R. 712 at 748-49.

32 James B. Kelly, "The Courts, the Charter, and Federalism," in Herman Bakvis and Grace Skogstad, eds., *Canadian Federalism: Performance, Effectiveness, and Legitimacy,* 2nd edition (Don Mills, ON: Oxford University Press, 2008), 52.

33 *Société des Acadiens v. Association of Parents,* [1986] 1 S.C.R. 549 [*Société des Acadiens*]; and *R. v. Beaulac,* [1999] 1 S.C.R. 768 [*Beaulac*].

34 *Société des Acadiens, supra* note 33. Cited in Russell, Knopff, and Morton, *supra* note 28, 651.

35 *Beaulac, supra* note 33, para. 25.

36 Ibid.

37 *Canada (Attorney General) v. Viola,* [1991] 1 F.C. 373 at 386-87.

38 *Forum des maires de la Péninsule acadienne v. Canada (Food Inspection Agency),* [2005] 3 S.C.R. 906.

39 *Beaulac, supra* note 33, para. 22.

40 *Attorney General (Quebec) v. Quebec Protestant School Boards,* [1984] 2 S.C.R. 66.

41 Ibid., para. 17.

42 *Gosselin (Tutor of) v. Quebec (Attorney General),* [2005] 1 S.C.R. 238 [*Gosselin*]. *Charter of Human Rights and Freedoms,* R.S.Q., c. C-12.

43 Minutes of Proceedings and Evidence of the Special Joint Committee of the Senate and of the House of Commons on the Constitution of Canada (January 29, 1981), 108. Cited in *Gosselin, supra* note 42, para. 29.

44 *Gosselin, supra* note 42, para. 30.

45 *Solski (Tutor of) v. Quebec (Attorney General),* [2005] 1 S.C.R. 201.

46 Ibid., para. 9.

47 Ibid., para. 50.

48 Ibid., para. 34.

49 F.R. Scott, "Language Rights and Language Policy," *Manitoba Law Journal* 4 (1971): 243-57.

50 Ibid.

51   *Mahé v. Alberta*, [1990] 1 S.C.R. 342.
52   Richard Goreham, *Language Rights and the Court Challenges Program: A Review of Its Accomplishments and Impact of Its Abolition* (Ottawa: Office of the Commissioner of Official Languages, 1992).
53   Ingride Roy, *Study of the Legal Impact of the Elimination of the Court Challenges Program* (Ottawa: Office of the Commissioner of Official Languages, October 2007), 13.
54   *Doucet-Boudreau v. Nova Scotia (Minister of Education)*, [2003] 3 S.C.R. 3; and *Arsenault-Cameron v. Prince Edward Island*, [2000] 1 S.C.R. 3.

10
Explaining the Impact of Legal Mobilization and Judicial Decisions: Official Minority Language Education Rights outside Quebec
Troy Riddell

Supporters of official minority language education (OMLE) in Canada cele-brated the twenty-fifth anniversary of the *Canadian Charter of Rights and Freedoms* by pointing out the significant policy advances that had occurred since 1982.[1] Limits on access to English-language schooling in Quebec were struck down under the *Charter*, and, outside Quebec, francophone com-munities came to enjoy access to homogenous French schools with manage-ment and control powers. It is easy to view such developments as the natural consequence of entrenching OMLE rights in section 23 of the *Charter*. After all, section 23 was the cornerstone of former Prime Minister Trudeau's plan to use the *Charter* to promote a pan-Canadian nationalism (so much so that section 23 is exempt from the override clause). However, scratching the historical surface reveals that the current policy regime was anything but inevitable. The wording of section 23 deliberately did not include manage-ment and control powers for official minority language communities in order to appease provincial officials. Moreover, years after the Supreme Court of Canada released its landmark *Mahé v. Alberta* decision in 1990, which declared that section 23 did include a right to management and control at the upper end of the scale of "where numbers warrant," a number of OMLE supporters complained that the decision was not being implemented.[2] Meanwhile, there were significant numbers of francophones outside Quebec who were fighting against a vision of section 23 that promoted what they considered to be an overly segregated approach to language education (which had the potential to undermine Catholic education in some areas).

This chapter does not seek to address the normative arguments surround-ing OMLE policy. Rather, it seeks to explain how OMLE policies developed under the *Charter*. The chapter, therefore, serves as both a review of OMLE policy since the entrenchment of section 23 of the *Charter* and as a case study for studying the policy impact of legal mobilization and judicial deci-sions. Although OMLE developments in Quebec are included, the focus of the chapter is on OMLE policies outside Quebec. A primary reason for this is that Quebec's education system, despite some misgivings expressed by English-speaking communities in the province, was seen as a model for other provinces to follow in providing education to its linguistic minority.[3] More puzzling is why the provinces outside of Quebec, which, with few exceptions, did not feature homogenous francophone schools or francophone school boards prior to the *Charter*, all came to develop very similar OMLE regimes characterized by francophone schools and francophone school boards.

The next section of the chapter provides a descriptive overview of the evolution of OMLE policy in Canada. This section is followed by a brief overview of judicial impact literature. Two contrasting theoretical frameworks are highlighted. One views judicial impact as being dependent on such "top-down" factors as Supreme Court of Canada victories, the provision of resources for implementation, and public opinion. The other views judicial impact from more of a "bottom-up" perspective, which highlights discourse and emphasizes the inherently contingent nature of the impact of legal mobilization by groups. The penultimate section of the chapter analyzes OMLE policy development through the theoretical frameworks. It concludes that OMLE policy would not have changed as it did without certain "top-down" structural factors such as the entrenchment of section 23, judicial victories, and federal government funding, but that such an analysis would be incomplete and even misleading if it did not take into account the activities of official minority language interest groups, policy and legal discourse, and contingent historical dynamics.

OMLE Legal and Policy Development

This overview of OMLE policy development begins with a snapshot of the time period just prior to the *Charter*'s enactment (1978-82), then reviews the time period from the introduction of the *Charter* until the Supreme Court of Canada's 1990 decision in *Mahé*, and finishes by reviewing developments since *Mahé*. OMLE policy in each of the three time periods is evaluated with respect to the nature of instruction (French as a first language (FFL) programs as opposed to immersion); the type of facilities provided ("homogenous" French schools that offer FFL programs in distinct physical settings as opposed to "bilingual" or mixed schools); and how much management and control, if any, francophone parents have over FFL programs and French schools.[4]

Prior to the entrenchment of OMLE rights in the *Charter*, all ten provincial premiers at the 1978 premier's conference in Montreal agreed that each child of the official language minority is entitled to first-language education where numbers warrant but that the implementation of this principle would be up to the discretion of each province.[5] In Quebec, this pledge did not lead Premier Rene Lévesque to suspend provisions of Bill 101 that limited access to English-language education to the children of parents who were educated in English in Quebec (and children who had already started their education in English). Did other provinces outside of Quebec change their OMLE policies before the *Charter*'s introduction? Table 10.1 reveals that more provinces outside Quebec began to recognize the concept of FFL instruction and homogenous French schools after the 1978 declaration. However, only New Brunswick opted to give management and control powers to its francophone minority.

Table 10.1, however, may exaggerate somewhat the development of policy "on the ground." French immersion programs and FFL programs were often fused in their implementation, and, if schools provided FFL programming, it was frequently in conjunction with immersion programs, with some children even sharing the same classes.[6] There was little or no increase in the number of homogenous French schools in most provinces. For instance, although Nova Scotia's legislation was changed in 1981 to allow the minister to designate a school an "Acadian" school, no such designations were made until 1984 – two years after the introduction of the *Charter*.

When the proposed *Charter* was being examined by the Special Joint Committee on the Constitution of Canada in 1980-81, a number of actors urged the Trudeau government to add the right to administer schools and instructional programs to the official minority-language education guarantees. The Association culturelle franco-canadienne de la Saskatchewan, for example, called for the "recognition of the principle of control over, and management of, Francophone schools by Francophones."[7] The government did not accede to such requests. Justice minister Jean Chrétien informed the committee: "We did not go that far [providing the right to manage institutions] in the sense that education remains the responsibility of the province."[8] The final version of section 23 of the *Charter* grants the right to instruction in the minority language, which includes the right to facilities for such instruction where the numbers warrant, with such instruction and facilities to be paid out of public funds. The rights are attached to parents who must meet two qualifications: (1) the parent must be a Canadian citizen and (2) (a) the parent must have learned French first and still understand it (this goes for English in Quebec); or (b) the parent's primary school instruction must have been in the relevant minority language in Canada; or (c) the parent must have (or had) children in the relevant minority language primary or secondary schools in Canada.[9] Section 23 was used immediately by Quebec's English language school boards to challenge Quebec's Bill 101. In *Attorney General of Quebec v. Quebec Association of Protestant School Boards,* the Supreme Court of Canada struck down the law for denying parents (or children) who were educated in English in Canada access to English-language schooling in Quebec.[10] Since section 23 was designed at least in part to trump Bill 101, the decision was not a surprise.

Table 10.1

OLME policy 1978-82

	Instruction	Homogenous facilities	Management
	"Discretionary": the provision of FFL instruction is purely at the discretion of the minister or school board.	"Qualified No": some schools were de facto homogenous francophone schools.	"Qualified No": some schools were under the de facto control of francophone parents.
	"Qualified Mandatory": the right to FFL instruction is triggered upon a certain numerical threshold.	"Qualified Yes": homogenous FFL schools recognized in law and schools could be designated as such.	"Qualified Yes": francophone representation on existing school boards or territorial coverage of francophone school boards is relatively limited.
	"Mandatory": FFL instruction provided without numerical qualification.	"Yes": more positive recognition of homogenous schools in law and policy.	"Yes": school boards organized along linguistic lines, cover most of or the entire province, and are exclusively responsible for FFL programs and schools.

Policy changes from previous period are denoted by italics

BC	*Qualified Mandatory* (1978)	No	No
AB	Discretionary	No	No
SK	*Qualified Mandatory* (1978)	*Qualified Yes* (1978)	No
MB	Qualified Mandatory	Qualified No	Qualified No
ON	Qualified Mandatory	*Yes* (1979)	Qualified No
NB	Qualified Mandatory	*Yes* (1981)	*Yes* (1981)
NS	Discretionary (recognized in law 1981)	*Qualified Yes* (1981)	No
PE	*Qualified Mandatory* (1980)	*Qualified No* (1980)	*Qualified No* (1980)
NF	Discretionary (no law or regulation)	No	No

	Instruction	Homogenous facilities	Management
Totals*	Discretionary = 3 provinces (–3) Qualified Mandatory = 6 provinces (+3) Mandatory = 0 provinces	No = 3 provinces (–3) Qualified No = 2 provinces (+1) Qualified Yes = 2 provinces (0) Yes = 2 provinces (+2)	No = 5 provinces (–1) Qualified No = 3 provinces (0) Qualified Yes = 0 provinces (0) Yes = 1 province (+1)

* (n) = net change in this period

There was more variability in the political and legal responses to section 23 outside of Quebec. Whereas the Association canadienne-francophone de l'Alberta (ACFA) was rather slow to demand distinct French schools and management and control of schools, the Commission des écoles fransaskoises presented early in 1984 a detailed proposal to the Saskatchewan government for a province-wide French language school board with parent committees at each school. A period of (unsuccessful) negotiations with the government followed before litigation was commenced. Ontario francophone groups quickly launched litigation in May 1983 under section 23 for management and control rights, even though the Ontario government had released a white paper indicating a willingness to provide proportional francophone representation on school boards. In some provinces, there were tensions between francophone groups over OMLE policy leadership, and, in many provinces outside Quebec, there were disagreements within francophone communities about the desirability of homogenous French schools and francophone school governance. Some francophone parents were concerned about the implications of francophone schools and school governance for financial and human resources, the religious (Catholic) dimension of education, and the ability of their children to work and socialize in an English environment. Others, like a group of parents in Edmonton who called themselves the Bugnet group, favoured francophone schools and school boards because of problems with assimilation in mixed school environments and the deficiencies of French immersion programs.[11]

Citing the aforementioned problems with existing policy and section 23 of the *Charter*, the Bugnet group requested a French school in Edmonton to be operated by a francophone school board. After their requests were rebuffed at both the provincial and local levels, they launched a legal challenge (*Mahé v. Alberta*). Judicial decisions, such as the lower court decisions in *Mahé*, tended to emphasize that section 23 entailed the right to FFL instruction and included the right to homogenous French schools, although FFL instruction in distinct physical settings within a shared building could also be appropriate, depending on such factors as the number of section 23 students, costs, and so forth.[12] Moreover, a trial court judge in Ontario ruled that section 23 required that minority facilities be equal to those of the majority and ordered the government and the local school board to improve the industrial arts facilities at the francophone high school in Penetanguishene.[13]

The courts differed somewhat over the question of whether section 23 provided management and control rights. The responses ranged from "no" (Manitoba Court of Appeal); to the opinion that section 23 allowed francophone parents to "participate in French language programme development and its delivery" but did not require an autonomous school system (Prince Edward Island Supreme Court, Appeal Division); to the opinion that management and control powers were included in section 23 but could be met with proportional representation on existing school boards (Ontario Court of Appeal); to the opinion that section 23 contemplated distinct francophone school boards but that the numbers in Edmonton did not warrant a separate board (a "sliding scale" approach was rejected) (Alberta Court of Appeal).[14] What were the provincial-level policy responses in the wake of the introduction of the *Charter* and the subsequent legal and political mobilization by francophone groups and some francophone parents? Table 10.2 shows a significant increase in the recognition of homogenous French schools, but little movement in giving management and control powers to francophone parents.

As for FFL instruction, the Alberta government formally recognized the distinction between FFL and French immersion in its 1988 document "Language Policy for Alberta."[15] However, because implementation was left largely to school boards, Alberta's policy on FFL instruction remained "discretionary." Conversely, late in 1984, Ontario amended its *Education Act* to guarantee access to FFL instruction for any child eligible under section 23 of the *Charter*.[16] In the late 1980s, both Prince Edward Island and Nova Scotia recognized in law the right to FFL instruction where numbers warranted. Prior to the legislative change in Nova Scotia, a trial judge had upheld a local school board's decision not to offer a FFL program or a French school after a survey revealed that fifty students would enroll in the program. On appeal, though, the appellate court argued that, owing to the remedial nature of section 23, a FFL program should be provided, but it would not necessarily have to be in a completely separate facility.

As indicated by Table 10.2, there was a significant increase in the number of provinces that recognized the concept of a homogenous French school. British Columbia, Manitoba, and Alberta did so in policy documents and encouraged school boards to create such schools where numbers warranted. Whether local boards established homogenous French schools often depended on factors such as costs, their beliefs about what the *Charter* required, and the state of majority and minority public opinion. Unlike the aforementioned provinces, Nova Scotia followed the model that Saskatchewan had introduced in 1978-79 by passing legislation that gave the minister of education the authority to designate a school as a homogenous French school depending on certain factors, particularly the number of students. All of these provinces were counted as being a "qualified yes," partly because of the discretion given to school boards or ministers and partly because the ratio of homogenous French schools compared to the number of total schools that offered FFL programs was relatively low. In Alberta, for example, the number of schools providing FFL programs grew to twenty by 1988-89, although only three of these were homogenous French schools. Ontario and Prince Edward Island were counted as being "yes" to the idea of homogenous schools because, although there was a certain amount of discretion,

Table 10.2

OMLE policy 1982-90

Instruction	Homogenous facilities	Management
"Discretionary": the provision of FFL instruction is purely at the discretion of the minister or school board.	"Qualified No": some schools were de facto homogenous francophone schools.	"Qualified No": some schools were under the de facto control of francophone parents.
"Qualified Mandatory": the right to FFL instruction is triggered upon a certain numerical threshold.	"Qualified Yes": homogenous FFL schools recognized in law and schools could be designated as such.	"Qualified Yes": francophone representation on existing school boards or territorial coverage of francophone school boards is relatively limited.
"Mandatory": FFL instruction provided without numerical qualification.	"Yes": more positive recognition of homogenous schools in law and policy.	"Yes": school boards organized along linguistic lines, cover most of or the entire province, and are exclusively responsible for FFLprograms and schools.

Policy changes from previous period are denoted by italics

	Instruction	Homogenous facilities	Management
BC	Qualified Mandatory	*Qualified Yes* (1987)	No
AB	Discretionary *(recognized in law 1988)*	*Qualified Yes* (1988)	No
SK	Qualified Mandatory	Qualified Yes	No
MB	Qualified Mandatory	*Qualified Yes* (1984)	Qualified No
ON	*Mandatory* (1984)	Yes	*Qualified Yes* (1986)
NB	Qualified Mandatory	Yes	Yes
NS	*Qualified Mandatory* (1989)	*Yes* (1989)	Qualified No
PE	*Qualified Mandatory* (improved 1989)	*Yes* (1989)	*Yes* (1989-90)
NF	Discretionary (no law or regulation)	*Qualified No* (1986)	No

Totals*			
	Discretionary = 2 provinces (–1) Qualified Mandatory = 6 provinces (0) Mandatory = 1 province (+1)	No = 0 provinces (–3) Qualified No = 1 province (–1) Qualified Yes = 4 provinces (+2) Yes = 4 provinces (+2)	No = 4 provinces (–1) Qualified No = 2 provinces (–1) Qualified Yes = 1 province (+1) Yes = 2 provinces (+1)

* (n) = net change from last period

when a school offered a FFL program, it was most often a homogenous French school rather than a "mixed" school. New Brunswick was a "yes" because schools and school districts were organized along linguistic lines by law.

During this time frame, only Ontario and Prince Edward Island joined New Brunswick in enshrining some form of management and control rights into law. Ontario provided for proportional francophone representation on school boards in 1986 and then created separate francophone boards for Metropolitan Toronto and Ottawa-Carleton in 1988-89. Prince Edward Island passed a law in 1989 providing for the participation of francophones in French language instruction program development and delivery – a regulation would be passed the next year to establish a francophone school board. Other provinces, however, were insistent that section 23 provided no management and control rights to francophone parents.

Indeed, when the *Mahé* case reached the Supreme Court of Canada, Alberta was joined by Manitoba and Saskatchewan in arguing that section 23 included no right to management and control. Alberta's submission to the Court quoted heavily from the legislative history of section 23 to back its argument that the section did not provide the right to management and control. The Quebec government claimed that section 23 parents should have input into creating a "proper linguistic environment" but not their own school boards. The federal government, as it had in *Reference Re Education Act of Ontario and Minority Language Education Rights,* supported reading section 23 as containing the right to management and control but acknowledged that implementation of the right could be achieved by a variety of methods depending on local circumstances.[17] The Ontario government now also endorsed this reasoning.

A number of francophone groups, including the ACFA, intervened to support the Bugnet group's contention, as did Alliance Quebec – the major anglophone rights group in Quebec. Not all of the OMLE intervenors went as far as the Bugnet group in calling for a mandatory injunction and almost complete administrative autonomy (to the point of having a separate department of education), though even the ACFA suggested that francophone school boards were required. The Supreme Court of Canada handed down its unanimous decision in March 1990.[18] The Court began by stating that section 23 was remedial in nature and deserved a large and liberal interpretation before arguing that section 23 encompassed a sliding scale with management and control at the upper end of the scale. The "where the numbers warrant" test, according to the Court, should take into account both existing and future demand, pedagogical considerations, and financial requirements (though costs should not be given undue emphasis given the remedial nature of section 23) – in Edmonton, this would entitle section 23 parents to management and control of distinct facilities but not a completely distinct school board. The Court suggested that perhaps there be minority representation on the existing school board but noted that it was up to provinces to implement schemes to satisfy section 23. As such, the remedy provided in *Mahé* left more flexibility for government decision makers than the mandatory injunction called for by the Bugnet group. The Court did not declare the *School Act* unconstitutional but called upon the government to provide a method by which those parents in Edmonton, and others so situated, could enjoy their section 23 rights as declared by the Court.[19] The Alberta government, according to the judgment of Chief Justice Brian Dickson, "must delay no longer" in discharging its constitutional obligations.[20]

Table 10.3 reveals dramatic changes in OMLE policy outside Quebec following the *Mahé* decision. By 2000, all provinces had in place a system of francophone school governance that covered the entire province. With the exception of Manitoba, the francophone school boards were given the exclusive authority to operate FFL programs and francophone schools.[21] Moreover, when provinces adopted these systems, they normally made access to FFL instruction easier and recognized the concept of the francophone schools in legislation or regulation. For example, Alberta's *School Amendment Act, 1993,* provided that if a pupil eligible under section 23 resides in an area controlled by a francophone regional school authority (school board) then that pupil is entitled to receive FFL instruction – since the extension of francophone authorities in 2000 to cover the province made access to instruction mandatory.[22] Some provinces still retain some form of qualification before FFL instruction will be provided ("qualified mandatory"), although the Supreme Court of Canada's decision in 2000, *Arsenault-Cameron v. Prince Edward Island,* signalled that the power of these governments to deny FFL instruction would be constrained, particularly if a program was recommended by a francophone school board. The Court ordered Prince Edward Island to abide by the recommendation of the provincial francophone school board to provide for FFL instruction in a francophone facility in Summerside over a government objection that the numbers did not warrant such a solution and that students could attend an appropriate school twenty-nine kilometres away.[23]

The number of francophone schools continued to increase in a number of provinces even though both the number of eligible children and the francophone population outside Quebec declined during this period.[24] In Alberta, for example, by 1998, there were twenty-four schools providing FFL programs, seventeen of which were homogenous French schools. In 2007, there were twenty-nine francophone schools. In Nova Scotia, a trial judge in 1999 found that the government was not proceeding quickly enough to provide francophone schools in five areas. He therefore ordered the province and the francophone school board to build schools according to a certain timeline. The judge retained jurisdiction over the case and required provincial authorities to report to him about their progress.

Table 10.3

OMLE policy 1990-		
Instruction	Homogenous facilities	Management
"Discretionary": the provision of FFL instruction is purely at the discretion of the minister or school board.	"Qualified No": some schools were de facto homogenous francophone schools.	"Qualified No": some schools were under the de facto control of francophone parents.
"Qualified Mandatory": the right to FFL instruction is triggered upon a certain numerical threshold.	"Qualified Yes": homogenous FFL schools recognized in law and schools could be designated as such.	"Qualified Yes": francophone representation on existing school boards or territorial coverage of francophone school boards is relatively limited.
"Mandatory": FFL instruction provided without numerical qualification.	"Yes": more positive recognition of homogenous schools in law and policy.	"Yes": school boards organized along linguistic lines, cover most of or the entire province, and are exclusively responsible for FFL programs and schools.

Policy changes from previous period are denoted by italics

	Instruction	Homogenous facilities	Management
BC	*Mandatory* (1996)	*Yes* (1996)	*Qualified Yes* (1995, 96) *Yes* (1999)
AB	*Mandatory* (1993*, 2000)	*Yes* (1993)	*Qualified Yes* (1993) *Yes* (2000)
SK	Qualified Mandatory (improved 1993, 2000)	*Yes* (1993)	*Yes* (1993) (modified 1999)
MB	*Qualified Mandatory* (improved 1993)	*Yes* (1993)	*Qualified Yes* (1994)
ON	Mandatory	Yes	*Yes* (1997)
NB	*Mandatory* (1997)	Yes	Yes (modified 1997)
NS	*Qualified Mandatory* (1991)	Yes	*Yes* (1995)
PE	Qualified Mandatory	Yes	Yes
NF	*Qualified Mandatory* (1996)	*Yes* (1996)	*Yes* (1996)

Totals**		
Discretionary = 0 provinces (-2) Qualified Mandatory = 5 provinces (-1) Mandatory = 4 provinces (+3)	No = 0 provinces (0) Qualified No = 0 provinces (-1) Qualified Yes = 0 provinces (-5) Yes = 9 provinces (+ 6)	No = 0 provinces (-4) Qualified No = 0 provinces (-2) Qualified Yes = 1 province Yes = 8 provinces (+6)

*   Mandatory within Francophone Regional School Authorities. The geographic scope of the Authorities was extended in 2000 to effectively make access mandatory.

** (+) = net change from last period

In *Doucet-Boudreau v. Nova Scotia (Minister of Education)*, this unique remedy was later upheld by a (slim) majority of the Supreme Court of Canada.[25] In doing so, the majority indicated that section 24(1), which empowers courts to provide remedies that are "appropriate and just in the circumstances," requires judges to be flexible and responsive in order to vindicate *Charter* rights, while respecting the roles of the different branches in a constitutional democracy and potential limits on judicial expertise. Although the dissent argued that the trial judge's remedy violated the constitutional separation of powers, the majority disagreed, emphasizing that the section 23 rights in question were remedial in nature and designed to address linguistic assimilation and a history of delay in providing francophone education.

As francophone proponents of school governance (with French schools and FFL instruction) were consolidating their policy victories, legal challenges were being made in Quebec against the law that was used to determine eligibility for English-language schooling under section 23 of the *Charter*. In *Solski (Tutor of) v. Quebec (Attorney General)*, the Supreme Court of Canada ruled that children who had participated in French immersion classes outside of Quebec should not be disqualified from access to English-language schooling in Quebec.[26] More generally, the Court informed Quebec that a less mechanical interpretation of eligibility requirements would be needed to ensure the law's constitutionality. The qualitative aspect of the assessment, according to the Court, must consider all of the circumstances of the child, including the time spent in each program, at what stage of education the choice of language of instruction was made, what programs are or were available, and whether learning disabilities or other difficulties existed. Estimates of how many children this rule will affect have varied and will depend on the Quebec government's reaction.[27] However, no matter how the government responds, any change in Quebec's policy will not be as dramatic as the policy changes that occurred outside of Quebec in the first couple of decades following the *Charter*'s introduction. The question becomes: how can the substance and timing of the major policy changes outside of Quebec – in FFL instruction, homogenous French schools, and francophone school governance – be explained?

Theories of Judicial Impact

Surprisingly, although there has been much written on judicial policy-making and the *Charter* over the last twenty-five years, relatively little attention has been paid to explaining and predicting the policy impact of legal mobilization and *Charter* decisions. Much of the literature on judicial policy-making revolves around the normative question of "judicial power" under the *Charter*. Although the now well-known "dialogue" literature analyzes legislative responses to judicial decisions, the focus of the dialogue debate is on how much power courts do, and should, have *vis-à-vis* legislatures in the *Charter* era. Dialogue scholars have not tried, for instance, to generate and test hypotheses about under what conditions legislatures will ignore or modify *Charter* decisions. Although there are some exceptions,[28] the literature on judicial impact is much more developed in the United States.

Stephen Wasby's early overview of the judicial impact literature by contained over a hundred hypotheses about the relationship between courts and policy change, some of which Wasby acknowledged were mutually contradictory. The general factors that he identified as determining judicial impact are: *the characteristics of cases* (a decision clearly based on the Constitution will produce greater compliance and so on); *communication* (reporting on immediate negative reaction tends to increase non-compliance and so on); *political environment* (the greater the number of levels of government or the number of people affected, for instance); *follow-up* (impact will be greater when efforts are made to follow up a decision than when such efforts are not made); *those responding* (the greater the power and the higher the status of those responding to a Court decision and so on); and *beliefs and values* (compliance will be higher in the absence of personal preferences and behaviour supporting an invalidated practice).[29]

Later, Gerald Rosenberg offered a more parsimonious model of impact.[30] Rosenberg proposed that because courts are "constrained" by a variety of institutional limitations, particularly their lack of enforcement tools, courts can only produce social change when the following conditions are met: (1) there is ample legal precedent for change; (2) there is support for change from Congress and the executive branch; and (3) there is support or low opposition in the public and costs/benefits are offered to implementers to induce compliance (or administrators are willing to hide behind decisions to implement reforms). While Rosenberg's model can be critiqued for leaving out potential explanatory factors, such as the clarity and forcefulness of a judicial decision, a more fundamental critique of Rosenberg's theoretical model comes from those scholars, particularly Michael McCann, who argue that the model assumes a "top-down" and "positivist" perspective, whereby the impact of Supreme Court of Canada decisions is correlated to the presence or absence of certain factors.[31] An alternative approach to evaluating judicial impact is one that analyzes legal and political disputes more contextually with the assumption that law, judicial decisions, and institutions more generally are "constitutive" in that they can shape norms and goals that guide behaviour. This "bottom-up" approach seeks to analyze how legal claims and judicial decisions are received, interpreted, utilized, and/or circumvented by various legal, social, and political actors.[32] Although scholars in this camp tend to be skeptical about how much legal mobilization and courts can alter the existing social and political power dynamics, many argue that disadvantaged groups can use legal mobilization and courts as part of a broader strategy to further their cause at least incrementally.

Explaining OMLE Policy Development

To assess the policy-related impact of section 23 and judicial decisions, this review of OMLE policy relies on both of the methodological approaches outlined earlier – the "top-down," factor-oriented approach exemplified by Rosenberg and the "bottom-up," dispute-centred approach exemplified by McCann. The analysis begins with the "top-down" approach. First, as suggested by Rosenberg and others, a victory in the Supreme Court of Canada was pivotal to OMLE policy development, particularly the establishment of francophone school governance. Prior to the Supreme Court of Canada's (unanimous) *Mahé* decision, which determined that there was a right to management and control in section 23, emphasized the remedial nature of section 23, and declared that the Alberta government should "delay no longer" in implementing section 23 rights, only three provinces had introduced management and control powers for section 23 parents. In two of these provinces (Ontario and Prince Edward Island), this came after their courts of appeal ruled that section 23 included some management and control rights. The refusal of other governments to act, sometimes coupled with explicit rejections of the idea that section 23 contained the right to management and control, suggest that the *Mahé* ruling was crucial. Jim Dinning, Alberta's minister of education at the time, said that the *Mahé* decision was "a catalyst" for the Alberta government to act and that francophone school governance "*might*" have been introduced without the decision, though the process would have taken "a lot" longer.[33]

Rosenberg argues that a Supreme Court victory is more likely if the Court has the support of the federal government.[34] The federal government not only funded section 23 litigation and interventions – the federal government's Court Challenges Program granted the Budget group $100,000 to usher the *Mahé* case to the Supreme Court, and the program spent nearly $2.5 million dollars on section 23 cases and interventions by early 1999 – it also intervened to support francophone groups in *Mahé*.[35] The somewhat flexible approach advanced by the federal government factum was adopted by the Court. The "sliding scale" framework led the Court to suggest that proportional representation on the existing board with control over those aspects of education pertaining to language and culture would be an appropriate solution in Edmonton.

The ACFA was concerned that the Court did not better specify the "where numbers warrant" formula and thought that it might lead to delays and more litigation.[36] The director of Alberta's Language Services Branch in the Department of Education attributed at least part of the delay in Alberta's response to the lack of "specific requirements" in the *Mahé* decision, except as they applied to remedy the rights violation in Edmonton.[37] As noted earlier, Rosenberg's model does not formally take into consideration the "forcefulness" or "clarity" of a judicial decision, but this factor may have some utility in explaining why most provinces took longer to implement robust systems of francophone governance than the francophone advocates wanted.

Rosenberg's model does include resources and incentives for implementation, and these were critical to OMLE policy development. Since the introduction of the *Charter*, the federal Official Languages in Education (OLE) program has channelled hundreds of millions of dollars to the provinces in order to supplement the additional costs associated with providing official minority first-language programs. Under a recent protocol agreement, for example, the federal government gave the provinces just over $170 million for minority language education for 2005-6 (approximately $50 million of which was for English-language education in Quebec).[38] Evaluations of the OLE in 1992 and again in 2003, which featured consultations with various stakeholders in the policy community, confirmed the importance of these monies to the maintenance of existing programs and the development of new programs.[39] These same stakeholders also pointed to the significance of the supplementary agreements that were made between the federal government and provinces to implement francophone school governance. Under these agreements, the federal government agreed to pay for half of the implementation costs of francophone school governance (and, in some cases, certain additional costs for improving FFL programs and francophone schools). The Alberta-Canada agreement, for example, provided that each level of government would contribute $5.385 million for the establishment of francophone school authorities, $6.35 million for the development of FFL programs, and $4.5 million for the establishment of fancophone schools/ community centres in Fort McMurray and Calgary. With the exception of New Brunswick and Prince Edward Island, no province established a comprehensive system of francophone school boards prior to a promise of federal funding. The 2003 evaluation of federal funding for minority language education, which was prepared for Heritage Canada, reported that "[t]he consultations indicate that, despite the existence of a clear obligation on the part of the provincial and territorial governments to implement this right to school governance, it is almost certain that the progress made during the past ten years would not have happened without federal support, provided largely through the Special Agreements."[40]

The importance of funding and incentives in implementation was underscored by the refusal of some local school boards, prior to the establishment of francophone boards, to create francophone schools without assurances of provincial funding, even if they generally favoured the concept.[41] The degree to which local and provincial administrators and elected officials favoured FFL instruction, francophone schools, and francophone school governance and how much of an effect this may have had upon the implementation of section 23 is difficult to assess. There is some evidence that supports the claim made by Rosenberg and others that the attitudes of imple-menters matter (and judicial decisions could be used to hide behind). At the local level in Alberta, for example, the St. Isadore school district, led by superintendent Jacques Moquin, who was described as a "passionate defender of French language and culture," established a homogenous francophone school in 1988 despite financial challenges. The school district cited section 23 of the *Charter* to justify its decision.[42] Conversely, the Alberta govern-ment's hesitation in introducing significant OMLE policy change prior to and after *Mahé* could be attributed to some degree to the attitudes of the political leadership. A number of cabinet ministers and caucus members were opposed to the *Mahé* decision and did not want to grant "special rights" to francophones.[43] Moreover, Premier Don Getty spoke out against enforced bilingualism shortly before his retirement, and his successor, Ralph Klein, specifically said that proposed legislation to give Alberta francophones management and control of schools fostered "discrimination."[44]

Nevertheless, the Alberta government of Premier Ralph Klein did introduce francophone school governance and did so before governments in other provinces that, in principle, were more supportive of such a policy. The incoming New Democratic Party (NDP) government in British Columbia, for example, had publicly come out in favour of francophone school govern-ance in 1991, yet, it was not until 1995 that it enacted a limited regulatory scheme and was faced with (renewed) litigation shortly thereafter.[45] In On-tario, despite the fact that Premier Bob Rae expressed support for creating more francophone school boards when he was sworn in in 1990, and the minister of education, Marion Boyd, was personally predisposed to the creation of more such boards,[46] only one additional board was created when the NDP was in power. Boyd attributes the lack of policy movement in Ontario at least in part to concerns over how the public might react to the creation of a more robust system of francophone school governance: "The NDP caucus was ambivalent, to say the least. Members were aware of the policy position but were leery of how following that policy might affect them in their particular ridings."[47] Likewise, in British Columbia, the NDP government had been "tiptoeing through a political minefield" by trying "to avoid riling Anglophone communities across the province, especially those ... mainly rural communities [that] have been openly hostile to poli-cies promoting bilingualism and French-language rights."[48] Therefore, fears about public opinion, as predicted by the "top-down" models, could have contributed to the delays and problems in implementing court decisions, even among the implementers who were sympathetic to policy change.[49] In the case of OMLE, differences of opinion within the minority francophone communities outside of Quebec also likely affected the nature and timing of OMLE policy change, as disagreements within francophone communities in most provinces outside Quebec posed difficulties for local school boards and provincial governments in deciding how to proceed with OMLE policy.[50]

What about the possible "indirect" effects that Rosenberg allows for in his own case studies relating to interest group mobilization, media attention, and public attitudes? The *Mahé* case did cause francophone groups at the provincial and national level to accelerate their efforts to develop francophone school management models and to pursue their implementation through political and legal means.[51] The commissioner of official languages in his 1985 report noted that minority language education was "often in the headlines" in the wake of court cases or legal action, and Paul Dubé of the Bugnet group claimed that the *Mahé* case "put us on the front pages of newspapers and in the media quite often," although it is difficult to determine whether media coverage had any sustained influence.[52] It is unlikely that the *Mahé* decision and related news coverage influenced majority public opinion, however, since an Alberta survey in the latter half of the 1990s revealed that just over 60 percent of respondents were not aware that the Supreme Court of Canada had made a decision in favour of francophone school governance rights.[53]

As McCann argues, though, even when including indirect effects, Rosenberg's model still focuses primarily on the judicial capacity to initiate behavioural changes rather than on the constitutive influence of law and the relational dynamics generated over time by legal mobilization and judicial decisions. Indeed, while Rosenberg's approach is helpful for understanding OMLE policy change, it does leave some important questions unanswered. In particular, it does not explain why all of the provinces outside Quebec adopted province-wide systems of francophone school governance when the *Mahé* decision emphasized flexibility and the Supreme Court of Canada indicated that only the situation in Edmonton called for proportional representation on the existing board. A "bottom-up" approach is required for a more complete and accurate understanding of OMLE policy development.

Even before the Supreme Court of Canada's *Mahé* decision, the use of legal mobilization and rights discourse as part of a larger political strategy contributed to OMLE policy change. Prince Edward Island introduced systems of francophone school governance, for example, even though the province's appellate court said that francophones had only a right to "participate" in program development and delivery. And while the Ontario government had been supportive of some system of proportional francophone representation on existing boards prior to the 1984 Ontario Court of Appeal decision, a lawyer who represented francophone groups in that case claimed that the decision "accelerated and reinforced" the expansion of French-language education rights.[54] According to Angéline Martel, legal mobilization and *Charter* rights discourse helped within Alberta to legitimate francophone schools and school governance as policy options within the francophone community and encouraged the established ACFA group to actively support these policy goals when it was previously reluctant to do so.[55] In response to lobbying from the ACFA and other francophone groups, the Alberta government's 1988 policy paper recognized the uniqueness of FFL instruction for francophones and the importance of French schools where numbers warranted. Some school boards in Alberta, such as the Edmonton Catholic School Board, eventually established francophone schools or FFL programs after being convinced over time of their constitutional and cultural necessity by francophone proponents who used legal and political tactics to pursue their goals. The *Mahé* decision then served to raise the profile of the OMLE issue (the Council of Ministers of Education, for instance, discussed OMLE policy for the first time in 1991), gave francophone groups greater access to the policy process when they were invited to sit on committees formed by governments to study the issue, laid the legal groundwork for the federal government to provide provinces with money to establish francophone school governance, and further legitimated the concept of francophone school governance.

OMLE policy development in Alberta illustrates the contingent and relational processes that followed *Mahé*. In response to the decision, the Alberta government established the French Language Working Group, which included representatives from Alberta francophone groups. Although there was some suspicion that the working group might have been created with the hope that it would be divided and result in delays,[56] the committee came back with an unanimous report – in part because the Alberta School Trustees Association, which had intervened against section 23 claimants in *Mahé*, came to support the francophone position.[57] The committee's report highlighted the Supreme Court of Canada's emphasis on the remedial nature of section 23 and recommended a system of francophone school boards rather than proportional representation on existing school boards.[58] This report largely reflected another report that had been prepared for the ACFA and the Alberta provincial francophone parents' association in anticipation of the *Mahé* decision, which was designed to inform and consult the francophone community about French-language rights.[59] In turn, Alberta's legislation in 1993 reflected the report of the French Language Working Group by creating francophone school boards in most parts of the province.

In other provinces, the process of establishing francophone school governance proceeded along different paths and at a different pace than in Alberta. The establishment of a system of francophone school boards in Ontario also reveals the kind of dynamics highlighted by the "bottom-up" perspective. Although various advisory committees and the province's Royal Commission on Learning had recommended in 1994 that a system of francophone school boards be set up across the province, a province-wide system of francophone school boards was not put in place until 1997, after the Conservative government concluded that ongoing section 23 litigation could complicate or undermine large parts of the significant educational reforms that they were planning if those plans did not include more francophone school boards.[60]

By the year 2000, all provinces had francophone governance structures that covered the entire province, and, except for Manitoba, all provided for exclusive management and control over FFL programs and schools. After this point, OMLE policy outside of Quebec moved into more of a consolidation phase. As noted earlier, francophones in Prince Edward Island succeeded in having the decision of the francophone school board override the decision of the minister of education about the establishment of FFL instruction in Summerside, and a trial judge in Nova Scotia oversaw the creation of more francophone (Acadian) schools. In various localities, francophone proponents of French schools and school boards were often successful in using rights discourse and threats of litigation to achieve their policy goals in the face of divergent views of decision makers or others in the francophone community.[61] These developments suggest that there has been a cumulative effect of legal and political mobilization – a possibility posited by "bottom-up" scholars.

Conclusion

According to OMLE researcher Stacy Churchill, there has been an "almost inconceivable transformation of minority education for Francophones [since the Charter was introduced]."[62] In most provinces outside of Quebec, section 23 of the *Charter* and the Supreme Court of Canada's *Mahé* decision were necessary to achieve robust francophone school governance. They were not sufficient, however. Federal government funding and the ability of francophone proponents to effectively use their political and legal resources to shape the policy process were integral to the establishment of francophone school boards. After OMLE policy change accelerated, judicial decisions and remedies for section 23 violations provided less latitude to decision makers, as exemplified in *Doucet-Boudreau*. The OMLE case study, therefore, suggests that the exercise of judicial power both shapes and reflects political developments.

Since accomplishing their major policy goals, francophone groups have focused on building on those policy achievements. Programs for pre-school-aged children, remedial FFL programs, and schools used as cultural centres are some of the current priorities.[63] Litigation, though, has not been a dominant tactic in the pursuit of these goals. In their brief to a parliamentary committee protesting the cancellation of the Court Challenges Program in 2006, the Fédération des communautés francophones et acadienne du Canada mentioned only one recent section 23 initiative – the Court Challenges Program had paid for preparing the groundwork for litigation against the regional municipality of Halifax.[64] The regional municipality subsequently agreed to share proceeds of its school surtax with the Acadian school board of Nova Scotia.[65] While the larger policy battles are over, the issue of "equivalency" that the Halifax tax raises – that the minority's educational system and the experience of students will be similar in value to that of the majority – has the potential to generate some political and legal conflict due to resource implications and the scope for disagreement over what is "equivalent."[66] Indeed, in August 2007, a Nova Scotia trial judge declared that the province's Tuition Support Program, which helps children with special needs attend private schools, violated section 23 because it did not adequately consider the needs of francophone students to attend FFL schools.[67] Taking into consideration the Supreme Court of Canada's criteria for fashioning remedies to section 23 violations, which were outlined in *Doucet-Boudreau*, the trial judge left it to the government, the francophone school board, and parents' groups to fashion an appropriate response to this rights violation.

While not insignificant, current and future OMLE policy skirmishes will pale in comparison to previous OMLE policy change – the striking down of Bill 101 in Quebec and the development of francophone school boards outside of Quebec. Underlying these policy developments is a vision of pan-Canadian nationalism that seeks to promote national unity by enforcing educational separation between French- and English-speakers in the name of linguistic minority preservation and promotion. This strategy is still contested on occasion, however. Ironically, weeks after the twenty-fifth anniversary of the *Charter*, Justin Trudeau, the son of the individual most responsible for the *Charter* and for section 23, told a teacher's conference in Saint John that New Brunswick should dismantle its separate school systems based on language. "The segregation of French and English in schools is something to be looked at seriously ... it is dividing people and affixing labels to people," the younger Trudeau was quoted as saying.[68] Although the teachers reportedly gave Trudeau a standing ovation, Acadian leaders and members of his own party quickly denounced the speech.[69] Trudeau's decision to quickly backtrack on his remarks suggests that the "separate but equal" vision of section 23, which has been enshrined in law and policy over the last twenty-five years, will remain the dominant paradigm that shapes OMLE policy for the foreseeable future.

Acknowledgments
I would like to thank Daniel Lester for his research assistance on this chapter.

Notes
1 *Canadian Charter of Rights and Freedoms*, Part 1 of the *Constitution Act, 1982,* being Schedule B to the *Canada Act 1982* (U.K.), 1982, c. 11.
2 *Mahé v. Alberta*, [1990] 1 S.C.R. 342. For complaints about the slow and contested implementation of *Mahé*, see Commissioner of Official Languages, *Annual Report 1992* (Ottawa: Supply and Services Canada, 1993), 18.

3   For a description of Quebec's system, which was described as "by far the best minority language education system in Canada," see Michael Mandel, *The Charter of Rights and the Legalization of Politics* (Toronto: Thomson Educational Publishing, 1989), 106-7.

4   See Angéline Martel, *Official Minority Education Rights in Canada* (Ottawa: Supply and Services Canada, 1991).

5   Canada, Council of Ministers of Education, *The State of Minority Language Education in Canada* (Toronto: Council of Ministers of Education, 1983), 1-2.

6   Martel, *supra* note 4 at 56-57.

7   *Minutes of the Special Joint Committee on the Constitution 1980-81* (Ottawa: Queen's Printer, 1981) at 12:11; see also l' Association Canadienne-Française de l'Ontario at 8:33; la Societé Franco-Manitobaine at 10:27; Fédération des Francophones hors Québec at 13:30; Positive Action Committee, Quebec at 7:57; and the Commissioner of Official Languages at 6:13.

8   Ibid., 38:108.

9   See Joseph Magnet, *Official Languages of Canada* (Cowansville, QC: Éditions Yvon Blais, 1995), 47. Parents in Quebec cannot qualify under the maternal language stipulation until that province assents. *Constitution Act, 1982* (U.K.), 1982, c. 11, s. 59.

10 *Attorney General of Quebec v. Quebec Association of Protestant School Boards*, [1984] 2 S.C.R. 66.

11 For details, see Troy Riddell, *The Courts and Policy Change: The Impact of Legal Mobilization on Official Minority-Language Education Policy outside Quebec* (Ph.D. dissertation, McGill University, 2002) [unpublished]. See also Michael Behiels, *Canada's Francophone Minority Communities* (Montreal and Kingston: McGill-Queen's University Press, 2004).

12 Martel, *supra* note 4, 41-42.

13 *Marchand v. Simcoe County Board of Education et al.*, [1986] 55 O.R. (2d) 638.

14 *Reference re Manitoba Public Schools Act*, [1990] 2 W.W.R. 289 (Man. C.A.); *Reference re Minority Language Education Rights* (1988), Nfld. and P.E.I.R. 236 (Sup. Ct. (A.D.) (PEI)); *Reference re Education Act of Ontario and Minority Language Education Rights*, [1984] 10 D.L.R. (4th) 491 (Ont. C.A.) [*Reference re Education Act of Ontario*]; and *Mahé v. Alberta* (1987), 42 D.L.R. (4th) 514 (Alta. C.A.).

15 "Language Policy for Alberta" (Edmonton: Alberta Education, 1988).

16 *Education Act*, R.S.O. 1990, c. E-2.

17 *Reference re Education Act of Ontario*, *supra* note 14.

18 *Mahé v. Alberta*, [1990] 1 S.C.R. 342.

19 *School Act*, R.S.A. 2000, c. S-3.

20 *Mahé*, *supra* note 2.

21 The Supreme Court of Canada indicated that choice was acceptable under section 23 but that allowing choice must not hamper the francophone school board in providing equal educational services. *Reference re Manitoba Public Schools Act*, [1993] 1 S.C.R. 839.

22 *School Amendment Act, 1993*, S.A. 1993, c.24.

23 *Arsenault-Cameron v. Prince Edward Island*, [2000] 1 S.C.R. 3.

24 See Angéline Martel, *Rights, Schools and Communities in Minority Contexts: 1986-2002* (Ottawa: Minister of Government Services, 2001).

25 *Doucet-Boudreau v. Nova Scotia (Minister of Education)*, [2003] 3 S.C.R. 3.

26 *Solski (Tutor of) v. Quebec (Attorney General)*, [2005] 1 S.C.R. 201. On the same day that it released its *Solski* decision, the Court rejected an attempt by francophone parents to gain access to English schools in Quebec. See *Gosselin (Tutor of) v. Quebec (Attorney General)*, [2005] 1 S.C.R. 238.

27 Also, in June 2007, the Court of Appeal of Quebec struck down Bill 104, which had amended a section of the Quebec *Charter of French Language*, R.S.Q., c.C-11, that had made it relatively easy for a child who had gone to an English-language private school for a year to transfer to the English-language public school. *T.B. c. Québec (Ministre de l'Éducation)*, 2007 QCCA 1112 (CanLII). See CBC News, "Families Win Challenge of Quebec's Language Law" (August 22, 2007), http://www.cbc.ca/canada/montreal/story/2007/08/22/english-schools.html.

28 See Ian Urquhart, "Federalism, Ideology, and Charter Review: Alberta's Response to Morgentaler," *Canadian Journal of Law and Society* 4 (1989): 157-73; Miriam Smith, "Recognizing Same-Sex Relationships: The Evolution of Recent Federal and Provincial Policies," *Canadian*

Public Administration 45 (2002): 1-23; and Christopher Manfredi and Antonia Maioni, "Litigating Innovation: Health Care Policy and the Canadian Charter of Rights and Freedoms," Annual Meeting, Canadian Political Science Association (2005).

29 Stephen Wasby, *The Impact of the United States Supreme Court* (Homewood, IL: Dorsey Press, 1970), ch. 8.

30 Gerald Rosenberg, *The Hollow Hope* (Chicago: University of Chicago Press, 1991).

31 Michael W. McCann, "Reform Litigation on Trial," *Law and Social Inquiry* 17 (1992): 715-43.

32 Stuart Scheingold, *The Politics of Rights* (New Haven, CT: Yale University Press, 1974); Marc Galanter, "The Radiating Effects of Courts," in Keith D. Brown and Lynn Mather, eds., *Empirical Theories of Courts* (New York: Longman, 1983); and Michael W. McCann, *Rights at Work* (Chicago: University of Chicago Press, 1994).

33 Interview with the Hon. Jim Dinning (June 15, 2001).

34 Rosenberg, *supra* note 30, 31-32.

35 Interview with Paul Dubé, co-founder of the Bugnet group (May 16, 2001); and Martel, *supra* note 24, 14, n. 26.

36 Interview with France Levasseur-Ouimet, former president of l'Association canadienne-française de l'Alberta (December 16, 1998). The Bugnet group representatives thought it was advantageous to have flexibility in the numbers requirement, especially for smaller francophone communities. Interview with Paul Dubé (May 16, 2001).

37 Interview with Gérard Bissonnette (December 16, 1998).

38 Department of Canadian Heritage, *Official Languages Annual Report, 2005-2006,* volume 1, Appendix 1.1, Table 1, http://www.pch.gc.ca/pgm/lo-ol/reports/2005-2006/vol1/110-eng.cfm.

39 Pageau Skuce Vézina, *Official Languages in Education Program: An Evaluation – Summary* (Ottawa: Secretary of State, 1992). Department of Canadian Heritage. *Evaluation of the Official Languages in Education Program* (June 25, 2003), http://www.canadianheritage.gc.ca/progs/em-cr/eval/2003/2003_09/4_e.cfm.

40 Department of Canadian Heritage. Evaluation of the Official Languages in Education Program (June 25, 2003), http://www.canadianheritage.gc.ca/progs/em-cr/eval/2003/2003_09/4_e.cfm. The quote is taken from page 18 after the web document was converted to a PDF format.

41 Richard Julien, "The Quest for All-French Schools in Alberta," *Canadian Ethnic Studies* 25 (1993): 25-49.

42 Wink Barron, "The High Cost of Héritage," *Alberta Report* (January 14, 1991), 25-26.

43 Interview with France Levasseur-Ouimet (December 16, 1998). Interview with Jim Dinning (June 15, 2001).

44 Joan Crockatt, "Klein Wants Francophone Bill Altered," *Edmonton Journal* (November 14, 1992), A7.

45 Commissioner of Official Languages, *Annual Report 1991* (Ottawa: Supply and Services Canada, 1992), 125.

46 Commissioner of Official Languages, *Annual Report 1990* (Ottawa: Supply and Services Canada, 1991), 242. Interview by e-mail with the Hon. Marion Boyd, former minister of education and attorney general of Ontario (June 2001).

47 Interview with Marion Boyd (June 2001).

48 Robert Matas, "B.C. Bows to Francophone-School Order," *Globe and Mail* (June 20, 1997).

49 For a more thorough discussion of public opinion on OMLE, including reference and analysis of public opinion polling on the subject, see Riddell, *supra* note 11.

50 See Riddell, *supra* note 11; and Behiels, *supra* note 11.

51 Commissioner of Official Languages, *Annual Report 1990, supra,* note 46, 214.

52 Commissioner of Official Languages, *Annual Report 1985* (Ottawa: Supply and Services Canada, 1986), 77; and interview with Paul Dubé (May 16, 2001).

53 The survey questions were created by the author and were part of the 1998 Alberta Advantage survey.

54 Confidential interview (June 26, 2001).

55   Interview with Angéline Martel (June 2, 1998). See also Angéline Martel, *Profil de la Francophonie d'Edmonton et Opinions des Francophones sur l'Éducation Française* (Edmonton: Bugnet Group, 1988).

56   Interview by phone with Georges Arès, former executive-director of l'Association canadienne-française de l'Alberta and former president of la Commission nationale des parents francophone (May 26, 2001).

57   Interview with France Levasseur-Ouimet (December 16, 1998).

58   Alberta, "Report of the French Language Working Group to the Minister of Education the Honourable Jim Dinning," (May 1991).

59   P.A. Lamoureux and D. Tardif, *An Educational System for Franco-Albertans*, prepared for l'Association Canadienne-Française de l'Alberta and la Fédération des Parents Francophones de l'Alberta, 1990.

60   Confidential interview with OMLE activist, Ontario (June 26, 2001).

61   For example, see Chris Morris, "Acadians to Keep Their Schools," *Globe and Mail* (July 5, 1997), A10; and Colette Derworiz, *Calgary Herald*, "New Board Formed for One School" (June 27, 2000), B1.

62   Stacy Churchill, *New Canadian Perspectives: Official Languages in Canada* (Ottawa: Department of Canadian Heritage, 1998), 31.

63   Fédération nationale des conseils scolaires francophones, *Plan d'action – Article 23: Afin de compléter le système scolaire* (Ottawa: Fédération nationale des conseils scolaires francophones, 2006). Behiels, *supra* note 11, ch. 8.

64   The Fédération des communautés francophones et acadienne du Canada launched a lawsuit under the *Official Languages Act*, R.S.C. 1985, c. 31, to try to reverse the government's decision to eliminate the Court Challenges Program. In exchange for the federation dropping its lawsuit, the government agreed to establish a "Program to Support Linguistic Rights" that would provide $1.5 million annually for official minority language groups inside and outside of Quebec to press their linguistic rights claims. Unlike the Court Challenges Program, however, the new program puts more emphasis on trying to solve rights claims first through mediation. See Elizabeth Thompson, "Court Challenges Program Revived; Funding Is Restricted to Language Cases," *The Gazette (Montreal)* (June 20, 2008), A1.

65   Brief submitted by the Fédération des communautés francophones et acadienne du Canada on the impact of cancellation of funding for the Court Challenges Program. It was submitted to the Standing Committee on Canadian Heritage (December 6, 2006), http://www.fcfa.ca/media_uploads/pdf/415.pdf.

66   See Nicolas Rouleau, "Section 23 of the Charter: Minority-Language Education Rights," in Joseph Eliot Magnet, ed., *Official Languages of Canada: New Essays* (Toronto: Butterworths, 2008).

67   *Dauphinee v. Conseil Scolaire Acadien Provincial*, 2007 NSSC 238.

68   Daniel Leblanc, "Trudeau Gets First Taste of Controversy," *Globe and Mail* (May 8, 2007), A4.

69   John Wishart, "Bold Step Possible If We Dare to Dream," *The Times (Moncton, NB)* (May 11, 2007), D9.

11
Reference re Same-Sex Marriage: Making Sense of the Government's Litigation Strategy
Matthew Hennigar

Only a few short years before the adoption of *the Canadian Charter of Rights and Freedoms*, the Supreme Court of Canada rendered its now infamous ruling in *Bliss v. Canada (Attorney General)* that discrimination on the basis of pregnancy did not violate the statutory 1960 *Canadian Bill of Rights'* guarantee of sexual equality.[1] *Bliss* was simply another example of what had become a well-established pattern of judicial rulings on equality rights, characterized by a narrow, "formalist" approach that tolerated significant levels of social inequality. The framers of the *Charter*, spurred, in particular, by women's groups, clearly intended to avoid such narrow interpretations of equality when they drafted the *Charter*'s equality rights in section 15, with its explicit references to equality "before and under the law" and "equal protection and equal benefit of the law."

During the entrenchment of the *Constitution Act, 1982*, however, it was unlikely that the *Charter*'s framers foresaw the remarkable events that would occur in the spring of 2003, when the highest courts of two Canadian provinces declared the traditional definition of marriage unconstitutional, arguing that the common-law definition of marriage as "the voluntary union for life of one man and one woman, to the exclusion of all others" violated the equality rights of gays and lesbians under section 15 of the *Charter*.[2] It would have been virtually unthinkable to the politicians negotiating the 1982 constitutional amendment – and even less so to the judges of the highest courts – that the *Charter* would in only twenty-five years be used to redefine a social institution so fundamental as marriage, particularly on the basis of sexual orientation, which the framers had deliberately excluded from the enumerated grounds of section 15.[3] Not that the decisions were uncontroversial – the rulings sent a shock wave through Canadian politics, sparking renewed criticisms of judicial activism and demands for the Canadian federal government to appeal the rulings to the Supreme Court of Canada. After hinting publicly that it would appeal, the Liberal government of Jean Chrétien reversed its opposition to same-sex marriage and, instead, drafted a bill legalizing it and, on July 17, 2003, referred its constitutionality to the Court (see appendix at the end of this chapter for timeline).[4]

This chapter seeks to explain the Chrétien government's response to the lower court decisions in *Barbeau/EGALE v. Canada (Attorney General)* and *Halpern v. Canada (Attorney General)*, including the reversal of its opposition to same-sex marriage and the decision to refer a draft bill to the Supreme Court of Canada rather than to simply appeal the rulings.[5] As will be explained later in this chapter, even if we accept that the Liberal government truly supported same-sex marriage, the decision not to appeal was apparently "suboptimal" from a strategic perspective. An appeal to the Supreme Court of Canada would almost certainly have resulted in the legalization of same-sex marriage, without the government having to take responsibility for the highly controversial change – one that divided not only the voting public but also the Liberal caucus itself. George Tsebelis' concept of "nested games" is used to illustrate that the government's litigation strategy must be understood as the product of decision making within several overlapping contexts ("games"), including partisan competition, the executive's desire to retain policy-making authority, and the Liberal leadership struggle.[6] In short, in addition to the principled rights issues raised by same-sex marriage, the personal and partisan considerations of the political centre played a crucial role in the government's *Charter* litigation strategy. The chapter proceeds as follows. First, the same-sex marriage cases are detailed, including the jurisprudential developments related to equality rights during the past twenty-five years, which structured the courts' rulings. The government's response is also explained in more detail. Next, Tsebelis' theory of "nested games" is briefly summarized, before the chapter details the various simultaneous "games" involving the federal government with respect to same-sex marriage during the summer of 2003.

Same-Sex Marriage Cases: EGALE and Halpern

In 2003, the institution of monogamous heterosexual marriage had existed for several centuries, but the existing common-law definition dated to the 1866 British case *Hyde v. Hyde and Woodmansee*.[7] There was no statutory definition of marriage until 2000, most likely because the common-law definition was widely taken for granted, as the BC Court of Appeal noted in *EGALE*: "[S]ame-sex conduct constituted a criminal offence in Canada until 1969. Thus, the prospect of same-sex marriages did not realistically arise in Canada until some time thereafter."[8] Moreover, legislative jurisdiction over marriage is somewhat unclear in Canada, due to the wording of Canada's founding document, the *Constitution Act, 1867*.[9] Under section 91(26) of this act, which relates to "marriage and divorce," the federal government has jurisdiction over marriage, including the capacity to marry. However, section 92(12) grants the provinces jurisdiction to legislate with respect to the conditions governing the celebration of marriage, under the heading "The Solemnization of Marriage in the Province," as well as authority over "Property and Civil Rights in the Province" via section 92(13).

The only federal statutory references to marriage appear in the *Modernization of Benefits and Obligations Act (MBOA)*[10] and the *Federal Law-Civil Law Harmonization Act No. 1 (FCHA)*.[11] The *MBOA* is an omnibus bill amending sixty-eight federal statutes to extend benefits and obligations available to heterosexual common-law spouses to same-sex couples, in response to the Supreme Court of Canada's ruling in *M. v. II.* declaring the opposite-sex definition of "spouse" unconstitutional.[12] However, section 1.1 of the *MBOA* states: "For greater certainty, the amendments made by the Act do not affect the meaning of the word 'marriage' that is, the lawful union of one man and one woman to the exclusion of all others." Similarly, section 5 of the *FCHA*, which harmonizes federal law with the civil law of Quebec, states that "[m]arriage requires the free and enlightened consent of a man and a woman to be the spouse of the other."

Given the explicitly heterosexual wording of the *MBOA*, it is surprising that it was not challenged in either *EGALE* or *Halpern* (as the *FCHA* only applies to Quebec, it was not applicable in either case). As the BC Court of Appeal noted in *EGALE*, all of the parties to the case agreed that the *MBOA* simply "states Parliament's view as to what marriage is" and "does not purport to be an exercise of Parliament's power to legislate in relation to marriage under s. 91(26) of the *Constitution Act, 1867*."[13] Similarly, in *Halpern*, the parties concurred that "s. 1.1 [of the *MBOA*] does not purport to be a federal statutory definition of marriage. Rather, s. 1.1 simply affirms that the Act does not change the common-law definition of marriage."[14] The cases focused instead on the 1866 common-law definition, but, as the preceding statement makes clear, there would be obvious and immediate implications for these federal statutes.

Both *EGALE* and *Halpern* turned on the question of whether the common-law definition of marriage violated the *Charter*'s section 15 right to equality. Sexual orientation is conspicuous by its absence from the enumerated grounds in section 15, and its exclusion was indeed deliberate, reflecting the opposition of many of the *Charter*'s drafters to recognizing gays and lesbians in Canada's supreme law. However, then-federal justice minister Jean Chrétien testified before the Special Joint Committee on the Constitution of Canada that section 15's wording was sufficiently open-ended to allow future *courts* to include sexual orientation.[15] The Supreme Court of Canada eventually agreed fourteen years later in *Egan v. Canada* that sexual orientation required constitutional protection.[16] In *Egan*, the Court considered whether the federal *Old Age Security Act* was unconstitutional because it limited spousal benefits to heterosexual couples.[17] Interestingly, the Court upheld the act, concluding that it was intended to benefit female widows who, because many of them had left the workforce to raise children, were financially dependent on their husbands – a situation not faced by most homosexual couples, including Egan and his partner. However, the Court did rule that equality rights protected sexual orientation.

The Court had set the stage for *Egan* in its first decision regarding section 15, *Andrews v. Law Society of British Columbia*, by ruling, as Chrétien had suggested, that the enumerated grounds of section 15 were not exhaustive.[18] This ruling was largely common sense – there is nothing in the wording of section 15 to suggest that *only* people belonging to the enumerated groups should be protected. In *Andrews,* the Court determined that section 15 protection can be extended when a legal distinction causes harm to (or evidences prejudice against) an "analogous ground" – a characteristic similar to an enumerated ground. This means that the group must be clearly defined, such as a "discrete and insular minority," and be "historically disadvantaged." As Chrétien's comments indicate, sexual orientation was recognized as a probable analogous ground even at the time of the *Charter's* drafting in 1981. The Court has refined the analogous ground concept since *Andrews*, most notably in *Law v. Canada (Minister of Employment and Immigration)*, placing greater emphasis on the adverse effects of legal distinctions on human dignity rather than just material harm.[19]

In light of these developments and, in particular, the ruling in *M. v. H.* on the definition of "spouse," the rulings on same-sex marriage were not entirely surprising. Both the BC and Ontario Courts of Appeal found that the marriage law makes a distinction on the basis of sexual orientation, a prohibited analogous ground. Moreover, this distinction is discriminatory, following *Andrews* and *Law*, because it perpetuates the view that same-sex couples are not capable of forming loving and lasting relationships and, thus, that same-sex relationships are not worthy of the same respect and recognition as opposite-sex relationships. The courts rejected the attorney general's argument that "marriage relates to the capacities, needs and circumstances of opposite-sex couples. The concept of marriage – across time, societies and legal cultures – is that of an institution to facilitate, shelter and nurture the unique union of a man and woman who, together, have the possibility to bear children from their relationship and shelter them within it."[20]

Both courts observed that same-sex couples can in fact choose to have children through adoption, surrogacy, and donor insemination, and, as the attorney general itself had acknowledged in its facta, procreation and child rearing are not the only purposes of marriage or the only reason that couples choose to marry. Both courts of appeal also rejected the attorney general's second line of argument, that the heterosexual definition of marriage is not discriminatory because of the convergence, since *M. v. H.* and the *MBOA*, of the legal treatment of same-sex and opposite-sex common-law couples, with the attendant benefits and responsibilities. Common-law spouses must cohabit for a specified period of time, unlike married couples, and not all marital rights and obligations have been extended to cohabiting.[21]

Notably, the attorney general advanced an additional argument in the Ontario Court of Appeal, that "marriage is not simply a shopping list of functional attributes but a unique opposite-sex bond [that] is not truly a common-law concept, but one that predates our legal framework, through its long existence outside of it."[22] The Ontario Court of Appeal categorically rejected this argument, stating bluntly that "the fact that the common law adopted, rather than invented, the opposite-sex feature of marriage is irrelevant."[23] Rather, the legal distinction was the crux of the matter. Furthermore, the court criticized the attorney general's "argument that marriage is heterosexual because it 'just is'" as being circular reasoning that sidesteps the entire section 15(1) analysis.[24]

Having found a violation of section 15, the courts next needed to address whether the violation was a reasonable limitation under section 1 of the *Charter* as laid down by the Supreme Court of Canada in *R. v. Oakes*.[25] Both courts of appeal concluded that the common-law definition of marriage fails the second and third parts of the *Oakes* test and could not be upheld. They argued that the attorney general did not demonstrate any pressing and substantial objective for maintaining marriage as an exclusively heterosexual institution, since encouraging procreation does not require excluding same-sex couples from marriage. Heterosexual couples will not stop having or raising children because same-sex couples are permitted to marry, and an increasing percentage of children are born to, and raised by, same-sex couples. By the same token – namely, the absence of a rational connection – the means are not proportional. Similarly, the exclusion of same-sex couples is not rationally connected to the "companionship" dimension of marriage since "gay men and lesbians are as capable of providing companionship to their partners as persons in opposite-sex relationships."[26] Furthermore, the common-law bar to same-sex marriage is not a "minimal impairment," most importantly because "same-sex couples are completely excluded from a fundamental societal institution" and "complete exclusion cannot constitute minimal impairment."[27] The courts also found the law both over-inclusive and under-inclusive: "The ability to 'naturally' procreate and the willingness to raise children are not prerequisites of marriage for opposite-sex couples. Indeed, many opposite-sex couples that marry are unable to have children or choose not to do so. Simultaneously, the law is under-inclusive because it excludes same-sex couples that have and raise children."[28]

The only disagreement between the BC and Ontario Courts of Appeal was over the appropriate remedy under section 24(1) of the *Charter*. Both courts opted for "reading in," which Chief Justice Antonio Lamer characterized in *Schachter v. Canada* as applicable when a rights violation is rooted in "what the statute wrongly *excludes* rather than what it wrongly *includes*."[29] In this instance, the courts reformulated the common-law definition of marriage as "the lawful union of *two persons* to the exclusion of all others"[30] (in British Columbia) and as "the voluntary union for life of *two persons* to the exclusion of all others"[31] (in Ontario). However, the BC Court of Appeal initially suspended this remedy for a period of twenty-four months to allow Parliament time to devise a response. In contrast, the Ontario Court of Appeal took the more activist route, declaring the new definition of marriage effective immediately and instructing that marriage licences be issued to those same-sex couples who had been denied them. Prompted by the Ontario court, and with the consent of the attorney general, the BC Court of Appeal revised its remedy so as to take immediate effect.[32]

The Government's Response and Fallout

After the BC Court of Appeal's ruling in *EGALE*, the Attorney General hinted that he would appeal to the Supreme Court of Canada. However, he did not file immediately, although there is a sixty-day window of opportunity for appeals to the highest court.[33] During this period, the Ontario Court of Appeal rendered its decision in *Halpern*, and the government announced that it would not appeal either decision. Instead, the Liberal government drafted a bill (which was not tabled in the House of Commons) legalizing same-sex marriage, and on July 17, 2003, it referred its constitutionality to the Court (see the appendix at the end of this chapter). The reference posed three questions: (1) is the statutory definition of marriage solely within federal jurisdiction; (2) is the proposed legislation consistent with the *Charter*; and (3) does the *Charter*'s freedom of religion protect religious officials from being compelled to perform a marriage between two persons of the same sex that is contrary to their religious beliefs? Notably, the second issue was a foregone conclusion. It was inconceivable that *including* same-sex couples would violate the *Charter*. The more pertinent question, which the reference neatly avoided, is whether *barring* same-sex couples from marrying is permissible under the *Charter*'s equality rights or the reasonable limits provision of section 1. In September 2003, the government narrowly defeated an opposition motion by the Canadian Alliance to reaffirm the traditional heterosexual definition of marriage, as committed to by the Liberal government only two years before in section 1.1 of the *MBOA*. An identical motion by the opposition party in 1999 had been overwhelmingly approved by the Liberal government.[34] This show of opposition – including within the Liberal caucus – to the government's draft bill recognizing gay marriage forced the leadership to alter the reference, and on January 28, 2004, Justice Minister Irwin Cotler, under the direction of now Prime Minister Paul Martin, included a question explicitly asking the Court whether the heterosexual definition of marriage violates the *Charter*.

Before the Court could rule on the same-sex marriage question, two key political events intervened. The first was the Liberal sponsorship scandal, in which Prime Minister Martin was marginally implicated in his capacity as a senior Quebec minister and the former finance minister. The second was Martin's decision to call a federal election, which on June 28, 2004, returned the Liberals to power, albeit with a minority government. Central features of Martin's campaign were his endorsement of the lower court rulings legalizing same-sex marriage and his portrayal of Stephen Harper, the new leader of the recently created Conservative Party, as "scary" and a threat to *Charter* rights because of his opposition to same-sex marriage and judicial activism. The strategy to use same-sex marriage as a "wedge issue" was at least partially successful, as Conservative support in the polls, which had been surging, stalled late in the campaign immediately after a series of Liberal attack ads targeted Harper's "extremism."[35] Two months after the election, Martin filled two vacancies on the Supreme Court by appointing Justices Rosalie Abella and Louise Charron, both of whom had supported equality rights claims by gays and lesbians when they sat on the Ontario Court of Appeal.

The Court's decision in *Reference re Same-Sex Marriage*, handed down on December 9, 2004, proved anti-climactic yet surprising.[36] The Court clarified that (not surprisingly) the draft bill would not violate the *Charter* and that the definition of marriage was federal jurisdiction. However, while the justices concluded that the *Charter*'s religious freedoms would prevent the state from compelling churches to marry gay couples, legislative guarantees to that effect fall under provincial, not federal, jurisdiction. On the key question of whether the *Charter* required recognizing same-sex marriages, the Court surprised observers by refusing to answer the question on the grounds that it was unnecessary to do so since Parliament had already decided to grant such recognition. The Liberal government finally tabled the bill (B-38, the *Civil Marriage Act*) in February 2005, and, after defeating a motion by the opposition Conservatives to deny a second reading in April, it was narrowly passed on June 28, 2005.

Nested Games and Government Litigation: A Theoretical Overview

Tsebelis developed his concept of "nested games" to analyze "cases in which an actor confronted with a series of choices does not pick the alternative that appears to be the best."[37] According to Tsebelis, "[i]f, with adequate information, an actor's choices appear to be suboptimal, it is because the observer's perspective is incomplete. The observer focuses attention on only one game, but the actor is involved in a whole network of games – what I call *nested games*. What appears suboptimal from the perspective of only one game is in fact optimal when the whole network of games is considered."[38] In simpler terms, a decision or choice that does not appear to be the best one may be explained when we fully understand all of the factors facing the decision maker. As this language suggests, the nested games approach belongs to the broader school of rational choice theory, which assumes that actors behave logically to achieve their goals. As I demonstrate elsewhere, litigation decisions by the federal government regarding appeals to the Supreme Court of Canada are made rationally, with lawyers and political officials weighing the costs and benefits of appealing, and the competing interests of those parties directly involved, within a context of institutionally bounded choice.[39] Among the strongest factors influencing the decision to appeal is whether the lower court's ruling could constrain the government's policy-making authority in significant or novel ways. Similarly, officials and documents from the Department of Justice speak of considering a variety of strategic factors in their decision making, including the likelihood that the Supreme Court of Canada will grant leave, maintaining the government's reputation with the Court, and resolving jurisprudential conflict in the lower courts.[40]

In this chapter, the analysis is extended in a more qualitative direction, to provide a thicker account of the political and partisan environment in which the same-sex marriage cases occurred. It is also important to stress that litigation decisions by the federal government are quite centralized in regard to high-profile, controversial cases before the senior appeal courts. Such litigation can be understood as a central agency function, in light of the attorney general's virtual monopoly over legal representation of line departments and agencies and the potential for strong direction from the prime minister. The latter was certainly realized in the same-sex marriage cases.[41] The federal government's litigation decision-making process for potential appeals to the Supreme Court of Canada is, in summary, as follows.[42] The counsel who litigates the case before the lower court – usually a lawyer in one of over a dozen regional offices across Canada – seeks formal approval from the attorney general. This approval involves a process of review and recommendation by the National Litigation Committee (NLC), with the final decision by the attorney general. The NLC is composed of several senior Department of Justice lawyers, who consult with affected line departments and agencies. The NLC recommends appealing only where "the public interest *requires* an appeal," such as in cases in which the impact is widespread, lower court rulings are conflicting, or an important policy will be undermined.[43] The NLC's recommendation is forwarded to the attorney general – who is simultaneously the minister of justice – and his or her deputy. At this level, the attorney general's decision may be influenced by the political interests of his or her Cabinet colleagues, including the prime minister. For example, sources inside the Liberal government have revealed that the response to the *EGALE* and *Halpern* rulings was debated at the highest levels of the political executive, including by Cabinet and then Prime Minister

Jean Chrétien.[44] In short, at this level, senior political figures may influence the decision to appeal.

The Nested Games of Same-Sex Marriage

The federal government's response to the lower court same-sex marriage rulings raises two related questions. The first is why the government vigorously opposed recognizing same-sex marriage in its arguments before the courts in *Halpern* and *EGALE* but reversed itself shortly after the decisions and openly supported it. The simplest explanation is that, as Chrétien has repeatedly stated, he had a conversion on the road to Damascus, so to speak – he changed his mind. In both earlier interviews and in his new autobiography, he speaks of putting aside his own views, which were rooted in his traditional Catholic upbringing in rural Quebec and doing what he thought was "right." Notably, however, in his autobiography, he does not actually claim that he was persuaded by rights-based arguments but, rather, by the human element – he discusses actual people he knew, fellow politicians who had experienced hardship living in the closet, and how coming out had changed their lives for the better. As with many aspects of Chrétien's public life, the political was personal. While it is an important point that *Charter* politics can be so influenced by the personality of individuals at the centre of power, this explanation is quite incomplete, as it does *not* explain the strategy that the Chrétien government then took.

This fact brings us to the second question: why did the government produce a draft bill complying with the rulings but refer it to the Supreme Court of Canada (the *Reference re Same-Sex Marriage*) without tabling it in the House of Commons? At least three other options were available that should have resulted in a quicker recognition of same-sex marriage. First, the government could have simply done nothing and allowed the lower court rulings to stand. One drawback of this approach would have been that, as provincial appeal court decisions, *EGALE* and *Halpern* technically only applied in their respective provinces. Another drawback was that there was pressure from external actors and within caucus (albeit much of it conflicting) on the government to act. A second option would have been to move immediately to pass the legislation, foregoing the reference or an appeal altogether. As will be more fully explained later in this chapter, there was obviously some political currency to be had in acquiring the Court's "approval" for the bill. As such, the third option of appealing the lower court rulings to the Supreme Court of Canada appears to have been the optimal strategy. It would have immediately put the issue before the highest court, and it was *extremely* likely that it would have upheld the lower courts, in light of its previous rulings on sexual orientation and section 15 discussed earlier. Moreover, a Supreme Court of Canada ruling would have had national application. Finally, and perhaps most importantly, an appeal and subsequent Supreme Court of Canada decision legalizing same-sex marriage would have achieved Chrétien's goal fairly quickly, while shifting political responsibility onto the Court for a controversial and divisive issue.

Same-sex marriage seemed to present the Liberals with what Mark Graber terms the "non-majoritarian dilemma."[45] Such a dilemma occurs when an issue is so polarizing for the voting public that there is no clear majority position (or the majority of voters are ambivalent or indifferent), but the existence of vocal minorities on either side of the issue ensures that any action the government takes will provoke strident opposition. This division also split the Liberal caucus and Cabinet, as evidenced by the strong support in both for maintaining the traditional definition of marriage in recent votes in the House of Commons. As alluded to earlier, in 1999, the Liberals had overwhelmingly supported a motion by the Canadian Alliance to affirm the traditional heterosexual definition of marriage, not long before passing the *MBOA* and the *FCHA*. Shortly after the lower court rulings on same-sex marriage, the Canadian Alliance introduced the identical motion, but this time Chrétien required cabinet ministers to oppose it while ostensibly allowing other members of his caucus to vote according to their conscience. Although opposed by the New Democratic Party and Bloc Québécois (and some members of the Conservative Party), the motion was defeated – only by five votes (137-132) – thanks to this partial invocation of party discipline and the absence of nineteen Liberal members of parliament. One-third of the government caucus (fifty-three MPs) defected to support the motion.[46]

What all of this implies is that the government seemed to take responsibility unnecessarily for a policy change when it was risky politically, while not pursuing its goal of legalizing same-sex marriage in as speedy a manner as was possible. Thus, the decision to draft a bill and refer it to the Supreme Court of Canada appears to have been a "suboptimal" choice, in rational choice terms. Using Tsebelis' nested games approach, however, we can see that Chrétien and the Liberals were operating in an even more complex decision-making environment than the foregoing analysis suggests. I contend that Chrétien and his closest advisors were simultaneously involved in at least the following six "games" with their respective preferences after his decision to support same-sex marriage.

Sexual Orientation Equality Game

This is the most obvious game in which the government found itself, with the goal of extending the legal protections, benefits, and responsibilities of marriage to gay and lesbian individuals and couples – in short, to promote equality on the basis of sexual orientation. As discussed earlier, an immediate move to recognize same-sex marriage through legislation, or even an appeal to the Supreme Court of Canada, could have achieved this goal more quickly.

This assumes, however, that the government *could* have passed such legislation, which brings us to the second nested game.

Liberal Party Caucus Game

Chrétien almost certainly knew that he might lose a vote in the House of Commons if it came soon after the lower court rulings because of resistance within his own party to same-sex marriage. This fact was evidenced by the strong support within the government caucus in September 2003 for the opposition's motion to retain the traditional definition of marriage. Proceeding through the court system would have bought the government some time, as the case made its way through argumentation before the Court and the justices deliberated – a process that often takes over a year. According to Grant Huscroft, "[i]n terms of crass partisan advantage, the government [used] the Court to fend off political criticism and buy time."[47] However, this could have been accomplished through an appeal, without the political risks associated with a reference. Moreover, if the attorney general had maintained his opposition to same-sex marriage in his submission to the Court – that is, defended the existing policy – this strategy should have eased pressure from the opponents of same-sex marriage within the Liberal caucus. Liberals who supported same-sex marriage, including then Attorney General Martin Cauchon, might have drawn some comfort from the likely prospect that the Court would uphold the rulings in *EGALE* and *Halpern* and that use of the section 33 notwithstanding clause was extremely unlikely.[48] So why use a draft bill and reference instead?

Two possible answers lie in the terms of the reference itself. The first is the essentially rigged question of whether recognizing same-sex marriage would violate the *Charter* rather than whether failing to do so would. As Grant Huscroft has observed, this question was "simply disingenuous."[49] It was inconceivable that *including* same-sex couples would violate the *Charter*. It is thus likely that the government hoped this question would elicit a Supreme Court of Canada ruling that appeared to support, and thus legitimize, the government's new position while silencing critics within the caucus, Parliament, and the public. The gambit failed, however, as critics in the caucus and elsewhere saw through the ploy and demanded the "real" question be put to the Court, which the Liberals' new leader and attorney general did the following winter. The second is the question of whether the *Charter*'s freedom of religion protects religious officials from being compelled to perform same-sex marriages. By signalling its intent to protect such institutions, the government probably hoped to assuage the caucus (and other) critics of gay marriage. While it is helpful to consider the internal politics of the Liberal caucus to explain Chrétien's strategy, we also need to look at what else the government was trying to accomplish with this reference, as illustrated by the following nested games.

Partisan Competition Game

Many of the factors raised by divisions in the Liberal caucus apply equally to the government's calculations regarding partisan competition. Beginning with the Liberals' rivals on the political right, Chrétien admittedly took a risk by taking a contentious position in support of same-sex marriage. While the Harper-led Canadian Alliance was gaining in the polls – at the Progressive Conservative Party's expense – they were eclipsed by the popularity of the Liberals under Paul Martin, who was still only the heir-apparent of the party, before the sponsorship scandal broke. So, in July 2003, there was no credible threat from the political right, which remained fragmented with unpopular leaders. Nonetheless, endorsing same-sex marriage did help to create a "wedge issue" for the Liberals against the Right-wing parties, by emphasizing the Canadian Alliance's conservative stance on moral issues – a platform on which the Alliance was relatively weak in vote-rich Ontario and Quebec, where the Liberals enjoyed their greatest support.

The draft bill and reference were also wise in light of the Liberals' rivals on the Left, including the New Democratic Party and the Bloc Québécois, both of whom supported same-sex marriage. Endorsing same-sex marriage allowed the Liberals to shore up support within their Left wing, including potential defectors to the New Democratic Party on this issue. It would also appeal to Leftist voters in Quebec – where same-sex marriage was more accepted than in English Canada – who had already begun to abandon the Bloc Québécois in the previous election. It is perhaps not surprising that a politician of Chrétien's partisan inclination and experience found that his personal values corresponded with a sound position in the perpetual game of party politics.

Election Game

Distinct from the partisan competition game, this game refers to the Liberals' desire to manage the agenda, given that an election was anticipated soon after Martin took over from Chrétien in early 2004. Even after the rulings in *Halpern* and *EGALE*, it is reported that then Prime Minister Chrétien was reluctant to legally recognize same-sex marriage not only because of his personal values as "a 69-year-old Catholic from rural Quebec" but also because he knew many rural members of parliament in the Liberal caucus "would have a tougher time" in an election that was anticipated within the year "if the government rushed passage of a law."[50] The draft bill and reference thus not only allowed Chrétien to take an advantageous position *vis-à-vis* the Liberals' partisan rivals but also to create enough of a delay – and hopefully obtain the Court's backing in the process – to allow the issue to "cool off." An appeal would have achieved a delay but without the benefits of partisan positioning. As noted earlier, same-sex marriage did indeed become a wedge issue that the Liberals, under Martin, desperately needed in the next election when the party was struggling with the sponsorship scandal. While it is unlikely that Chrétien foresaw this exact series of events, the scandal highlights the political reality – which competent leaders know well – that partisan competition is continuous and it is wise to guard your flanks when possible.

Executive Policy-Making Authority Game

Although there can be political advantages to shifting responsibility for policy change to the courts, it is generally the case that political leaders seek to enhance their influence over policy, which includes protecting their policy-making authority from incursions by other actors, including, paradoxically, the judiciary. This is one reason that political leaders are reluctant to relinquish control over judicial appointment, and, of course, why our *Charter* has a notwithstanding clause.[51] Senior lawyers in the attorney general's office whom I have interviewed openly acknowledged this mindset. Consider the following statements:

> Invalidation of statutes always reduces Parliament's room to manoeuver, so we'll always be concerned about that.

> I think the overriding concern in the non-criminal area, is, if not actually winning the case, minimizing the loss, so that Parliament can have a range of policy options.

> Usually reading in or reading down is going to be one of the most intrusive remedies. When you just strike down, usually you're giving Parliament a little leeway to devise a solution. You may be saying this one solution is bad, but you've still got all the others to choose from, whereas when they read in they're saying this is what the law shall be henceforth. It may not be legally impossible ... to come along with a different solution, but it's going to be politically very difficult.

Although the lawyers speak of "Parliament," students of Canadian politics know full well that, with rare exceptions, Parliament does not "devise solutions" – the government does, thanks to our Westminster system of fused executive and legislature, in tandem with our single-member-plurality electoral system's tendency to produce majority governments. Moreover, the same lawyers have stated that their "client" is the respective minister responsible for the policy or the minister of justice. Nonetheless, the comments provide an interesting insight into the way Department of Justice lawyers perceive their own role, which is that they have a responsibility to protect the policy-making authority of the elected branches.

The Chrétien government's strategy regarding same-sex marriage suggests an attempt to keep its options open, namely by not tabling the bill for debate and by referring the bill rather than appealing the lower court losses. With respect to the latter, although reference decisions are commonly treated as judicial rulings, technically they are not, and the government emphasized that it was seeking the Court's non-binding "advice." In contrast, a decision on appeal from *Halpern* and *EGALE* would have been legally binding on Parliament and provincial legislatures, government officials (including justices of the peace and marriage commissioners), and lower courts. The Court's likely remedy of a *Charter* violation might also have concerned members of the government.

In recent cases involving legislation and sexual orientation, the Supreme Court of Canada signalled that it would not refrain from enforcing its rulings in favour of rights claimants. In *Vriend v. Alberta*, the Court chose to "read in" to Alberta's human rights code explicit protection against discrimination on the basis of sexual orientation.[52] In effect, the Court re-wrote the province's legislation and ordered its human rights tribunal to enforce the changes immediately. The following year, in *M. v. H.*, the Court employed the somewhat less-intrusive remedy of invalidating the heterosexual definition of "spouse" in part of Ontario's family law regime and then suspending the ruling for six months to allow the province time to respond.[53] Where *Halpern* and *EGALE* dealt with the judge-made common law rather than legislation, judicial revision of the law, if found discriminatory, would have been a certainty.

So what options did the Liberals want to preserve? An internal policy review by the Department of Justice,[54] which Attorney General Cauchon had successfully lobbied Chrétien for in 2002,[55] identified several possibilities, which Chrétien repeated in his recent autobiography. While recognizing same-sex marriage through federal legislation was one option, the Department of Justice advised the government that, as the Supreme Court of Canada would observe in *Reference re Same-Sex Marriage*, Parliament did not have jurisdiction under the federal division of powers to exclude religious institutions from having to perform same-sex marriages (due to provincial authority over "the solemnization of marriage" in section 92(12)). Nonetheless, the government put this issue to the Supreme Court of Canada in the reference, possibly for greater clarity but probably also to signal to voters and members of its own caucus its desire to enact such protections.

A second option that was considered was legalizing sex-neutral "civil unions" (open also to opposite-sex common-law couples), which had been created in Denmark, Belgium, France, and Vermont,[56] and retaining "marriage" as an exclusively heterosexual institution but making the two relationships identical in terms of legal benefits and responsibilities. Justice raised the concern that proved to be central in *Halpern* and *EGALE*, namely that the very fact of treating same-sex couples who *wanted* to marry differently from heterosexual couples probably constituted discrimination under section 15.[57] Moreover, the review concluded that because of the constitutional division of powers, "neither the federal Parliament nor a provincial or territorial legislature acting alone has the jurisdiction to create a new form of legal relationship beyond marriage (such as a civil union or a domestic partnership) that will have predictable legal consequences under both federal law and provincial or territorial law."[58]

A third option was for the federal government to get out of the "marriage" business altogether, leaving it to religious institutions (whose ceremonies would no longer have binding *legal* status) and creating a single, sex-neutral institution (such as "civil unions" or "registered partnerships") for legal unions. This option also raised division of power concerns since it would require the provinces to change their laws regarding solemnization. In addition, without legal marriage, the federal laws regarding divorce would become moot, leaving a legal vacuum regarding dissolution of relationships. In any case, the review argued, denying legal recognition to purely religious marriages would offend many religious institutions and adherents.

The logic of the lower court rulings in *Halpern* and *EGALE*, which came after the Department of Justice's review, would have precluded the option of retaining traditional marriage and creating parallel civil unions. In addition, an appeal to the Supreme Court of Canada, upholding the lower courts, would similarly constrain the government. As such an outcome was highly probable, the decision to refer, rather than appeal, can be understood as an attempt to preserve the political centre's policy discretion. It is important to note that the federal government's ultimate decision not to pursue any of the policy options that differed from the lower courts does not in itself contradict this argument. Political leaders, as noted earlier, generally seek to enhance their discretion and control over policy and will act to do so – even when it ultimately proves unsuccessful.

Liberal Leadership Game

By the summer of 2003, the Liberal Party had been riven by a protracted and extremely public leadership struggle between its existing leader, Jean Chrétien, and his increasingly impatient heir-apparent Paul Martin. At this point in time, Chrétien had already announced that he would step down in February 2004 – he was ultimately pushed out by the party in December 2003 – and had introduced several bold legislative measures that he saw as his personal legacy, which were broadly consistent with the "just society" envisioned by his mentor, former prime minister Pierre Trudeau. These measures included partial decriminalization of marijuana; political financing reform (prohibiting or sharply limiting corporate donations to political parties and candidates); creating an independent ethics commissioner;

negotiating a comprehensive deal with Aboriginals on improving govern-ance and social welfare; introducing controls on assisted human reproduction while encouraging stem cell research; establishing a national sex offender registry; and recognizing same-sex marriage.[59]

From this perspective, the draft bill and initial reference may have reflected in part Chrétien's desire to take credit for this reform before he left office – something he could not have done via a regular appeal to the Supreme Court of Canada. While some of these measures were adopted by the House of Commons and/or Senate before Chrétien stepped down (most notably campaign finance reform), most of these initiatives had little chance of passing in the time that he had remaining in office. Given this situation, the fact that each of the measures was highly controversial and that an elec-tion was expected shortly after Martin took over, one has to wonder whether these measures were also motivated in part by Chrétien's desire to complicate the leadership of his rival and successor. The fact that some of these initia-tives languished under Martin – in particular, the "pot law" – suggests they were not welcomed by the new Liberal leadership, although the prime min-ister and his staff were soon preoccupied with the sponsorship scandal.

As the preceding analysis illustrates, the government was operating in an environment rich with competing goals and incentive structures. Chrétien's *volte-face* on same-sex marriage may have been ultimately based on his per-sonal attitudes, but his strategic decisions in the months that followed the lower court rulings suggest a keen awareness of more traditional political factors. Several of these fall under the umbrella of party politics, including managing divisions within his own Liberal caucus, positioning his party advantageously *vis-à-vis* its competitors on both the Left and the Right, and attempting to influence the grounds upon which the next federal election would be fought. The picture that emerges is of a Liberal leadership at once trying to take credit for a policy change regarding same-sex marriage while also using the Supreme Court of Canada to simultaneously enhance the legitimacy of, but to delay, this change.

A similar tension is reflected in the government's apparent desire to en-hance the judiciary's influence on this issue, but also to protect the execu-tive's policy-making authority by maintaining its policy options through delay and a non-binding reference. While the government may have ultim-ately embraced the lower court rulings, the bill doing so (the *Civil Marriage Act*) was not introduced to Parliament until a year and half after the rulings, and it did not become law for almost another six months.[60] Notwithstanding the stated desire of two consecutive prime ministers to recognize same-sex marriage and end this form of legal discrimination, neither moved to ac-complish it in the fastest means available. This fact can only be explained by taking a broader view of the political and partisan context in which the same-sex marriage issue arose, one in which concerns about "rights" were only one part of a much bigger picture.

Conclusion

One possible criticism of the foregoing argument is that it gives the Chrétien government and his advisors too much credit and that their decision not to appeal is less the product of calculated strategy than tactical errors. One might argue that they simply did not appreciate that not appealing was, in fact, counter-productive to their goal of promoting equality for gays and lesbians. Tsebelis emphasizes that his theory assumes actors are working with "adequate information" in each game – for example, that they did not just "guess wrong" on the Supreme Court of Canada's likely rulings on appeal.[61] Such a possibility cannot be refuted with the available information, but it is highly improbable that the prime minister, the prime minister's office, and the attorney general's office are that politically or legally unsophisticated. The attorney general's office, for example, boasts an impressive roster of highly experienced counsel in a wide range of legal specializations, an extensive consultation process surrounding appeals to the Supreme Court of Canada, and access to the highest levels of political leadership. Chrétien proved himself a more than capable partisan tactician in his long political career, including winning three consecutive majority governments.

There is thus a strong case for using a nested games approach to understand the litigation decisions concerning same-sex marriage in the summer of 2003. It should be stressed, however, that it is not suggested that the government conceptualizes its decisions explicitly in terms of these "nested games." Rather, it is a heuristic tool for the observer in order to help make sense of the different demands and interests shaping the government's behaviour. This approach, when applied to the same-sex marriage reference, reveals the importance of personal views at the political centre in high-profile cases as well as of calculations about partisan advantage, issue-agenda management, and protecting policy-making authority. This should not be surprising, as the reference power is typically exercised in a highly politicized manner, at the behest, or with the approval, of the prime minister. This fact alone suggests that it is reasonable to look to the goals of the prime minister when trying to understand the government's litigation strategy in high-profile cases. The facts and arguments presented throughout this chapter illustrate not only how *Charter* cases can "judicialize" politics – by influencing public policy, elections, the political agenda, and public discourse – but also how litigation and judicial processes regarding the *Charter* can be thoroughly politicized in the traditional sense.[62] It is important to bear this point in mind when assessing the transformative potential of the *Charter* after twenty-five years and beyond.

Appendix

Same-Sex marriage timeline

Sept. 6, 2002	Superior Court of the District of Montreal declares in *Hendrick* that section 5 of the *Federal Law-Civil Law Harmonization Act, No. 1 (FCHA)*, section 1.1 of the *Modernization of Benefits and Obligations Act (MBOA)*, and part of paragraph 2 of article 365 of the *Civil Code of Quebec (CCQ)* (providing that marriage can only be solemnized between a man and a woman) are inoperative but suspends the declarations of invalidity for a period of two years.
May 1, 2003	B.C. Court of Appeal rules in *EGALE*; remedy delayed until July 12, 2004
June 10, 2003	Ontario Court of Appeal rules in *Halpern*; remedy immediate
June 17, 2003	AG Canada Cauchon announces Ottawa will not appeal either decision
July 8, 2003	AG Canada lifts suspension of B.C.C.A. remedy
July 15, 2003	AG Canada withdraws appeal in *Hendrick* (case continues anyway, as appeal brought by 3rd party, the Catholic Civil Rights League)
July 17, 2003	Draft legislation legalizing same-sex marriage referred to Supreme Court
Sept. 16, 2003	By one vote, House of Commons defeats Opposition motion by the Canadian Alliance to reaffirm the traditional heterosexual definition of marriage. Fifty-two Liberals vote for motion, 31 abstain, and Cabinet is forced by PM Chrétien to oppose motion.
December 12, 2003	Paul Martin officially replaces Jean Chrétien as Prime Minister
January 26, 2004	Arguments heard before Q.C.A. in *Hendrick*
January 28, 2004	Revised terms of same-sex marriage reference to Supreme Court announced (whether status quo violates Charter)
March 19, 2004	Q.C.A. strikes down *FCHA, MBOA,* and *CCQ* provisions in *Hendrick*
June 28, 2004	Martin and Liberals re-elected but with minority government
August 30, 2004	Justices Abella and Charron of O.C.A. appointed to Supreme Court

▶

◄ *Appendix*

Same-Sex marriage timeline

October 6-7, 2004	*Same-sex Marriage Reference* case heard by Supreme Court
December 9, 2004	*Same-sex Marriage Reference* decision rendered by Court, which refuses to rule on whether the opposite-sex requirement for marriage in civil and common law violates Charter
February 1, 2005	Liberal government tables Bill C-38, the *Civil Marriage Act,* which recognizes same-sex marriage
April 13, 2005	Proposed amendment to Bill C-38 by Opposition Conservative Party, which would have denied the bill second reading, defeated
June 28, 2005	Final Reading of Bill C-38 passed by vote of 158-133
July 20, 2005	Royal Assent given to *Civil Marriage Act*

Notes

1 *Bliss v. Canada (Attorney General)*, [1979] 1 S.C.R. 183. *Canadian Charter of Rights and Freedoms,* Part 1 of the *Constitution Act, 1982,* being Schedule B to the *Canada Act 1982* (U.K.), 1982, c. 11. *Canadian Bill of Rights*, S.C. 1960, c. 44.

2 *Barbeau/EGALE v. Canada (Attorney General)*, 2003 BCCA 251 (B.C. C.A.) [*Barbeau/EGALE*]; *Halpern v. Canada (Attorney General)*, [2003] O.J. No. 2268 (Ont. C.A.) [*Halpern*]. EGALE (Equality for Gays and Lesbians Everywhere) is an organization that promotes civil and equality rights for gays and lesbians.

3 The protections afforded by section 15 were given an open-ended wording, however, as the enumerated grounds ("race, national or ethnic origin, colour, religion, sex, age, or mental or physical disability") were only protected "in particular," not exclusively.

4 Under section 53 of the *Supreme Court Act*, R.S.C. 1985, c. S-26, the Supreme Court of Canada can be asked to provide "advisory opinions" on legal (typically constitutional) questions submitted by the federal government. Provincial legislation similarly authorizes references by provincial governments to the highest court of appeal in each respective province.

5 *Barbeau/EGALE, supra* note 2; and *Halpern, supra* note 2.

6 George Tsebelis, *Nested Games: Rational Choice in Comparative Politics* (Berkeley: University of California Press, 1990).

7 *Hyde v. Hyde and Woodmansee* (1866), L.R. 1 P.and D. 130 at 133 (Lord Penzance).

8 *Barbeau/EGALE, supra* note 2, para. 41.

9 *Constitution Act, 1867* (U.K.), 30 and 31 Victoria, c. 3.

10 *Modernization of Benefits and Obligations Act*, S.C. 2000, c. 12.

11 *Federal Law-Civil Law Harmonization Act No. 1*, S.C. 2001, c. 4.

12 *M. v. H.*, [1999] 2 S.C.R. 3.

13 *Barbeau/EGALE, supra* note 2, para. 44.

14 *Halpern, supra* note 2, para. 28.

15 Special Joint Committee on the Constitution of Canada, November 1980, *Minutes of Proceedings*, Jean Chrétien 36 (January 1981): 14-15 [emphasis added].

16 *Egan v. Canada*, [1995] 2 S.C.R. 513.

17 *Old Age Security Act*, R.S.C. 1985, c. O-9.

18 *Andrews v. Law Society of British Columbia*, [1989] 1 S.C.R. 143.

19 *Law v. Canada (Minister of Employment and Immigration)*, [1999] 1 S.C.R. 497.

20 Quoted in *Halpern, supra* note 2, para. 82.

21 This distinction was upheld in 2002 by the Supreme Court of Canada in *Nova Scotia (Attorney General) v. Walsh*, 2002 SCC 83.

22 Roslyn Levine, Attorney General of Canada factum in *Halpern, supra* note 2, cited in Shannon Kari, "Marriage Exists outside Canada's Law, Ottawa Argues," *Gazette (Montreal)* (April 19, 2003), A14.

23 *Halpern, supra* note 2, para. 68.

24 Ibid., para. 71.

25 *R. v. Oakes*, [1986] 1 S.C.R. 103. The three part *Oakes* test is as follows:

1 Was the violation prescribed by law? (This excludes from section 1 protection "policies embedded in administrative practice, rather than explicit legislation" or "vague enabling legislation" where "the actual standards used by the law's administrators are *their* standards, not the law's.")

2 Is the violation justified by a "pressing and substantial objective"?

3 Are the legal means "proportional" to the objective?: are they (1) "rationally connected"; (2) is there a "minimal impairment" of the rights, that is, are the "least drastic means" used; and (3) does the benefit to general welfare outweigh the cost to the individual's rights?

26 *Halpern, supra* note 2, para. 131.

27 Ibid., para. 139.

28 Ibid., para. 130.

29 Ibid., para. 681 (Lamer C.J.) [emphasis in original]. *Schachter v. Canada*, [1992] 2 S.C.R. 679.

30 *Bearbeau/EGALE, supra* note 2, para. 159.
31 *Halpern, supra* note 2, para. 148 [emphasis added].
32 *Bearbeau/EGALE, supra* note 2.
33 *Supreme Court Act, supra* note 4, s. 58.
34 Kim Lunman and Drew Fagan, "Marriage Divides the House," *Globe and Mail* (September 17, 2003), A1 and A4.
35 According to the Canada Election Study, the importance of the attack ads should not be overstated, but the study's authors note that Liberal support surged among those who were only "somewhat angry" about the sponsorship scandal. It seems likely that these voters were mobilized by the attack ads. Elisabeth Gidengil, Andre Blais, Joanna Everitt, Patrick Fournier, and Neil Nevitte, "How the Race was Won," *Globe and Mail* (July 14, 2004), A15.
36 *Reference re Same-Sex Marriage*, [2004] 3 S.C.R. 698.
37 George Tsebelis, *supra* note 6, 1.
38 Ibid., 7.
39 Matthew Hennigar, "Why Does the Federal Government Appeal to the Supreme Court of Canada in Charter of Rights Cases? A Strategic Explanation," *Law and Society Review* 41, 1 (March 2007): 225-50.
40 Mary Dawson, "The Impact of the Charter on the Public Policy Process and the Department of Justice," *Osgoode Hall Law Journal* 30 (1992): 595-603; Department of Justice Canada, *Federal Prosecution Service Deskbook* (Ottawa: Department of Justice Canada, 2000), V-22-3-6, cited in Hennigar, *supra* note 39.
41 Matthew Hennigar, "Conceptualizing Attorney General Conduct in Charter Litigation: From Independence to Central Agency," *Canadian Public Administration* 51, 2 (Summer 2008): 193-215.
42 This is adapted from Matthew Hennigar, "Players and the Process: Charter Litigation and the Federal Government," *Windsor Yearbook of Access to Justice* 21 (2002): 91-109.
43 Department of Justice Canada, *supra* note 40.
44 Tonda MacCharles, "It Was an Issue of Rights," *Toronto Star* (October 2, 2004), H1 and H4. Jean Chrétien confirmed this in his recent autobiography, *My Years as Prime Minister* (Toronto: Knopf Canada, 2007).
45 Mark Graber, "The Non-Majoritarian Difficulty: Legislative Deference to the Judiciary," *Studies in American Political Development* 7 (1993): 35-72.
46 Brian Laghi, "MPs' Debate Mirrors National Turmoil," *Globe and Mail* (September 17, 2003), A4; and Lunman and Fagan, *supra* note 35, A1 and A4.
47 Grant Huscroft, "'Thank God We're Here': Judicial Exclusivity in Charter Interpretation and Its Consequences," *Supreme Court Law Review* (2d) 25 (2004): 258.
48 Tonda MacCharles, "Cauchon Takes Stand on Social Issues," *Toronto Star* (October 4, 2004), A4; and Martin Cauchon, speech to Equality Forum International Business Colloquium Dinner, Philadelphia, PA (May 1, 2004), excerpted at http://www.samesexmarriage.ca/advocacy/EF040504.htm.
49 Huscroft, *supra* note 47.
50 MacCharles, *supra* note 44, H4.
51 Two exceptions are explained by Ran Hirschl ("hegemonic preservation") and Tom Ginsburg ("insurance model of judicial review"). Ran Hirschl, *Towards Juristocracy: The Origins and Consequences of the New Constitutionalism* (Cambridge, MA: Harvard University Press, 2004); and Tom Ginsburg, *Judicial Review in New Democracies: Constitutional Courts in Asian Cases* (Cambridge: Cambridge University Press, 2003).
52 *Vriend v. Alberta*, [1998] 1 S.C.R. 493.
53 *M. v. H., supra* note 12. Which it did by passing legislation in 1999 that did not extend the definition of "spouse" to same-sex couples and, instead, created a new legal relationship of "same-sex partners" with parallel benefits and responsibilities (*Family Law Act*, R.S.O. 1999, c. F.3, s. 1(1)). This approach, which had already been ruled unconstitutional by a federal court (*Moore and Akerstrom v. Treasury Board*, [1998] T-1677-96 (F.C.T.D.)) was abandoned in 2005 under the Liberal government, which adopted a sex-neutral definition of "spouse" (*Spousal Relationships Statute Law Amendment Act*, S.O. 2005, c. 5).

54 Department of Justice Canada, *Marriage and Legal Recognition of Same-Sex Unions: A Discussion Paper* (Ottawa: Department of Justice Canada, 2002).

55 MacCharles, *supra* note 44, H4.

56 Hawaii also had allowed civil unions, except that they were *only* available to same-sex couples, meaning there was no legally recognized alternative to marriage for heterosexuals.

57 Notably, this would not be true of opposite-sex couples that choose civil union, as they *could* marry if they wished to do so.

58 Department of Justice Canada, *supra* note 54, 9-10.

59 See, for example, CBC News, "Some Important Legislation in Danger of Dying" (November 7, 2003), http://www.cbc.ca/canada/ story/2003/11/07/house031107.html.

60 *Civil Marriage Act,* S.C. 2005, c. 33.

61 Tsebelis, *supra* note 6, 7.

62 C. Neal Tate and Torbjörn Vallinder, eds., *The Global Expansion of Judicial Power* (New York: New York University Press, 1995).

Part 3: Citizenship and Identity

12
Bills of Rights as Instruments of Nation Building in Multinational States: The Canadian *Charter* and Quebec Nationalism

Sujit Choudhry[1]

On the eve of the twenty-fifth anniversary of the *Canadian Charter of Rights and Freedoms*, Canada was plunged once again into an existential debate over the very nature of the Canadian political community.[1] As has happened so often in the past, the issue was Quebec. The triggering event for this latest round of constitutional introspection was a question put to Prime Minister Stephen Harper in Quebec City on June 23, 2006. Quebec's political elites have long referred to the province, its institutions, its symbols, and its collective goals in national terms. The provincial legislature is the National Assembly, its head of government the prime minister as opposed to a mere premier, its national holiday called la Fête Nationale, a range of public policies promoting French as Quebec's public language publicly described as tools of nation building, and the question of Quebec's continuing membership in the Canadian federation the "national question" – the nation in each instance not being Canada. The occasion for the prime minister's visit to Quebec was la Fête Nationale. The prime minister was asked whether celebrating Quebec's national holiday signified his acceptance of the notion that Quebec was a nation. The prime minister declined to answer, stating that the debate over whether Quebec is a nation was "semantic" and "doesn't serve any purpose."[2]

The issue would probably have died there. Yet, a few days later, then-Liberal leadership candidate Michael Ignatieff stated in a speech that Quebec was indeed a nation within Canada.[3] In his policy platform, he went even further. Since Quebecers "have come to understand themselves as a nation, with a language, history, culture and territory that marks them out as a separate people," Ignatieff called for the Constitution to be amended to explicitly acknowledge "the national status of Quebec."[4] Ignatieff's proposal provoked an immediate and hostile reaction from his two leading rivals, Stéphane Dion and Bob Rae. Neither was opposed in principle to the idea that Quebec

---

1 The copyright for this chapter resides with the author.

was a nation. Rather, their objections were strategic. Ignatieff had argued that the constitutional recognition of Quebec as a nation would not come with any additional powers and had as its goal the dampening of nationalist sentiment. However, Dion and Rae feared that it would perversely have exactly the opposite effect.[5] At the very least, it would serve as constitutional encouragement for a series of demands to reconstitute Canada around two nations, Quebec and Canada. The goal would be dramatically enhanced powers for Quebec on an asymmetric basis that would reflect its unique status as a province *and* a nation – *un province pas comme les autres*.[6] Others opined that it could also serve as a springboard to statehood, a prospect made more likely by the probable failure of constitutional negotiations.[7]

Ignatieff's proposals dominated the Liberal leadership race over the course of the fall and badly divided the party. The party's Quebec wing complicated matters further when it passed a resolution in October that made the recognition of Quebec as a nation official party policy and mandated the consideration of options to "officialize" this status.[8] The resolution raised the spectre of open civil war on the eve of the Liberal leadership vote in December. The Bloc Québécois sought to exploit these divisions by indicating in November that it would table a motion in the House of Commons that would "recognize that Quebeckers form a nation."[9] It was a win-win proposition for the Bloc Québécois. Facing dissension from within his own caucus, Prime Minister Harper responded with a resolution of his own, to recognize the "Québécois" as "a nation within a united Canada."[10] The New Democratic Party and the Liberals immediately announced their support for the resolution. In an instant, the Bloc Québécois' coup became a blunder. Ultimately, it capitulated, which led to the motion being easily passed by the House of Commons at the end of November.[11] The passage of the motion by the House in turn led to the withdrawal of the Liberal policy resolution before it was debated.

It would be tempting to analyze this episode in purely political terms. But, instead, this chapter draws attention to a puzzle and a curious omission. Dion's reaction to Ignatieff's proposal states the puzzle: "Do we want this recognition to be purely symbolic, or do we want it to lead to concrete consequences on, say, the division of powers or the allocation of public funds? And how does this approach square with the previous question? It is contradictory to affirm that the recognition of Quebec as a nation is necessary but purely symbolic."[12]

Dion's puzzlement stems from the fact that although the constitutional recognition of Quebec as a nation generated heated debates, it was strictly a symbolic measure that would have had no legal effect. To Dion, a constitutional symbol, "although desirable, is not necessary."[13] In this respect, the proposed amendment was quite unlike the distinct society clauses in the Meech Lake and Charlottetown Accords, which were interpretive provisions.

However, even in these earlier episodes, the concrete legal effect, if any, of those clauses ultimately mattered less than their explicit acknowledgment of Quebec's distinctiveness. And the most trenchant opponents of Ignatieff's proposals joined the debate on the terrain of constitutional symbolism. As they put it, to constitutionally entrench the recognition of Quebec's national status would be an assault on the idea of a single Canadian nation.[14] Constitutional symbols mattered centrally to both the proposal's proponents and its detractors. The question is why?

The curious omission is the *Charter*. The notion of one Canada was most closely associated with Pierre Trudeau. The *Charter* was Trudeau's central instrument for nation building. Moreover, the *Charter* was a direct response to the centrifugal pressures of Quebec nationalism. So, not surprisingly, it was Quebec that objected most to the *Charter*. And it was the adoption of the *Charter* over Quebec's objections that sparked two decades of constitutional politics to reach a constitutional accommodation with that province, including Ignatieff's proposals. In short, the *Charter* is an integral part of why Canada found itself debating Quebec's status as a nation nearly twenty-five years after it was adopted. Yet, the *Charter* was hardly mentioned at all during the debate over Ignatieff's proposal.

The objective of this chapter is to link the puzzle and omission – that is, to tie the debate over the constitutional recognition of Quebec as a nation to the impact of the *Charter* on Canadian constitutional culture. One of the debate's most striking features is that support for Ignatieff's initiative was sharply polarized on linguistic grounds. Francophones within Quebec were its most enthusiastic supporters, whereas anglophones outside of Quebec were its most vociferous critics. This pattern of political opinion reflects differing underlying patterns of national identification. Francophones inside Quebec tend to view Quebec as their primary national political community, whereas anglophones outside Quebec tend to identify with Canada.

It will be argued that these competing patterns of national identification reflect the rather mixed legacy of the *Charter*. The *Charter* was intended to serve as the centrepiece of a common Canadian nationality that transcended the linguistic divide. Yet, while the *Charter* has been an effective tool for anglophone nation building, it has been unsuccessful in combating Quebec (read francophone) nationalism. Indeed, not only did the *Charter* not offset Quebec's nationalism, it may also have made things worse. This is a cautionary tale to plurinational polities faced with the same challenge as Canada – of building a common political identity against the backdrop of competing nationalisms and attempting to do so through a bill of rights.

Quebec Nationalism and the *Charter* Project

In the academic literature, the idea that there was a direct link between the genesis of the *Charter* project and Quebec nationalism no longer commands significant attention. Canadian debates about the *Charter* now take as their starting point the Bickelian charge that judicial review is a deviant institution in a liberal democracy that is in need of justification. The theory of dialogue as an account and justification of the Canadian practice of judicial review – potentially applicable to other jurisdictions as an alternative to American-style judicial supremacy – is the latest turn in this constitutional conversation.[15] What the actual political forces were that gave rise to the *Charter* is no longer at the forefront of scholarship.

However, it was not always this way. To recover the connection between the *Charter* and the rise of nationalism in Quebec, we need to return to the scholarship produced in the wake of the adoption of the *Charter* and the following decade of constitutional politics. The link was perhaps most famously made by Peter Russell.[16] Russell's question was why federal politicians, principally Trudeau, made the *Charter* their major constitutional priority between 1968 and 1981. Until that point, the federal goal had been the patriation of the Constitution – in other words, the adoption of a domestic amending formula that would terminate the imperial role in formal constitutional change. Placing the *Charter* front and centre was therefore a dramatic change. Russell's answer was the rise of Quebec nationalism or, more precisely, a significant shift in the character of Quebec's constitutional demands. Until the 1960s, Quebec's constitutional claims – advanced in constitutional politics and before the courts – had been defensive, aimed at safeguarding the existing areas of jurisdiction granted to Quebec by the *Constitution Act, 1867*.[17] However, in the 1960s, Quebec's goals shifted to the expansion of its jurisdiction over social and economic policy in order to enable the province to engage in a nation-building enterprise and construct a modern Quebec, the major institutions of which operated in French.

Why this shift in Quebec took place is itself a complex story.[18] To a considerable extent, it was a defensive response to the dramatically increased role of Ottawa in economic and social policies after the Second World War. Federal policy activism meant an increase in the importance of federal institutions, especially the federal bureaucracy, which worked in English and in which francophone Quebeckers were a small minority. Another factor was the enormous social change within Quebec. After the war, there was massive urbanization and industrialization, in a context where anglophones dominated positions of economic leadership and many of the professions. These demographic and economic shifts underlined and reinforced the role of language as the basis for the unequal distribution of economic power within the province, which was documented so vividly by the Royal Commission on Bilingualism and Biculturalism.[19] Quebec's political elites responded by mobilizing francophones around the nationalist project of *maîtres chez nous*, which encompassed both the expansion of Quebec's jurisdiction and the use of these new tools to construct a modern set of economic and political institutions to ensure the survival of a modern, francophone society. The upgrading in the status of Quebec overtook the older idea of *la nation canadienne-française,* which resided both inside and outside the province, because of the necessity for territorial jurisdiction to engage in a modern project of nation building.

The *Charter* was the federal government's defensive response to these centrifugal pressures. To be sure, as Alan Cairns has noted, the domestic and international forces that led to the adoption of the *Charter* were much broader than just the need to respond to Quebec.[20] Yet, Russell persuasively argues that the desire to combat Quebec nationalism was central to the federal government. The primary sources support Russell's analysis. The most important federal document was *Federalism for the Future,* which was released in February 1968 in conjunction with the Confederation of Tomorrow Conference.[21] The document acknowledges that the impetus for constitutional reform was Quebec, specifically "the dissatisfaction of the people of Canada of the French language and culture with the relative positions of the two linguistic groups within our Confederation."[22]

However, the response was not to meet Quebec's demands for enhanced autonomy on the terrain of federalism. Rather, the federal government's view was that "first priority should be given to that part of the Constitution which should deal with the rights of the individual – both his rights as a citizen of a democratic federal state and his rights as a member of the linguistic community in which he has chosen to live."[23] This choice was initially presented as a matter of logic since "the rights of people must precede the rights of governments."[24] Yet, *Federalism for the Future* goes on to emphasize the contribution of a constitutional bill of rights as the basis for national unity. The constitutional entrenchment of "individual human rights for all Canadians ... is a fundamental condition of nationhood" and rights "are ... fundamental to the will of the nation to survive."[25] "[T]ake these rights away," it continued, "and few Canadians would think their country worth preserving."[26]

Constitutions, Nationalism, and Nation Building

So how exactly was the *Charter* supposed to further national unity? We can get a handle on the nation-building function of the *Charter* and bills of rights more generally by making three sets of distinctions. The first is the distinction between two varieties of nationalism. On the one hand, nationalism is often paired with claims of self-determination and sovereignty. This is the nationalism of national minorities, such as the Quebecois, the Scots, and the Catalans. The political goal underlying the kinds of nationalist movements ranges from autonomy to states of their own. This is the dominant understanding of nationalism in the legal imagination. Accordingly, the regulation of nationalist politics becomes a matter for international law, with the principal question being under what circumstances peoples' right to self-determination encompasses the right to statehood. International law has generally been very resistant to these claims.[27] The centrality of this conception of nationalism to the legal imagination became clear during the debate over Ignatieff's proposal. For example, some argued that choice of the term "nation" over "distinct society" carried legal significance because a nation possesses the right to self-determination under international law.[28]

On the other hand, nationalism can be understood as "nationalizing nationalism."[29] The goals of this variety of nationalism are neither internal autonomy nor statehood. Rather, the energy of nationalism is directed at an existing political community in a process whereby states, already extant, create nations. At its core, nationalizing nationalism consists of a set of policies that are designed to homogenize the national culture and language to coincide with those of the dominant ethnolinguistic group and to centralize political and legal power in institutions dominated by the majority group and which operate in its language. In states that contain minority nations, such as Quebec, these minorities respond to nationalizing nationalism by engaging in defensive nation-building projects of their own. Indeed, many Quebec federalists who harbour no desire to secede nonetheless supported the Ignatieff proposal precisely because it reinforced defensive claims of jurisdiction by Quebec in the service of preserving and promoting its unique linguistic identity.

Legal scholars have focused on the first form of nationalism but not on the second, which brings us to the second distinction – between different ways in which constitutions can serve as instruments of nationalizing nationalism.[30] Historically, the most direct way has been to centralize legal and political power. This centralization occurred, for example, in Spain with the abolition of the *Generalitat* in Catalonia in 1714 and the *Fueros* of the Basque province and Navarre in the early nineteenth century. The state would possess jurisdiction over language and education, which would allow it to set the majority's language as the official language of the state and of instruction in schools. Another mechanism was the elimination of pre-existing forms of legal pluralism, to require all ethnolinguistic groups to participate in a common legal-constitutional order, organized around common judicial institutions dominated by members of the majority group, applying the legal system of the dominant group (as occurred in settler societies in North America). In other words, one way of responding to Quebec's nationalism would have been to engage in a centralizing project of this sort. The use of constitutional design in the service of nationalizing nationalism in fact was attempted in the colonial period in Canada between 1840 and 1867. It was a spectacular failure.

However, the *Charter* project points to the use of a constitutional bill of rights to engage in a similar nationalizing project. At first blush, this action seems bizarre since the first set of nationalizing strategies involves the centralization of political and legal power, whereas a bill of rights sets limits on such policies. Yet, a bill of rights can nonetheless serve this role, and now we get to the final distinction. There are two ways to think about the nation-building role of a bill of rights: the *regulative* conception and the *constitutive* conception. On the regulative conception, the function of a bill of rights is to enable individuals to invoke the machinery of the courts to set binding constraints on political decision making. Serving this function does not depend on a bill of rights having any effect on citizens' political identities. On the constitutive conception, a bill of rights constitutes the demos that it also constrains. It encodes and projects a certain vision of political community – in particular, the idea of a political community as consisting of rights-bearing citizens of equal status. To serve as an instrument of nation building, a bill of rights must alter the very self-understanding of citizens.

This is the idea of civic citizenship, most famously presented by Ernest Renan.[31] I have characterized the argument for civic citizenship previously in the following way.[32] A constitutional order must meet two constraints, the *legitimacy* constraint and the *stability* constraint. The legitimacy constraint is normative, while the stability constraint is sociological. The ambition of liberal constitutionalism is that a constitutional order must both be legitimate and must enjoy the allegiance of a sufficient number of its citizens to work. On the liberal conception, the conditions for the legitimate exercise of public power are the rights and institutions of representative government that one finds in a typical liberal-democratic constitution. The ambition of the civic conception of citizenship is that these same conditions also supply the necessary motivational element for those institutions to work. Additionally, the connection between legitimacy (normative) and stability (sociological) is not contingent. Rather, it is conceptual – in other words, it is the ambition of the civic conception of citizenship that citizens view themselves as part of the same constitutional-legal order, *precisely because* that order is legitimate.

The *Charter* as a Nation-Building Instrument

The *Charter* relies on both the regulative and constitutive conceptions of a bill of rights to serve as an instrument of nation building. In regulatory terms, the *Charter* imposes legal restraints on minority nation building by Quebec, through the rights to inter-provincial mobility and to minority language education for children. The centrality of the mobility and minority language education rights provisions to the nation-building project of the *Charter* is underlined by their exemption from the notwithstanding clause, unlike most *Charter* rights. Both rights can be understood as a response to potential or actual policies of linguistic nation building by Quebec, and, indeed, Quebec has objected to both.[33] The *Charter* prohibits the use of disincentives to inter-provincial migration by guaranteeing the right to "move and take up residence in any province" and "to pursue the gaining of a livelihood in any province."[34] These rights are subject to laws of general application "other than those that discriminate among persons primarily on the basis of province of present or previous residence" and "laws setting down reasonable residency requirements for the receipt of social services.[35] Quebec objected because the province "legitimately discriminates in its legislation to preserve and enhance its integrity as a culturally differend [sic] society operating within the context of the dominant Anglophone culture of the continent."[36]

Far more important as a tool of minority nation building in Canada is the linguistic assimilation of international and inter-provincial migrants. The key tool in this case is education. Under the Canadian Constitution, education lies in the provincial jurisdiction and encompasses power over the language of instruction and curriculum.[37] This power has been crucial for Quebec because it has permitted that province to establish and operate a primary and secondary educational system that works in French, which is a centrepiece of linguistic nation building. It has also enabled Quebec to create French-language universities, an indispensable support for the use of French in economic and political life, which is the source of considerable controversy in other plurinational states. Conversely, it has denied to the federal government the power to set a standard curriculum in a shared national language, a common instrument of nation building in many countries.

Absent the *Charter*, Quebec could have mandated that the exclusive language of public education in Quebec – at all levels – be French. Yet, the *Charter* granted the right to certain categories of citizens to receive minority language primary and secondary education for their children where numbers warrant. The federal government justified this right by reframing the problem of linguistic disadvantage. For Quebec, the problem was the diminished status of French within Quebec. The federal government responded by attempting to break the equation of French with Quebec, by making the issue the status of francophones across Canada. As *Federalism for the Future* puts it, "the people of the French language and culture do not have the same opportunities as do those of the English language to live their lives, to raise their children ... in their own language *in all parts of Canada*."[38] The goal was to make Canada the home for francophones from coast to coast. The minority language education provisions were the centrepiece of this strategy. Yet, the language rights applied symmetrically to Quebec's Anglophone minority.

The flashpoint of controversy within Quebec has been the right of anglophones who received their primary school instruction anywhere in Canada in English to have their children educated in English in Quebec – the so-called "Canada Clause."[39] This provision was sharply attacked by Premier

René Levesque as undermining "the capacity of our National Assembly to protect French culture in Quebec."[40] Quebec's *Charter of the French Language* attempted to limit this right to parents who had been educated in English in Quebec.[41] The Canadian *Charter* was drafted specifically to render this policy unconstitutional, which the Supreme Court of Canada did in one of its first *Charter* judgments.[42] Another provision of the *Charter*, which grants citizens whose children have received their schooling in English anywhere in Canada the right to English-language education for their children in Quebec, also limits Quebec's ability to linguistically integrate migrants from other provinces.[43] An attempt to construe this right narrowly was recently found to be unconstitutional.[44] For Quebec, minority language education rights are very controversial, precisely because they limit Quebec's ability to encourage the linguistic integration of migrants to Quebec from other parts of Canada, not just immigrants to Canada.

Russell was rightly skeptical of the language rights provisions as a tool of nation building. Despite the entrenchment of the right to minority language education, French outside Quebec continues to decline, as does English within Quebec. In other words, the territorialization of language communities has continued apace. In addition, although the *Charter* grants the right to interact with the federal government and New Brunswick in French, these rights do not apply to dealings with other governments.[45] Francophones must still use English to interact with provincial governments. Moreover, even if such rights had been entrenched, the practical reality remains that the major economic and political opportunities are only open to those who speak English. As Jean Laponce has argued, if a language is not the language of the public sphere and is only spoken at home, it will eventually decline.[46]

Although the *Charter* grants the right to minority language, it does not grant the right to lead a complete life in French. Parallel forces have occurred in Quebec, reinforced by the emigration of anglophones. As Russell notes, as European settlement extended into western Canada in the late nineteenth and early twentieth century, it may have been possible to create a truly bilingual society in the Canadian west. Instead, the federal government took exactly the opposite position, most infamously in the Manitoba schools crisis.[47] Thus, Ken McRoberts is correct when he argues that the dream of a bilingual Canada from sea to sea is now over.[48] If the goal of the language rights provisions of the *Charter* was to roll back the clock on linguistic assimilation, they are "too little too late."[49]

However, the *Charter* was also intended to function constitutively as the germ of pan-Canadian constitutional patriotism. As *Federalism for the Future* states, "a constitution is more than a legal document; it is an expression of how the people within a state may achieve their social, economic and cultural aspirations through the exercise and control of political authority."[50]

In a federal state such as Canada, since citizens share these rights irrespective of language or province of residence, a bill of rights serves as a transcendent form of political identification – the spine of common citizenship that unites members of a linguistically diverse and geographically dispersed polity across the country as a whole. Cairns puts this point well: "[T]he *Charter* fosters a conception of citizenship that defines Canadians as equal bearers of rights independent of provincial location. This legitimizes a citizen [sic] concern for the treatment of fellow Canadians by other than one's own provincial government."[51]

Russell's skepticism of the constitutive effects of a bill of rights – which is shared by Dion – stems from an underlying skepticism regarding the efficacy of symbolic constitutionalism.[52] For both individuals, a constitution can only become a source of political identification and the basis of a national identity because of its concrete effects on public policy. Subsequent experience has proven that Russell was right and wrong. Outside of Quebec, the *Charter* has generated a new pan-Canadian patriotism, likely much more quickly than even the most optimistic predictions suggested. However, within Quebec, the *Charter* has decidedly not had this effect. The *Charter* has not served to bind francophone Quebeckers to the Canadian constitutional order. Indeed, the sharply differentiated effect of the *Charter* on Canadian constitutional culture suggests that it may now be harder, because of the *Charter*, to build a unifying account of the Canadian constitutional order that transcends linguistic and regional divides.

The conflicting reactions to the Meech Lake Accord within and outside Quebec powerfully illustrate these points. Outside of Quebec, the public reaction to Meech Lake was very hostile, as famously described by Alan Cairns.[53] There were two points of criticism. The first was the process whereby the accord was reached. The proposed constitutional amendments were arrived at as the result of closed-door negotiations between the premiers and the prime minister. The complete package was then presented to the Canadian public as a *fait accompli*, a seamless whole that could not be altered for fear that the whole deal would unravel. As a legal matter, this approach grew out of the relevant procedures for constitutional amendment themselves, which required the consent of the two chambers of federal Parliament and the provincial legislatures.[54]

During the Meech Lake process, citizens outside Quebec rejected this process for constitutional change by rejecting its underlying theory. They asserted themselves, not the governments, as the constituent actors in the constitutional process. The Constitution did not belong to governments; it belonged to them. In the language of Trudeau, the rights of citizens precede the rights of governments. This was dramatically different from the way in which citizens had situated themselves *vis-à-vis* the Constitution before the *Charter*. The *Charter* had transformed Canadians outside Quebec into constitutional actors and the basic agents of constitutional change. As the Charlottetown process made clear, Canadian constitutional culture would not permit constitutional amendments without widespread public consultation.

The transformative effect of the *Charter* on constitutional culture also explains the hostile reaction to perhaps the central provision in the Meech Lake Accord – the distinct society clause. The clause would have mandated that the Constitution be interpreted to recognize "that Quebec constitutes within Canada a distinct society" and would have affirmed "[t]he role of the legislature and Government of Quebec to preserve and promote the distinct identity of Quebec."[55] The clause did not identify in what precise respects Quebec was distinct from the rest of Canada and, indeed, the precise legal effect of the clause was the subject of widespread contestation. Outside Quebec, the fear was that the clause would provide for the unequal application of the *Charter*, by authorizing Quebec to limit the *Charter* in a manner not open to other provincial governments. In particular, there was a concern that it would provide additional constitutional support for linguistic nation building on the part of Quebec.

Now the question is why the unequal effect of the *Charter* mattered at all. Canadian public policy has long been differentiated on a provincial or regional basis because of vast differences in demography and the structure of the economy. The answer was that for Canadians outside Quebec the *Charter* was what made Canada a country and was the spine of a Canadian citizenship that was shared by all Canadians, both those within and outside Quebec. Consequently, the potential for its unequal application across Canada was an assault on a basic, non-negotiable term of the Canadian social contract and the very identity of the country. As Cairns puts it, "the *Charter* norm is ... sustained by a citizenry that views the possibility of a distinct and weaker *Charter* regime in another province as a constitutional affront. It offends the norm of an equal rights-possessing citizenry uniformly present in the federal, ten provincial and two territorial arenas. The *Charter* generates a roving normative Canadianism oblivious to provincial boundaries, and thus hostile to constitutional stratagems such as the Meech Lake 'distinct society' that might vary the *Charter*'s availability in one province."[56]

However, within Quebec, the view on the distinct society clause was exactly the opposite, rooted in a particular account of the history and origins of Canada. For Quebec, the adoption of federalism and the creation of Quebec was a direct response to the failure of the United Province of Canada, a British colony that resulted from the merger of the previous colonies of Lower Canada (later Quebec) and Upper Canada (later Ontario), which existed between 1840 and 1867. The history here is complex.[57] In brief, citizens of both Lower and Upper Canada elected equal numbers of representatives to a legislative assembly, although the largely francophone citizens of the former outnumbered the largely anglophone citizens of the latter.[58] The language of government was meant to be English.[59] The goal behind the merger and departure from representation by population was to facilitate the assimilation of francophones – that is, to engage in English language nation building even before anglophones were a majority. As time went on, Upper Canada became more populous and demanded greater representation in the joint legislature, which was resisted by francophones who feared they would be outvoted on matters important to their identity. The result was political paralysis. Federalism was the solution – providing for representation by population at the federal level but also creating a Quebec with jurisdiction over those matters crucial to the survival of a francophone society in that province, such as education through institutions that operated in French.

So, to Quebec, Canada is unintelligible except against the backdrop of the idea that the institutions of federalism are designed to protect Quebec's linguistic distinctiveness. This idea is at the heart of the "two nations" or "dualist" theory of Canada. Yet, the odd thing about the Canadian Constitution is that it lacks express recognition of this fact and treats Quebec on a basis of juridical equality to the other provinces. On the symbolic front, the Constitution is absolutely silent on who Canadians were, or were not, to be.[60] This silence may be nothing more than a function of the peculiar legal character and political function of the *British North America Act, 1867 (BNA Act)* as a statute of the British Parliament that granted Canada extensive powers of internal self-government but not independence. It may also reflect a lack of agreement on such a shared account at the time Canada came into being. Yet, as Charles Taylor has perceptively argued, whatever the reasons for this silence, the lack of such a statement did not come without its costs.[61]

It was accompanied by a political culture outside of Quebec that refused to acknowledge the French-Canadian understanding of Confederation. The formal juridical equality of the provinces reinforced this refusal, setting up the dominant constitutional conversation as the contest between province building and pan-Canadian nation building. The distinct society clause therefore mattered a great deal because it was the first time the Constitution would explicitly acknowledge a view of what Canada was for. The concrete legal effect of the clause counted for a whole lot less than this simple statement. Indeed, by the end of the Meech Lake process, the clause mattered much less for what it did than for what it said.[62] And so the repudiation of the clause on the basis of a theory of Canada that was grounded in the *Charter* set up the *Charter* as an obstacle to, rather than as a central component of, how many Quebecers understood the nature of their relationship with Canada.

Now this is not the only reason that the *Charter* has failed to take in Quebec as the seed of pan-Canadian nationalism. Another strike against the *Charter* was the process whereby it was adopted, over Quebec's insistence that there was a constitutional convention granting it a veto over constitutional change. Patriation in the face of the asserted veto damaged the legitimacy of the 1982 Constitution in the eyes of many Quebecers.[63] The claim of a veto for Quebec again derived from a constitutive account of the Canadian constitutional order, in which Canada was understood as a plurinational federation in which Quebec was a constituent actor. So any constitutional amendments that af-·fected Quebec's ability to safeguard its linguistic identity (including its role in central institutions) would require its consent. And competing views over popular involvement in the constitutional amendment procedure *after* 1982 have made it difficult for the *Charter* to serve as the basis for a shared Canadian identity. The *Charter* fuels a view of Canadian citizens irrespective of province of residence as the constituent actors in the amending process. This position is largely irreconcilable with a veto for Quebec and sets up another disjunction between the notion of Canada constituted by the *Charter* and Quebec's account of a plurinational Canada. This gap between these two views of the amending process is illustrated by the referendum over the Charlottetown Accord, which was, in effect, two referenda held simultaneously – one in Quebec and one in the rest of Canada, with differing views on what the relevant majorities were.

The second reason is language. The stated aim of the *Charter* project was to serve as a common basis of citizenship that transcended the linguistic divide. The principal mechanism for doing so was minority language education rights provisions. These provisions were more than regulative measures that constrained linguistic nation building by Quebec. They communicated a conception about the place of language in Canada, with two components. First, they were designed to inculcate a self-understanding in francophones that Canada as a whole was their home, not simply Quebec, and a corresponding set of understandings for anglophones in Quebec. Second, by detaching linguistic identity from a province of residence, by opting for personality over territoriality as the basis of language of education, and by granting a right for linguistic minorities to choose their linguistic identity, the *Charter* adopted a stance of neutrality on matters of linguistic choice.

This position challenged the very legitimacy of linguistic nation building by Quebec. Moreover, this constitutional choice was likely to be non-neutral in its effect on Quebec's ability to protect and promote the French language. Although the minority language rights provisions apply symmetrically to francophone minorities outside Quebec and the anglophone minority in Quebec, they are rather unequal in their impact. The reason is that English is the dominant language of North America and, indeed, is now the dominant language of international economic life. So the economic pressures for francophones to assimilate are great. What this means is that for Quebec to continue as a French-speaking community in the modern world, it must adopt linguistic policies that in other provinces are unnecessary. The symmetrical character of the minority language education rights provisions conceals a lack of symmetry in fact. This lack of symmetry is symbolically important because it marks a repudiation of Quebec's understanding of what Canada is for.

Conclusion: Bills of Rights as Nation-Building Instruments in Plurinational Places

Had the *Charter* been effective at combating Quebec nationalism and serving as the glue of a pan-Canadian national identity, the last twenty-five years of constitutional politics would not have happened. There would have been no Meech Lake Accord, no Charlottetown Accord, and no referendum in 1995 in which the country came close to break-up because of the threat of a unilateral declaration of independence in the event of a yes vote. And there would have been no proposal for, let alone a vote in favour of, a motion of the House of Commons recognizing the "Québécois" as a nation, even within a united Canada. Yet, because all of these things have happened, one of the basic political purposes of the *Charter* was not met. I would go even further and suggest that it was the role of the *Charter* as the central element of a pan-Canadian patriotism outside of Quebec that explains the vehemence of those who rejected Ignatieff's proposal that Quebec's national status be recognized in the Constitution for principled, not pragmatic, reasons. Andrew Coyne, for example, argues that the recognition of Quebec as a nation cut against an account of Canadian national identity under which "we are tied together by something more than blood, something higher than ethnicity."[64] To be sure, Coyne draws on a view of Canada that dates back to the founding of Canada itself, when George-Étienne Cartier famously proclaimed that Confederation would constitute "a political nationality with which neither the national origin, nor the religion of any individual, [will] interfere."[65] However, this view of Canada was strengthened by the *Charter*, which furthered its logic by guaranteeing all Canadians a set of rights independent of race and ethnic background.

So, to invoke the notion of one Canada was inevitably to invoke the legacy of Trudeau. And it was the *Charter* that lay behind the criticisms of the use of the term "Québécois" in the House of Commons resolution, as opposed to "Quebecker," because the former is ambiguous on whether it refers to a political community defined by ethnicity, language, or territory. The suggestion was that if ethnicity or language were the shared element of political identity of the nation recognized by the House of Commons and the definition of citizenship embodied therein, it cut against the grain of the transethnic and linguistic notion of equal citizenship embedded in the *Charter*. Indeed, the power of the Trudeau vision was so great outside Quebec that the Ignatieff campaign was forced to respond by releasing a remarkable document that attempted to reconcile Ignatieff's proposals with Trudeau's views.[66]

The Canadian experience holds more general lessons. Canada is a particular kind of divided society, in which there are competing nationalisms within the same political place. These places are variously referred to as multinational polities,[67] plurinational polities,[68] or, most recently, plurinational places.[69] In some cases, these places are states, such as Bosnia Herzegovina, Sudan, Sri Lanka, and Cyprus. In other cases, it falls within part of a state, as does northern Ireland. In yet other cases, it traverses the boundaries of a state, as does Kurdistan, which straddles the borders of Turkey, Iraq, and Iran. In all of these situations, ethnic, religious, and/or linguistic identities have served as the basis for nationalist mobilization, and each national group is engaging in competing nation-building projects that often conflict. For majorities, the goal is nationalizing nationalism; for minorities, it is state-seeking nationalism, leading to autonomy or secession, irredentist or otherwise. The *Charter* project was an attempt to use a bill of rights as a nation-building instrument to build a shared political identity that transcends the linguistic divide in a plurinational context. Moreover, the *Charter* was adopted as part of a process of constitutional *transition*, as Canada severed its final legal connections with the United Kingdom and adopted an indigenous source of title for the Canadian constitutional order. In other plurinational places, bills of rights are also looked to at moments of constitutional transition to serve as the basis of a shared political identity. The question is whether this reliance is realistic.

It is very difficult for bills of rights on their own to serve a constituting role in defining a new political identity. Contrary to those who argue for the possibility of a pure "constitutional patriotism" based on the commitment to universalistic principles of political morality, a bill of rights must be nested in a contingent context – a constitutional narrative drawing on a web of political memory forged by shared experiences, challenges, failures, and triumphs.[70] The Canadian experience tells us that in plurinational places, there is an additional hurdle. The task is not simply to situate a bill of rights in a contingent historical and political context. The task is to do so in a context in which the existence of competing nationalisms makes the dominant question of constitutional politics the conflict between competing national narratives. If the ambition of a bill of rights as a constitutive instrument of nation building is to serve as a central element of an overarching narrative, by standing apart from, and transcending, these competing narratives, a plurinational context is a particularly difficult environment in which to do so. Indeed, there is the danger that rather than transcending those national narratives, a bill of rights will be drawn back into it. This is what has happened in Canada. And if this would happen in Canada, where we have managed our nationalist politics peacefully and within the rule of law, the difficulties may be greater still for countries emerging from violent conflict.

There are many reasons to value a bill of rights. Following John Hart Ely, we may argue that a bill of rights is required to protect the preconditions of the democratic process.[71] We could be Dworkinians and claim that rights are the conditions for the legitimate exercise of public power, and a bill of rights enforced by judicial review is the best means for implementing this commitment.[72] With Mark Tushnet and Jeremy Waldron, we could dispute whether judicial supremacy is the best institutional arrangement through which we can realize our commitment to liberal democracy.[73] Yet, whatever the reasons for adopting a bill of rights, constituting a nation by a bill of rights alone is not one of them.

Acknowledgments

An earlier version of this chapter was presented at the Harvard Law School in April 2007 and appears as an Social Science Research Network working paper at http://papers.ssrn.com/sol3/papers.cfm?abstract_id=1006905. Thanks to Bill Alford, Eddie Goldenberg, Richard Goldstone, Janet Hiebert, and Richard Simeon for helpful questions and comments. Thanks to Bryan Thomas and Tiffany Tsun for excellent research assistance. All remaining errors are mine.

Notes

1   *Canadian Charter of Rights and Freedoms,* Part 1 of the *Constitution Act, 1982,* being Schedule B to the *Canada Act 1982* (U.K.), 1982, c. 11 [*Charter*].
2   Bill Curry, "PM Dodges 'Semantic Debate' on Quebec: On Eve of Province's Holiday Festivities, Harper and Cabinet Meet at the Citadel," *Globe and Mail (Toronto)* (June 24, 2006), A7.
3   Herbert Bauch, "Quebec Is a Nation within Canada: Ignatieff – Federal Liberal leadership Contender Says He's Open to New Constitutional Talks," *Montreal Gazette* (June 28, 2006), A9.
4   Michael Ignatieff, *Agenda for Nation Building: Liberal Leadership for the Twenty-First Century,* 2006), 27 and 29.
5   Stéphane Dion, "What, Exactly, Do We Mean by 'Nation'?" *National Post* (October 26, 2006), A14; and Bob Rae, "Careless Rhetoric Is Not What Quebec Needs," *National Post* (November 7, 2006), A18.
6   See, for example, the proposals of Claude Morin, set out in "Reconnaissance de la nation québécoise – De quoi s'agit-il?" *Le Devoir* (October 24, 2006), A7.
7   Lysiane Gagnon, "Reopening a Constitutional Can of Worms," *Globe and Mail* (September 25, 2006), A15.
8   The resolution was adopted on October 21, 2006. The text of the resolution can be found online at http://www.cbc.ca/news/background/liberals/quebec-nationalunity.html#resolution.
9   The motion was ultimately introduced by Gilles Duceppe, leader of the Bloc Québécois on November 23, 2006, one day after the prime minister introduced his motion in the House of Commons. *House of Commons Debates,* 39th Parl., 1st Sess, No. 85 (November 23, 2006) at 5234.
10 *House of Commons Debates,* 39th Parl., 1st Sess, No. 84 (November 22, 2006) at 5197.
11 *House of Commons Debates,* 39th Parl., 1st Sess, No. 87 (November 27, 2006) at 5412.
12 Dion, *supra* note 5.
13 Ibid.
14 Norman Spector, "Playing the Constitutional Card Betrays Trudeau's Vision," *Globe and Mail (Toronto)* (October 30, 200), A19; Andrew Coyne, "The Real Question: Is Canada a Nation?" *National Post* (November 15, 2006), A1; Roy Romanow and John Whyte, "Stephen

Harper Traded the Peaceable Kingdom for a Trojan Horse," *Globe and Mail (Toronto)* (December 8, 2006), A25.

15 From an extensive literature, see Peter Hogg and Allison Bushell, "The Charter Dialogue between Courts and Legislatures (Or Perhaps the Charter of Rights Isn't Such a Bad Thing after All)" *Osgoode Hall Law Journal* 35 (1997): 75; Christopher Manfredi and James Kelly, "Six Degrees of Dialogue: A Response to Hogg and Bushell," *Osgoode Hall Law Journal* 37 (1999): 513; F.L. Morton and Rainer Knopff, *The Charter Revolution and the Court Party* (Peterborough: Broadview Press, 2000); Kent Roach, *The Supreme Court on Trial: Judicial Activism or Democratic Dialogue* (Toronto: Irwin Law, 2001); and Jeremy Waldron, "Some Models of Dialogue between Judges and Legislators," *Supreme Court Law Review* (2d) 23 (2004): 7.

16 Peter H. Russell, "The Political Purposes of the Charter of Rights and Freedoms," *Canadian Bar Review* 61 (1983): 30.

17 *Constitution Act, 1867* (U.K.), 30 and 31 Victoria, c. 3.

18 See generally Kenneth McRoberts, *Quebec: Social Change and Political Crisis* (Toronto: McLelland and Stewart, 1988).

19 Canada, *Final Report of the Royal Commission on Bilingualism and Biculturalism* (Ottawa: Queens Printer, 1967), vol. 3.

20 Alan Cairns, "Barriers to Constitutional Renewal in Canada," in Douglas Williams, ed., *Reconfigurations: Canadian Citizenship and Constitutional Change* (Toronto: McLelland and Stewart, 1995), 142.

21 Canada, *Federalism for the Future* (Ottawa: Queen's Printer, 1968).

22 Ibid. at 2.

23 Ibid. at 8.

24 Ibid.

25 Ibid. at 18.

26 Ibid.

27 Antonio Cassese, *Self-Determination of Peoples: A Legal Reappraisal* (New York: Cambridge University Press, 1995).

28 "Ignatieff's Folly," *Globe and Mail (Toronto)* (September 8, 2006), A22. For a similar view from Quebec sovereignists, see Robert Dutrisac, "'Le code génétique du Canada vient d'être modifié,' dit Boisclair," *Le Devoir* (November 25, 2006), A3.

29 Rogers Brubaker, *Nationalism Reframed* (New York: Cambridge University Press, 1996).

30 Michael Hechter, *Containing Nationalism* (Oxford: Oxford University Press, 2000); Will Kymlicka, *Multicultural Odysseys: Navigating the New International Politics of Diversity* (Oxford: Oxford University Press, 2007); and Wayne Norman, *Negotiating Nationalism: Nationbuilding, Federalism, and Secession in the Multinational State* (Oxford: Oxford University Press, 2006).

31 Ernest Renan, *Qu'est-ce qu'une nation,* 1882, http://archives.vigile.net/04-1/renan.pdf.

32 Sujit Choudhry, "Citizenship and Federations: Some Preliminary Reflections," in Kalypso Nicolaidis and Robert Howse, eds., *The Federal Vision: Legitimacy and Levels of Governance in the US and the EU* (Oxford: Oxford University Press, 2001), 377-402.

33 See, for example, Letter from Premier René Lévesque to Prime Minister Margaret Thatcher, December 19, 1981, reprinted in *McGill Law Journal* 30 (1985): 645 at 708-14.

34 *Charter, supra* note 1, s. 6(2).

35 Ibid. at s. 6(3).

36 Letter from Premier René Lévesque to Prime Minister Margaret Thatcher, *supra* note 33, 710.

37 *Constitution Act, supra* note 17.

38 Canada, *supra* note 21, 4.

39 *Charter, supra* note 1, s. 23(1)(b).

40 Letter from Premier René Lévesque to Prime Minister Margaret Thatcher, *supra* note 33, 710.

41 *Charter of the French Language,* R.S.Q. c. C-11.

42 *Attorney General of Quebec v. Quebec Protestant School Boards,* [1984] 2 S.C.R. 66.

43 *Charter, supra* note 1, s. 23(2).

44 *Solski (Tutor of) v. Quebec (Attorney General),* 2005 SCC 14.

45 *Charter, supra* note 1, s. 20.
46 Jean Laponce, *Languages and Their Territories* (Toronto: University of Toronto Press, 1987).
47 W.L. Morton, "Manitoba Schools and Canadian Nationality," *Report of the Annual Meeting of the Canadian Historical Association* 30:1 (1951): 351.
48 Kenneth McRoberts, *Misconceiving Canada: The Struggle for National Unity* (Toronto: Oxford University Press, 1997).
49 Russell, *supra* note 16, 40.
50 Canada, *supra* note 21, 10.
51 Cairns, *supra* note 20, 218.
52 Russell, *supra* note 16, 36.
53 Alan Cairns, "Citizens (Outsiders) and Governments (Insiders) in Constitution-Making: The Case of Meech Lake," *Canadian Public Policy* 14 (1988): S121.
54 *Constitution Act, 1982* (U.K.), 1982, c. 11, ss. 38, 41, and 43.
55 *Motion for a Resolution to Authorize an Amendment to the Constitution of Canada* (Ottawa: Queen's Printer, 1987) ss. 2(1)(b) and 2(3).
56 Cairns, *supra* note 20, 218-19.
57 McRoberts, *supra* note 48.
58 *An Act to Reunite the Provinces of Upper and Lower Canada, and for the Government of Canada*, 3 and 4 Vict., c. 35 (U.K.), s. XII.
59 Ibid. at s. XLI.
60 Sujit Choudhry, Jean-François Gaudreault-DesBiens, and Lorne Sossin, "Afterword: Solidarity between Modesty and Boldness," in Sujit Choudhry, Jean-François Gaudreault-Desbiens, and Lorne Sossin, eds., *Dilemmas of Solidarity: Rethinking Redistribution in the Canadian Federation* (Toronto: University of Toronto Press, 2006), 206.
61 Charles Taylor, "Shared and Divergent Values," in Charles Taylor, ed., *Reconciling the Solitudes: Essays on Canadian Federalism and Nationalism* (Montreal and Kingston: McGill-Queen's University Press, 1993), 155.
62 Patrick Monahan, *Meech Lake: The Inside Story* (Toronto: University of Toronto Press, 1991).
63 Sujit Choudhry and Jean-François Gaudreault-DesBiens, "Frank Iacobucci as Constitution-Maker: From the *Quebec Veto Reference* to the Meech Lake Accord and the *Quebec Secession Reference*," *University of Toronto Law Journal* 57 (2007): 165.
64 Andrew Coyne, "And with That, We're Well on Our Way to Belgiumhood," *National Post* (November 23, 2006), A1.
65 Canada, Legislature, *Parliamentary Debates on the Subject of the Confederation of the British North American Provinces*, 8th Parl., 3rd Sess. (Quebec: Hunter, Rose, 1865), 60.
66 Alfred Apps, "The New Treason of Old Ideas," PDF document on the Democratic SPACE Web site, http://democraticspace.com/blog/alfred-apps-op-ed.pdf.
67 Will Kymlicka, *Multicultural Citizenship* (Oxford: Oxford University Press, 1995).
68 Michael Keating, *Plurinational Democracy* (Oxford: Oxford University Press, 2001).
69 John McGarry and Brendan O'Leary, "Consociational Theory and Plurinational Places: Northern Ireland and Other Cases" in Guy Ben-Porat, *Failure of the Middle East Peace Process: A Comparative Analysis of Peace Implementation in Israel/Palestine, Northern Ireland and South Africa* (New York: Palgrave Macmillan, 2008), 70.
70 Jürgen Habermas, "Citizenship and National Identity," in Jürgen Habermas, ed., *Between Facts and Norms* (Cambridge, MA: MIT Press, 1996), 491; and Bernard Yack, "The Myth of the Civic Nation," *Critical Review* 10 (1996): 193. For an overview, see Jan-Werner Müller, *Constitutional Patriotism* (Princeton: Princeton University Press, 2007).
71 John Hart Ely, *Democracy and Distrust* (Cambridge, MA: Harvard University Press, 1980).
72 Ronald Dworkin, *Freedom's Law: The Moral Reading of the American Constitution* (Cambridge, MA: Harvard University Press, 1996).
73 Mark Tushnet, *Taking the Constitution Away from the Courts* (Princeton: Princeton University Press, 2000); and Jeremy Waldron, "The Core of the Case against Judicial Review," *Yale Law Journal* 115 (2006): 1346.

13

The Internal Exile of Quebecers in the Canada of the Charter

Guy Laforest

I will begin this chapter on a personal note. More than twenty-five years ago, when the *Canadian Charter of Rights and Freedoms* came into effect, I was living in Montreal and studying at McGill University.[1] Among my professors were two great intellectuals who were also great idealists, Charles Taylor and James Tully.[2] I learned much from them, and, over time, they became friends of mine. Other professors influenced me perhaps less directly but just as meaningfully, namely Blema Steinberg, Daniel Latouche, James Mallory, and Harold Waller. Their approach was tinged with realism, and it perfectly offset Taylor's and Tully's approach. In philosophy, the realist approach is that of liberalism without illusions, as expounded by Judith Shklar, Raymond Aron, Isaiah Berlin, and Karl Popper among others. In politics, according to these authors, one must first and foremost avoid the worst and must understand that cruelty, fear, terror, and violence can crush the human person and attack his or her dignity and privacy. In this respect, I share the judgment of Irvin Studin, who recently wrote that Canada is a tremendous success on the scale of humanity, one of the countries among the most "peaceful, just and civilized."[3] A country where, to add my own voice, the strong as well as the weak can sleep soundly in a decent, comfortable and humane social environment without fear of the worst. All of this counts, therefore, for a tremendous development in the history of mankind.

I start on this note to provide a sense of proportion for the analysis that will be developed regarding the internal exile of Quebecers in the Canada of the *Charter*. Like a number of other people in Quebec, in terms of political identity and belonging, I am not a happy citizen in the Canada of the *Charter*.[4] Beyond my personal feelings, I think this sentiment is explained by the fact that Quebec is not properly integrated into the new Canada that has arisen since the constitutional reforms of 1982. Paradoxically, this reform saw the light of day, to a large extent, due to the dynamism and pressure exerted by Quebec on Canada in the aftermath of the Quiet Revolution. This chapter will argue that instead of improving the situation, constitutional reform in 1982 worsened it and resulted in the internal exile of Quebecers within the Canada of the *Charter*. The term *internal exile* describes very well the basis of my thoughts – someone who is exiled from the inside is someone who feels uncomfortable and who lives like a stranger in his own country.

This chapter will be divided into three sections. The first section argues that the first twenty-five years of the *Charter* has led to the exile of Quebecers within Canada. The Trudeau vision of the Constitution embraced Canadian sovereignty as the means to challenge Quebec nationalism, and this action led to the end of the Canadian dream that was created through the Confederation of the British North American colonies in 1867. The second section contends that the exile of Quebecers can be ended by amending the *Charter* to recognize the distinct status of Quebec within section 1 of the *Charter*, the reasonable limits clause, and section 27, the interpretive clause that requires the *Charter* to be applied in a manner consistent with Canada's multicultural heritage. The final section reflects on the virtues of the *Charter* but concludes that its implementation without the consent of the Quebec National Assembly represents, to invoke Donald Smiley, a dangerous deed – one that has led to the internal exile of Quebecers within the Canada of the *Charter*, which continues to be a fundamental obstacle to Canada as a just federal society.[5]

Pierre Trudeau, the Exile of Quebecers, and the *Charter*

And once again, it means an even greater tendency, a greater weight on the side of provincialism, at the expense of a federal institution or legislation that, up until now, has given Canadians a feeling of belonging to one Canada. In the same way, the Charter was important to Canadian unity, as was the patriation of the Constitution and the new Canadian flag. All of these things have been important in the sense that they have helped Canadians to realize that they share with all other Canadians, throughout the country, the same set of fundamental values.[6]

The internal exile of Quebecers is made immensely more complex if we add the dominant role played by Pierre Elliott Trudeau, undoubtedly one of the greatest political figures of Quebec and Canada in the twentieth century. In terms of belonging and identity, Quebecers were to some extent exiled by one of their own. Federalism held an important position in Trudeau's life – except that a study of his actions and writings in the 1980s, juxtaposed against the overall horizon of his political-intellectual life, reveals him to be a nationalist and a Canadian sovereigntist more than a federalist.[7] This fact is clearly illustrated in an important book that André Burelle, philosopher and former speechwriter for the former prime minister, recently devoted to Pierre Elliott Trudeau's work.[8] I will return to Burelle's analysis in a moment.

At the end of his career, Pierre Trudeau dreamed of establishing once and for all the sovereignty of both the Canadian nation and the central government. In the debate over the Meech Lake Accord, he often wondered: "How do you make a country stronger by weakening the only government that can talk for all Canadians?"[9] Rather than trying to find in federalism and its institutions a balance between a design for a Canadian nation and a Quebec nation, he decided after the 1980 referendum to resort to Canadian nationalism to change the country and to prevail over Quebec sovereigntists once and for all.[10] The *Charter* was the instrument that he used to carry out such a plan, as political scientist Alan Cairns recalls in an interview with the historian Robert Bothwell:

> The prime one, the obvious one, is what the Charter appears to be on its face, a way of protecting citizens' rights against the state. From Trudeau's perspective, however, the much more important goal was the attempt to generate a national identity, and this really meant an attack on provincialism. It was a way of trying to get Canadians to think of themselves as possessors of a common body of rights independent of geographical location, which would constitute a lens through which they would then view what all governments were doing. So it was really a de-provincializing strategy, primarily aimed at Quebec nationalists, but also at the general centrifugal pressures that were developing across the federal system.[11]

In his 2005 book, Burelle lucidly explains the political events in 1980 that led Trudeau to break the delicate balance that had previously prevailed in his mind between the community-minded personalism of the Citélibrist period – the views of Jacques Maritain and Emmanuel Mounier – which were reconcilable with the federalism of 1867 and a certain acceptance of the difference of the Quebec nation, and, second, an ultra-individualist and symmetrical liberalism that was making the case for Canadian nation building.[12] In the spirit of Burelle, the "one nation" federalism of the *Constitution Act, 1982,* draws upon Republican unitarism and starts from the premise of an individualistic and anti-communitarian liberalism.[13] According to Burelle, this federalism is operationalized in the following manner: "(a) All individuals are brought into a single civic nation, which delegates to the federal parliament the whole of its national sovereignty; (b) Invested with this sovereignty, the central Parliament entrusts to the provinces the functional powers better exercised by them."[14]

What kind of federalism flows from such logic? According to Burelle, a federalism that does not respect the Quebec difference, which disregards the principle of non-subordination between two levels of government, both sovereign in their respective jurisdictions – in other words, a federalism that moves away from what the founders of the Canadian federation wanted to build in 1867. According to Burelle, the spirit of 1982 flouts that of 1867 by way of the intersecting operation of the following principles: "(a) the practice of a misguided subsidiarity – i.e., devolution of downward sovereignty (top-down) from the central government; (b) the existence of a senior 'national' government and junior 'provincial governments'; (c) the granting to Ottawa the right to intervene to ensure 'the national interest' in areas of provincial jurisdiction; (d) the identity of law and treatment of individuals and provinces merged within a single and republican nation."[15] On the whole, Burelle's interpretation strikes me as being quite fair. However, he said this somewhat differently in his 1994 book when he spoke of government by judges via a "national Charter" and a government by the "Canadian people," enabling Ottawa to circumvent the division of powers.[16] In response to this argument, however, I would introduce an important nuance. A distinction must be made between the vision of the *Charter* promoted by Trudeau and the actual content of the document.

I think Burelle understands Trudeau and his vision of the *Charter* as well as the content of the *Charter*, since the document is not simply limited to individual rights. There is room in the *Charter* for the multicultural heritage of Canadians and for the collective rights of indigenous peoples. However, there is not room for the idea of Quebec's difference and for the principle that should flow from the legal consequences of this difference. Before exploring in the next section the means that might bring an end to the internal exile of Quebecers in the Canada of the *Charter*, I will conclude with two analyses of the spirit of 1982 by Eugénie Brouillet and José Woehrling, two of the best public law professors in Quebec today. According to Brouillet, the *Charter* cannot accommodate Quebec's differences because judicial review in a federal system results in centralization: "It is precisely because of the Canadian Charter's potential to integrate that the federal government made it the cornerstone of the constitutional reform of 1982. On the political level, the recognition of super-legislative rights and freedoms for all Canadian citizens would form the basis of their common identity and strengthen the unity of the Canadian nation. On the legal level, this amounted to the transfer into the courts' hands of the power to implement those rights and freedoms and the development of positive and negative standards which would result in a centralizing direction."[17] This position is supported by Woehrling but in a more indirect manner. Woehrling, argues that human rights projects are used by the majority culture to regulate the activities of minority groups within a federal state:

> To the extent that the protection of rights by a constitutional instrument is an anti-majoritarian tool, it limits the political autonomy of minorities who have one or more territorial entities. The minority who controls such an entity sees its political power restricted to its own minorities and its own

members ... The majority at the national level could give in to the temptation to use its power to impose on its minority the respect for excessive guarantees for the benefit of the minority 'within the minority.' One has the impression sometimes that the majority group at the national level defends its own interests under the pretext of human rights and minority rights.[18]

To End the Exile

At the beginning of 2008, the political situation was in flux in Canada and Quebec with the presence of two minority governments, and all indications were that this state of affairs would continue in the coming months. This is what I call a second-degree equation of several unknowns, creating a fog in the minds of most experts. Several positive developments of the last several years must also be clearly recognized: the asymmetrical Canada-Quebec health agreement signed in 2004 by the governments of Paul Martin and Jean Charest; Stephen Harper's declaration of the doctrine of open federalism during the January 2006 electoral campaign, which led to the election of a Conservative government in Ottawa; the Harper-Charest agreement in May 2006 that accepted the principle of a special international role for Quebec and incorporated a representative of the government of Quebec into the Canadian delegation to UN Educational, Scientific, and Cultural Organization; the House of Commons resolution in November 2006 stating that the Quebecois form a nation within a united Canada (despite the ambiguities that persist between the English and French versions of the text); and, finally, the fiscal imbalance was a cornerstone of the 2007 budget.[19]

In my view, there is no doubt that these developments served to help alleviate the discomfort and to change the climate in which we have operated our political life. They do not, however, take into account the issue of Quebec's place in Canada's constitutional architecture. To make progress in this direction, one has to amend the *Constitution Act, 1982*, and the *Charter*. The first section of the *Charter* states that rights are "subject only to such reasonable limits prescribed by law as can be demonstrably justified in a free and democratic society." Since the Supreme Court of Canada recognized federalism as the premier arrangement of the Canadian political community and the principle normative pillar of our constitutional structure in the *Reference re Secession of Quebec*, an amended section 1 of the *Charter* should refer to a "free and democratic *federation*" rather than to a "free and democratic *society*."[20] This small change would have two major effects. First, it would instruct judges of the need to take into account the neuralgic nature of the federal principle in their understanding of the rules that govern our legal system, and, second, it would have educational value since it would invite the public to better understand the importance of federalism in the Canadian political identity. This action would have the additional result that Quebecers would feel less alone in taking federalism seriously in their understanding of Canada!

The second change that I propose flows logically from the debate that marked Canadian public life in the fall of 2006 – the desirability of recognizing the Quebec nation. Launched by Michael Ignatieff during his candidacy for the leadership of the Liberal Party of Canada, the debate ended with a modified motion presented by Prime Minister Stephen Harper in the House of Commons, which recognized the Quebecois as a nation within a united Canada. To end the internal exile of Quebecers, I believe, we need to place their way of defining themselves in a text that really matters to Canadians, the *Charter*. Section 1 of the *Charter* could be amended to recognize that Quebec forms a distinct society in Canada as well as explicitly stating that the government of Quebec and the National Assembly have the obligation to protect and promote Quebec as a distinct society. This is the phrase that was preferred by Claude Ryan and André Laurendeau during the proceedings of the Royal Commission on Bilingualism and Biculturalism over forty years ago.

Some would suggest that this proposal represents the ghost of the distinct society clause from the failed Meech Lake Accord. They are not wrong. Many Quebecers see the *Charter* – principally, section 1 – as an attempt to create a single great Canadian nation that would incorporate all other affiliations, particularly those flowing from modern Quebec nationalism. In this respect, the adoption of the Meech Lake Accord would have rectified the issue and the internal exile of Quebecers. One day in the future, the question will resurface, and it will be part of the constitutional doctrine of a future government of Quebec. It is interesting to recall, with respect to the issue of the distinct society clause and its recognition, what the former Liberal leader, Stéphane Dion, said when he was minister in the government of Jean Chrétien in 1996:

> What is the essence of the distinct society clause? This provision would be a section for interpretation, similar to section 27 of the Charter of Rights and Freedoms, which recognizes multiculturalism. It guarantees that in the grey areas of the Constitution, in areas where it is necessary to interpret the rules, the Supreme Court will take into account the distinct nature of Quebec in areas such as language, culture and civil law. This will be a useful clarification, but one that would not alter the division of powers under the Constitution. This is not a request for special status or unique privileges.[21]

Since the end of British rule in the eighteenth century, we have refused to implement the policy of assimilation and homogenization that has generally dominated the period of consolidation of the modern nation-state in Europe. The *Quebec Act* of 1774 guaranteed Her Majesty's new subjects of

French origin religious freedom and the maintenance of their civil law.[22] When Canada became a federal dominion in 1867, a similar spirit of openness, recognition of diversity, and respect for minority rights was expressed in the division of powers, which provided the provinces jurisdiction over property and civil rights, as well as the sections protecting religious minorities. This was clearly a demand not only from Canada-Est – the former name of Quebec – but also from other British North American colonies that entered Confederation in 1867. It is quite possible to trace the historical and legal origins of asymmetrical federalism in Canada to the wording of section 94 of the *Constitution Act, 1867,* which omitted Quebec from the harmonization of laws related to property and civil rights between the federal government and the common-law provinces during Confederation (Ontario, Nova Scotia, and New Brunswick).[23] This Canadian originality in the history of the modern nation-state was notably expressed in 1982 in the wording of section 27 of the *Charter,* which stipulates that "[t]his Charter shall be interpreted in a manner consistent with the preservation and enhancement of the multicultural heritage of Canadians."

The third change that I believe is needed to put an end to the internal exile of Quebecers in the Canada of the *Charter* deals with section 27. If the debate on the Quebec nation has raised significant interest in the country's English and French media, just as much can be said for the work of the Consultation Commission on Accommodation Practices Related to Cultural Differences, which was co-chaired in the province of Quebec by Gerard Bouchard and Charles Taylor. Although one cannot prejudge the direction of the final report, the preliminary consultation document clearly shows that the commission has chosen to give a broad interpretation to its mandate, thereby agreeing to consider the question of the relationship between the majority and the minority.[24] Canada and Quebec are lands of immigration. This history has accelerated in the second half of the twentieth century and will not change. I believe that this social phenomenon is good and that it honours all of the people who live in Canada and who have had to confront this troubled world of ours. However, I also believe that in its portrayal of the rights and obligations that flow from section 27 regarding the multicultural heritage of Canadians, the *Charter* misses a fundamental reality, namely that this heritage is embodied in Canada in the institutional networks of two host societies. In addition to the Canadian society, the Quebec society with its predominance of the French language is seeing its social life challenged by globalization flows. Such a clarification of section 27 of the *Charter* strikes me as being essential for both the fair and stable integration of Quebec in Canada today.

Canada is a free and democratic federation integrating Quebec's distinct national society and a multicultural heritage embodied in two host societies, one of which communicates mainly in French. This is what is lacking in the

Charter, if I understand the situation, in order to go beyond the political alienation of Quebecers. Such changes would not end political conflicts in the Canadian federal system, including those between Quebec and its Confederation partners. Those who want to put an end, once and for all, to "political-constitutional squabbles" must accept that political life will always be a matter of dialogue and debate that may lead to clashes. However, such changes would have the effect of healing an injury and restoring confidence in the Constitution as higher law and in Canadian institutions. As Catalans and many federated states of the world have done, Quebecers must also demonstrate daring and imagination by acquiring, in an autonomous manner, an internal constitution that is strengthened by the backbone of the institutions of their society.[25] Finally, Quebecers that are more confident in their future and better integrated will also be more open to the desire for constitutional change of other Canadians, which is certainly as legitimate as their own desire for such modifications. Quebecers, once they are no longer internally exiled, should be capable of proclaiming their allegiance to Canada and of engaging as well in joint efforts for the next century.

Conclusion

In the context of the twenty-fifth anniversary of the adoption of the *Charter*, I will try one last time to render comprehensible this notion of the internal exile of Quebecers by recalling another historical event, the famous cry of General Charles de Gaulle on the balcony of Montreal's City Hall in July 1967: "Vive le Québec libre!" It is appropriate to be a little nostalgic when one remembers the year 1967. It was the era of the centenary of the Canadian Confederation and the World's Fair in Montreal, a time when people from here and abroad were invited to live with hope and idealism in the spirit of the "Terre des Hommes" of Saint-Exupery. It seems to me that if General de Gaulle's speech had such an impact in Montreal in 1967, it was because it responded to three deep aspirations of Quebec's society: it solemnly affirmed Quebec's right to be different within Canada and North America, it gave a strong taste of political freedom, which could take several forms in the modern world, and, finally, it answered a universal desire for recognition. In 1967, Charles de Gaulle gave a planetary dimension to the Quebec question. When we attempt to understand the deep significance of the *Charter* to Canada, we realize that it has reinforced similar aspirations for the majority of those Canadians living outside Quebec – just as it has for a substantial minority within Quebec.

By proposing an intelligent balance between individual rights, collective rights, and rights for people within minority communities, and doing so in an original way when compared to the American *Bill of Rights*, the *Charter* has represented a strong affirmation of the Canadian difference within Western liberal democracies.[26] Second, the *Charter* has helped to complete, on the axis of political freedom, the absolute independence of the Canadian nation-state. Finally, the *Charter*, and its influence on the world, has fuelled Canadians' desire for recognition, by making their country the vanguard of a different kind of civilization for the twenty-first century. This perspective is what we can conclude when we read the best thinkers of Canada's idealist school, from Charles Taylor to James Tully as well as Will Kymlicka, John Ralston Saul, and Michael Ignatieff. The chief justice of the Supreme Court of Canada, Beverley McLachlin, was writing in this tradition in a speech that she delivered on April 17, 2002, on the occasion of the twentieth anniversary of the proclamation of the *Charter*: "We have a Charter that reflects our most fundamental values, that tells us who and what we are as a people. We have a Charter that the world admires. Most important of all, we have a Charter that Canadians in the last two decades have come to embrace as their own. La Charte: c'est à nous. La Charte: c'est nous."[27]

We can therefore understand that the *Charter* is a source of great pride in Canada. Many people have the urge to say, like the chief justice in 2002, that the *Charter* belongs to us and that the *Charter* is us. With the exception that, as seen by Quebec, this *Charter* was adopted in an anti-democratic way without its consent, in defiance of the opposition, its government, and the National Assembly. Commenting on the patriation of the *Constitution Act, 1982*, without the consent of Quebec, Claude Ryan stated: "We must conclude with great certainty that each time the essential prerogatives of the National Assembly are attacked, the people of Quebec are themselves attacked. To be indifferent to such an attack on the powers of the National Assembly is to be indifferent to, or to make light of, the aspirations and the fundamental reality of the people of Quebec themselves."[28]

Quebec's legislative autonomy in language matters was reduced, the federal principle in our institutions was weakened, and, in our political culture, Quebec's right to difference was not included in the *Charter*. More specifically, the Canada of 1982 and the *Charter* do not explicitly recognize either Quebec's difference or the fact that this difference should lead to political and legal consequences. Canadian idealism, which sees in our political system and especially in the *Charter* a standard-bearer for humanity in its whole, seems condemned to remain deeply inauthentic as long as we have not found a fair and reasonable way to recognize the Quebec difference, in law as well as in symbols.[29] Without being able to deal in this chapter with all aspects of this issue, it seems clear to me that Quebecers have chosen to live their quest for identity and freedom in Canada. Quebec is in Canada to stay, except if it recognizes itself too imperfectly reflected, represented, and respected in Canadian institutions. A great mind of McGill University and Quebec, Charles Taylor once stressed in reflecting on Quebec's nationalism that we need to be ruthless toward our essentialist myths. Canada's majoritarian nationalism has locked itself into a similar essentialist myth when it imagines that it can hide the deep political alienation of Quebecers that resulted from the entrenchment of the Charter of Rights and Freedoms over the objections of the National Assembly. As long as this situation continues, Canada's efforts to present itself to the world as the harbinger of a "civilization of difference" will look somewhat incoherent. Another great mind of Western humanism, Paul Ricoeur, wrote that the historical memory of the people must strive to be fair and happy. The internal exile of Quebecers, therefore, is a fundamental obstacle to the development of a fair and happy historical memory in Canada after more than twenty-five years of the *Charter*.

Acknowledgments

This chapter is a translation of Guy Laforest, "L'exil intérieur des Québécois dans le Canada de la Charte" prepared for *Contested Constitutionalism*. James Kelly and Christopher Manfredi would like to thank Tamara Levy and Michèle Friel for the translation of this chapter. Translated by permission from *Constitutional Forum constitutionnel* 16, 2 (2007).

Notes

1 *Canadian Charter of Rights and Freedoms*, Part 1 of the *Constitution Act, 1982*, being Schedule B to the *Canada Act 1982* (U.K.), 1982, c. 11.

2 We will find analyses of the current situation in Canada inspired by the work carried out by Charles Taylor and James Tully in Alain-G. Gagnon, *Au-delà de la nation unificatrice: plaidoyer pour le fédéralisme multinational* (Barcelona and Montreal: Institut d'estudis autonomics et Boréal, 2007); see also Guy Laforest, *Pour la liberté d'une société distincte* (Quebec City: Presses de l'Univesité Laval, 2004).

3 Irvin Studin, ed., *What Is a Canadian? Forty-Three Thought-Provoking Responses* (Toronto: McClelland and Stewart, 2006), 184.

4 My thesis is also advanced in the work of André Burelle. See, for instance, André Burelle, *Le mal canadien* (Montreal: Fides, 1994); see also Christian Dufour, *Lettre aux souverainistes québécois et aux fédéralistes canadiens qui sont restés fidèles au Québec* (Montreal: Stanké, 2000).

5 Donald Smiley, "A Dangerous Deed: The Constitution Act, 1982," in Keith Banting and Richard Simeon, eds., *And No One Cheered: Federalism, Democracy and the Constitution Act* (Toronto: Methuen, 1983), 78 and 90.

6 P.E. Trudeau, "There Must Be a Sense of Belonging," in D. Johnston, ed., *Pierre Trudeau Speaks Out on Meech Lake* (Toronto: Stoddart, 1990), 31.

7 Ibid.

8 André Burelle, *Pierre-Elliott Trudeau: l'intellectuel et le politique* (Montreal: Fides, 2005).

9 P.E. Trudeau, "We, the People of Canada," in Johnston, *supra* note 6, 94.

10 I have written extensively on these questions. See notably Guy Laforest, *Trudeau et la fin d'un rêve canadien* (Quebec City: Septentrion, 1992); see also Guy Laforest, "La vraie nature de la souveraineté: réponse à mes critiques à propos de Trudeau et la fin d'un rêve canadien," in Guy Laforest, ed., *Pour la liberté d'une société distincte* (Quebec City: Presses de l'Université Laval, 2004), 219-36.

11 Robert Bothwell, *Canada and Quebec: One Country, Two Histories* (Vancouver: UBC Press, 1995), 180.

12 Burelle, *supra* note 8, 68-70.

13 *Constitution Act, 1982* (U.K.), 1982, c. 11, s. 59.

14 Burelle, supra note 8 at 459. Translation of the original: "(a) Tous les individus y sont fondus en une seule nation civique qui délègue au Parlement fédéral la totalité de sa souveraineté nationale; (b) Investi de cette souveraineté, le Parlement central confie aux provinces les pouvoirs fonctionnellement mieux exercés par elles."

The Internal Exile of Quebecers in the Canada of the Charter 261

15 Ibid. at 459. Translation of the original: "(a) la pratique d'une subsidiarité dévoyée i.e. d'une dévolution de souveraineté descendante (top down) qui part de l'Etat central; (b) l'existence d'un gouvernement senior "national" et de gouvernements juniors "provinciaux"; (c) l'attribution à Ottawa d'un droit d'ingérence pour garantir "l'intérêt national" dans les champs de compétence provinciale."

16 Burelle, *supra* note 8, 64.

17 Eugénie Brouillet, *La négation de la nation: l'identité culturelle québécoise et le fédéralisme canadien* (Quebec: Septentrion, 2005), 325. Translation of the original: "[C]'est précisément en raison du potentiel intégrateur de la charte canadienne que le gouvernement fédéral en a fait la pierre angulaire de la réforme constitutionnelle de 1982. Sur le plan politique, la reconnaissance de droits et libertés supralégislatifs à chacun des citoyens canadiens constituerait le fondement de leur identité commune et renforcerait ainsi l'unité de la nation canadienne. Sur le plan juridique, le transfert entre les mains des tribunaux du pouvoir de mise en œuvre de ces droits et libertés et le développement de normes nationales positives et négatives qui en découleraient joueraient dans un sens centralisateur."

18 José Woehrling, "La Charte canadienne des droits et libertés et ses répercussions sur la vie politique," in Réjean Pelletier and Manon Tremblay, eds., *Le parlementarisme canadien, troisième édition revue et augmentée* (Quebec City: Presses de l'Université Laval, 2005), 115. Translation of the original: "Dans la mesure où la protection des droits par un instrument constitutionnel est un dispositif antimajoritaire, elle vient limiter l'autonomie politique des minorités qui disposent d'une ou de plusieurs entités territoriales. La minorité qui contrôle une telle entité voit son pouvoir politique limité au profit de ses propres minorités et de ses propres membres ... La majorité au niveau national peut alors céder à la tentation d'utiliser son pouvoir pour imposer à sa minorité le respect de garanties excessives au profit de "la minorité dans la minorité". On a l'impression, parfois, que le groupe majoritaire au niveau national défend ses propres intérêts sous le prétexte des droits de la personne et des droits des minorités."

19 Guy Laforest and Eric Montigny, "Le fédéralisme exécutif: problèmes et actualité," in Pelletier and Tremblay, *supra* note 18, 364-68; see also Keith Banting et al., *Open federalism: Interpretations, Significance* (Kingston: Institut des relations intergouvernementales, 2006), in particular, the chapter authored by Alain Noël, "Il suffisait de presque rien: promises and pitfalls of open federalism," 25-37. For an overview, see Michael Murphy, ed., *Canada: The State of the Federation 2005: Quebec and Canada in the New Century* (Montreal and Kingston: McGill-Queen's University Press, 2007), and, finally, see Alain-G. Gagnon, ed., *Le fédéralisme canadien contemporain: fondements, traditions, institutions* (Montreal: Presses de l'Université de Montréal, 2006).

20 *Reference re Secession of Quebec*, [1998] 2 S.C.R. 217.

21 Stéphane Dion, "Notre pays est en danger," *La Presse* (March 8, 1996), B-7. Translation of the original: "Quelle est l'essence de la disposition sur la société distincte? Cette disposition serait un article d'interprétation, semblable à l'article 27 de la Charte des droits et libertés, qui reconnaît le multiculturalisme. Elle garantit que, dans les zones grises de la Constitution, dans les domaines où il faut interpréter les règles, la Cour suprême tiendra compte du caractère distinct du Québec dans des domaines comme la langue, la culture et le droit civil. Ce sera une clarification utile, mais qui ne modifiera en rien le partage des pouvoirs prévu par la Constitution. Il ne s'agit pas d'une demande de statut spécial ni de privilèges particuliers."

22 For a philosophical interpretation of this idea, see James Tully, *Une étrange multiplicité: le constitutionnalisme à une époque de diversité* (Quebec City: Presses de l'Université Laval, 1999), 142-45. On the Quebec Act, see Alain Gagnon and Laurent-Mehdi Chokri, *Le régime politique canadien, revised and augmented,* 3rd ed. (Quebec City: Presses de l'Université Laval, 2005), 16.

23 See Janet Ajzenstat, Paul Romney, Ian Gentles, and William D. Gairdner, eds. *Débats sur la fondation du Canada,* French edition prepared by Stéphane Kelly et Guy Laforest (Quebec City: Presses de l'Université Laval, 2004), 336-37 and 378. I find therein the speeches of two members of the Legislative Assembly, M.C. Cameron and Christopher Dunkin, clearly establishing a connection between Article 94 and a strong asymmetrical status for Quebec,

all of which has been neglected by many generations of Quebec constitutionalists! *Constitution Act, 1867* (U.K.), 30 and 31 Victoria, c. 3, s. 93.

24 Quebec, Commission de consultation sur les pratiques d'accommodement reliées aux différences culturelles, *Accommodements et différences: vers un terrain d'entente, la parole aux citoyens*, consultation document (Quebec City: Éditeur officiel du Québec, 2007), v.

25 Laforest, *supra* note 10, 256.

26 US *Bill of Rights*, 1789.

27 Beverley McLachlin, "En pleine maturité: l'identité nationale canadienne et la Charte des droits," speech presented at a seminar in Ottawa on the *Rights and Freedoms in Canada, Twenty Years after the Adoption of the Charter* (April 17, 2002), http://www.scc-csc.gc.ca/aboutcourt/judges/speeches/charter_f.asp. This quote is taken from the English version of the original speech: http://www.scc-csc.gc.ca/AboutCourt/judges/speeches/charter_e.asp.

28 Passages from a speech by Claude Ryan during a debate at the National Assembly on September 30, 1981. Cited in Réal Bélanger, Richard Jones, and Marc Vallières, *Les grands débats parlementaires 1792-1992* (Quebec City: Presses de l'Université Laval, 1994), 39. Translation of the original: "Nous devons conclure avec beaucoup de fermeté que chaque fois que l'Assemblée nationale est atteinte dans ses prérogatives essentielles, c'est le peuple du Québec lui-même qui est atteint. Être indifférent à une atteinte faite aux pouvoirs de l'Assemblée nationale, c'est être indifférent ou traiter à la légère les aspirations et la réalité fondamentale du peuple québécois lui-même."

29 Christian Dufour, *Lettre aux souverainistes québécois et aux fédéralistes qui sont restés fidèles au Québec* (Montreal: Stanké, 2000), 114.

14

The Road Not Taken: Aboriginal Rights after the Re-Imagining of the Canadian Constitutional Order

Kiera L. Ladner and Michael McCrossan

Indigenous nations have a history with constitutional renewal and entrenched rights that began long before the prelude to the patriation of the Canadian Constitution in 1982. In fact, the constitutional histories and rights discourses of Aboriginal peoples predate the Canadian constitutional negotiation of 1867, and many predate the creation of the British constitutional order with the signing of the Magna Carta in 1215. Neither rights nor constitutional renewal were alien to Aboriginal peoples when they entered the foray of Canadian constitutional politics in the late seventies. What was alien, however, were the constitutional order and rights discourses historically rooted in the political, philosophical, and legal traditions of a far off land – traditions and philosophies that claim to be universal, despite the fact that they are specific to Western-Eurocentric history and the thinkers and politics that it produced. Meanwhile, Aboriginal constitutional orders and their corresponding conceptualization of rights were created in a specific territory and, as such, are an expression of how a nation has decided to live in this territory and to construct relations (among themselves and with others) in the best way possible under its natural laws.[1]

Many have contended that Aboriginal politics – both prior to and after colonization – was collectivist in nature and void of both individualism and a rights discourse.[2] Though a strong collectivist orientation permeated the political systems and political philosophies of Aboriginal nations, Aboriginal politics was not devoid of individualism. Aboriginal peoples have their own traditions of individualism and rights that vary according to nation. These traditions of rights and individualism are extremely different from, and are quite incompatible with, Western-Eurocentric traditions. Any discussion of individualism, rights, and responsibilities within an Indigenous context must begin with Creation and the relationship between individuals and Creation. Individual rights were typically seen as responsibilities resulting from power or individual manifestations of the Creator's essence and Creation's teachings.

Power involves the gifts or potentials of Creation, which are given to and/or obtained by individuals and for which individuals are responsible. Understood in terms of Creation and power, individualism results from the idea (and the corresponding doctrine of non-interference) that individuals are free to live out their responsibilities resulting from their gifts and to discover and realize their potentials without interference since each individual is an autonomous being with separate and distinct gifts. Contrary to what some might think, the Royal Commission on Aboriginal Peoples (RCAP) argued that this radical individualism is compatible with a collectivist orientation.[3]

While a tradition of individual rights and responsibilities has always existed among Aboriginal peoples, such traditions and philosophies are inconsistent with Western-Eurocetric conceptualizations of rights and freedoms.[4] In large part, it was these inconsistencies and a desire to protect Indigenous philosophies, traditions, Aboriginal communities, and Aboriginal and treaty rights that caused Aboriginal leaders to take a stance against Trudeau's constitutional vision and to involve themselves in Canada's mega-constitutional politics.[5] Aboriginal people involved themselves in Canada's constitutional renewal to protect their different philosophical, political, and legal traditions from both the *Canadian Charter of Rights and Freedoms* and further infringement by federal and/or provincial governments.[6] Their involvement went far beyond the confines of the constitutional talks and was spurred on by much more than a desire to have Aboriginal and treaty rights recognized and affirmed in the Constitution. Indigenous leaders and constitutional visionaries saw a window of opportunity to re-imagine the Canadian constitutional order, to constitutionalize their sovereignty, and to create the opportunities necessary for their decolonization. Remarkably, they succeeded, or so they thought.

This chapter explores Indigenous constitutional visions *circa* 1982 and contrasts Aboriginal readings of the *Constitution Act, 1982,* with the jurisprudence of the Supreme Court of Canada in the area of Aboriginal and treaty rights.[7] It argues that although the early literature signalled an acceptance of this reading and a commitment to decolonization, the courts have nevertheless abandoned the path set before them in favour of sustaining Canada's colonial legacy. This chapter begins with an exploration of Indigenous constitutional visions. It then turns to a discussion of the literature and assesses how the courts have departed from the post-colonial vision of the *Constitution Act, 1982,* that was offered to Aboriginal peoples. Finally, the chapter concludes by assessing how the courts have attempted to deny Aboriginal sovereignty and obliterate Aboriginal constitutional orders. Understood in this light, section 35(1) of the *Constitution Act, 1982,* is an affirmation of treaty constitutionalism, and, as such, Aboriginal rights and responsibilities are vested in, and limited by, Indigenous constitutional orders. They are, therefore, *merely* "recognized and affirmed" and not *created* by the Canadian constitutional order.

Indigenous Constitutional Visions

Aboriginal nations had (and continue to have) their own constitutional orders or what James (Sa'ke'j) Youngblood Henderson terms legal and political orders, which comprise and define their distinct political, economic, educational, property, and legal systems. These legal and political orders are comprised of oral "documents" such as orations, stories, songs, and ceremonies and written "documents" such as wampum and pictographs. Such constitutional orders are not based on declarations of Crown sovereignty, claims of absolute ownership, or the existence of a hierarchical regime that exercises and enforces what remains of the Crown's sovereignty. Rather, they were intentionally constructed over generations as an expression of their relationship with the world around them and as a means of maintaining peace and friendship among all beings (both human and non-human) in that territory. They did not assume a right to assert claims of sovereignty, ownership, or jurisdiction over the beings that shared the territory. Instead, these constitutional orders speak of a relationship that entails responsibilities for governing and/or managing the relationship among and between themselves and other beings in order to protect their territory.[8]

Examples of Indigenous constitutions include the Blackfoot system of Okahn and the teachings of the bundles that lay out the laws and responsibilities of the clans, societies, and nations that comprise the confederacy[9] as well as the the Mi'kmaq teachings of the seven districts that comprise the Grand Council and the rights and responsibilities of individuals, families, clans, and leadership within each district.[10] Like other nations, Indigenous nations have their own written and/or unwritten constitutional orders. Each of these distinct constitutional orders sets forth a system of government, provides a defined and limited ability to make, interpret, and enforce "law" within a given territory, sets forth the rules of the "political game," and defines the roles and responsibilities of all members of the nation. The legal and political orders that comprise Indigenous constitutional orders were not subject to the authority of another nation or another government but were, instead, subject to the people of the nation and the manner in which they decided to live within, and relate to, their territory (and other beings in their territory). This did not change with colonization.

Aboriginal peoples did not cede their sovereignty, surrender their constitutional orders, or subject themselves to the powers of foreign authorities.[11] Rather, Indigenous laws, sovereignty, and constitutional orders were maintained and protected by the treaties between Aboriginal nations and settler societies. Aboriginal peoples negotiated treaties to formalize relationships and to deal with such matters as creating and maintaining peace and friend-ship between nations, establishing favourable trading relationships, sharing resources within one's territory, and respecting the terms or laws that would govern their relationship. Treaties were not only negotiated on a nation-to-nation basis, but they also formalized a commitment to a nation-to-nation relationship. This commitment allowed the newcomers (and their perpetual offspring) and Aboriginal peoples to peacefully co-exist as self-governing, autonomous nations within the same (Indigenous) territory.[12]

The treaties established a relationship of non-interference between co-equals that allowed each nation to govern its own peoples within the shared territory in accordance with its own traditions.[13] Viewed in this light, any jurisdiction that was not explicitly delegated or shared was maintained within the Indigenous constitutional order. Aboriginal sovereignty was unimpeded and could not be infringed upon by claims of Crown sovereignty except where explicitly agreed to by means of delegated authority or shared sovereignty. In situations where no treaties were negotiated, Aboriginal constitutions were quite often recognized, affirmed, and protected by the terms of the original relationship between Aboriginal nations and the new-comers. However, in situations where no treaties were negotiated, Indigenous constitutional orders remained intact since Aboriginal peoples never agreed to delegate any powers or responsibilities to the Crown.

Despite promises to the contrary, the Canadian government (and its im-perial predecessors) interfered in Indigenous politics. Under the cloak of the *Indian Act*, the federal government pursued policies tantamount to political genocide.[14] In an attempt to eliminate Aboriginal sovereignty and Indigenous constitutional orders, the federal government institutionalized a system of "civilized government" or band councils. Modelled after municipalities with very limited scope and delegated authority, band councils were created pri-marily to serve as puppet governments of the federal government. This system of administration also provided the federal government with the opportunity to ready band councils for governing themselves. Since the primary goal of the *Indian Act* was assimilation – not just civilization – the idea was that once enough experience had been gained, First Nations would be granted "self-government" by way of remodelling band councils as regular municipal governments.[15]

Viewed in this light, the 1969 white paper was not simply an attempt to eliminate Aboriginal rights and the special status of Indians. Rather, it was an affront to Indigenous constitutional orders and a final attempt to elimin-ate any remnants of nationhood and sovereignty. This affront mobilized Aboriginal peoples and provided new life and organizational capacity to Aboriginal movements such as the Indian Association of Alberta, which was created in the 1930s with a vision dating back to Big Bear's attempts to mobilize the Plains Cree in the 1880s.[16] With renewed vigour and capacity, national Aboriginal organizations mobilized to protect their special status and to fight for recognition of their rights, including Aboriginal title and self-determination.

1982: Seeing beyond the *Charter*

One such political opportunity that became available for Aboriginal peoples to press for their collective rights was Trudeau's attempt to patriate the Constitution that "was part of a settler-state constitutional agenda"[17] driven by Quebec, Western alienation, and inter-governmental conflict.[18] However, Aboriginal peoples were never direct players in the constitutional process and were only permitted observer status and were never fully able to participate in the first minister talks (although they were permitted limited participation in ministerial-level talks.) Instead, they engaged in an uncoordinated strategy of international and domestic lobbying of the United Nations and the Parliament of Canada, demonstrations, education campaigns, and legal action in the United Kingdom, which, according to Roger Gibbins, resulted in significant constitutional gains.[19]

The majority of Aboriginal political organizations, however, did not support the *Constitution Act, 1982*. Only one provincial organization – the Metis Association of Alberta – agreed to the wording of section 35(1), but only after the word "existing" was added to the Aboriginal provisions therein. There was much confusion (or so it was claimed), and, in the end, even Trudeau was left wondering "what do Aboriginal peoples want?"[20] Given national and historical differences among Aboriginal peoples and their experiences, this was not a simple question. So what did they want? What was the Aboriginal constitutional vision? The simple answer is that no singular vision existed among all Aboriginal peoples, just as no singular vision existed among all Canadians. However, there were points of clarity and consensus among this diversity of vision.

For instance, the Native Council of Canada (NCC), representing Metis and non-status Indians, sought constitutional recognition of Metis and non-status Indians as Aboriginal peoples and recognition of their special status. Indeed, this recognition was vital as no such recognition or rights had been accorded these peoples, with the exception of Alberta's Metis settlements. The Inuit Committee on National Issues (ICNI), on the other hand, sought recognition of their land rights. Meanwhile, the National Indian Brotherhood/Assembly of First Nations (NIB/AFN) (representing status Indians) viewed the Constitution as an opportunity to negotiate "the terms and conditions" of their relationship with Canada. All agreed, however, that they needed to protect their rights from constitutional infringement, from the *Charter* itself, and from further encroachments by the provincial and federal governments. In a joint submission to Parliament in 1980, all three organizations agreed that the Constitution had to "entrench treaty and aboriginal rights, recognize aboriginal self-government, and require Aboriginal consent to constitutional amendments affecting their rights."[21]

In January 1981, they achieved fleeting success when the special joint parliamentary committee recommended the inclusion of section 25 to protect Aboriginal and treaty rights from the *Charter*[22] and section 34 in Part II of the act (what became section 35), which both recognized and affirmed Aboriginal and treaty rights and provided constitutional recognition to all Aboriginal peoples (Metis, Inuit, and Indians). This success was short lived since the inclusion of a consent clause was denied and the NIB withdrew its support. However, these sections were eventually restored, albeit as section 35, but modified by the inclusion of "existing" Aboriginal and treaty rights at the insistence of the federal New Democratic Party and the governments of Saskatchewan, Manitoba, Ontario, and Alberta.[23] With this modification of Aboriginal and treaty rights, the ICNI and the NCC joined the NIB in their opposition, and only the Metis Association of Alberta supported the *Constitution Act, 1982*.

Throughout these constitutional talks, there was disagreement as to whether Aboriginal peoples should be participating in the constitutional discussions, as this strategy seemed to contradict claims of nationhood and the international nature of Aboriginal rights claims. Further, there was disagreement over whether it was desirable to spell out the meaning of Aboriginal and treaty rights. Despite the disagreements and the lack of support for the constitutional package, there was nonetheless a unifying Aboriginal constitutional vision and some semblance of consensus as to the meaning of sections 25 and 35. What unified Aboriginal peoples was the consensus on the origins of their distinctive rights: they were derived from their own constitutional orders and not dependent on the *Canadian* constitutional order. What unified Aboriginal leadership were the stories of their ancestors and a vision to continue the journeys of the likes of Membertou, Deskaheh, and Big Bear, who sought to protect and live within their own constitutional orders. What unified Aboriginal peoples were the possibilities that constitutional talks offered for envisioning decolonization and concluding their struggles with colonialism. Twenty-five years later, scholars, politicians, and judges still have a hard time imagining decolonization and understanding that the possibility for realizing decolonization lies within the Canadian Constitution in somewhat of an encrypted code.

Although rejected out of fear that the level of protection needed for Aboriginal and treaty rights was not attained, sections 25 and 35 achieved the impossible. Encrypted as Aboriginal and treaty rights, these sections represented the recognition and affirmation of Indigenous constitutional orders within the Canadian Constitution and their subsequent protection from the *Charter*.[24] As James (Sa'ke'j) Youngblood Henderson, Marjorie Benson, and Isobel Findlay argue, "the spirit and the intent of section 35(1), then, should be interpreted as 'recognizing and affirming' Aboriginal legal orders, laws and jurisdictions unfolded through Aboriginal and treaty rights."[25] In essence, Aboriginal and treaty rights are the manifestation of Indigenous constitutional orders and the means by which these orders are recognized and affirmed in the Canadian Constitution.

Scholars React

> I honestly don't know what the Indians want. I just don't know.
> Pierre Elliott Trudeau

While many Canadians and government officials may have had difficulty envisioning the rights contained within section 35(1), most scholars of the day had an understanding that was fairly consistent with the positions advanced by the Aboriginal visionaries. For Douglas Sanders, Aboriginal and treaty rights found their origins in separate constitutional orders that had existed prior to the arrival of European settlers. In Sanders' view, a comprehensive recognition of the rights contained within section 35(1) "would involve (a) recognition of self-government, (b) recognition of Aboriginal customary law, (c) recognition of Aboriginal land rights, and (d) recognition of land based rights."[26] Indeed, it was only in 1982 that such legal systems (and the bundles of rights attached to them) became protected under Canadian law from further encroachment by settler governments.

Brian Slattery also recognized the continuing existence of Aboriginal constitutional orders but argued that Indigenous legal orders were received into Canadian law through the common-law doctrine of Aboriginal rights derived from the customary practices of European governments and their interactions with Aboriginal nations at the time of contact. The governing principle underpinning this doctrine was one of "continuity," "whereby the property rights, customary laws, and government institutions of the native people were presumed to survive" unless such rights were deemed to be inconsistent with the Crown's assertion of sovereignty.[27] These principles formed the foundation of British Imperial policy and were formally sanctioned by the Royal Proclamation of 1763. The views regarding the origins of Aboriginal and treaty rights, if accepted by Canadian governments and their courts, would hold much promise for decolonizing the Canadian constitutional order. By showing that Aboriginal rights derived from legal systems outside of the colonial order, these authors re-imagined legal structures that had been selectively ignored by colonial governments – a vision of parallel constitutional orders "united under one Crown but not under one law."[28]

There was, however, less agreement as to the level of protection accorded these rights under sections 25 and 35(1). For Aboriginal peoples engaged in constitutional renewal, one of the quintessential issues involved protecting their constitutional orders and treaties from the proposed *Charter*, from legislative infringement, and from bureaucratic and judicial neglect. Although many rejected the *Constitution Act, 1982,* as being insufficient to protect Aboriginal and treaty rights, many scholars argued that such protection had been achieved. For example, William Pentney argued that section 25 of the *Charter* would act as an "interpretive prism" in cases where the enforcement of *Charter* rights could potentially infringe upon the rights of Aboriginal people.[29] Mary Ellen Turpel-Lafond, on the other hand, argued that the two rights traditions were so fundamentally at odds that they could never be interpreted to co-exist under the *Charter*. As a result of this fundamental disjuncture, Turpel-Lafond argued that Aboriginal rights should never be subject to the conceptual frameworks, philosophical paradigms, and legal traditions of the other's discourse of rights.[30]

Much to the relief of the Aboriginal visionaries, the early legal scholarship also envisioned that the shield that protected Aboriginal and treaty rights from abrogation was not strictly confined to section 25. For scholars such as Sanders, the constitutionalization of Aboriginal and treaty rights under section 35(1) shielded these "existing" rights from legislative infringement. In Sanders' view, the only way that Aboriginal rights could be modified by Canadian governments would be through either constitutional amendment or by the express consent of Aboriginal people themselves.[31] Similarly, Kent McNeil argued that the constitutionalization of Aboriginal and treaty rights was shielded to such an extent that it could only be modified through constitutional amendment.[32]

Slattery arrived at a slightly different conclusion by arguing that the entrenchment of Aboriginal and treaty rights ensured that such rights were legally enforceable in the courts and protected against statutory override.[33] However, he postulated that courts would ultimately be "guided by standards of reasonableness" in their definition of Aboriginal rights. Accordingly, Aboriginal rights could be justifiably limited by governments in cases of emergency and/or for "pressing public needs."[34] While Slattery did not specifically outline reasons for arriving at this notion of "reasonableness," he nevertheless unknowingly predicted the manner in which the Supreme Court of Canada would come to interpret Aboriginal and treaty rights under section 35(1).

Aboriginal Rights and the Supreme Court of Canada

Although Slattery provided an opening for the Court to abrogate and derogate from the constitutional visions advanced by Aboriginal people, it is unlikely that the Court was waiting for such an invitation. Immediately, the Court began its quest to whittle away what seemed to be impenetrable rights by determining the substance and strength of Aboriginal and treaty rights.

In so doing, the Court fundamentally altered the "shield" surrounding these rights, discarded its own inherited common-law traditions, ignored principles of treaty constitutionalism, and attempted to interfere with Aboriginal constitutional orders by cutting away the impenetrable rights of Aboriginal people. The first case in which the Court engaged the scope of section 35(1) was *R. v. Sparrow*.[35] Recognizing that Aboriginal rights were derived from the "distinctive cultures" of Aboriginal peoples, the Court set out to find whether the Musqueam nation held an Aboriginal right to fish for food and ceremonial purposes that could supersede federal fishing regulations. To do so, the Court relied on the work of legal scholars such as Slattery, McNeil, and Pentney to establish the meaning of section 35 and the validity of such an interpretation. The Court determined that the word "existing" meant that rights that had been previously extinguished by governmental action were not revived when the *Constitution Act, 1982,* came into being. The Court acknowledged that Aboriginal rights could be extinguished in the past in so far as the legislation or statute in question demonstrated "a clear and plain intention" to legitimately extinguish Aboriginal rights.[36]

When viewed alongside an Indigenous reading of the spirit and intent of the constitutional provisions, the idea that these rights could be legitimately extinguished prior to 1982 completely obfuscates Aboriginal legal orders and jurisdictions. It not only violates the principle of non-interference but also denies Aboriginal people the power to govern their territorial space in accordance with their own laws by permitting the Crown to infringe upon rights that find their origins in separate constitutional orders. As such, the rights that the Aboriginal visionaries thought they had achieved at the constitutional table were drastically undercut.

Although the Court violated the Aboriginal reading of the Constitution prior to 1982, there was still hope that section 35(1) offered "existing" Aboriginal rights substantive protection against legislative infringement or regulation. This was not to be realized. The Court ruled that "existing" Aboriginal rights could be justifiably infringed if it was established that the legislation in question was directed toward "valid objectives," and this reasoning led the Court to develop what has come to be known as the *Sparrow* test. Under this two-part test, Aboriginal rights can be justifiably infringed if the legislative objective is found to be "compelling and substantial."[37] Such objectives were deemed to be those oriented toward the goals of conservation and resource management. Given the often precarious existence of Aboriginal interests, the Court argued that its justificatory standard for legislative infringements would serve to uphold the honour of the Crown by promoting "reconciliation."[38]

While *Sparrow* has often been described as a "landmark" decision, a number of scholars have argued that the decision contains its own inherent limits, which conceptually exclude Aboriginal rights to sovereignty from the space of legal possibilities.[39] For instance, the Court asserted in its judgement that "there was from the outset never any doubt that sovereignty and legislative power, and indeed the underlying title, to such lands [is] vested in the Crown."[40] Although the Court does indeed make reference to the unquestioned nature of Crown sovereignty, this discussion is used to contrast between claims to sovereignty both prior to, and after, the constitutionalization of Aboriginal rights. For the Court, section 35(1) ushered in a new constitutional era unbound by traditional assumptions. While *Sparrow* does not directly challenge the sovereignty of the Crown, when citing the words of Noel Lyon, the Court does briefly discuss the "significance" of entrenching Aboriginal and treaty rights within the Canadian Constitution: "[T]he context of 1982 is surely enough to tell us that this is not just a codification of the case law on [A]boriginal rights that had accumulated by 1982. Section 35 calls for a just settlement for [A]boriginal peoples. It renounces the old rules of the game under which the Crown established courts of law and denied those courts the authority to question sovereign claims made by the Crown."[41] This statement suggests that members of the judiciary might be willing to reflexively consider the role that courts have played in faithfully deferring to the sovereign power of the Crown. Understanding *Sparrow* in the context of 1982 provides an opportunity to establish a post-colonial order in Canada.[42] While *Sparrow* unfortunately followed some of the "old rules of the game" by upholding parliamentary supremacy and the power of the Crown to infringe upon Aboriginal rights, the decision nevertheless provides an opening to question the legitimacy of Crown sovereignty over Aboriginal peoples.

This tentative opening was quickly closed as the Court retreated along a well-established path littered with colonial remnants and assumptions of Crown sovereignty. Six years after *Sparrow*, writing for a majority of the Court in *R. v. Van der Peet*, then Chief Justice Antonio Lamer argued that the purpose behind recognizing and affirming Aboriginal rights in section 35(1) of the *Constitution Act, 1982,* was to achieve a "reconciliation of the pre-existence of Aboriginal societies with the sovereignty of the Crown."[43] Such an understanding of section 35 undermined its potential for decolonization as it served to naturalize Crown sovereignty and take it as a given rather than as a power of the Crown whose legitimacy over Aboriginal people had yet to be determined.

Using the notion in *Sparrow* that Aboriginal rights were "integral to the distinctive culture" of Aboriginal people as his starting point, Chief Justice Lamer developed a test to locate and identify the "rights" recognized and affirmed under section 35 of the Constitution: "[I]n order to be an [A]boriginal right an activity must be an element of a practice, custom, or tradition integral to the distinctive culture of the [A]boriginal group claiming the right."[44] By privileging a conception of Aboriginal rights that was oriented toward the past or "pre-existence" of Aboriginal societies, Chief Justice Lamer ultimately incorporated a temporal restriction into his distinctive culture test. In so doing, Lamer's test requires Aboriginal people to demonstrate that the activities for which they seek constitutional protection are a continuous, "central and significant part of the society's distinctive culture" from contact onwards.[45] The Court also stated that the claimed rights must not have been clearly extinguished by the Crown at the time at which sovereignty was asserted, thus excluding those practices, customs, or traditions that may have come into existence as a result of, or in response to, European contact.[46] As Russel Barsh and James (Sa'ke'j) Youngblood Henderson have argued, reconciliation is a constitutional "doctrine plucked from thin air."[47] Not only is Chief Justice Lamer's conception of reconciliation fundamentally at odds with its presentation in *Sparrow*, but, "[t]aken to its logical extreme, the 'reconciliation' test has the effect of extinguishing everything that had not already been judicially recognized prior to 1982."[48]

In formulating this distinctive culture test, the Court ignored both the academic literature and the constitutional visions of Aboriginal people and ultimately charted its own path. The concern expressed by Barsh and Henderson in regard to extinguishment can be readily observed in *R. v. Gladstone*, where the Court was faced with an Aboriginal claim to possess a right to fish for commercial purposes.[49] In this instance, when faced with the prospect of recognizing a commercial fishing right, Chief Justice Lamer began the process of discursively subsuming Aboriginal peoples and their legal orders within the larger Canadian community: "Because, however, distinctive [A]boriginal societies exist within, and are a part of, a broader social, political and economic community, over which the Crown is sovereign, there are circumstances in which, in order to pursue objectives of compelling and substantial importance to that community as a whole (taking into account the fact that [A]boriginal societies are a part of that community), some limitation of those rights will be justifiable."[50]

Chief Justice Lamer's doctrine justifies additional limitations on Aboriginal rights based on the grounds of the common good of all Canadians and implicitly ignores Indigenous constitutional visions.[51] Since Aboriginal peoples have been defined within the text of the decision as "Canadians," Chief Justice Lamer is able to present his common good standard as a logical "goal" and one that "is consistent with the reconciliation of [A]boriginal societies with the larger Canadian society of which they are a part."[52] It is important to note that this understanding of reconciliation implicitly obfuscates Aboriginal readings of the spirit and intent of the *Constitution Act, 1982*, and denies Aboriginal people their rights and sovereignty in harmony with their own constitutional orders. This can be further observed in *R. v. Pamajewon,* wherein Chief Justice Lamer's test was used to preclude claims to self-government by the Shawanaga and Eagle Lake First Nations.[53]

The Court's Aboriginal rights jurisprudence dramatically rendered Indigenous constitutional visions obsolete. The judiciary untethered Aboriginal rights from their separate constitutional orders and permitted governments to legally infringe upon these rights in the name of the common good. This development is particularly problematic as these Aboriginal nations did not agree to share sovereignty with Canadian society or delegate any responsibility for their rights to the federal government. By not engaging with the idea that Aboriginal rights are defined (and limited) by Aboriginal constitutional orders, the Court continued to walk the colonial path of denying the existence and applicability of Aboriginal laws and jurisdictions. Simply put, the Court continued the tradition of colonizing Indigenous constitutional orders and engaging in acts of political genocide.

Treaty Rights and the Supreme Court of Canada

While early judicial determinations allowed for justifiable limitations on the exercise of Aboriginal rights, it was unclear how the Supreme Court of Canada would assess the level of protection accorded to Aboriginal treaty rights under the "new" Canadian constitutional order. Given that treaty rights were now officially "recognized and affirmed," there was hope that Indigenous visions of treaty constitutionalism would be respected. Indeed, treaties had already reconciled contested sovereignties and afforded protection to Aboriginal constitutional orders at the time of negotiation. Remarkably, the Court continued to deny the applicability of Aboriginal laws and jurisdictions and, in the process, strengthened the power of Parliament to unilaterally alter the rights of Aboriginal people recognized under treaty.

The first case in which the Court examined the effect of section 35(1) on Aboriginal treaty rights was *R. v. Badger.*[54] The Court not only distinguished between Aboriginal and treaty rights but also articulated a number of interpretive principles. According to the Court, these principles developed out of case law and currently serve as interpretive guides for assessing Aboriginal treaty claims. Since treaties represent "an exchange of solemn promises" between Aboriginal peoples and the Crown, the Court argued "the honour of the Crown is always at stake" in their interpretation.[55] Further, because treaties were written solely by representatives of the Crown, and it is often unclear as to the extent to which these written documents correspond to the oral promises made between Aboriginal people and the Crown, "any uncertainties, ambiguities or doubtful expressions should be resolved in favour of the Indians."[56] This principle was highly significant, as it acknowledged the importance of moving beyond a literal or positivistic reading of the written terms, toward an understanding of the treaties that would allow for both Crown and Aboriginal perspectives to be taken into account. Viewed from this perspective, any rights that were not explicitly delegated remained within and were regulated by Indigenous constitutional orders. Although the Court acknowledged the "solemn" nature of treaties and the fact that they resulted from mutual agreements, it nevertheless argued that Aboriginal and treaty rights were similar in the sense that both could be unilaterally infringed.[57] In the Court's view, the justificatory framework advanced in *Sparrow* for the infringement of Aboriginal rights "should, in most cases, apply equally to the infringement of treaty rights."[58]

The principles advanced in *Badger* have continued to shape the Court's jurisprudence on treaty rights. *R. v. Marshall* was one of the most controversial decisions to employ these principles.[59] Not only did the decision itself generate criticism, but the impartiality of the Court was also questioned after the Court issued a clarification of its judgment two months after the original decision was released.[60] The majority decision in *Marshall I* determined that the treaty produced a "broader agreement" that recognized the Mi'kmaq's right to obtain goods to trade and to continue exercising the hunting and fishing rights as governed by their own constitutional order. Despite the Court recognizing a right to trade, it argued that such a right did "not extend to the openended accumulation of wealth."[61] Instead, it was a regulated right "subject to restrictions that can be justified under the *Badger* test."[62] However, since *Badger* never specifically outlined a justification test for limiting the treaty rights of Aboriginal people, it remained unclear how the Court would assess the degree to which treaty rights were "shielded" from legislative infringement.

The decision rendered two months later by a unanimous Court in *Marshall II* provides important insights into the degree to which the Court respects the "solemn" nature of Aboriginal treaties. As a result of the Court's reasoning in *Marshall II*, governments may no longer be required to justify the infringement of Aboriginal treaty rights: "[R]egulations that do no more than reasonably define the Mi'kmaq treaty right in terms that can be administered by the regulator and understood by the Mi'kmaq community that holds the treaty rights do not impair the exercise of the treaty right and therefore do not have to meet the *Badger* standard of justification."[63] Simply put, the Court dramatically reduced the level of constitutional protection that was to have been given Mi'kmaw treaty rights by section 35. It did so by opening the possibility for the federal government to unilaterally impose regulations or restrictions on those rights in the absence of any standard or justification. Barsh and Henderson argue that the Court has created the opportunity for the governments of Canada to unilaterally alter or redefine treaties and other agreements with Aboriginal peoples at whim: "*Marshall II* vindicates a kind of *administrative* supremacy over Aboriginal peoples, in which ministerial discretion can unilaterally override fundamental constitutional rights without the need for justification or compensation."[64] Under this framework, governments are now able to legislatively infringe upon treaty rights and Aboriginal jurisdictions despite the fact that the treaties have recognized the jurisdictional separation of the parties. This ability ultimately means that the constitutional recognition and affirmation granted to treaties under section 35 is nothing but a permeable shield that can be displaced and overridden by parliamentary sovereignty.

The Road Not Taken

Although embraced in large part by the early literature and early decisions such as *Sparrow*, the Aboriginal understanding of sections 25 and 35 as encrypted rights has been abandoned. The courts have not only discarded the idea that Aboriginal and treaty rights are the constitutional manifestation of Indigenous constitutional orders, but also completely cast aside key principles of their own constitutional traditions. As Barsh has argued, a key principle in the British common-law tradition is the doctrine of *lex loci*, which holds that the local laws and governing institutions of a territory are respected and become incorporated under the common law.[65] Regardless of how a previously occupied territory becomes part of the Crown's dominion, the local laws currently in place remain in force unless they are deemed to be inconsistent with the sovereignty of the Crown.[66] However, even if such inconsistency is found, the local laws remain in place until they are expressly changed or modified. This has not only been the case for territorial acquisitions such as Scotland, Ireland, India, and British North America, but it has also been applied to Aboriginal governments and their laws in British North America. This principle has had the effect of enabling separate legal orders to co-exist within, and be applied to, different communities sharing the same territorial space. While British settlers brought their laws to the "new" world, the local laws of Indigenous communities were not displaced by the arrival of this new legal regime but, instead, were acknowledged as "law" and continued to remain in force, protected under the functioning of British common law. This is most evident in the oft-cited 1867 case, *Connelly v. Woolrich*, which upheld Cree customary law.[67]

While respect for legal pluralism and the *lex loci* are fundamental tenets of the common-law tradition, they were further institutionalized in the *Constitution Act, 1982*. According to Henderson, 1982 established a postcolonial order in Canada by bringing "Aboriginal legal orders, laws and jurisdictions unfolded through Aboriginal and treaty rights" into the Constitution.[68] The significance of respecting legal pluralism and embracing the post-colonial opportunities afforded by the *Constitution Act, 1982,* has also been expressed by Peter Russell, John Borrows, and Patrick Macklem.[69] In particular, both Borrows and Macklem demonstrate that the foundation of Canada's constitutional order originated in the treaty relations between Aboriginal nations and the British Crown, which were often negotiated according to Indigenous laws and customary practices. It was this treaty relationship that delineated the boundaries over which settler governments could exercise their own constitutional authority. As noted by Borrows, "Indigenous legal values form the hidden but underlying bedrock upon which the Crown and its assignees have built their claims.[70] Further, not only are Aboriginal constitutional orders recognized and affirmed as Aboriginal and treaty rights, they are also now part of the supreme law of the land and can no longer be overridden. Henderson eloquently explains the importance of the post-colonial context of 1982: "In the post-colonial order of Canada, these rights have now been given full constitutional authority, becoming an integral part of unwritten federal common law operating in the constitution of Canada. Thus, it is no longer sufficient to rely solely on existing colonial precedents or statutory provisions in unravelling Aboriginal and treaty issues. The worldviews and the languages of First Nations are as relevant in determining the spirit and contexts of Aboriginal and treaty issues as are the Anglocentric traditions of England."[71] The courts have neither followed their own constitutional principles nor embraced this post-colonial trajectory. Rather, the courts have engaged in the selective deployment of the common-law tradition.

While the *Constitution Act, 1982,* signifies an explicit acknowledgment of the *lex loci*, the courts have stood steadfast in ignoring the *lex loci* and, thus, denying Aboriginal legal orders, laws, and jurisdictions when rendering their decisions. While they suggest that the common-law doctrine of Aboriginal rights takes into account both European and Aboriginal perspectives on the rights under dispute, the reality is a reading of the common law that has privileged British/Canadian legal systems to the extent that it all but ignores Indigenous constitutional orders. Justice Ian Binnie's concurring judgement in *R. v. Mitchell* clearly demonstrates this idea: "The *Constitution Act, 1982* ushered in a new chapter but it did not start a new book. Within the framework of s. 35(1) regard is to be had to the common law ('what the law has historically accepted') to enable a court to determine what constitutes an [A]boriginal right."[72] In other words, it is as if 1982 had changed nothing.

Legal scholars have argued that 1982 marked the dawning of a new era of constitutional supremacy, one that included Indigenous constitutional orders unfolded through Aboriginal and treaty rights as part of the supreme law of Canada. Instead, the Court has continued its tradition of defending parliamentary supremacy and negating or ignoring doctrines of constitutional supremacy. This is most evident in decisions such as *Sparrow, Van der Peet,* and *Marshall I* and *II.* While section 35 was envisioned as making treaties part of Canadian constitutional law, and, thus, Aboriginal constitutions and jurisdictions as part of the supreme law, in *Marshall*, the Court provided legislatures with ample opportunity to ignore or infringe upon the rights and jurisdictions of nations such as the Mi'kmaq. As such, the Court created greater opportunties for limiting treaty rights through assertions of the common good and Crown sovereignty. In the end, we are left with Canada claiming the right to regulate the Mi'kmaw fishery and the Mi'kmaw are, once again, searching for ways to operationalize their vision that the *Constitution Act, 1982*, starts a new chapter and creates a post-colonial order.

By deploying the common law in a manner that leaves little or no room for considerations of Aboriginal law and/or Indigenous constitutional orders, the Court has ultimately crafted a vigorous defence of Crown sovereignty that situates Aboriginal peoples firmly under the territorial control of the Crown. The Court has continued to ignore Aboriginal visions of both separate constitutional orders and co-existing sovereignties. Through its interpretation, the Court has continuously dealt with contestations of sovereignty by situating Aboriginal people as part of the Canadian collective and by creating a unified vision of sovereignty that subsumes Aboriginal nations under the Crown. In Justice Binnie's concurring judgement in *Mitchell*, a vision of the constitutional order is advanced in which both sovereignty and territorial space are reified and represented as immutable. In part, this reification is based on the questioning of the strength of Chief Mitchell's claim to possess an Aboriginal right that derives from an alternate legal order, namely the Haudenosaunee constitutional order and the subsequent treaties that protected it. Mitchell's understanding of the two-row wampum is interpreted not as an attempt to legally assert Mohawk sovereignty over their territories in accordance with their own laws, but, rather, as an attempt "to live as if the international boundary did not exist."[73]

In rendering this decision, Aboriginal understandings of history, law, and jurisdiction are denied legitimacy within a cognitive framework that perceives the place of Aboriginal peoples in relation to Canadian sovereignty as being no different than that of any other "Canadian" community: "I accept that this crisscrossing of borders through the Mohawk community goes beyond mere inconvenience and does constitute a significant burden on everyday living. It is, of course, a burden to border communities everywhere. Jurisdictional patchworks, and their ability to complicate one's existence, are not special to [A]boriginal communities. Elsewhere in Quebec, there are similar difficulties. In Estcourt, the international boundary runs through the living-room of the Bechard family. In Stanhope, Quebec, the billiard room of the Dundee Line Hotel is neatly bifurcated by the boundary with New York State."[74] As this passage attests, Justice Binnie perceives the Canadian border as an objective and neutral line that treats all communities equally. By comparing the situation faced by the Mohawks to that of a bifurcated billiard room in a Quebec hotel, Justice Binnie completely effaces both the diversity and the legitimacy of the territorial claims existing within this region in favour of a unified and totalizing vision of Canadian sovereignty and territorial space.[75]

The destructive effects of just such a totalizing vision can be seen in Justice Binnie's treatment of the interplay between Haudenosaunee and Canadian constitutional orders and the treaties that recognized their continued existence. In this regard, Justice Binnie presents an understanding of the Gus-Wen-Tah, or the two-row wampum, which has no prior existence outside of the text of the decision itself: "The modern embodiment of the "two-row" wampum concept, modified to reflect some of the realities of a modern state, is the idea of a 'merged' or 'shared' sovereignty. 'Merged sovereignty' asserts that First Nations were not wholly subordinated to non-[A]boriginal sovereignty but over time became merger partners."[76] What is interesting about this understanding of the two-row (the Gus-Wen-Tah) is that Justice Binnie attributes the notion of "merged sovereignty" to the RCAP. According to Justice Binnie, "[i]f the principle of 'merged sovereignty' articulated by the Royal Commission on Aboriginal Peoples is to have any meaning, it must include at least the idea that [A]boriginal and non-[A]boriginal Canadians *together* form a sovereign entity with a measure of common purpose and united effort."[77] However, a search for the term "merged sovereignty" within the RCAP reveals that the phrase does not appear anywhere in the document.[78] Instead, it would appear that this phrase – and its attribution to the RCAP – is nothing more than a judicially crafted attempt to bolster support for a particular understanding of the constitutional order. In this regard, by collapsing the two-row into a single, unified row and, thus, a vision of one national integrated community, Justice Binnie leaves Crown sovereignty intact (and unquestioned) as the primary organizing force within the juridical domain.[79]

This structuring effect can be observed in Justice Binnie's description of the purpose behind including Aboriginal rights within section 35(1) of the Constitution. As with *Van der Peet* and *Gladstone*, Justice Binnie repeatedly asserts that the primary objective at the core of section 35(1) is "the reconciliation of the interests of [A]boriginal peoples with Crown sovereignty."[80] This continual assertion of sovereignty is much more than a "mere incantation."[81] Every time the Court invokes the sovereignty of the Crown, it simultaneously solidifies the sovereign authority of the Canadian state as well as redirects and retranslates Crown sovereignty over Aboriginal peoples, their laws, their governments, and their constitutional orders. This definitional force of "sovereignty" extends beyond demarcations of the Crown's territorial domain to the place of Aboriginal and treaty rights within the constitutional order itself. For Justice Binnie, section 35(1) does more than simply recognize and affirm Aboriginal and treaty rights. The Canadian Constitution itself brings these rights into existence: "If the respondent's claimed

[A]boriginal right is to prevail, it does so not because of its own inherent strength, but because the *Constitution Act, 1982* brings about the result."[82] As such, the ability of Aboriginal peoples to renew Indigenous constitutional orders, Aboriginal governance, relationships with their territories, and a decolonized relationship with Canada, is fundamentally diminished by this reassertion of "sovereignty."

Conclusion

After twenty-five years of opportunity for decolonization, there have been few gains made in realizing this potential. Simply put, the Court has rendered obsolete everything Aboriginal people fought to achieve in the *Constitution Act, 1982*, and in subsequent constitutional negotiations. The Court has replaced the idea that sections 25 and 35 recognized, affirmed, and *protected* Aboriginal law, sovereignty, and Indigenous constitutional orders with the idea that section 35 protects Crown sovereignty and parliamentary supremacy while recreating Aboriginal people as Canadian citizens. This development simply repackages the assimilationist goals that the Canadian government established in the *Indian Act* of 1876, reiterated in its 1969 white paper, and retranslates them into constitutional law. In effect, this jurisprudential development is, as Paul McHugh suggests, "as much an expression of the road not taken as that which remained in place."[83] As scholars such as James Henderson, John Borrows, Patrick Macklem, and Peter Russell remind us, there is another road that the courts could easily rediscover. To fundamentally alter their understanding of the Constitution and sections 25 and 35, Crown sovereignty, and constitutional/parliamentary supremacy, the courts need to embrace the post-colonial opportunities provided by the framers of the *Constitution Act, 1982*.

Acknowledgments

Part of the research presented in this chapter is the result of a project funded by the Social Science and Humanities Research Council (SSHRC) on Indigenous constitutional visions. We wish to thank the Ontario Graduate Scholarship (OGS), the SSHRC, the National Centre on First Nations Governance, and the Canada Research Chair (CRC) program for funding our research endeavours. We also wish to thank Susan Hill, Frances Abele, and the editors of this collection for their comments on the various iterations of this chapter. We also wish to thank Sa'ke'j Henderson and Leroy Little Bear for sharing their constitutional journeys over the years.

Notes

1   For a discussion of natural law as a foundation of Aboriginal legal and political orders (what we call constitutional orders), see James (Sa'ke'j) Youngblood Henderson, *First Nations Jurisprudence and Aboriginal Rights* (Saskatoon: University of Saskatchewan, Native Law Centre, 2006), 116-77. For a discussion of how Indigenous constitutional orders and political systems were constructed as a relationship to the ecological order and with the intent of living the best possible way, see Kiera L. Ladner, "Up the Creek: Fishing for a New Constitutional Order," *Canadian Journal of Political Science* 38 (2005): 923-55.

2 Menno Boldt, *Surviving as Indians: The Challenge of Self-Government* (Toronto: University of Toronto Press, 1993), 150.

3 Royal Commission on Aboriginal Peoples, *Report of the Royal Commission on Aboriginal Peoples*, volume 1 (Ottawa: Canada Communications Group, 1996), 119.

4 Mary-Ellen Turpel, "Aboriginal Peoples and the Canadian Charter: Interpretive Monopolies, Cultural Differences," *Canadian Human Rights Yearbook* 3 (1989-1990): 4-45.

5 Peter Russell, *Constitutional Odyssey*, 3rd edition (Toronto: University of Toronto Press, 2004).

6 *Canadian Charter of Rights and Freedoms*, Part 1 of the *Constitution Act, 1982*, being Schedule B to the *Canada Act 1982* (U.K.), 1982, c. 11.

7 *Constitution Act, 1982* (U.K.), 1982, c. 11, s. 59.

8 James (Sa'ke'j) Youngblood Henderson, "Mi'kmaq Tenure in Atlantic Canada," *Dalhousie Law Journal* 18 (1995): 196-300.

9 Kiera L. Ladner, "Governing within an Ecological Context: Creating an AlterNative Understanding of Blackfoot Governance," *Studies in Political Economy* 70 (Spring 2003): 125-52.

10 James (Sa'ke'j) Youngblood Henderson, *The Mikmaw Concordat* (Halifax: Fernwood, 1997).

11 Patrick Macklem, *Indigenous Difference and the Constitution of Canada* (Toronto: University of Toronto Press, 2001).

12 James (Sa'ke'j) Youngblood Henderson, "Empowering Treaty Federalism," *Saskatchewan Law Review* 58 (1994): 247.

13 Ibid., 241-332. See also Kiera L. Ladner, "Treaty Federalism: An Indigenous Vision of Canadian Federalisms," in Miriam Smith and Francois Rocher, eds., *New Trends in Canadian Federalism* (Peterborough: Broadview Press, 2003).

14 *Indian Act*, R.S.C. 1985, c. I-5.

15 Kiera L. Ladner and Michael Orsini, "The Persistence of Paradigm Paralysis: The *First Nations Governance Act* as the Continuation of Colonial Policy," in Michael Murphy, ed., *Canada: State of the Federation 2005* (Montreal and Kingston: McGill-Queen's University Press, 2005).

16 Kiera L. Ladner, "*Aysaka,paykinit*: Contesting the Rope around the Nations' Neck," in Miriam Smith, ed., *Group Politics and Social Movements in Canada* (Peterborough: Broadview Press, 2007).

17 P.G. McHugh, *Aboriginal Societies and the Common Law: A History of Sovereignty, Status and Self-Determination* (New York: Oxford University Press, 2004), 94.

18 Russell, *supra* note 5, 92-127.

19 See Douglas E. Sanders, "The Indian Lobby," in Keith Banting and Richard Simeon, eds., *And No One Cheered: Federalism, Democracy and the Constitution Act* (Toronto: Methuen, 1983), 301; and Roger Gibbins, "Canadian Indians and the Canadian Constitution: A Difficult Passage toward an Uncertain Destination," in J. Rick Ponting, ed., *Arduous Journey: Canadian Indians and Decolonization* (Toronto: McClelland and Stewart, 1986), 304.

20 Sanders, *supra* note 19, 327.

21 Sanders, *supra* note 19, 313-14.

22 Section 25 reads as follows: "The guarantee in this Charter of certain rights and freedoms shall not be construed so as to abrogate or derogate from any aboriginal, treaty or other rights or freedoms that pertain to the Aboriginal peoples of Canada."

23 Section 35(1) reads as follows: "The existing aboriginal and treaty rights of aboriginal peoples are hereby recognized and affirmed."

24 We use the term "encrypted rights" to refer to the fact that the Aboriginal leadership was speaking about, and fighting for, the same Indigenous constitutional orders that their ancestors had fought to protect in the treaties and through other means. Seizing this window of opportunity, the Aboriginal leaders embraced and used the rights discourse of the colonizers as a way to continue the battle and to protect their constitutional orders and treaties. While we use the term "encrypted," other authors such as Henderson, Marjorie Benson, and Isobel Findlay use the term "unfolded" to convey a similar idea.

25 James (Sa'ke'j) Youngblood Henderson, Marjorie L. Benson, and Isobel M. Findlay, *Aboriginal Tenure in the Constitution of Canada* (Scarborough: Carswell, 2000), 432-34.

26 Douglas Sanders, "The Rights of the Aboriginal Peoples of Canada," *Canadian Bar Review* 61 (1983): 328.

27   Brian Slattery, "The Hidden Constitution: Aboriginal Rights in Canada," *American Journal of Comparative Law* 32 (1984): 366.
28   Russel Lawrence Barsh and James (Sa'ke'j) Youngblood Henderson, "Aboriginal Rights, Treaty Rights, and Human Rights: Indian Tribes and 'Constitutional Renewal,'" *Journal of Canadian Studies* 17 (1982): 59.
29   William Pentney, "The Rights of the Aboriginal Peoples of Canada in the Constitution Act, 1982: Part 1 – The Interpretive Prism of Section 25," *University of British Columbia Law Review* 22 (1988): 57.
30   Turpel, *supra* note 4, 33.
31   Sanders, *supra* note 26, 334; see also Sanders, "Pre-Existing Rights: The Aboriginal Peoples of Canada," in Gerald A. Beaudoin and Ed Ratushny, eds., *The Canadian Charter of Rights and Freedoms* (Toronto: Carswell, 1989), 733.
32   Kent McNeil, "The Constitutional Rights of the Aboriginal Peoples of Canada," *Supreme Court Law Review* 4 (1982): 255.
33   In his early writings, Slattery stated that section 35 rendered Aboriginal rights "sure and unavoidable." See Brian Slattery, "The Constitutional Guarantee of Aboriginal and Treaty Rights," *Queen's Law Journal* 8 (1982-83): 2.
34   Slattery, *supra* note 27, 384.
35   *R. v. Sparrow*, [1990] I S.C.R. 1075 [*Sparrow*].
36   Ibid., 1099.
37   Ibid., 1033.
38   Ibid., 1109.
39   Michael Asch and Patrick Macklem, "Aboriginal Rights and Canadian Sovereignty: An Essay on *R. v. Sparrow*," *Alberta Law Review* 24 (1991): 507.
40   *Sparrow*, *supra* note 35, 1135.
41   Ibid., 1106.
42   See also Henderson, *supra* note 1.
43   *R. v. Van der Peet*, [1996] 2 S.C.R 507 at para. 31.
44   Ibid., para. 46.
45   Ibid., para. 55.
46   Michael Murphy, "Culture and the Courts: A New Direction in Canadian Jurisprudence on Aboriginal Rights?" *Canadian Journal of Political Science* 34 (2001): 109-29.
47   Russel Lawrence Barsh and James Youngblood Henderson, "The Supreme Court's *Van der Peet* Trilogy: Naive Imperialism and Ropes of Sand," *McGill Law Journal* 42 (1997): 998.
48   Ibid., 999.
49   *R. v. Gladstone*, [1996] 2 S.C.R. 723 [*Gladstone*].
50   Ibid., para. 73.
51   See Gordon Christie, "Judicial Justification of Recent Developments in Aboriginal Law," *Canadian Journal of Law and Society* 17 (2002): 41-71.
52   *Gladstone*, *supra* note 49, para. 74.
53   *R. v. Pamajewon*, [1996] 2 S.C.R. 821.
54   *R. v. Badger*, [1996] 1 S.C.R. 771.
55   Ibid., para. 41.
56   Ibid., para. 52.
57   Ibid., para. 77.
58   Ibid., para. 75.
59   *R. v. Marshall*, [1999] 3 S.C.R. 456 [*Marshall I*].
60   *R. v. Marshall*, [1999] 3 S.C.R. 533 [*Marshall II*].
61   *Marshall I*, *supra* note 59, para. 7.
62   Ibid., para. 56.
63   *Marshall II*, *supra* note 60, para. 37.
64   Russel Lawrence Barsh and James Youngblood Henderson, "Marshalling the Rule of Law in Canada: Of Eels and Honour," *Constitutional Forum* 11 (1999): 17.
65   Russel Lawrence Barsh, "Indigenous Rights and the *Lex Loci* in British Imperial Law," in Kerry Wilkins, ed., *Advancing Aboriginal Claims: Visions, Strategies, Directions* (Saskatoon: Purich Publishing, 2004), 91-126.

66 Brian Slattery, "Understanding Aboriginal Rights," *Canadian Bar Review* 66 (1987): 738.
67 For a discussion of *Connelly v. Woolrich*, see Slattery, *supra* note 27, 367.
68 Henderson, Benson, and Findlay, *supra* note 25, 434.
69 See Peter H. Russell, *Recognizing Aboriginal Title: The Mabo Case and Indigenous Resistance to English-Settler Colonialism* (Toronto: University of Toronto Press, 2006); John Borrows, "Constitutional Law from a First Nation Perspective: Self-Government and the Royal Proclamation," *University of British Columbia Law Review* 28 (1994): 1-47; Patrick Macklem, *Indigenous Difference and the Constitution of Canada* (Toronto: University of Toronto Press, 2001).
70 John Borrows, *Recovering Canada: The Resurgence of Indigenous Law* (Toronto: University of Toronto Press, 2002).
71 James (Sa'ke'j) Youngblood Henderson, "Empowering Treaty Federalism," *Saskatchewan Law Review* 58 (1994): 281-82.
72 *Mitchell v. M.N.R*, 2001 SCC 33 at para. 115 [*Mitchell*].
73 Ibid., para. 125.
74 Ibid., para. 79.
75 For a discussion of how law can serve to constitute spatial structures, see Nicholas Blomley, *Law, Space, and the Geographies of Power* (New York: Guilford Press, 1994).
76 *Mitchell, supra* note 72 at para. 129.
77 Ibid., para. 129 [emphasis in original].
78 *Report of the Royal Commission on Aboriginal Peoples*. 5 vols. (Ottawa: Canada Communication Group Publishing, 1996).
79 For a discussion of how the Court invokes Crown sovereignty in relation to Aboriginal title, see John Borrows, "Sovereignty's Alchemy: An Analysis of *Delgamuukw v. British Columbia*," *Osgoode Hall Law Journal* 37 (1999): 537-96.
80 *Mitchell, supra* note 72, para. 164, see also paras. 74, 76, 80, 123, 133, and 155.
81 See Chief Justice McLachlin's comments on the "honour of the Crown" in *Haida Nation v. British Columbia (Minister of Forests)*, [2004] 3 S.C.R. 511 at para. 16.
82 *Mitchell, supra* note 72, para. 70.
83 McHugh, *supra* note 17, 481.

Conclusion

15
The *Charter* and Canadian Democracy
Peter H. Russell

More than twenty-five years ago, as the Canadian constitutional process was giving birth to the *Canadian Charter of Rights and Freedoms*, I wrote an article about the political purposes of the *Charter*, as conceived by its political sponsors, and its likely consequences for Canadian democracy.[1] On the latter, I noted how the *Charter* was bound to involve the judiciary in making important decisions on contentious issues of public policy and went on to make the following comment on the democratic implications of this empowerment of the judiciary: "The danger here is not so much that non-elected judges will impose their will on a democratic majority, but that questions of social and political justice will be transformed into technical legal issues and the great bulk of the citizenry who are not judges and lawyers will abdicate their responsibility for working out mutually acceptable resolutions of the issues which divide them."[2] In this chapter, I will reflect on this comment in light of the quarter-century of experience we have now had with the *Charter*. How serious has the danger that I apprehended been? What about the most widely anticipated threat to democracy – policy-making by non-elected judges? Have there been more serious threats to Canadians that have nothing to do with the *Charter*? Has the *Charter* affected the quality of Canadian democracy in ways that were hoped for and in other ways that were not anticipated twenty-five years ago? These are the questions I will pursue in this concluding chapter of *Contested Constitutionalism: Reflections on the Canadian Charter of Rights and Freedoms*.

The *Charter* and the Sinews of Canadian Democracy
The apprehension about the *Charter*'s implications for the quality of our democratic life that I voiced more than twenty-five years ago related to what I call "the sinews of democracy." By this phrase, I mean the capacity of our Canadian body politic to debate and resolve over time divisive normative issues that arise in our political life. A healthy and vibrant democratic polity

should be muscular enough to engage with these issues through public discussion and debate and eventually arrive at positions that, although they leave some people deeply dissatisfied, provide ways of dealing with the issue that are relatively consensual. Back in 1982, I feared that, by judicializing such issues, the *Charter* might have the effect of turning them into technical legal matters, with the consequence that the bulk of the citizenry would cease to debate them and leave their resolution to lawyers and the courts, thus reducing Canada's capacity to function as a deliberative democracy.[3]

Looking back now over the last twenty-five years, how did the *Charter* affect how Canada as a democratic community dealt with the big, controversial questions of social and political justice that arose during the period? I have in mind issues such as Sunday closing, abortion, euthanasia, the rights of gays and lesbians, the rights of linguistic and religious minorities especially with respect to education, the reasonable accommodation of ethnic minorities, and mandatory retirement – to mention only those that come to the top of my mind. All of these issues were litigated under the *Charter*. *Charter* aficionados can rattle off the relevant cases. The *Charter* decisions of the courts – above all, the decisions of the Supreme Court of Canada – undoubtedly influenced public policy on all of these issues. In many cases, a judicial decision on the *Charter* was a crucial factor in bringing about a particular policy outcome. For example, Supreme Court of Canada decisions on the first two items on my list – Sunday closing and abortion – clearly had the effect of ending the criminalization of commercial activities on the Christian Sabbath and the criminalization of abortion. Although most of the Court's decisions on such issues supported rights claimants and overturned existing legislation or called for changes in government practice, such outcomes were not always the case. The Supreme Court of Canada's 1990 decision in *McKinney v. University of Guelph*, upholding mandatory retirement, went the other way and impeded legislative reform in this area for a number of years.[4] Yet, while *Charter* litigation made the judiciary a major player in these hotly contested areas of public policy, the question is whether it shut down debate and discussion of these issues within the body politic or made our discourse about the moral issues raised by the *Charter* unduly legalistic?

My impression – and that is really all one can have on such a broad question – is that court decisions on these matters, even when they have had a decisive impact on them, generally did not close off political debate and discussion. With abortion, for example, I saw no sign of the right-to-life movement backing down nor of the pro-choice movement abandoning their support for birth control and for those who seek and provide abortion. Catch phrases from Supreme Court of Canada decisions, such as Justice Bertha Wilson's use of the right to liberty, could now be heard in confrontations between the contending groups, but, by and large, the debate was not dominated by legalistic technicalities. Similarly, long before the Supreme Court of Canada shot down the *Lord's Day Act* and opened up Sunday to commercial activity, it had long ceased to be a religious issue and was instead a social policy debate about the value of maintaining a common day of rest and recreation for working families.[5] This issue continued to be debated and worked on at the community level and in labour relations. As for mandatory retirement, the losing side in the Supreme Court of Canada carrried on its struggle, totally unpersuaded by the reasoning of the Court's majority, and, with the help of changing demographics, labour shortages, and political lobbying, it eventually began to get rid of mandatory retirement province by province. In the case that dealt with euthanasia, *Rodriquez v. British Columbia (Attorney General)*, Justice Frank Iacobucci, writing for the Court's majority, was deferential to public deliberation and ruled that the Court should not deal with such a difficult moral issue until public opinion on it was better formed.[6]

Same-sex marriage was one issue on which *Charter* decisions of the courts threatened to smother reasoned debate among parliamentarians – although not among the public. After the Ontario Court of Appeal found no reasonable justification for denying the equal benefit of law to same-sex unions,[7] and the Supreme Court of Canada found no constitutional flaw in federal legislation proposing to extend the status of civil marriage to couples of the same sex,[8] Prime Minister Paul Martin's reaction was that since the matter had been decided by the courts it was now beyond debate and discussion. His government would go ahead with the same-sex marriage legislation, and use of the *Charter*'s notwithstanding clause was out of the question because "Canadians don't want to see governments taking away their rights."[9] Not for a minute was he willing to articulate and defend the very strong reasons advanced by the Court against denying the status of marriage to unions of gays and lesbians. As a Roman Catholic, Martin clearly had difficulty recognizing the legitimacy of same-sex marriages. Nevertheless, he had no choice but to comply with the *Charter*. His treatment of the issue was devoid of the spirit of that great Liberal statesman Wilfrid Laurier, who had taught his Catholic fellow citizens to accept the democratic imperative of a secular state.[10] The *Charter*, through its judicial oracle, had spoken, and that, for Mr. Martin, was the end of the matter.

Stephen Harper was no improvement on Martin. He was ill at ease with same-sex marriage, although he would not tell us why. It seemed that, on the one hand, he did not want to offend the fundamentalist Christian rump of his party, but, on the other hand, because he was trying to expand the base of his party, he did not want the fundamentalists' position to become the Conservative Party's official position. As prime minister, Harper kept his promise to allow a free parliamentary vote on a motion calling on the government to restore the traditional definition of marriage. Yet, at the same time, by refusing to use the *Charter*'s override clause, he made sure this parliamentary initiative would have no legislative effect. Even if Parliament voted to restore the traditional definition of marriage, the judicial rulings that the *Charter* requires a legal definition of marriage that includes same-sex unions would still stand. The lack of any coherence in Harper's position did not stop him from declaring at the conclusion of the short parliamentary debate that the contentious issue of same-sex marriage was "permanently closed."[11]

However, despite Martin's *Charter* baby talk and Harper's declaration of closure, same-sex marriage continues to be discussed and debated in the country. Margaret Sommerville, the founding director of McGill's Centre for Medicine, Ethics and Law, in the 2006 Massey lectures and in newspaper opinion-editorial essays, has advanced carefully reasoned arguments against recognizing same-sex marriages.[12] However, the balance of opinion and practice in Canada now clearly favours giving same-sex couples access to civil marriage, although some religious groups continue to resist giving such marriages the blessing of their faith. Those individuals of Sommerville's persuasion encounter resistance not from the *Charter* and its application to the issue by the judiciary but, rather, from a more pervasive threat to free public discussion – political correctness. Within my university, there was considerable resistance to allowing Sommerville a platform to espouse her views. Although Sommerville has not persuaded me that the conservation of family life requires the denial of "marriage" status to same-sex unions, I deplore the efforts to silence her. Branding disagreeable positions as "offensive" and denying them a public forum poses a grave threat to Canadian liberal democracy. This kind of thinking was becoming all too prevalent, particularly among younger members of the political Left, well before the *Charter*. In generating litigation leading to decisions that are in line with the views of the political correctness crowd, the *Charter* may have added an ounce or two to their moral arrogance. But I doubt that the *Charter* has been a major factor in fostering these illiberal attitudes. And I note that in the end, Sommerville, as so often is the case with the targets of political correctness, was not denied a platform. I conclude that, by and large, despite my fears, the sinews of Canadian democracy have not been significantly weakened by the *Charter*.

The False Spectre of Activism
The most widespread democratic concern about the *Charter*, both before and after its adoption, was the spectre of unelected judges making decisions about important matters of public policy. I was among the first to voice this concern when Pierre Trudeau began to press for an entrenched bill of rights as his top priority for constitutional reform in Canada.[13] The important policy-making role that the *Charter* would bestow on the judiciary was the main theme of my submission to the Special Joint Committee of the Senate

and the House of Commons on the Constitution in January 1981.[14] This insight – a prosaic and obvious point for political science scholars – seemed to come as a shock to members of the committee. A member of the committee asked me about the *Charter's* implications for the abortion issue. I responded that the issue was bound to be dealt with by the courts once the *Charter* became law and went on to tell them about the Supreme Court of the United States' decision in *Roe v. Wade*.[15] However, I said that I did not have a clue as to how Canadian judges would approach the issue. I described the huge swings of opinion that had taken place in the United States Supreme Court on interpreting constitutional rights and stressed how impossible it was for me (or anyone else) to predict the movements in judicial interpretation of the *Charter* over time. The one thing the so-called "framers of the constitution" should be clear about, I said, is that the actual, effective meaning in law of the *Charter's* abstract words would be determined not by them but, rather, by Canada's judges, above all by the nine members of the Supreme Court of Canada. The parliamentarians did not seem thrilled with this news.

Once the *Charter* became law and the Supreme Court of Canada began to render decisions on it, there was a tremendous outburst of concern about the anti-democratic implications of this expansion of judicial power. The Supreme Court of Canada helped launch this outburst by showing in its first dozen or so *Charter* decisions that it was going to take the *Charter* seriously and would not shy away from overturning legislation or executive actions that violated its terms. The Court adopted interpretative approaches that shocked some of its critics. In its very first decision on the *Charter*, Justice Willard Estey, harking back to Lord Sankey's metaphor in the *Persons* case, said the *Charter*, like the rest of the Constitution, must be adapted to the changing needs of the country it serves and treated as a "living tree."[16] In *Big M Drug Mart,* the decision that overturned the *Lord's Day Act*, Chief Justice Brian Dickson espoused a purposive approach to finding the meaning of the right to religious freedom.[17] This approach required a judicial exploration of the reasons that led Western, liberal societies to dismantle state-supported religions. In *Singh v. Minister of Employment and Immigration*, Justice Bertha Wilson's majority decision ruled out administrative cost and inconvenience as justification in a free and democratic society for abridging the constitutional right of persons seeking refugee status in Canada.[18] In *Operation Dismantle, Inc. v. R.*, the Supreme Court of Canada rejected the Supreme Court of the United States' "political questions doctrine," which rendered some issues non-justiciable solely because of their controversial political nature.[19] Our highest court would not duck an issue solely because it is a political hot potato. In *Reference re B.C. Motor Vehicle Act*, the Court refused to comply with the "original intent" of the *Charter's* framers to limit the principles of fundamental justice in section 7 to procedural matters.[20] In

Andrews v. Law Society of British Columbia, the Court's first decision interpreting the *Charter*'s equality rights, the Supreme Court of Canada made it clear that the right to "equality before and under the law" and to "equal protection and benefit of the law without discrimination" would be interpreted as substantive rights and not confined to the grounds of discrimination explicitly included in the prohibition of discrimination.[21]

All of these interpretative stances by the Court as well as the specter of its invalidating legislation such as the abortion provisions of the *Criminal Code* caused one great hullabaloo.[22] Academics on both the Left and the Right and some leading journalists began to attack the Court for its "activism." Judicial activism became the scourge of the land. Phrases such as "judicial supremacy," "rule by judges," and "jurocracy" were becoming standard usage in the rhetoric of the Supreme Court of Canada's critics. I began to receive invitations to address groups, attend conferences, and write papers on judicial activism's threat to Canadian democracy. My responses to these attacks on the Court's "judicial activism" disappointed and surprised many colleagues and former students who had been influenced by the alarm bells I rang in the pre-*Charter* period about how a constitutional bill of rights would lead to a major increase in judicial power. Why was I now apparently pulling in my horns?

There were three immediate reasons that I found I could not join the critics of "judicial acivism." First, I was a big fan and supporter of the *Charter*'s notwithstanding clause. I thought it would serve as a democratic safety valve, ensuring that neither the judiciary nor parliamentarians would have the last word on difficult decisions relating to the metes and bounds of constitutionally protected rights.[23] What I obviously did not foresee is that politicians – at least at the federal level – would be too fearful of how the use of the override would spin politically to ever contemplate using it. The Bourassa government's use of section 33 to overcome the Supreme Court of Canada's decision in *Ford v. Quebec* and restore the Quebec law prohibiting outdoor signs in English gravely undermined support for the notwithstanding clause in English Canada.[24]

I came to appreciate the value of the clause even when it was not used. I happened to be visiting Edmonton at the time the Supreme Court of Canada rendered its decision in *Vriend v. Alberta*, extending to gays and lesbians the protection against discrimination afforded by Alberta's *Individual's Rights Protection Act*.[25] Premier Ralph Klein was immediately under pressure to use section 33 to override the Supreme Court of Canada. Yet, when editorials in Alberta newspapers and members of his own caucus began to express concern about the implications of continuing to permit discrimination against Albertans in employment and other areas solely because of their sexual orientation, Klein backed down and said Alberta would live with the Court's decision. The availability of the legislative override meant that the elected government accepted responsibility for leaving intact the expansion of equality called for by the Court. Alberta's premier could not blame this change in Alberta law on the Court.

I remain a strong supporter of the override clause.[26] It should be used only in those rare situations when a Supreme Court of Canada decision, especially one rendered by a badly divided court and based on a very contentious interpretation of the *Charter*, has struck down legislation that is clearly valued by a large popular majority. I hope that our federal politicians would use it if a Court majority ever adopted the position that three members of the Court took in *Chaoulli v. Quebec (Attorney General)* when they held that a provincial ban on private insurance for publicly insured health services violates principles of fundamental justice in section 7 of the Charter.[27] Public opinion research recently conducted by Nik Nanos indicates that among the minority of Canadians who have heard of the notwithstanding clause there is no majority position on its use or non-use.[28] My guess is that there would surely have been strong public support for using the notwithstanding clause to preserve Canada's public medical insurance plan. Canadians may well value their medicare system even more than their *Charter*.

Another, more fundamental, reason for not jumping on the anti-activist bandwagon was the popularity of the *Charter*. I got a sense of this sentiment when the Conservatives asked me to be one of their two individual present- ers to the Special Joint Committee of the Senate and the House of Commons on the Constitution. They explained that while they shared my concern about the *Charter* increasing judicial power, it was not a point they wanted to raise themselves because they did not want to be seen as opposing a *Charter* for which their polls showed there was overwhelming popular sup- port. After the *Charter* became law and the Supreme Court of Canada began to interpret it, the popularity of the *Charter* was evident in poll after poll. An in-depth study of public opinion on the *Charter* and the issues associated with it that I carried out with three colleagues in the late 1980s showed that both English-speaking and French-speaking Canadians were overwhelmingly positive about the *Charter*.[29] Our survey also showed that ordinary Canadians knew virtually nothing about the contents of the *Charter*. The *Charter* was revered fundamentally as a symbol of justice and human rights. The level of support for the *Charter* (and knowledge about it) was even higher among politicians.

Being in favour of the *Charter* is not, of course, the same thing as being in favour of a robust and liberal application of it by the judiciary. Indeed, when we asked questions about issues that the Supreme Court of Canada has dealt with in *Charter* cases, we found that in some instances the public did not support the Court's position. For example, in a drunk-driving case in which the police administered a breathalyzer without allowing the driver to contact a lawyer, the public would not support excluding breathalyzer evidence under section 24(2) of the *Charter*. However, in *R. v. Therens*, the Court's first decision on the *Charter*'s exclusion of evidence provision, the Court took the opposite position, holding that such evidence must be excluded because the way it was acquired infringed the accused's *Charter* right and admitting it would "bring the administration of justice into disrepute."[30] On the other hand, there were plenty of situations and contexts, especially equality issues, in which public opinion was in line with positions taken by the Court.

Social science research has shown that public support for the judiciary is diffuse and remains high even when there is not majority support for a particular decision.[31] The *Charter*'s popularity does not mean that Canadian judges have a mandate to give the widest possible interpretation of the *Charter*. But, by the same token, there is no democratic mandate requiring judges to take the narrowest possible approach to the *Charter*. Our research shows that the public, unlike politicians, trust courts more than legislatures to make decisions about their rights and freedoms.[32] If the Supreme Court of Canada had been strongly restrained in its interpretation of the *Charter* and consistently inclined to give government and legislatures the benefit of the doubt when they became subject to *Charter* challenge, I believe the Court would have been denying the will of the Canadian people and their elected leaders.

A third factor in my acceptance of *Charter*-based judicial review is that it quickly became apparent that it was not the decisions of elected legislatures but, rather, the activities of the executive branch of government, particularly the police, that most often were subject to *Charter* review in the courts. Between 1977 and 1981, I had served as director of research for the Royal Commission on Certain Activities of the Royal Canadian Mounted Police (RCMP). While much of the commission's work focused on the RCMP's security intelligence activities, the commission's mandate extended to examining illegal and improper activities of the RCMP's criminal investigation branch. The commission reported that in many cases in which police evidence had been illegally or improperly gathered, it was accepted by the courts. Evidence of a coerced confession was about the only exception to the dictum enunciated by Justice Meredith of the Ontario Court of Appeal that, in Canada, "it is still quite permissible to 'set a thief to catch a thief.'"[33] The commission found that the police took the absence of judicial criticism of the way they obtained their evidence as judicial authorization for techniques such as breaking into private premises without a warrant and interrogating suspects without allowing them to contact a lawyer. It recommended that Canada adopt a law such as exists in Australia and Scotland that gives judges a discretion to exclude evidence obtained through means that seriously breach human dignity and social values.[34] I was pleased to see that the *Charter* included an enforcement section requiring judges to exclude evidence obtained in a manner that infringes the rights guaranteed by the *Charter* and if, "having regard to all the circumstances," admitting the evidence would in the judge's view "bring the administration of justice into disrepute."[35]

Judicial review of police conduct is an essential practice of *liberal* democracy. In deciding when evidence must be excluded, judges are guided by the standards they believe ought to be upheld in the criminal justice system and, if violated, ought to bring the criminal justice system into disrepute. In making these determinations, the judiciary does not take their cues from popular political opinion. And this is just as well. In the inquiry into public opinion about rights that our research team carried out in the late 1980s, we found that on issues that pit civil rights against considerations of public order, justice against crime control, the main cleavages in our society are not between the general public and their leaders but, rather, between partisan, ideological political groups.[36] Citizens and political elites on the right side of politics are more inclined than their counterparts on the left to support the rights of the individual if doing so is seen as jeopardizing public security. Lawyers, from whose ranks judges are chosen, overwhelmingly give a high priority to supporting the rights of the individual under investigation by the police. Liberal democracy is enhanced when lawyer-judges play a lead role in ensuring that citizens' rights are adequately protected in the criminal justice system.

Finally, my research on the Supreme Court of Canada's *Charter* decisions and consideration of its jurisprudence did not support the charges of its anti-activist critics. To begin with, the term "activist" was frequently used as a vague pejorative term of abuse rather than as a well-defined analytical concept. In my writing on constitutional judicial review, I defined judicial activism as "judicial vigour in enforcing constitutional limitations on the other branches of government and a readiness to veto the policies of other branches of government on constitutional grounds." Judicial self-restraint, I defined as "a judicial predisposition to find room within the constitution for the policies of democratically accountable decision-makers."[37] This is how these terms were used in the American literature on judicial review when I first began studying the subject fifty years ago. In applying these concepts both to the constitutional decisions of the Judicial Committee of the Privy Council and the Supreme Court of Canada on both federalism and rights issues, I found that, at certain times and on certain issues, our highest constitutional court tended to be quite activist – for example, in enforcing its understanding of provincial rights against the federal government – while, at other times and on other issues, Canada's highest constitutional adjudicator was quite restrained – for instance, in interpreting the *Canadian Bill of Rights*.[38]

The same fluctuating pattern was evident in the Supreme Court of Canada's treatment of the *Charter*. Its first few decisions on the *Charter* were markedly activist, sending a message to the nation that it would be giving much more effect to the constitutional *Charter* than it had given to the statutory *Canadian Bill of Rights*. Yet, in the years that followed, this thoroughly activist stance was not sustained. On some issues, for instance, criminal justice rights, its decisions were remarkably activist.[39] On others, such as legislation and government-supported activities restricting the rights of labour unions, the Court was remarkably restrained.[40] Statistical studies of the Supreme Court of Canada that I carried out with my colleagues showed that the Court was settling into a markedly balanced approach to *Charter* interpretation. Of the 119 statutes challenged in the Court's first 195 *Charter* cases, seventy-nine were upheld, while forty-one were nullified.[41] Some justices, such as Antonio Lamer and Bertha Wilson were remarkably activist, while others, like Charles Gonthier and Gerard La Forest were remarkably restrained.[42] The majority were hard to predict. The empirical evidence simply did not support the charge that the Supreme Court of Canada as a whole was systematically inclined to be activist in interpreting the *Charter*.

Activism also fails as a normative basis for assessing judicial interpretation of the *Charter*. In a constitutional democracy, a court's ruling that a law or government act is invalid because it violates the *Charter* (or any other provision of the Constitution) should not be judged solely on the basis of that activist result but, rather, on the basis of the reasons given by the court for reaching that conclusion. Let me illustrate this point by indicating considerations that might lead one to oppose an activist approach in one case but support such an approach in another. In *Reference re B.C. Motor Vehicle Act*, for instance, I was not persuaded by the opinion that Justice Lamer wrote for an unanimous Court that section 7 of the *Charter* should be interpreted as requiring substantive as well as procedural justice in laws that encroach on the right to life, liberty, and security of the person. I thought the evidence of the drafting and parliamentary discussion of section 7 submitted to the Court made it clear that the framers' intention was that it should be confined to procedural fairness. I took some comfort from Justice Lamer's qualification that a substantive interpretation of section 7 was limited to criminal law and legal rights. Over many years, courts have developed well-articulated standards of procedural justice, but, if judges apply "principles of fundamental justice" to the substance of social and economic policy, they are inviting themselves into policy-making work for which they lack both the capacity and a democratic mandate. I heaved a huge sigh of relief when the present chief justice in *Chaoulli* failed to win a majority for her effort to use a substantive justice approach to section 7 as grounds for overturning Quebec's legislation banning private insurance for services covered by public medicare.[43]

An example of an activist decision that I supported is the position that the Court took in *Andrews*, its first decision on equality rights in section 15, that the right to be protected from harmful discrimination ought not to be confined to the enumerated categories in section 15, as well as its subsequent finding in *Egan v. Canada* that gays and lesbians are an example of a discrete and insular minority who merit the protection of section 15.[44] The language of section 15 makes it clear that the enumerated categories at the end of the section are only examples of unconstitutional discrimination. There is massive evidence of Canadian citizens suffering harmful effects of discrimination because of their sexual orientation. Moreover, the allegation that the framers intended that gays and lesbians not enjoy the protection of section 15 is not supported by the parliamentary evidence.[45]

Other commentators might contest my reasons for opposing or agreeing with the Court's reasoning. But the point is that in assessing the wisdom and legitimacy of judicial decisions, it is the reasoning of the judges that must be considered and assessed – not the fact that the decision's result is activist or restrained. Judicial decisions on the *Charter* and our evaluation of them are exercises in practical reasoning – reasoning about what is right and just and required by our Constitution. When human beings reason about such issues they cannot reach the level of certainty or objectivity that may be theoretically possible in mathematics or empirical science. An element of subjectivity is inescapable in the way we deal with these issues. However, this does not mean that when judges or citizens make decisions about them they do nothing more than give effect to their personal whims. When judges, politicians, and citizens advance arguments to justify the positions they take on contested normative issues, they engage in a public process of deliberation. It is the social, public quality of this deliberative process that saves it from radical subjectivity. The quality of our democratic life can be enhanced rather than reduced by *Charter* litigation that puts important questions about the shape and limits of fundamental rights and freedoms on the agenda of public affairs. Unfortunately, media treatment of Supreme Court of Canada decisions on these issues all too often focuses entirely on the bare result, rather than on the reasons that the judges advance for reaching this result.[46] This unfortunate occurence is what happens when concerns about judicial activism come to dominate popular discussion of court decisions on the *Charter*.

Barking Up the Wrong Tree

At the very time judicial activism and its implications for democracy were being debated in the academy and the media, a very different kind of threat to the quality of Canadian democracy was emerging. I refer to the trend toward a tremendous centralization of power in the operation of Canada's system of parliamentary/Cabinet government. Over the last fifty years, control of government and policy, especially at the federal level, has been increasingly concentrated in the prime minister's office (PMO). This central-izing trend began with the emergence of the Privy Council Office, the De-partment of Finance, and the Treasury Board after the Second World War as powerful "central agencies" coordinating the work of government depart-ments. Yet, it is another central agency, the PMO, that has been crucial in shifting power within the executive from the Cabinet to the prime minister. Unlike other central agencies, the PMO is staffed not by career civil servants but by political appointees, hand-picked by the prime minister and dedicated to making his or her reign a political success. Although it is the most power-ful office of government and is funded by taxpayers' money, the federal government considers it to be immune from Canada's *Access to Information Act*.[47] The head of the PMO is the prime minister's chief of staff, who is, next to the prime minister, the most powerful person in Ottawa.

This strengthening of the PMO began in the Trudeau years when the prime minister's political staff more than doubled to over ninety people.[48] Donald Savoie's books, which chart the centralizing of power in Ottawa, show that Trudeau's successors have found that they too need a strong PMO.[49] They need it, above all, as a means of controlling communication of the govern-ment's message. In the age of television, when opinion is shaped by ten-second clips, prime ministers and their political advisers emulate large corporations in trying to market themselves and their government's product. The PMO's job is to try to ensure that news about government remains fo-cused, stays "on message," and has a positive spin. The centralization of power in the PMO undermines Cabinet and parliamentary government. Cabinet ministers in their communications with the public are instructed by political staffers from the PMO. Savoie describes how Cabinet has become essentially a focus group for testing support for the policy initiatives of the prime minister and his political staff. The systematic effort at central control of the government's message has little tolerance for parliamentary discussion of policy or legislation. Members of the government caucus are under par-ticularly tight control from central command. Parliamentarians have pushed backed with "democratic renewal" reforms aimed especially at strengthening the legislative role of parliamentary committees. Yet, scholars studying the impact of these reforms report that prime ministerial controls have prevented much of their potential from being realized.[50]

Our system of Cabinet/parliamentary government has become increasingly presidential. The phrase *primus inter pares* (first among equals) as a descrip-tion of the prime minister's position had some cogency in days gone by but cannot be used today. The prime minister is in a separate stratosphere from his Cabinet and parliamentary colleagues. In the poignant words of Jeffrey Simpson, today "the prime minister is the Sun King around whom all revolves and to whom all must pay homage."[51] Simpson's book *The Friendly Dictatorship,* written during the Chrétien years, provides an incisive account of the unchecked power of Canada's prime minister. The style of leadership was becoming truly presidential. The danger is that when the governing party has a majority in the House of Commons, we have a presidential government without the checks and balances that limit presidential power in the American system of government. As Denis Smith warned, "we seemed to have created in Canada a presidential system without its congressional advantages."[52] This increase in prime ministerial power has been experienced throughout the parliamentary world, but a recent comparative study of prime ministerial power in twenty-seven parliamentary democracies places Canada at the very top of the table.[53]

It is remarkable that the debate and discussion about the dangers to democracy posed by judicial activism has showed so little awareness of the centralization of power that was occurring in our parliamentary system. Those who have been concerned about appointed judges dealing with policy issues that are properly the business of elected legislators tended to assume that elected legislators freely discuss and debate legislative proposals and whether they comply with fundamental rights and freedoms. Given the realities of parliamentary life, such an assumption is pure fantasy. The dialogue debate about interaction between the courts and legislators in deciding *Charter* issues also paid little attention to executive domination of Parliament. There are some notable exceptions, such as Janet Hiebert's analysis of the stunted consideration that *Charter* issues receive in the Canadian Parliament[54] and James Kelly's incisive account of how the Department of Justice has emerged as a new powerful central agency in controlling parliamentary discussion of *Charter* matters.[55] Yet, for the most part, debate about judicial activism has been too judge-centred to take any notice of what actually goes on in the House of Commons.

Those whose main concern during the *Charter's* first quarter-century was the danger it posed to Canadian democracy were barking up the wrong tree. The main threat to Canadian democracy during this period came not from the *Charter* but from the evolution of our Cabinet/parliamentary system of government toward a presidential system of government – a presidential system without the checks and balances of Congress. The *Charter* pushed the Canadian judiciary into making decisions on a number of controversial moral issues and increased its capacity for supervising the administration of criminal justice. However, even in its most activist moments, such activity does not mean that Canadians are in danger of being governed by appointed judges rather than elected politicians. The big decisions of government on domestic and foreign policy are not made by our judges but, rather, by the prime minister and his hand-picked political advisers. I kick myself for not being sufficiently alert to this danger to Canadian democracy and hope to have made amends in a recent book that heralds minority government as the most effective way of sustaining parliamentary government and countering the drift to prime ministerial government.[56]

Charter Patriotism

The *Charter* is more than just popular. In English Canada, it has become a major source of civic pride and has achieved truly iconic status. Survey data show that the *Charter* is also popular in Quebec, although I doubt that for the francophone majority it has achieved anything like the importance it has for civic identity in the rest of the country. Quebec has its own *Charter of Human Rights and Freedoms,* and the Quebecois have their own nationalist symbols and myths, including, for many of them, the "night of the long knives" and a sense that they were betrayed in the politics of constitutional patriation in 1981.[57] Still, those of us who care about the unity of our country should be thankful that the Canadian *Charter* has not been a source of disunity. During the Meech Lake debacle, the *Charter* came dangerously close to being a divisive force when political elites in English Canada argued that recognizing Quebec as a "distinct society" would diminish *Charter* protection of rights and freedoms in *la belle province.*[58] Fortunately, this ugly chapter in our constitutional odyssey left no permanent fissure.

No one was more prescient about the effect the *Charter* would have on Canada's constitutional culture than political scientist Alan Cairns. In a series of articles written during the period when the *Charter* was being added to the Constitution and the years immediately following its adoption, Cairns advanced the thesis that the *Charter* would bring about a profound change in how Canadians think about their Constitution. Before the *Charter*, federalism and parliamentary government were the twin pillars of Canada's constitutional order. Cairns predicted that after the *Charter,* these traditional notions would have to "jostle with notions of citizenship expressed in the guarantees of the Charter."[59] The *Charter* gave the Canadian citizen "a new status as a bearer of rights." Adding a *Charter* to the Constitution meant that Canada's Constitution would no longer be all about governments – it would be equally about citizens and their rights.

It is difficult to assess empirically the extent to which the *Charter* has changed Canada's constitutional culture in the direction predicted by Cairns. Canadians are certainly less deferential than they were in the past. Indeed, Michael Adams' research shows that today Americans, who have lived with a constitutional bill of rights since their country's founding, are more respectful of authority than Canadians.[60] How much of this change can be attributed to the *Charter* is difficult to say. The demand for better protection of rights – for women, for visible minorities, for gays and lesbians, for Indigenous peoples – has contributed to the *Charter*'s political sponsors' enthusiasm for their project. The continuing stream of well-publicized *Charter* cases about rights claims has increased the penetration of our public discourse by rights talk. The idea that a fundamental purpose of the Constitution is to protect the rights of citizens goes hand in hand with a constitutional philosophy of popular sovereignty. Cairns suggests that if the *Charter* had been entrenched at the time we were developing a formula for amending the Constitution in Canada, adoption of the existing amending process would have been inconceivable."[61] Indeed, in the constitutional struggles that followed patriation, pressure for a more democratic constitutional process became irresistible, and, for any major changes in Canada's Constitution, holding a referendum is now virtually a convention of the Constitution.[62]

The *Charter* has certainly contributed to the emergence of a more rights-conscious and democratic constitutionalism in Canada. This part of Cairns' thesis seems well supported by the evidence. Yet, his contention that the new emphasis on citizens' rights would reduce, if not supplant, the old emphasis on provincial identity is much more dubious. Provincial governments continue to find popular support for challenging Ottawa. Federal-provincial issues continue to be near the top of the political agenda. Canadians, and not just Quebeckers, contest issues of federal power versus provincial rights today just as much as they did in pre-*Charter* days. Witness the current controversies over the fiscal imbalance and the use of spending power. In *Clash of Rights,* we show that in democratic politics, rights claims are inherently contestable. Citizens' thinking about rights issues (including provincial rights) is not dichotomized in an either/or fashion. Most citizens have latent support for freedom and order, equality and competitiveness, provincial rights, and an effective federal government.[63] How they will resolve the clash of values in their own heads will depend on the political context in which the conflict between rights claims is played out. In the post-*Charter* era, there are still contexts in which, for significant numbers of Canadians, provincial identities will trump their attachment to rights.

So *Charter* patriotism is not the quick fix for national unity that its political sponsors envisaged. Nor is it anything like the "constitutional patriotism" that Jürgen Habermas saw as a deliberative process of building a democratic constitutional consensus.[64] Love of the *Charter* is more like flag waving and anthem singing. Calling it the *Charter* has enhanced its symbolic capability. It is difficult to imagine people getting as dewy-eyed about a bill of rights or a human rights act. The *Charter* rings like a bell. And when the *Charter* bell rings, it does not bring to mind its actual provisions or applications by the courts. Reverence for the *Charter* is detached from its contents and its beneficiaries. *Charter*-worshippers look at me in puzzlement when I tell them that the group in our society that has benefited most from the *Charter* is the one that is charged with criminal offences. *Charter* patriotism has probably contributed to the dumbing-down of the Canadian demos.

Conclusion: Liberty and Equality after Twenty-Five Years

While national unity is clearly what drove Pierre Trudeau to make the *Charter* his number one constitutional priority, it was not the basis of the *Charter*'s popularity with many citizens and civil rights groups. Those who made submissions to the special joint committee on the constitution and who so warmly embraced the *Charter* expected that it would actually increase the enjoyment of liberty and equality in Canada. The *Charter* was not envisaged as a stand-pat instrument that would simply protect the liberty and equality that Canadians already enjoyed. No, the *Charter* was to increase liberty and enhance equality and, thereby, improve the quality of Canadian democracy.

These normative impulses underlying the *Charter*'s popularity – a desire for greater liberty and also for more equality – call for a *Charter* that will promote two very different kinds of rights: "blue rights" that will limit what the state can do to its citizens and "red rights" that require the state to do more for its citizens. However incoherent ideologically inclined commentators on the Right and on the Left may find this amalgam of expectations, the evidence is that most citizens desire a good deal of liberty and equality.[65] Has the *Charter* delivered on these normative expectations?

After hundreds of Supreme Court of Canada decisions on the *Charter*, thousands of lower court decisions, and tens of thousands of decisions made every day by lawmakers, governments, administrators, and police officers on how the *Charter* should affect their work, it is a daunting task to add up the score on the net result of the *Charter*'s impact on Canadians' liberty and equality. There have certainly been ups and downs. For every *Charter*-based act or decision that advanced a liberty or equality claim, one can think of a counter-example where the courts or government went the other way. Liberty-lovers may well argue that, from their perspective, the *Charter* has been a failure, partly because it has done so much for equality. Equality-seekers may argue just as strenuously that, from their perspective, the *Charter* has been a real disappointment, delivering little real substantive equality while encouraging citizens to think of government as the enemy rather than as the agent of social reform. For what it is worth, I conclude this article by offering my own, highly impressionistic assessment of what the *Charter* has contributed to Canadians' liberty and equality.

On the liberty front, the *Charter*'s impact on freedom of speech and religion – the classic liberal freedoms – has been minimal. The commercial freedom to advertise has been advanced[66] and a pornographer's freedom to amuse himself secured.[67] Yet, these are hardly the freedoms we go to war to defend. On the other hand, the core of our laws against obscene and pornographic expression,[68] the prohibition of anti-hate propaganda, and Canada's most significant limit on political speech have been upheld.[69] School prayers of any kind have been ruled unconstitutional,[70] but this decision is in line with a broad societal push for the secularization of public institutions. The significant liberty gains that can be attributed to the *Charter* are in the criminal justice area. There have certainly been setbacks, most recently in upholding the police power of investigative detention,[71] but, on balance, the *Charter* has increased the rights of those who have come into contact with the police as suspects and with prosecutors and judges as accused. The *Charter* has certainly removed some of the harshest provisions of our criminal law – for instance, the minimal seven-year imprisonment for bringing the tiniest amount of narcotics into the country[72] – and has tilted a little toward the liberty side in reviewing anti-terrorist legislation.[73] These liberty gains in the criminal justice area may or may not be welcomed by a majority of Canadians. Yet, Canadians, I hope, wish to live in a liberal democracy, not a simple majoritarian democracy.

As for equality, economic inequality – the gap between the income and living conditions of the poor and the comfortable – has widened during the *Charter* years.[74] However, I disagree with those who have argued that the *Charter*, by deflecting political action away from egalitarian politics, has something to do with the widening of economic disparities. In the 1980s and 1990s, the political forces of neo-conservatism were rolling back the welfare state in all of the industrialized Western democracies. The absence of a constitutional charter of rights and freedoms would not have insulated Canada from these forces. While the *Charter* did nothing to arrest the policy impact of neo-conservatism in Canada, it did assist some of the groups in Canadian society that were pressing to overcome inequalities inflicted on them by discriminatory laws and practices. Gays and lesbians are the biggest beneficiary of the *Charter's* equality rights. David Rayside's recent comparative study shows convincingly that the *Charter* has been an important factor in contributing to the relatively greater gains that gays and lesbians have made in Canada in widening their rights and opportunities.[75] The equality gains of women attributable to the *Charter* are more difficult to assess. Feminist groups were the most vociferous advocates of a strong equality section in the *Charter* and of a provision that all of the rights and freedoms in the *Charter* "are guaranteed equally to male and female persons."[76] Yet, while there have certainly been some feminist gains – notably, the decriminalization of abortion and the better protection of rape victims in the criminal justice system – there have also been some significant setbacks – notably, the failure to have working women's child care expenses treated as an income tax deduction.[77] And, of course, many women do not share feminist views of what should count as improving the lives of women. Sections of society that have clearly made equality gains through the *Charter* are the official language minorities and some groups of disabled people – I have in mind deaf people who, after *Eldridge v. British Columbia*, have a right to be assisted by sign language translators when they seek access to public health services.[78] At the margin, the *Charter* has contributed to making Canadian democracy more generous and inclusive. Two cheers for the *Charter*!

Notes

1 *Canadian Charter of Rights and Freedoms*, Part 1 of the *Constitution Act, 1982*, being Schedule B to the *Canada Act 1982* (U.K.), 1982, c. 11 [*Charter*].
2 Peter H. Russell, "The Political Purposes of the Canadian Charter of Rights and Freedoms," *Canadian Bar Review* 61 (1983): 52.
3 On the nature of deliberative democracy, see Simone Chambers, "Deliberative Democratic Theory," *American Review of Political Science* (2003): 307-26.
4 *McKinney v. University of Guelph*, [1990] 3 S.C.R. 229.
5 *Lord's Day Act*, S.C. 1906, c. 27.
6 *Rodriquez v. British Columbia (Attorney General)*, [1993] 3 S.C.R. 519.
7 *Halpern v. Canada (Attorney General)* (2003), 65 O.R. (3rd) 161.
8 *Reference re Same-Sex Marriage*, 2004 SCC 79.
9 *Globe and Mail* (December 10, 2004), A1.
10 On the struggle to wean Quebec Catholics from supporting a secular state, see Rainer Knopff, "Quebec's 'Holy War' as 'Regime Politics': Reflections on the Guibord Case," *Canadian Journal of Political Science* 12 (1979): 315-31.
11 Gloria Galloway, "Same-Sex Marriage File Closed for Good, PM Says," *Globe and Mail* (December 8, 2006), A1.
12 Margaret Sommerville, *The Ethical Imagination: Broadcast Lectures* (Toronto: Anansi, 2006).
13 Peter H. Russell, "A Democratic Approach to Civil Liberties," *University of Toronto Law Journal* 19 (1969): 109-31.
14 Special Joint Committee on the Constitution of Canada, November 1980, *Minutes of Proceedings*, Jean Chrétien 36 (January 1981): 14-15.
15 *Roe v. Wade*, 410 U.S. 113 (1973).
16 *Law Society of Upper Canada v. Skapinker*, [1984] 1 S.C.R. 357.
17 *R. v. Big M Drug Mart*, [1985] 1 S.C.R. 295 [*Big M Drug Mart*].
18 *Singh v. Minister of Employment and Immigration*, [1985] 1 S.C.R. 177.
19 *Operation Dismantle, Inc. v. R.*, [1985] 1 S.C.R. 441.
20 *Reference re B.C. Motor Vehicle Act*, [1985] 2 S.C.R. 486 [*B.C. Motor Vehicle Act*].
21 *Andrews v. Law Society of British Columbia*, [1989] 1 S.C.R. 143.
22 *Criminal Code*, R.S.C. 1985, c. C-46, s. 264.
23 See Peter H. Russell, "Standing Up for Notwithstanding," *Alberta Law Review* 29 (1991): 293-309.
24 *Ford v. Quebec*, [1988] 2 S.C.R. 712.
25 *Vriend v. Alberta*, [1998] 1.S.C.R. 493. *Individual Rights Protection Act*, R.S.A. 1980, c.1-2.
26 See Peter H. Russell "The Charter's Homage to Parliamentary Democracy," *Policy Options* 28 (February 2007): 65-68.
27 *Chaoulli v. Quebec (Attorney General)*, [2005] 1 S.C.R. 791.
28 Nik Nanos, "Charter Values Don't Equal Canadian Values: Strong Support for Same-Sex and Property Rights," *Policy Options* 28 (February 2007): 50-55.
29 Paul M. Sniderman, Joseph F. Fletcher, Peter H. Russell, and Philip E. Tetlock, *The Clash of Rights: Liberty, Equality and Legitimacy in Pluralist Society* (New Haven, CT: Yale University Press, 1997), see especially 170, Table 6.2.
30 *R. v. Therens*, [1985] 1 S.C.R. 613.
31 See Joseph F. Fletcher and Paul Howe, "Public Opinion and Canada's Courts," in Paul Howe and Peter H. Russell, eds., *Judicial Power and Canadian Democracy* (Montreal and Kingston: McGill-Queen's University Press, 2001), 255-96.
32 Sniderman et al., *supra* note 29, 164, Figure 6.1.

33 Commission of Inquiry into Certain Activities of the Royal Canadian Mounted Police (the McDonald Commission), *Second Report, Freedom and Security under the Law*, volume 2 (Ottawa: Canadian Government Publishing Centre, 1981), 1037.
34 Ibid., 1046.
35 *Charter, supra* note 1, s. 24(2).
36 See Sniderman et al., *supra* note 29, particularly ch. 2.
37 "Introduction," in Peter H. Russell, Rainer Knopff, and Ted Morton, eds., *Federalism and the Charter: Leading Constitutional Decisions* (Ottawa: Carleton University Press, 1989), 19.
38 *Canadian Bill of Rights*, S.C. 1960, c. 44.
39 For instance, its decisions in *B.C. Motor Vehicle Act, supra* note 20, and *Big M Drug Mart, supra* note 17, and its decisions on the exclusion of evidence.
40 For example, *Retail, Wholesale and Dept. Store Union v. Dolphin Delivery*, [1986] 2 S.C.R. 573; and *Reference re Public Service Employee Relations Act (Alberta)*, [1987] 1 S.C.R. 313.
41 See F.L. Morton, Peter H. Russell, and Troy Riddell, "The *Canadian Charter of Rights and Freedom*: A Descriptive Analysis of the First Decade, 1982-1992," *National Journal of Constitutional Law* 5 (1994): 19.
42 Ibid., 38.
43 For a discussion of this issue, see Sujit Choudhry, "Worse Than Lochner," in Colleen M. Flood, Kent Roach, and Lorne Sossin, eds., *Access to Health, Access to Justice: The Legal Debate over Private Health Insurance in Canada* (Toronto: University of Toronto Press, 2005), 75-100.
44 *Egan v. Canada*, [1995] 2 S.C.R. 513.
45 See James B. Kelly, *Governing with the Charter: Legislative and Judicial Activism and Framers' Intent* (Vancouver: UBC Press, 2005), 98-102.
46 See Florian Sauvageau, David Taras, and David Schneiderman, *The Last Word: Media Coverage of the Supreme Court of Canada* (Vancouver: UBC Press, 2005).
47 Campbell Clark, "Khan Report Blocked, Despite Tory Promise on Secrecy," *Globe and Mail* (October 29, 2007), A4. *Access to Information Act*, R.S.C. 1985, c. A-1.
48 See R.M. Punnett, *The Prime Minister in Canadian Government and Politics* (Toronto: Macmillan Canada, 1977.)
49 Donald J. Savoie, *Governing from the Centre: The Concentration of Power in Canadian Politics* (Toronto: University of Toronto Press, 1999); and Donald J. Savoie, *Breaking the Bargain: Public Servants, Ministers and Parliament* (Toronto: University of Toronto Press, 2003).
50 See Michael M. Atkinson, "Parliamentary Government in Canada," in Michael S. Whittington and Glen Williams, eds., *Canadian Politics in the 1990s*, 3rd edition (Toronto: Nelson, 1990), 337-55; and David C. Docherty and Stephen White, "Parliamentary Democracy in Canada," *Parliamentary Affairs* 57 (2004): 613-29.
51 Jeffrey Simpson, *The Friendly Dictatorship* (Toronto: McClelland and Stewart, 2001), 4.
52 Denis Smith, "President and Parliament: The Transformation of Parliamentary Government in Canada," in Thomas A. Hocken, ed., *Apex of Power: The Prime Minister and Political Leadership in Canada* (Toronto: Prentice-Hall, 1971), 323.
53 Eoin O'Malley, "The Power of Prime Ministers: Results of an Experts Survey," *International Political Science Review* 28 (2007): 7-27.
54 Janet L. Hiebert, *Charter Conflicts: What Is Parliament's Role?* (Montreal and Kingston: McGill-Queen's University Press, 2002).
55 Kelly, *supra* note 45.
56 Peter H. Russell, *Two Cheers for Minority Government: The Evolution of Canadian Parliamentary Government* (Toronto: Emond/Montgomery, 2008).
57 *Charter of Human Rights and Freedoms*, R.S.Q., c. C-12.
58 See Peter H. Russell, *Constitutional Odyssey: Can Canadians Become a Sovereign People?* 3rd edition (Toronto: University of Toronto Press, 2004), 146-47.
59 Alan Cairns and Cynthia Williams, *Constitutionalism, Citizenship and Society in Canada* (Toronto: University of Toronto Press, 1985), 38.
60 Michael Adams, *Fire and Ice: The United States, Canada and the Myth of Converging Values* (Toronto: Penguin Books, 2003).
61 Alan C. Cairns, *Charter versus Federalism: The Dilemmas of Constitutional Reform* (Montreal and Kingston: McGill-Queen's University Press, 1992), 91.

62 Patrick Boyer, *Direct Democracy in Canada* (Toronto: Dundurn, 1992).

63 Sniderman et al., *supra* note 29.

64 Omid A. Payrow Shabani, *Democracy, Power, and Legitimacy: The Critical Theory of Jurgen Habermas.* (Toronto: University of Toronto Press, 2003), 170.

65 The evidence is presented in Sniderman et al., *supra* note 29.

66 *Rocket v. Royal College of Dental Surgeons*, [1990] 1 S.C.R. 232; and *RJR-MacDonald v. Canada*, [1995] 3 S.C.R. 199.

67 *R. v. Sharpe*, [2001] 1 S.C.R. 45.

68 *R. v. Butler*, [1992] 1 S.C.R. 452; and *R. v. Sharpe*, [2001] 1 S.C.R. 45.

69 *R. v. Keegstra*, [1990] 3 S.C.R. 697.

70 *Zylberberg v. Sudbury Board of Education* (1988), 65 O.R. (2nd) 641 (C.A.).

71 *R. v. Mann*, [2004] 3 S.C.R. 53.

72 *R. v. Smith*, [1987] 1 S.C.R. 1045.

73 *Charkaoui v. Canada (Citizenship and Immigration)*, [2007] S.C.R. 9.

74 Edward Broadbent, "Social Democracy or Liberalism in the New Millenium," in Peter H. Russell, ed., *The Future of Social Democracy* (Toronto: University of Toronto Press, 1999).

75 David Rayside, *Queer Inclusions: Continental Divide* (Toronto: University of Toronto Press, 2006).

76 *Charter, supra* note 1, s. 28.

77 *Symes v. Canada*, [1993] 4 S.C.R. 695.

78 *Eldridge v. British Columbia*, [1997] 3 S.C.R. 624.

Contributors

Dennis Baker is assistant professor of political science at the University of Guelph. His research focuses on the institutional separation of powers, particularly the relationship between the courts and the representative branches. He has co-authored papers regarding rules of evidence in sexual assault cases in the *Windsor Yearbook of Access to Justice* and has conducted research on the strategic manoeuvring behind the Supreme Court of Canada rulings on prisoners' voting rights.

Sujit Choudhry is Scholl professor in the Faculty of Law at the University of Toronto and associate dean (first year program). He holds law degrees from Oxford, Toronto, and Harvard, was a Rhodes Scholar, and served as law clerk to Chief Justice Antonio Lamer of the Supreme Court of Canada. He is the editor of *The Migration of Constitutional Ideas* (Cambridge University of Press, 2006), *Dilemmas of Solidarity* (University of Toronto Press, 2006), and *Constitutional Design for Divided Societies* (Oxford University Press, 2008) and is currently writing a book, *Rethinking Comparative Constitutional Law*. He appeared as counsel for Human Rights Watch before the Supreme Court of Canada in *Charkaoui v. Canada* (security certificate).

Graham Fraser is commissioner of official languages, a position he assumed in October 2006. Previously, he worked as a journalist for the *Toronto Star,* the *Globe and Mail, The Gazette,* and *Maclean's*. He is the author of five books, most recently, *Sorry I Don't Speak French: Confronting the Canadian Crisis That Won't Go Away* (McClelland and Stewart, 2006) and *René Lévesque and the Parti Québécois in Power* (McGill-Queen's University Press, 2001). He was educated at the University of Toronto, receiving his BA in 1968 and his MA in 1973.

Matthew Hennigar is associate professor of political science at Brock University. His research has appeared in such venues as the *Canadian Journal of Political Science, Law and Society Review,* and *University of Toronto Law Journal*, and focuses on the legal and institutional dimensions of Canadian politics, in particular, the judiciary's organization and impact on public policy, the federal government's legal bureaucracy, and rights litigation. His major current research project, funded by the Social Sciences and Humanities Research Council, is an analysis of the government of Canada's litigation strategy in *Charter* cases. He is also co-author of *Canadian Courts: Law, Politics, and Process* (Oxford University Press, 2008).

Janet L. Hiebert is professor in the Department of Political Studies, where she teaches Canadian and constitutional politics. She is author of two books, *Charter Conflicts: What Is Parliament's Role?* (McGill-Queen's University Press, 2002) and *Limiting Rights: The Dilemma of Judicial Review* (McGill-Queen's University Press, 1996), along with numerous journal articles and chapters on the politics of rights and on campaign finance laws in Canada. Her research interests focus on how recently introduced bills of rights alter political practices, policy development, and legislative behaviour in Canada, New Zealand, the United Kingdom, and Australia.

Grant Huscroft is professor in the Faculty of Law at the University of Western Ontario. He has written extensively on bills of rights and judicial review in Canada, the United States, New Zealand, and Australia. He is co-author of *The New Zealand Bill of Rights* (Oxford University Press, 2003) and has edited five collections of essays: *Expounding the Constitution: Essays in Constitutional Theory* (Cambridge University Press, 2008); *Inside and Outside Canadian Administrative Law* (University of Toronto Press, 2006); *Constitutionalism in the Charter Era* (LexisNexis-Butterworths, 2004); *Litigating Rights: Perspectives from Domestic and International Law* (Hart Publishing, 2002); and *Rights and Freedoms* (Brookers, 1995).

James B. Kelly is associate professor of political science at Concordia University and the 2006-7 Seagram Chair in Canadian Studies at the McGill Institute for the Study of Canada. He has published *Governing with the Charter* (UBC Press, 2003), which was short-listed for the 2005 Donner Prize for the best book on public policy.

Rainer Knopff is professor of political science at the University of Calgary. He has written widely in the areas of public law, human rights, and Canadian political thought. His books include *Human Rights and Social Technology: the New War on Discrimination* (Carleton University Press, 1989) (with T.E. Flanagan), *Charter Politics* (Nelson Canada, 1992) (with F.L. Morton), and *The Charter Revolution and the Court Party* (Broadview, 2000) (with F.L. Morton).

Kiera L. Ladner is assistant professor and Canada Research Chair in Indigenous Politics and Governance in the Department of Political Studies at the University of Manitoba. Her research interests include treaty constitutionalism, indigenist theory and methodology, decolonization, constitutional politics, Indigenous governance ("traditional," *Indian Act,* and self-government), and social movements. Her current community-based research attempts to create deeper understanding both within communities and between Indigenous nations and colonial societies in Canada and Hawaii. She has published in many journals, including the *Canadian Journal of Political Science, Politique et Societes*, and the *Journal of Canadian Studies*.

Guy Laforest is professor of political science at Université Laval. His most recent book is *Pour la liberté d'une société distincte: parcours d'un intellectuel engagé* (Presses de l'Université Laval, 2004). He has also just completed a major postface, "Lord Durham, French Canada and Quebec: Remembering the Past, Debating the Future," for the 2007 edition of *Lord Durham's Report* (McGill-Queen's University Press, forthcoming). His main areas of teaching and research are political theory, intellectual history of Canada and Quebec, constitutional politics, and federalism in Canada.

Sylvia LeRoy is a policy and communications consultant based in Vancouver and has worked at the Fraser Institute. Her publications have covered such topics as judicial reform and accountability, the legality of equalization and the federal spending power, welfare reform, private social service delivery, and charitable giving. During 2003-7, she managed the Donner Canadian Foundation Awards for Excellence in the Delivery of Social Services, which evaluate the management and delivery of social services in the non-profit sector. Her degrees in political science include a BA from the University of Western Ontario and a MA from the University of Calgary.

Antonia Maioni is director of the McGill Institute for the Study of Canada, William Dawson Scholar, and Associate Professor of Political Science at McGill University. Maioni has published extensively in the field of Canadian and comparative politics, with a particular focus on health policy. She is the author of *Parting at the Crossroads: The Emergence of Health Insurance in the United States and Canada* (Princeton University Press, 1998) and of numerous journal articles on health care and health care politics in Canada.

Christopher P. Manfredi is dean in the Faculty of Arts at McGill University and professor of political science. His research focuses on law and the courts with a particular emphasis on the political and policy impact of rights litigation. His books include *Judicial Power and the Charter: Canada and the Paradox of Liberal Constitutionalism* (Oxford University Press, 2001) and *Feminist Activism in the Supreme Court: Legal Mobilization and the Women's Legal Education and Action Fund* (UBC Press, 2004), which was nominated for the 2004 Donner Prize for the best book on public policy.

Michael McCrossan is a Ph.D. candidate in the Department of Political Science at Carleton University. His current research focuses on the spatialization of legal knowledge and the constitutional rights of Indigenous peoples.

Andrew Petter, Queen's Counsel, is former dean and professor of law at the University of Victoria. Prior to joining the University of Victoria in 1986, he practised with the Constitutional Branch of the Saskatchewan Department of Justice and taught at Osgoode Hall Law School at York University. From 1991 to 2001, he served as a member of the British Columbia Legislative Assembly and held numerous Cabinet portfolios, including attorney general. His major fields of interest are constitutional law, civil liberties, and legislative and regulatory processes.

Troy Riddell is associate professor in the Department of Political Science at the University of Guelph. He has teaching and research interests in constitutional and judicial politics. He has published articles in the *University of Toronto Law Journal* (with Lori Hausegger and Matthew Hennigar), the *Law and Society Review*, *Canadian Public Administration,* and the *Canadian Journal of Political Science*.

Kent Roach is professor of law at the University of Toronto, where he holds the Prichard-Wilson Chair in Law and Public Policy. He is also a Fellow of the Royal Society of Canada. He is the author of eight books, including *The Supreme Court on Trial: Democratic Dialogue or Judicial Activism* (Irwin Law, 2001) and *September 11: Consequences for Canada* (McGill-Queen's University Press, 2003). He has published articles on anti-terrorism law in Australia, Canada, Hong Kong, Singapore, South Africa, the United Kingdom, and the United States and has co-edited *The Security of Freedom: Essays on Canada's Anti-Terrorism Bill* (University of Toronto Press, 2001) and *Global Anti-Terrorism Law and Policy* (Cambridge University Press, 2005). He served on the research advisory committee of the Commission of Inquiry into the Actions of Canadian Officials in Relation to Maher Arar and as research director (legal studies) for the Commission of Inquiry into the Bombing of Air India Flight 182.

Peter H. Russell is professor emeritus at the University of Toronto, where he taught political science from 1958 to 1996. He has engaged as a scholar and citizen in three kinds of politics: the politics of constitutional change; the politics of judiciaries; and political relations between indigenous peoples and settler states. His most recent books in these fields are *Constitutional Odyssey: Can Canadians Be a Sovereign People?* 3rd edition (University of Toronto Press, 2004), *Canada's Trial Courts: Two Tiers or One?* (University of Toronto Press, 2007), and *Recognizing Aboriginal Title: The Mabo Case and Indigenous Resistance to Settler State Colonialism* (University of Toronto Press, 2005). He is a past-president of the Canadian Political Science Association and the Canadian Law and Society Association, a fellow of the Royal Society of Canada, and an officer of the Order of Canada.

Index

LAW AND
SOCIETY

Wayne V. McIntosh and Cynthia L. Cates
Multi-Party Litigation: The Strategic Context (2009)

Renisa Mawani
Colonial Proximities: Crossracial Encounters and Juridical Truths in British Columbia, 1871-1921 (2009)

Catherine E. Bell and Robert K. Paterson (eds.)
Protection of First Nations Cultural Heritage: Laws, Policy, and Reform (2008)

Hamar Foster, Benjamin L. Berger, and A.R. Buck (eds.)
The Grand Experiment: Law and Legal Culture in British Settler Societies (2008)

Richard J. Moon (ed.)
Law and Religious Pluralism in Canada (2008)

Catherine E. Bell and Val Napoleon (eds.)
First Nations Cultural Heritage and Law: Case Studies, Voices, and Perspectives (2008)

Douglas C. Harris
Landing Native Fisheries: Indian Reserves and Fishing Rights in British Columbia, 1849-1925 (2008)

Peggy J. Blair
Lament for a First Nation: The Williams Treaties in Southern Ontario (2008)

Lori G. Beaman
Defining Harm: Religious Freedom and the Limits of the Law (2007)

Stephen Tierney (ed.)
Multiculturalism and the Canadian Constitution (2007)

Julie Macfarlane
The New Lawyer: How Settlement Is Transforming the Practice of Law (2007)

Kimberley White
Negotiating Responsibility: Law, Murder, and States of Mind (2007)

Dawn Moore
Criminal Artefacts: Governing Drugs and Users (2007)

Hamar Foster, Heather Raven, and Jeremy Webber (eds.)
Let Right Be Done: Aboriginal Title, the Calder Case, and the Future of Indigenous Rights (2007)

Dorothy E. Chunn, Susan B. Boyd, and Hester Lessard (eds.)
Reaction and Resistance: Feminism, Law, and Social Change (2007)

Margot Young, Susan B. Boyd, Gwen Brodsky, and Shelagh Day (eds.)
Poverty: Rights, Social Citizenship, and Legal Activism (2007)

Rosanna L. Langer
Defining Rights and Wrongs: Bureaucracy, Human Rights, and Public Accountability (2007)

C.L. Ostberg and Matthew E. Wetstein
Attitudinal Decision Making in the Supreme Court of Canada (2007)

Chris Clarkson
Domestic Reforms: Political Visions and Family Regulation in British Columbia, 1862-1940 (2007)

Jean McKenzie Leiper
Bar Codes: Women in the Legal Profession (2006)

Gerald Baier
Courts and Federalism: Judicial Doctrine in the United States, Australia, and Canada (2006)

Avigail Eisenberg (ed.)
Diversity and Equality: The Changing Framework of Freedom in Canada (2006)

Randy K. Lippert
Sanctuary, Sovereignty, Sacrifice: Canadian Sanctuary Incidents, Power, and Law (2005)

James B. Kelly
Governing with the Charter: Legislative and Judicial Activism and Framers' Intent (2005)

Dianne Pothier and Richard Devlin (eds.)
Critical Disability Theory: Essays in Philosophy, Politics, Policy, and Law (2005)

Susan G. Drummond
Mapping Marriage Law in Spanish Gitano Communities (2005)

Louis A. Knafla and Jonathan Swainger (eds.)
Laws and Societies in the Canadian Prairie West, 1670-1940 (2005)

Ikechi Mgbeoji
Global Biopiracy: Patents, Plants, and Indigenous Knowledge (2005)

Florian Sauvageau, David Schneiderman, and David Taras, with Ruth Klinkhammer and Pierre Trudel
The Last Word: Media Coverage of the Supreme Court of Canada (2005)

Gerald Kernerman
Multicultural Nationalism: Civilizing Difference, Constituting Community (2005)

Pamela A. Jordan
Defending Rights in Russia: Lawyers, the State, and Legal Reform in the Post-Soviet Era (2005)

Anna Pratt
Securing Borders: Detention and Deportation in Canada (2005)

Kirsten Johnson Kramar
Unwilling Mothers, Unwanted Babies: Infanticide in Canada (2005)

W.A. Bogart
Good Government? Good Citizens? Courts, Politics, and Markets in a Changing Canada (2005)

David R. Boyd
Unnatural Law: Rethinking Canadian Environmental Law and Policy (2003)

Ikechi Mgbeoji
*Collective Insecurity: The Liberian Crisis, Unilateralism, and Global
Order* (2003)

Rebecca Johnson
*Taxing Choices: The Intersection of Class, Gender, Parenthood,
and the Law* (2002)

John McLaren, Robert Menzies, and Dorothy E. Chunn (eds.)
*Regulating Lives: Historical Essays on the State, Society, the Individual,
and the Law* (2002)

Joan Brockman
Gender in the Legal Profession: Fitting or Breaking the Mould (2001)

Printed and bound in Canada by Friesens

Set in Stone by Artegraphica Design Co. Ltd.

Copy editor: Stacy Belden

Proofreader: Dianne Tiefensee

Indexer: Christine Jacobs

ENVIRONMENTAL BENEFITS STATEMENT

UBC Press saved the following resources by printing the pages of this book on chlorine free paper made with 100% post-consumer waste.

TREES	WATER	ENERGY	SOLID WASTE	GREENHOUSE GASES
13	4,594	9	590	1,107
FULLY GROWN	GALLONS	MILLION BTUs	POUNDS	POUNDS

Calculations based on research by Environmental Defense and the Paper Task Force. Manufactured at Friesens Corporation